The Bodleian Library
A Subject Guide
to the Collections

The Bodleian Library
A Subject Guide
to the Collections

Edited by

GREGORY WALKER

MARY CLAPINSON

and LESLEY FORBES

2004

First published in 2004 by The Bodleian Library
Broad Street
Oxford OX1 3BG

ISBN 1-85124-079-9

Designed by Jessica Harvey and Baseline Arts Ltd

Printed and bound by The University Press, Cambridge

British Library Cataloguing in Publication Data
A CIP record of this publication is available from the British Library

FRONTISPIECE:

I. Portrait of Thomas Bodley

Portrait if the Library's Founder, said to have been painted in Venice on the late 1570s when
Bodley was in his thirties.

Purchased in 1635

Lane Poole 71

Contents

Foreword   7

Introduction   9

Editors, Contributors and Advisors   11

General Bibliography   12

1.   Building the Bodleian's Collections   16
2.   The Legal Deposit Collections   20
3.   Classical Studies   25
4.   British History and Politics   31
5.   English Literature and Language   42
6.   Children's Books   48
7.   Theology   51
8.   Philosophy   57
9.   Social Sciences   62
10.   Law   68
11.   Geography and Maps   75
12.   Music   80
13.   Science, Technology and Medicine   88
14.   German Studies   98
15.   French Studies   102
16.   Italian Studies   106
17.   Hispanic Studies   110
18.   Russia and Eastern Europe   115
      Russia and the Former USSR, Baltic States, Poland, Czech and Slovak Republics, Hungary, Yugoslavia and Successor States, Romania, Bulgaria, Albania
19.   Near and Middle East   121
      Hebrew, Yiddish, Aramaic, Egyptian and Coptic, Armenian, Georgian, Ethiopic, Syriac, Islamic Collections, Central Asia
20.   South, South East and Inner Asia   135
      South Asia, Tibet, South East Asia

21.   East Asia   141
         China, Japan, Korea, Mongolia
22.   North America   151
         United States, Canada
23.   Australia and New Zealand   157
24.   Sub-Saharan Africa   159
25.   Printed Ephemera   163
26.   Pictorial Resources   167
         Europe (Medieval and Renaissance Illuminated
         Manuscripts, Later Manuscripts, Heraldry, Illustrated
         Printed Books, Prints and Printed Ephemera,
         Photographs, Portraits); The Near and Middle East,
         Asia and Africa (Hebrew, the Christian Orient,
         Islamic Collections, Africa, South Asia, Tibet,
         South East Asia, China, Japan, Korea)
27.   Bindings   182
28.   Historical Bibliography and Book History   187
Bodleian Shelfmarks   192
Principal Special Collections   198
Index   223

Foreword

The history of any great library resides in the complex inter-relationships between the personalities which have shaped it, the buildings which have housed it, and the collections which have filled it. Each of these key elements – especially where their stories are long and full of interesting variety – brings its own fascination to the institutional 'mix', and serves to determine the particular features that characterise a library in its present form. In the case of the Bodleian Library, now entering its fifth century of continuous existence at the heart of one of the great universities of the world, it is probably its collections – unrivalled anywhere among academic institutions, in terms of their range, depth and quality – on which its worldwide reputation is rightly based. Yet, by a curious irony, the history of those great collections is perhaps the element about which least (comparatively speaking) has been written. Certainly, until this present volume, there has been no comprehensive overview of the development of the Bodleian's collections, and no means by which either the general or the specialist reader can come to appreciate, within the space of a single volume, the entire intellectual content of the Library, in all its many forms.

This book is therefore greatly to be welcomed, in that it fills an important *lacuna* in the history of the Bodleian. As a detailed account of the Library's collections, the *Guide* serves to explain the Bodleian's present remarkable character, both as a library of world significance and as a lasting monument to its visionary founder. There can be no doubt that Sir Thomas Bodley himself would be staggered – but, hopefully, gratified – to know that the institution which he (re)founded for his *alma mater*, and for the much wider 'republic of letters', has grown into a great deal more than the 'true ornament' which he envisaged for Oxford over four hundred years ago. Yet it is largely Bodley's founding principles for *his* library which have served to make the Bodleian's collections what they are today. Systematic, but large-scale, acquisition of the world's literature, the achievement of deposit status, the widespread support of benefactors and dedicated friends, the employment of expert staff, and a commitment to posterity, with statutes and regulations designed to promote the longevity of the collections – all these are an integral part of Bodley's enduring legacy to the Library on which he lavished both his fortune and his energies in the latter part of his distinguished life. Thus it is that the publication of this systematic survey of the Bodleian's collections, described four centuries after the Library's opening in 1602, serves as yet one more tribute to the exceptional individual who set the Library on its way so firmly and so well all those many years ago.

Although the production of this volume has proved to be a major undertaking, the work is now done, the yawning gap is filled, and the story is now finally told. And, for this, as in so many other respects, a huge debt of gratitude is owed to the Library staff, past and present, forty or more of whom have helped to make this book such a valuable and compelling account of the Bodleian's collections as they exist in the early part of the twenty-first century. The Editors in particular – Mary Clapinson, Lesley Forbes, and especially the Managing Editor, Gregory Walker – should take the lion's share of the credit for commissioning and shaping the form and content of the book. It is deeply gratifying for Bodley's twenty-third Librarian to be able to thank them all for this exceptional labour of love, and to be able to commend to the widest possible readership this long-awaited volume of insights into one of the greatest library collections of the world.

Reg Carr
Bodley's Librarian
October 2003

Introduction

Purposes of the Guide

This *Guide* provides, for the first time, a subject-based approach to the Bodleian Library's collections as a whole. It offers a systematic outline of the Library's present resources, relating them to the growth of the collections over four hundred years and giving particular attention to holdings of special or unique strength. This form of presentation is intended to serve three purposes.

Firstly, it aims to act as an introduction and point of departure for prospective users of the Library and for those advising them, supplementing the descriptive text with extensive references to further reading and specialised catalogues, and with a descriptive list of the principal special collections.

Secondly, it is hoped that the chapters will give existing users an informative context to their immediate topics of study and research, and the stimulus for a wider exploration of the Bodleian's resources.

Thirdly, the *Guide* is intended as a readable account for anyone interested in the principal components that now make up the country's oldest and second largest public research library, and in the processes which formed it.

Contents of the Guide

Each of the chapters which form the main body of the *Guide* characterises briefly a segment of the Bodleian's resources for study and research. Most chapters deal with the Library's holdings in a particular subject or field of study, but a few focus on other bodies of material which are the product of special factors in collection-building, such as legal deposit and printed ephemera. Particular emphasis is laid on those special collections and other concentrations of material which constitute notable – and in some cases unique – resources for research.

Contributors and editors have had to make difficult judgements over what to omit from the text of the *Guide*, what to highlight and what to touch on in passing. However, they have not avoided evaluative comment or comparison with libraries elsewhere. Individual works are mentioned selectively, to exemplify or emphasise the nature of the material being described.

The *Guide* is not in any way a catalogue of the Bodleian, but it does provide references to many catalogues and other finding aids, as well as to published treatments of the collections and their contents. These will be found in the General Bibliography (*pages 12–15*) and in the select bibliographies following each chapter. The list of principal special collections (*pages 198–223*) is intended as an additional key to resources, not least because it includes entries for collections which, by the nature of their contents, have not readily fitted into the scheme of chapters. It is preceded by an introduction to the complex structure of Bodleian shelfmarks.

Now that the Bodleian Library is a part of Oxford University Library Services, and is developing a closer and more integrated relationship with all OULS libraries, it should be noted that the coverage of this *Guide* is confined to the central Bodleian and those libraries – formerly called 'dependent libraries' – most closely associated with it. These are the Bodleian Japanese Library; the Bodleian Law Library; the Bodleian Library of Commonwealth and African Studies at Rhodes House; the Indian Institute Library; the Institute for Chinese Studies Library; the Oriental Institute Library; the Philosophy Library; the Radcliffe Science Library and Hooke Library; and the Vere Harmsworth Library.

Editors, Contributors and Advisors

All editors, contributors and advisors are present or former members of the Bodleian Library's staff except where otherwise indicated

Editors

Gregory Walker *Managing Editor*
Mary Clapinson
Lesley Forbes

Contributors and Advisors

Kate Alderson-Smith
Bruce Barker-Benfield
Reg Carr
Hannah Chandler
Mary Clapinson
Alan Coates
Gillian Evison
Jack Flavell
Lesley Forbes
Geoffrey Groom
David Helliwell
Clive Hurst
Mark Janes
Richard Judd
Martin Kauffmann
Ralf Kramer
Julie Anne Lambert
Helen Langley
Robert Logan
Robert McNeil
Nick Millea
Doris Nicholson

Amanda Peters
John Pinfold
Jan Piggott *Keeper of the Archives, Dulwich College*
Judith Priestman
Adrian Roberts
Julian Roberts
Timothy Rogers
Mary Sheldon-Williams
Christopher Skelton-Foord
Barbara Tearle
Steven Tomlinson
Michael Turner
Izumi Tytler
David Vaisey
Hilla Wait
Colin Wakefield
Gregory Walker
Peter Ward Jones
Judith Waring
Nigel Wilson *Fellow of Lincoln College*
Robert Wyatt

General Bibliography

Descriptions and catalogues relating principally to the subject matter of a single chapter will be found in the select bibliography at the end of that chapter. The bibliographies do not normally include articles dealing with individual items in the collections, but many of these can be found in the Library's journal, the *Bodleian Library Record* (1938 to date) and its predecessor, the *Bodleian Quarterly Record* (1914–38).

Descriptions and histories

W.D. Macray, *Annals of the Bodleian Library, Oxford* (2nd ed.; Oxford: Clarendon Press, 1890, repr. Bodleian Library, 1984).

Letters of Sir Thomas Bodley to Thomas James, ed. G.W. Wheeler (Oxford: Clarendon Press, 1926).

Sir Edmund Craster, *History of the Bodleian Library, 1845–1945* (Oxford: Clarendon Press, 1952, repr. Bodleian Library, 1981).

A.F.L. Beeston, 'The Oriental Manuscript Collections of the Bodleian Library', *Bodleian Library Record*, 5/2 (1954), 1–7.

The Bodleian Library Account Book 1614–1646, ed. Gwen Hampshire (Oxford Bibliographical Society, New Series, Vol. XXI; Oxford, 1983).

Ian Philip, *The Bodleian Library in the Seventeenth and Eighteenth Centuries* (Oxford: Clarendon Press, 1983).

D.M. Rogers, *The Bodleian Library and its Treasures 1320–1700* (Henley-on-Thames: Ellis, 1991).

A Directory of Rare Book and Special Collections in the United Kingdom and the Republic of Ireland, ed. B.C. Bloomfield, (2nd ed., London: Library Association Publishing, 1997), 493–520.

Volumes in *The History of the University of Oxford* (Oxford: Oxford University Press) include chapters on the history of the Bodleian and other Oxford libraries. See especially:

I.G. Philip and Paul Morgan, 'Libraries, Books and Printing' in Volume IV, *Seventeenth-Century Oxford*, ed. Nicholas Tyacke (1997), 659–85.

I.G. Philip, 'Libraries and the University Press', in Volume V, *The Eighteenth Century*, ed. L.S.S. Sutherland and L.G. Mitchell (1986), 725–55.

I.G. Philip, 'The Bodleian Library', in Volume VI, part I, *Nineteenth-Century Oxford*, ed. M.G. Brock and M.C. Curthoys (1997), 585–97.

Giles Barber, 'Libraries', in Volume VIII, *The Twentieth Century*, ed. Brian Harrison (1994), 471–84.

Catalogues of the collections

The OLIS (Online Libraries Information System) Online Catalogue is a union catalogue which contains entries for nearly all published material held in the Bodleian Library, as well as the holdings of many other Oxford libraries. Workstations for consulting the online catalogue are available in all Bodleian reading rooms. OLIS can also be accessed from outside the Library on the World Wide Web at: www.lib. ox.ac.uk/olis or by telnetting directly to library.ox.ac.uk.

A growing number of the Library's manuscript collections are also catalogued online and can be accessed at www.bodley.ox.ac.uk/dept/scwmss/wmss/online/online.htm. Many descriptions of individual collections can be found on the Archives Hub at www.archiveshub.ac.uk. Work is currently (2004) in progress on an Electronic Catalogue of Medieval and Renaissance Manuscripts, which will incorporate thousands of bibliographical references to Bodleian manuscripts at present held in the card file 'Bodley Refs' (published references to Bodleian Western manuscripts) in Duke Humfrey's Library.

Listed below are other, published catalogues giving access to major sectors of the collections. Further advice on finding materials and using the catalogues can be found in the Library's current *Reader's Guide*, in guides to particular departments and types of material, and on departmental web pages.

The 'Quarto' series of catalogues, first published between 1845 and 1900, cover the major manuscript collections acquired mainly in the 17th and 18th centuries. Vols.

I–V, IX–X cover the Western manuscript collections: Ashmole, Canonici (Greek and Latin, and Italian), Digby, Greek manuscripts, Laud, Rawlinson and Tanner. Vols. VI–VIII are catalogues of Oriental manuscripts.

Summary Catalogue of Western Manuscripts in the Bodleian Library at Oxford. (7 vols.; Oxford: Clarendon Press, 1895–1953, repr. Kraus-Thomson, 1980).

Otto Pächt and J.J.G. Alexander, *Illuminated Manuscripts in the Bodleian Library, Oxford* (3 vols.; Oxford: Clarendon Press, 1966–73). An unpublished supplement (1974) containing addenda and a concordance of shelfmarks is available in the Library.

A.C. de la Mare, *Catalogue of the Collection of Medieval Manuscripts Bequeathed to the Bodleian Library, Oxford by James P.R. Lyell* (Oxford: Clarendon Press, 1971).

Andrew G. Watson, *Catalogue of Dated and Datable Manuscripts c.435–1600 in Oxford Libraries* (2 vols.; Oxford: Clarendon Press, 1984).

Mary Clapinson and T.D. Rogers, *Summary Catalogue of Post-Medieval Western Manuscripts in the Bodleian Library, Oxford: Acquisitions 1916–1975* (3 vols.; Oxford: Clarendon Press, 1991). Post-1975 accessions are described in unpublished catalogues available in the Library and, increasingly, online. Current accessions are catalogued online.

Brian Ó Cuív, *Catalogue of Irish Language Manuscripts in the Bodleian Library at Oxford and Oxford College Libraries* (Dublin: Dublin Institute for Advanced Studies, 2001).

Peter Kidd, *Medieval Manuscripts from the Collection of T.R. Buchanan in the Bodleian Library, Oxford* (Oxford: Bodleian Library, 2002).

Barbara Crostini Lappin, *A Catalogue of Greek Manuscripts Acquired by the Bodleian Library since 1916* (Oxford: Bodleian Library, 2004).

R.T. Milford and D.M. Sutherland, *A Catalogue of English Newspapers and Periodicals in the Bodleian Library, 1622–1800* (Oxford: Oxford Bibliographical Society, 1936).

Bodleian Library, *Pre-1920 Catalogue of Printed Books on Compact Disc* (Oxford University Press, 1993).

A Guide to Microform Holdings in the Bodleian Library (5th ed.; Oxford: Bodleian Library, 2002).

A Catalogue of Books Printed in the Fifteenth Century now in the Bodleian Library, ed. Alan Coates et al. (Oxford, 2005, forthcoming).

Exhibition catalogues

Duke Humfrey's Library and the Divinity School 1488–1988 (Oxford: Bodleian Library, 1988).

A Continental Shelf: Books Across Europe From Ptolemy to Don Quixote (Oxford: Bodleian Library, 1994).

Sir Thomas Bodley and his Library (Oxford: Bodleian Library, 2002).

Wonderful Things From 400 Years of Collecting: The Bodleian Library 1602–2002 (Oxford: Bodleian Library, 2002).

1. Building the Bodleian's Collections

The Work of Four Centuries

Collection-building is the fundamental function of an active library. It is essential that a leading scholarly library such as the Bodleian should exert itself to keep abreast of current publications, fill gaps in its existing holdings, and at the same time judiciously seek and foster the donation of material that will enhance its strengths. Indeed, gifts and bequests have given the Bodleian much of its unique quality, and have added conspicuously to its glories in some of the thinnest times (financially speaking) in its history. We should nevertheless remember too that the Library's Curators and staff, in their repeated exercise of choice and their allocation of finite – often very finite – resources, have over the past four centuries created countless patterns in the texture of a collection of some seven million volumes. Many of the patterns – some broad and sketchy, others small and detailed – are traced in the rest of this book. This chapter looks at some of the past influences on the Bodleian's collection-building activity, and highlights issues now facing the Library as it considers how its holdings and services can most effectively be offered to users as part of an integrated library structure.

Thomas Bodley's best known, and perhaps most far-reaching, contribution to the future of his library's collections was the agreement of 1610 with the Stationers' Company which was the forerunner of the present provisions for legal deposit. The idea had in fact been suggested to him by his first Librarian, Thomas James. Bodley took a vigorous personal interest in all matters of book selection until his death, constantly discussed policy with James, sought benefactions, and arranged for agents across Europe and beyond to buy books for his library. The scope he gave to trusted representatives is illustrated by his comment on John Bill, who bought for him in France and Italy: 'His commission was large, his leasure very good, and his paiment sure at home'. Bodley intended that, after his death, the Librarian should follow the Curators' advice in book selection, and also solicit recommendations, subject to the Vice-Chancellor's permission to purchase. Unfortunately the assurance of what Bodley called 'some certaintie in revenewe' came to an end with the Civil War. By the later seventeenth century the shortage of funds was so acute that there could be no consistent approach to the buying of books. Deposit by the Stationers lapsed, and subsequent measures to revive it had only limited success for the next two hundred years. Exchanges – still today an important source of material – first figure in the Bodleian's history in 1691–92, when the University Press sent 55 volumes to an Amsterdam bookseller in return for books intended for the Bodleian. However, ordinary spending fell to around £10 a year in the 1690s, and to nothing at all in the first years of the eighteenth century. After Thomas Hyde resigned as Librarian in 1700 he complained of being 'chid and reproved' by the Vice-Chancellor for proposing more books for purchase than the University claimed to be able to afford.

For the greater part of the eighteenth century the Library depended for its growth far more on donations than on books bought. Lord Crewe's benefaction of £10 annually was the chief element in the book fund from 1750 until 1780, when the University at last recognised again the need for a substantial and assured income, and granted the Bodleian the proceeds arising from charges made to readers and from a share in students' matriculation fees. This 'new money', as it was called, effected a remarkable transformation in the Library's attitude to collection-building and in its procedures for selection. 'They have lately bought all the new foreign books' wrote one Oxford bookseller in 1789. The Curators met more frequently to select titles from book fair catalogues and other sources; and the records of 'Libri Desiderati', which we have from 1788, show that nearly all items that were recommended were being ordered. One interesting and successful innovation was the large purchase of early printed books from the Pinelli and Crevenna sales in 1789–90, when the Bodleian was able to spend nearly £2,600 by appealing to members of the University for interest-free loans.

The 'new money' made it possible, and not uncommon, for the Library to spend £1,000 or more on important collections – and this in a period when a Gutenberg Bible could be bought for £100, as the Bodleian's copy was in 1793. It was a time when Bodley's Librarian, Bulkeley Bandinel (described by Craster as 'watchful and usually ahead of his competitors') had the money to back his talent for making acquisitions which were unexpected, far-sighted, and sometimes inspired. The Canonici collection of manuscripts was bought in 1817, at £5,444 the most expensive purchase since the Library's foundation. In 1829 the Oppenheimer Library – the most important and magnificent Hebraica collection ever accumulated – was acquired at the bargain price of £2,200. The Library could afford to buy 43,000 foreign dissertations in 1827; over 19,000 English pamphlets in 1837; and 2,000 early Polish books in 1850. However, the value of the bookfund declined steadily from around mid-century. Large special purchases ended, periodical subscriptions began to consume an increasing share of expenditure; and by the late 1870s the Bodleian was spending only about £1,400 a year on books while the figure at the British Museum was around £10,000.

Throughout this period the selection of material was largely carried out by the Librarian and his senior staff. The 1856 Bodleian statute empowered the then librarian (H.O. Coxe) to take the advice of professors and others, 'but', records Craster, ' there is little to show how far the Librarian availed himself of the permission accorded to him'. Concern at the low level and slow receipt of acquisitions was voiced in a 'memorial' circulated in the University in 1888, and prompted the Curators to begin weekly meetings to consider book-lists, but these lapsed after a term due to the lack of a quorum. During the 1920s the Library was able to spend little more than £200 a year on foreign books, and the position improved only gradually up to the outbreak of the Second World War. The first 'dependent libraries' were added to the Bodleian in 1927 (the Radcliffe Science Library and the Indian Institute Library) and 1929 (Rhodes House Library), bringing to it the beginnings of specialisation in collecting by subject and area.

The thirty years after 1945 saw a rapid increase in the scale of the Bodleian's collection-building operations. The range of University research and teaching broadened, contributing to and in turn fed by the expansion of scholarly publishing around the world, and more generous funding allowed the Library to respond actively to both these trends, as well as to handle many major donations and retrospectively to fill many gaps in its earlier holdings. After a fairly stable period in the later 1970s and the 1980s, a combination of factors has in recent years worked against the Bodleian and other major research libraries in their efforts to maintain adequate levels of coverage and of access to resources. The rising cost of publications, notably of scientific periodicals, early printed books and manuscripts, is outstripping the funds available for acquisition. Competition for those funds has sharpened as the range of media required for research and teaching becomes more diverse, and as the University seeks to provide an expanding array of networked electronic services throughout the library system. Alongside these new developments, and indeed throughout the post-war period, legal deposit has continued to reflect the British publishing industry's record of growth by delivering more publications every year.

Every decision to buy or subscribe, every acceptance of a donation, every exchange agreement negotiated, makes assumptions about the purpose that a library serves. The Bodleian has – and has had – more roles attributed to it than perhaps any other library in the country. It is, of course, the University's central research library, and this status alone has carried with it a range of implied obligations with regard to collection-building. Over the centuries it has accumulated the largest, and often the richest, library resources for most fields of study represented in Oxford; but it has also come to owe, *de facto*, different duties to different subjects. College, faculty and departmental libraries, as they have been set up and developed, have assumed a variety of roles in providing for particular academic interests. Some of their collections have gained national and international repute in major areas of study, and are recognised as the University's leading holdings of material in those subjects. In an integrated library structure, collecting policies need to be clearly assigned and articulated. Collection-building in the Bodleian is now moving decisively away from extensive but largely informal collaboration with other Oxford libraries into a planned framework of collection management for the University Library Services as a whole.

Besides its duties to the University, the Bodleian has since Sir Thomas Bodley's days recognised a responsibility to have regard to the needs of scholarship in the world at large. Its Statute requires that it should be maintained 'not only as a university library but also as an institution of national and international importance'; and the Bodleian's efforts to meet these expectations have greatly influenced – as they still do – the character of the collections and the decisions which are adding to them. The privilege of legal deposit remains an essential element in collecting strategy. Over the years it has combined with supplementary procurement to form an archive of what the British Isles have produced in print since Caxton. Beyond this, the Library has always striven to collect over a broader canvas than the immediate research and teaching requirements of the University would dictate, with the future as much as the present in mind. This has stemmed from a perceived expectation that great libraries should lead as well as follow research; and that material – and it might from one occasion to the next be anything from a single pamphlet to a second Rawlinson Collection – should continue to be sought out and made accessible to enhance the unique qualities in the Bodleian's holdings that attract scholars from around the world.

The Bodleian has never lacked, and continues to welcome, the interest of users and others prepared to tell it what should be collected and to comment on the adequacy of its coverage. There has been a steady stream of personal critiques since at least the early eighteenth century, when the antiquary Thomas Hearne (perhaps the Library's most noted Janitor) accused it of being 'meanly…furnished with curious Classical Books, and Books of our English History and Antiquities'. The Bodleian's collections, like those of every large institutional library, are the product of countless acts of recommendation and judgement – scholarly or biased, short-term or long-sighted - made by thousands of people, from Sir Thomas Bodley himself, through twenty-three of his Librarians and thirteen generations of Curators, to the library staff and committees of today, and the readers and other specialists who advise them. After four hundred years of this great undertaking, we as librarians owe it to ourselves, and to the library we serve and build, to render an account to our readers, our benefactors, our parent body, and to Thomas Bodley's *Respublica literatorum*.

2. The Legal Deposit Collections

It is generally accepted that the origins of legal deposit can be traced back to France and the *Ordonnance de Montpellier* of 1537, which required the printer and publisher to forward a copy of every newly published book to the Royal Library at Blois. It is likely that Thomas James, Bodley's first Librarian, was aware of this requirement, and it was his suggestion that Sir Thomas Bodley might make a similar arrangement with the Stationers' Company in London. The Stationers' Company had, since 1557, kept a series of registers in which all books printed by members were entered, thus ensuring for the owner the exclusive right to print that book. There was, of course, another element to this, since the Stationers' Company charter, confirmed by Queen Elizabeth in 1559, gave the State a degree of control over what was printed. Bodley saw in this situation the opportunity to provide for his library the means of acquiring free of charge all the scholarly books published in England for the use of members of the University and for the scholarly community outside Oxford, and he managed to persuade the Master and Wardens of the Company to enter into a perpetual agreement to supply the Library with a free copy of every new book printed by members of the Company. The resulting deed was signed on 12 December 1610 and sealed in Convocation in Oxford on 27 February 1611.

The first book received under this arrangement, now at shelfmark 4° R 34 Th., with Bodley's inscription on the flyleaf, was an anonymous work printed in 1611 by Felix Kingston for Thomas Man, entitled *The Christian Religion Substantially, Methodicallie, Plainlie and Profitablie Treatised*. While Sir Thomas might well have approved of this title, he was disappointed by the nature of some of the other books received. Many were novels, romances, and almanacs, which he described as 'idle bookes and riffe-raffes' and James was encouraged not to add such material to the Library. Bodley also disapproved of books in English; and works in the vernacular, including what are now regarded as major works of literature, do not feature greatly in the catalogue of the Library's collections, published in 1620. The Bodleian Library's collections of literature in English of this period owe more to the acquisition of Robert Burton's books in 1640 than to the agreement with the Stationers' Company. In 1664, some books deposited under this agreement, including a copy of the First Folio of Shakespeare dating from 1623, were probably part of a batch of duplicates sold to an Oxford bookseller. Although the Bodleian later acquired another copy via the Malone collection, it was fortunate in being able to buy back its original copy of the First Folio from the Turbutt family in 1905.

While the agreement might not have affected the Master and Wardens of the Stationers' Company, the requirement to provide free books was resented by many printers and publishers, who made up the ordinary membership of the Company. From the beginning, there were problems in establishing a reliable supply of books, and the scale of deposit in these early years seems to have been limited. For example, the total number of items received within the period of a year in 1613–14 was 113, which represents no more than 20% of registered items and 15% of all publications during that period. The University's response was to enlist the aid of its Chancellor, Archbishop William Laud. This action resulted in a decree in the notorious Star Chamber in 1637 which stated that a copy of every new book had to be delivered to Stationers' Hall before any sale took place, and that this copy was then to be sent to the Bodleian Library for preservation there. Following the abolition of the Star Chamber in 1640, the agreement with the Stationers' Company became largely ineffective. In 1662, the Press Licensing Act confirmed the role of the Stationers' Company in licensing and registering new publications, and it required the deposit of three copies: one for the Royal Library, the others for the universities of Oxford and Cambridge. Although it was the duty of the Master of the Company to collect these copies, there was no requirement until 1665 for him to forward them to the libraries. In 1674, the two Universities consulted about joint action, and in 1688 Bodley's Librarian, Thomas Hyde, went to London personally to demand the copies due to the Library. The Act itself, seen as a means of controlling what was printed and published in a time of crisis, was allowed to lapse in 1679, and although it was revived in 1685, it finally expired in 1695. In the following fifteen years, the Library had to rely on the generosity of some London booksellers for books published in England.

The first Copyright Act of 1710 required printers to deposit copies of their works on the best paper in nine libraries, which by then included the Scottish universities and the Faculty of Advocates in Edinburgh. Publishers had originally claimed perpetual copyright in their works, but in this Act the term was limited to twenty-one years for existing works and fourteen years for works published after 1710. However, imprecise wording in the Act meant that printers could claim that they had only to deposit those works registered at Stationers' Hall. Expensive works, less prone to the likelihood of being pirated, were not registered, and thus avoided deposit. As a result, only 10% of published books were entered at Stationers' Hall in the period 1710 to 1726. During this period, J.P. Chalmers in his study of the survival of copyright books noted 1,257 items deposited at Stationers' Hall, and of these he could identify only 727 in the Bodleian. As a result of the continuing failure of publishers to deposit books under the terms of the Act, the Bodleian Curators appointed the booksellers John and William Innys to act as their agents in London in October

1726, but this had little long-term effect. In 1727, the Bodleian Library received only 27 items under the Act and relied much on the generosity of individual authors and of major benefactors such as the Reverend Charles Godwyn (who left to the Bodleian some 1,600 mainly eighteenth-century books and pamphlets on history) to make good the deficiencies of deposit. As in the past, not all deposits were added to stock, and the Library's records for 1768 and 1769 reveal that only 45% of items received in this way were catalogued.

A further Copyright Act of 1775 made little difference to this state of affairs, although in theory the publisher did not have legal protection unless nine copies were deposited at Stationers' Hall at the time of registration. A ruling in 1798 at the Court of King's Bench, *Beckford v. Hood*, reversed the general view that publishers had no copyright in a work unless it was registered at Stationers' Hall, and this led to a further decline in the number of registrations: from 651 in 1797 to 271 in 1812. In the early years of the nineteenth century, there was much discussion about copyright and deposit. Edward Christian, in his *Vindication of the Rights of the Universities...* (1807), argued that the intention was for all published books to be deposited and preserved for the use of posterity, while Robert Maugham in *A Treatise on the Laws of Literary Property* (1828) took the view that not everything need be kept. In 1812, Cambridge University sued a publisher for non-deposit, and obtained the ruling that eleven copies should be deposited at Stationers' Hall, whether or not the work was registered. A further Copyright Act of 1814 did little to change the situation for either side, but in the Copyright Act of 1836 the number of libraries entitled to deposit was reduced to five. Those five libraries were the British Museum, which inherited the right of the Royal Library, the Universities of Oxford and Cambridge, the Faculty of Advocates in Edinburgh, and Trinity College, Dublin. The British Museum's right was taken over in 1973 by the British Library. The right of the Faculty of Advocates Library passed to the National Library of Scotland in 1924. The National Library of Wales became the sixth library in 1911. A further Act in 1842 repealed much of the previous legislation and stipulated that the copy on the best paper should go to British Museum within one month of publication. The other libraries retained the right to demand a copy within twelve months of publication, which forms the basis of the current legislation.

Not only were there difficulties in interpreting and enforcing the legislation during this period, but the mechanism for deposit continued to be fallible. In its Keeper of Printed Books – later Librarian – Antonio Panizzi, the British Museum had someone determined to enforce the terms of the Act, and in the period 1850–55 the annual intake of deposits in that library rose from 9,834 to 25,818 items. The other libraries were forced to rely on Joseph Greenhill, the Stationers' Company Warehouse Keeper and Treasurer of the English Stock. Although he received fees from the libraries, Greenhill operated the registration and deposit system very much as a personal fiefdom.

As a result of his inefficiencies, representatives of the four libraries met in London in 1859 to plan a course of action, although the final break was not made until 1863 when those libraries appointed their own agent, Gregory W. Eccles of the British Museum. In the period 1799 to 1814, annual registrations at Stationers' Hall averaged 343; however, the annual number of items recorded in the *Nineteenth-Century Short Title Catalogue* averages 2,775 for the same period. The proportion of items registered in the period 1815 to 1842 improved markedly: an average of 1,231 compared to an average of 4,819 publications recorded in *NSTC*. In the period 1843–1862, the average declined: 1,005 publications registered, compared to an average of 7,674 items in *NSTC*. However, in 1852, the Bodleian recorded 3,711 volumes and 4,308 periodical parts received by deposit, and these figures had nearly doubled (to 6,067 and 8,550) by 1879. At this point, it was estimated that legal deposit accounted for 60–70% of the Bodleian Library's intake. In 1900, the value of the material received was calculated to be £2,000.

The Bodleian was now beginning to be concerned about the amount of material received under the Act, and in 1895 the libraries considered the possibility of joint action to limit the amount of material received, although no agreement was reached. Not only was more material received, but more was retained and added to stock. In contrast to the views of the founder, Bodley's Librarian E.W.B. Nicholson now argued that 'no printed matter which the Library receives under the Act is valueless to posterity'.

The current basis of legal deposit in the United Kingdom is the Copyright Act of 1911, which granted copyright protection without the need for registration, thus removing the role of the Stationers' Company. The six libraries have continued to exercise their rights to claim; five of them working together through the Copyright Agency based in London and the British Library through its Legal Deposit Office in Boston Spa. During the twentieth century, the number of legal deposit accessions in the Bodleian has fluctuated according to economic conditions and the output of the book trade. In the year 1914, it had reached 52,000 items, but declined in 1918 to 35,000. By 1931, legal deposit accessions had reached 58,000 items per annum, despite efforts to reduce the number of popular periodicals taken. By 1970, this figure had reached 92,000 items and, by 1990, the total was nearly 160,000 items. The current annual intake (in 2003) is in the region of 70,000 monograph titles and 100,000 periodical parts. This includes a high proportion of the books and periodicals available through trade sources in the United Kingdom and in Ireland, including many publications published in the United States and distributed in the United Kingdom. It also includes the publications of many smaller, non-commercial publishers, and embraces material in a wide diversity of physical formats. The Bodleian exercises some selectivity with regard to periodical titles, in co-operation with the other legal deposit libraries, but aims to take all titles of academic value.

Sir Thomas Bodley's agreement and the successive Acts of Parliament that followed have not always been successful in practice, as the statistics for receipts over the first two and a half centuries reveal. Bodley wished to be selective in adding deposited books to the Library and, consequently, he excluded much that we would now consider to be of great value. As the enforcement of the Act has become more effective, the libraries have aimed at a higher level of coverage. Bodley's original agreement, involving just one library, has evolved within a legal framework to embrace the concept of shared responsibility, with six libraries building and maintaining a national published archive. The legal deposit privilege, exercised albeit imperfectly over nearly four hundred years, has formed the cornerstone of the Bodleian Library's collecting policies, particularly in the last hundred years. The expectation that most British and Irish publications would be received under the Act has enabled the Library to devote most of its resources to the collection of foreign publications. The quality and depth of the collections thus amassed has encouraged donations of material to supplement and complement what has been acquired by deposit and purchase. Sir Thomas Bodley's original initiative – which was to endow the University of Oxford with the scholarly output of English publishing – has been an essential factor in the development of the Library's central role in the provision of resources for the University and for the national and international research community.

Select bibliography

R.C.B. Partridge, *The History of the Legal Deposit of Books Throughout the British Empire: A Thesis Approved for the Honours Diploma of the Library Association* (London: The Library Association, 1938).

J.P. Chalmers, 'Bodleian Copyright Survivors of the First Sixteen Years of the Copyright Act of Queen Anne, 10 April 1710 to 25 March 1726', M.Litt. thesis (University of Oxford, 1974). Permission to use information contained in this thesis is gratefully acknowledged.

David McKitterick, *Cambridge University Library: A History: The Eighteenth and Nineteenth Centuries* (Cambridge: Cambridge University Press, 1986). Chapter 14 is entitled 'The Copyright Agency'.

John Feather, *Publishing, Piracy and Politics: An Historical Study of Copyright in Britain* (London: Mansell, 1994). Chapter 4 is entitled 'The Legal Deposit of books'.

Simon Eliot, "'Mr Greenhill, whom you cannot get rid of": Copyright, Legal Deposit and the Stationers' Company in the Nineteenth Century', in Robin Myers et al., (eds.), *Libraries and the Book Trade: The Formation of Collections from the Sixteenth to the Twentieth Century* (New Castle, Delaware: Oak Knoll Press, 2000), 51–79.

3. Classical Studies

The Bodleian's inherited collections, both printed and manuscript, are a major source for classical studies. In close consultation with the Sackler Library, the other major classics research library in the University, the Bodleian pursues a broad-based collecting policy for current publications. Through the legal deposit system it receives the product of British and Irish publishers in the field, and it purchases extensively in Engli sh and European languages (principally German, French, Italian, Spanish and Greek), buying all standard continental editions of ancient authors and subscribing to many of the scholarly monograph series. The Bodleian develops its collections in classical language, literature, philosophy, history and inter-disciplinary studies. The Sackler Library incorporates the former Ashmolean Library and its collecting in classics reflects its origins as the library of a major museum, concentrating on art, archaeology, epigraphy and numismatics. Both libraries purchase antiquarian material in support of their prime fields.

The strength of the manuscript and rare book collections of the Bodleian is largely the result of its early foundation in a University whose curriculum was for centuries firmly based in the classics. (*See also the chapter on Theology.*)

Manuscripts

The classical papyri in the Bodleian are less extensive than those in the Ashmolean Museum, but include a number of major items. Chronologically the collection covers the Hellenistic to Byzantine periods, mostly in Greek but with a few Latin pieces. Most are documents relating to the public or private business of Graeco-Roman Egypt. The earliest and most important of these are the two rolls containing the Revenue Laws of Ptolemy II Philadelphus, as revised in 259–8 BC (MS. Gr. class. a. 4 (P)). By contrast, the most personal document is a letter of an Egyptian boy, Theon, from the second or third century AD, requiring his father to buy him a lyre at Alexandria (MS. Gr. class. f. 66 (P)).

The literary papyri include a number of unique (if fragmentary) text-carriers for Greek poetry: second-century AD fragments of the lyric poets Alcaeus and Sappho (MSS. Gr. class. a. 16 (P) and c. 76 (P)) and over 300 lines of Euripides' lost play *Hypsipyle* (MS. Gr. class. b. 13 (P)); from a papyrus codex of the fourth century, seven leaves of Callimachus' *Aetia* and *Iambi* (MS. Gr. class. c.72 (P)). Other papyri add ancient witnesses for texts already known from the medieval tradition: substantial remains of two second- and third-century rolls of Homer's *Iliad* (MSS. Gr. class. a. 1 (P) and a. 8 (P)); fragments of Plato's *Laches*, early third century BC, written probably less than a century after the author's death (MSS. Gr. class. d. 22–3 (P)); in Latin, small fragments of Livy and Sallust from the fourth and fifth centuries AD (MSS. Lat. class. f. 5 (P) and e. 20 (P)). There are a few biblical, theological and liturgical papyri in Greek. The most famous of these contains the *Sayings of Jesus*, in a single leaf from a papyrus codex of the third century AD (MS. Gr. th. e. 7 (P)), which was later identified from a parallel Coptic version as part of the Gospel of Thomas.

Although nearly all the Bodleian's papyri were acquired directly or indirectly from Egypt between 1878 and 1934, a group of four papyrus rolls from the library excavated at Herculaneum in 1752 had been given to the University in 1810 by the Prince of Wales. His gift included pencil transcripts of many of the other rolls which had been opened and copied at Naples where the originals remain (MSS. Gr. class. c. 1–7).

Besides the *unica* amongst its literary papyri, the Bodleian holds a few medieval manuscripts of classical texts which are famous either as paramount witnesses (Plato, Euclid, Catullus) or even as sole text-carrier (the Oxford Juvenal (MS. Canon. Class. Lat. 41) with its 36 unique lines). However the strength of its holdings lies in the broad coverage of many classical authors in a host of secondary witnesses, of greater or lesser importance for their respective texts. Assessed alongside those preserved in comparable libraries, such manuscripts are of value not only as sources of readings for modern editors but also as evidence for the history of their authors' medieval transmission and intellectual influence. Further sources for these topics are to be found in marginal glosses and in the separate commentaries and other secondary scholarship of medieval and later scholars.

The Bodleian holds a few Latin manuscripts from the fifth to the eighth centuries which are of interest for the history of Late Roman script and book-production simply by virtue of their date, though their texts are biblical or Christian rather than strictly classical. Among these is a fifth-century manuscript in uncial script of St. Jerome's translation of Eusebius' Chronicle (MS. Auct. T. 2. 26), one of the two oldest Latin manuscripts now in Britain. Many of the Bodleian's Carolingian manuscripts from France and Germany came as gifts from Archbishop Laud in the 1630s. Amongst these are ninth-century copies of a few early texts, including the earliest and most faithful witness to Sidonius Apollinaris (MS. Laud Lat. 104). Continental manuscripts of the ninth, tenth and eleventh centuries from other sources include copies of Virgil, Solinus, Priscian, Seneca, Terence, Horace, Cicero and Livy.

Manuscripts written in the British Isles form the backbone of the Bodleian's collections, and play a modest but distinctive role in the transmission of the Latin classics. From the Anglo-Saxon period, St. Dunstan's classbook (MS. Auct. F. 4. 32) includes a late ninth-century copy from Wales of the first book of Ovid's *Ars Amatoria*, one of the two earliest witnesses for the text. This was given to the Bodleian as a foundation gift by Thomas Allen in 1601. A similarly early gift of manuscripts from Exeter Cathedral (1602) included a copy of Boethius' *De consolatione philosophiae*, superbly written in English Caroline minuscule of the tenth century at Canterbury (MS. Auct. F. 1. 15). From elsewhere in Europe, the Bodleian's most important classical manuscript of the period following the Norman Conquest is the Oxford Juvenal (mentioned above), copied in Beneventan script at or near the abbey of Monte Cassino around the year 1100. It reached Oxford in 1817 in the purchase of over 2,000 manuscripts from the collection of Matteo Luigi Canonici. This acquisition was part of an active policy by the University to build up its classical holdings. Other collections which provided opportunities to buy classical manuscripts were those of J. P. D'Orville (bought 1804), E. D. Clarke (1809) and J. Meerman (1824).

The newly acquired collections were especially rich in later manuscripts from Italy. The Canonici collection yielded the famous Catullus, dating from the third quarter of the fourteenth century, the earliest complete surviving copy of the text (MS. Canon. Class. Lat. 30). Other ancient authors arrived in multiple copies made by humanistic scribes in fifteenth-century Italy. Two of the Library's most famous Greek manuscripts, the 'D'Orville Euclid' (MS. D'Orville 301) and the 'Patmos Plato' (MS. E. D. Clarke 39), reached Oxford in the early nineteenth century. Although derived from different sources, they were both made in Constantinople in the late ninth century for the same scholar-collector, Arethas of Patrae.

The earliest surviving manuscript of Photius' *Letters*, with their allusions to classical poetry, is of similar date (MS. Barocci 217). It came to the Bodleian in 1629 in the Library's first major acquisition of Greek manuscripts. Nearly 250 Greek manuscripts, collected by Francesco and Iacopo Barozzi of Crete and Venice in the sixteenth and early seventeenth centuries, were bought for the University in 1629 by its then Chancellor, William Herbert, 3rd Earl of Pembroke. The size of the Barocci Collection and its depth of coverage established the Bodleian as the major repository of Greek manuscripts in England. A further twenty-nine Greek manuscripts arrived at the same time from Sir Thomas Roe, English ambassador at Constantinople, and other groups followed from Archbishop Laud (1630s), Oliver Cromwell (1654) and John Selden (1659).

Although most of the texts in these smaller donations were patristic and theological rather than classical, the Barocci collection included a number of major witnesses for classical and Byzantine literature. MS. Barocci 50 is a tenth-century miscellany of Greek poetry and other texts, including the earliest surviving copies of Musaeus' *Hero and Leander* and of the Homeric parody, *Batrachomyomachia*. A vast collection of over 140 Greek texts is preserved in a volume of the thirteenth century (MS. Barocci 131). Amongst the Byzantine materials in the Bodleian's Greek collections are a few classical texts in manuscripts of the eleventh to fourteenth centuries. One of the most important is the eleventh-century archetype of Epictetus, from which all other surviving copies descend (MS. Auct. T. 4. 13). It is one of the 50 Greek manuscripts bought in 1820 from the eighteenth-century collection of Giovanni Saibante of Verona. By far the majority of the Bodleian's manuscripts of Greek classical authors date from the fifteenth and sixteenth centuries, many written in Italy by scribes who were Greek émigrés .

A major acquisition of Greek manuscripts arrived in 1954, with over 100 manuscripts bought from the library of the Earls of Leicester at Holkham Hall. Like Holkham itself, the Greek manuscripts were the product of the Grand Tour, as eighteenth-century members of the Coke family brought home classical treasures from the Renaissance libraries of the Continent. In 1717 Thomas Coke bought manuscripts from the library of San Giovanni di Verdara at Padua, which included fifteenth-century manuscripts of Homer's *Odyssey* and *Iliad*, the first book of Herodotus, and Philostratus (MSS. Holkham Gr. 84 and 116, 90 and 103).

Sources for classical scholarship from the sixteenth century onwards survive in several classes of material: scholarly commentaries and notes on classical topics and authors; academic correspondence; and marginal notes, including collations, in early printed editions of classical texts. Collections of *adversaria* by scholars of the sixteenth to eighteenth centuries include groups from Isaac Casaubon, J.E.Grabe, Gerard Langbaine and James St Amand. Manuscripts and annotated printed books from the collection of Nicolas Heinsius were bought at Leiden in 1683 by Edward Bernard, and were purchased in 1697–8 by the University with Bernard's own working papers (*S.C.* 8717–8886). In the first half of the eighteenth century, J.P.D'Orville corresponded from Holland in Latin, Dutch, French, English and Italian with the major classicists of his day, and acquired papers of earlier scholars and correspondence of Isaac Vossius and Nicolas Heinsius (MSS. D'Orville 468–76). These papers were purchased with D'Orville's classical manuscripts in 1804, along with his collection of annotated printed books. Letters from many other major scholars, often between England and the Continent, survive among the Bodleian's general collections of seventeenth- and eighteenth-century literary correspondence, one of the Library's special strengths.

Many editions of classical texts have been printed at Oxford over the centuries. An accumulation of the working papers, manuscripts and printed books associated with editions printed in the eighteenth and nineteenth centuries was built up at the Clarendon Press. These materials were deposited at, and later given to, the Bodleian between 1885 and 1922 (MSS. Clar. Press). Amongst the papers of nineteenth- and twentieth-century classicists may be noted those of Mark Pattison (1813–84), with his particular interest in the history of classical scholarship, and of two Regius Professors of Greek, Ingram Bywater (1840–1914) and Gilbert Murray (1866–1957).

Finally, the photographic collections of E.A. Lowe on early Latin manuscripts, of James Wardrop and Alfred Fairbank on humanistic Latin manuscripts, and of Edgar Lobel and Ruth Barbour on Greek manuscripts, bring the subject full circle.

Incunabula

The Bodleian was principally concerned in the late eighteenth and early nineteenth centuries with obtaining a comprehensive series of the earliest editions of the classics. This policy was motivated both by contemporary taste and by the classical curriculum of the University at the time. The Library bought early printed classical texts heavily at the Pinelli and Crevenna sales in 1789 and 1790, and many more were acquired by donation. The Bodleian obtained perhaps its grandest incunable of a classical (or, for that matter, any other) text through the bequest of Francis Douce (1757–1834), former Keeper of Manuscripts at the British Museum. This is a decorated copy of the 1476 edition of Cristoforo Landino's Italian translation of Pliny's *Natural History*, printed on vellum in Venice by Nicolaus Jenson (Douce 310). The incunable classics in the Library's collections include copies both of texts alone and texts with commentaries, many printed in Italy with finely hand-painted Italian initials and borders. The collection of both Latin and Greek texts printed by Aldus Manutius is strong; for example, of the sixteen editions printed by Aldus in Greek before 1500, the Bodleian has copies of thirteen.

Later Classical Scholarship

Legal deposit ensured that the Bodleian received the works of Oxford's own eminent classical scholars, such as Gaisford and Routh, from early in the nineteenth century onwards, and also the publications of other prominent British writers such as Gibbon, Bentley and Porson. The renaissance in classical studies on the Continent at that time was generating new scholarship of which Oxford was only dimly aware, and which found little representation on the Bodleian shelves. Many of the more serious lacunae of that period have since been made good by the acquisition of major collections, either by purchase or by bequest. An example of complementary purchase is the collection of foreign classical dissertations belonging to Friedrich Jacobs, editor of the *Anthologia Graeca* (1794–1814). By the end of the nineteenth century Oxford had regained its academic status, and classical scholarship flourished under major figures such as Bywater, Jowett, Conington, and Dean Liddell, the co-compiler of the standard *Greek-English Lexicon*. The Homer library of David Binning Monro (1836–1905) was purchased after his death for the Bodleian by his friends. In 1923 William Ewart Gladstone's son Henry presented to the Library his father's collection of pamphlets on Homer. (Before he achieved political fame, the elder Gladstone had already gained a considerable reputation as a classical scholar in Oxford, delivering the Romanes Lecture in 1892.) Another source of antiquarian acquisition has been through the good offices of the Friends of the Bodleian, founded in 1925. One of their earliest and most valuable gifts was Milton's copy of Euripides, published in Geneva in 1602.

Select bibliography

David Rogers, 'The Holkham Collection', *Bodleian Library Record*, 4/5 (1953), 255–67.

Ruth Barbour, 'Summary Description of the Greek Manuscripts from the Library at Holkham Hall', *Bodleian Library Record*, 6/5 (1960), 591–613.

Greek Manuscripts in the Bodleian Library [exhibition catalogue] (Oxford: Bodleian Library, 1966).

Reynolds Stone, 'The James Wardrop Collection of Prints and Negatives', *Bodleian Library Record*, 8/6 (1972), 297–337. Includes list of negatives by Bruce Barker-Benfield.

Nigel Wilson, *Mediaeval Greek Bookhands: Examples Selected from the Greek Manuscripts in Oxford Libraries*. 2 vols. (Cambridge, MA, 1973). Includes plates of many Bodleian manuscripts.

An Exhibition of Papyri, mainly in Greek [...] (Oxford: Bodleian Library, 1974).

The Survival of Ancient Literature [exhibition catalogue] (Oxford: Bodleian Library, 1975).

Repertorium der griechischen Kopisten 800–1600, erstellt von E. Gamillscheg und D. Harlfinger (Vienna, 1981). Vol. 1 covers manuscripts in British collections.

Printing Greek – A European Enterprise [exhibition catalogue] (Oxford: Bodleian Library, 1992).

A Continental Shelf: Books across Europe from Ptolemy to Don Quixote [exhibition catalogue] (Oxford: Bodleian Library, 1994), 32–61.

Christopher Stray, *Classics Transformed: Schools, Universities and Society in England, 1830–1960* (Oxford: Clarendon Press, 1998).

4. British History and Politics

The antiquary Thomas Hearne, writing in Oxford in the early eighteenth century, lamented that the Bodleian was, in contrast to its vast theological collections, 'meanly furnished' with 'books of our English history and antiquities'. As an indictment of the acquisitions made by the Bodleian's founder and first three librarians, this was, like so many of Hearne's opinions, unduly harsh.

The Middle Ages to the seventeenth century

The early years of the seventeenth century had witnessed the steady growth of the collections of English medieval manuscripts, many given by benefactors who saw in the Bodleian a safe haven for manuscripts which had been rescued from the earlier ravages of English monastic libraries. These included chronicles, among them early manuscripts of Higden's *Polychronicon*, of Nennius's *Historia Britonum*, and of saints' lives. The original manuscripts of John Leland's *Itinerary* and *Collectanea*, the results of his researches for a history of the nation, were given by William Burton in 1632. (It was Hearne himself who edited them for publication in 1710–15). Sir Kenelm Digby's collection of manuscripts, given by him in 1634, is rich in the early history of science in England, but also contains much relating to English history in general. Archbishop Laud's many benefactions included, in 1638, the 'Peterborough Chronicle' (MS. Laud Misc. 636), a version of that cornerstone of English history, the *Anglo-Saxon Chronicle*, written at Peterborough Abbey in *c.*1121 with additions to 1133. Robert Burton, author of *The Anatomy of Melancholy*, had been assiduous in collecting contemporary ephemeral works such as pamphlets, newsbooks and jestbooks, which came to the Bodleian on his death in 1640. The huge library of the jurist John Selden (1584–1654) was rich in works of history as in so many other subjects. The bequest of Thomas, Lord Fairfax (1612–71), the parliamentarian general credited with putting a guard on the library door to save the Bodleian from pillaging by his own army in 1646, bequeathed a small group of very important manuscripts, among them several works relating to the history of England, Scotland and Ireland. With the library of Thomas Barlow, Bishop of Lincoln (1607–91), came a fine collection of tracts of the Civil War and Interregnum.

Within a few years of Hearne's death in 1735, these collections, all in the Bodleian when Hearne castigated its history collections, were enormously augmented by the acquisition of four magnificent manuscript collections, which put the Library at the forefront of centres for the study of seventeenth-century British history and significantly enhanced its holdings of medieval manuscripts. The first was from Thomas Tanner, Bishop of St Asaph (1674–1735). His books included more Civil War and Interregnum tracts. The majority of his manuscripts were the more or less official papers of William Sancroft, Archbishop of Canterbury from 1678 to 1693, an invaluable source for studies of the Anglican church. They include an important series of letters, many to Speaker Lenthall, covering the period from the personal rule of Charles I to 1659. Another group was made up of papers of John Nalson, a royalist pamphleteer (1637?–86), who in the course of researching a political history of the decade from 1639 to 1649 was granted access to the office of the Clerk of Parliament, whence he 'borrowed' and never returned many state papers of the period. A further 25 volumes of Nalson's papers came as a deposit in 1945 and were allocated to the Library in 1987, having been accepted by HM Treasury in lieu of tax due on the estate of Ivy Cavendish Bentinck, Duchess of Portland. Tanner had also collected important medieval manuscripts, among them the oldest surviving manuscript of the Old English version of Bede's *Ecclesiastical History* (MS. Tanner 10).

Another historian, Thomas Carte (1686–1754), presented in 1753 his collection of the papers of James, 1st Duke of Ormonde, Lord Lieutenant of Ireland in the 1640s and after the Restoration. The Carte manuscripts are further enhanced as a major source for Irish history by papers of Sir William Fitzwilliam, Lord Deputy in Elizabeth's reign, and of Sir John Davies, James I's Attorney-General in Ireland. The mass of official papers includes the earliest extant journal of an Irish parliament (MS. Carte 61) and the original letter-book of the Council of Confederate Catholics at Kilkenny from 1642 to 1645 (MS. Carte 64).

The third great benefaction of the mid-eighteenth century was the collection of Richard Rawlinson, antiquarian and Bishop in the nonjuring Church of England (1690–1755). His manuscripts include state papers of John Thurloe, Secretary of State during the Protectorate, 25 volumes of Admiralty papers of Samuel Pepys, records of Sir John Coke relating to the Court of Arches, and all manner of individual volumes of official papers of the reigns of Charles II and James II. He had also acquired important manuscripts of Irish medieval chronicles, among them the *Annals of Inisfallen* (MS. Rawl. B. 503) and the *Annals of Ulster* (MS. Rawl. B. 489).

The fourth core collection of seventeenth-century manuscripts to reach the Bodleian was the Clarendon State Papers. Alongside material for the 1st Earl of Clarendon's *History of the Rebellion* are his official correspondence and papers, amassed during the Civil War, his exile with Charles II and his period as Lord Chancellor from 1660 to 1667. Most famous among this latter group is the wonderful series of notes passed between the King and his first minister during Council meetings (MSS. Clarendon 100–101).

By the middle of the eighteenth century the foundations of the Bodleian's great seventeenth-century manuscript collections were firmly laid. They have continued to be augmented to the present day. In 1860 the Visitors of the Ashmolean transferred the Museum's books and manuscripts, which included the collection of its founder Elias Ashmole (*d.*1692). Ashmole's interests are well represented in his manuscripts. Astrology, alchemy and medicine loom large, most notably in the papers of Simon Forman (*d.*1611) and the medical and astrological practice-books of Richard Napier (*d.*1634) – both a surprisingly useful source of biographical data. Ashmole's own manuscripts for a history of the Order of the Garter, and his own and Sir Robert Glover's (*d.*1588) heraldic and genealogical collectanea are a major source for early modern heraldry. There are also many manuscripts relating to the parliamentary history of the seventeenth century, and a few earlier manuscripts of historical interest, such as the letter-book for 1442 of Thomas Beckington, Bishop of Bath and Wells (MS. Ashmole 789), the Premonstratensian Register of Richard Redman, Bishop of Ely, for the years 1474–1503 (MS. Ashmole 1519) and a volume of original royal warrants and letters of the period from Henry VIII to Charles I (MS. Ashmole 1729). The transfer from the Ashmolean included 30 manuscripts of John Aubrey (1626–97), among them three volumes of his *Brief Lives* (MSS. Aubrey 6–9). Among more recent larger acquisitions are the departmental records of Sir John Bankes as Attorney-General to Charles I during the crucial years of his personal rule from 1629 to 1640 and the papers of Sir William Herrick as one of the Tellers of the Exchequer from 1616 to 1623. Notable among individual manuscripts is that of Edmund Ludlow's 'A Voyce from the Watch Tower' which was purchased in 1970 (MS. Eng. hist. c. 487), and edited by A.B. Worden as *Camden Fourth Series*, vol. 21 (1978).

From the seventeenth to the eighteenth century

The printed collections of primary and secondary works also grew apace, through gifts, purchases and legal deposit. The holdings of seventeenth- and early eighteenth-century pamphlets were notably increased with the transfer of the collections of Elias Ashmole and Anthony Wood (from the Ashmolean Museum in 1860) and Humphrey Bartholomew (from the Radcliffe Library in 1861). The almost complete sets of London newspapers of 1672 to 1737 collected by the publisher John Nichols were purchased from his son in 1865. Three years previously F.W. Hope had presented his father's collection of mainly eighteenth-century newspapers. The books bequeathed by Nathaniel Crynes in 1745 included a wide range of historical material from the sixteenth to the eighteenth century, while those bequeathed by Charles Godwyn in 1770 focussed on works of English civil and ecclesiastical history published in the eighteenth century. The magnificent bequest of Francis Douce (1757–1834) included over 19,000 volumes of all periods, many of them works of history, biography and antiquities. A substantial series of pamphlets, many relating to Irish history, collected by Edmund Malone was purchased in 1838 (G. Pamph. 327–402).

The eighteenth-century manuscript collections do not match those of the previous century. Their strength is more in the accumulation of single volumes and small groups, especially of diplomatic correspondence. Three collections are of particular interest. The papers of Edward Tucker of Weymouth and Melcombe Regis, MP (*d.*1737) and his sons document their running of the principal stone business and their holding of the office of surveyor of HM quarries in Portland for the greater part of the eighteenth century. The family papers of the Barons North and Earls of Guilford include a fine series of estate and personal papers of the 1st Earl of Guilford (1704–90), and almost 60 volumes of official papers of his son, the 2nd Earl, better known as Lord North, mainly concerned with imports and exports, customs and excise in the 1760s and 1770s. The papers of George, 1st Earl Macartney (1737–1806) are a major source for his time as governor and president of Fort St. George, Madras, between 1762 and 1792.

The nineteenth and twentieth centuries

The early nineteenth-century manuscript collections are particularly strong in political, military and diplomatic history, with papers of, among many others, William Wilberforce (1759–1833); John Francis Caradoc, 1st Baron Howden (1759–1839) as Commander-in-Chief at Madras and Lisbon, and as Governor of Gibraltar and of the Cape of Good Hope; General Sir Charles William Doyle (1770–1842) relating to Spain, 1808–15; Charles Russell as first assistant Resident at Hyderabad in 1810–11; and Frederick Douglas, MP for Banbury from 1812 to 1819.

The Library holds one of the UK's largest concentrations of modern British political papers from 1840 to the present day, with a breadth of coverage which makes it a resource of national and international significance. Running to over 400 collections which range in size from over 2,000 boxes of correspondence and papers to a single diary, the holdings are drawn from the personal papers of politicians, public servants (mainly diplomats), journalists, broadcasters and others active in public life. Most of the collections came to the Bodleian, by donation and deposit rather than by purchase, in the second half of the twentieth century. Many of the great names in British politics are represented including the archives of six Prime Ministers (Benjamin Disraeli, H.H. Asquith, Clement Attlee, Harold Macmillan, Harold Wilson and James Callaghan) as well as over 100 Cabinet Ministers and backbench MPs including George Villiers, 4th Earl of Clarendon (1800–70), John Wodehouse, 1st Earl of Kimberley (1826–1902), Sir William Harcourt (1827–1904) and his son Lewis Harcourt (1863–1922), Frederick Marquis, 1st Earl of Woolton

(1883–1964) and Sir Geoffrey (later Baron) Howe (*b*. 1926); distinguished diplomats like Sir John Crampton (1805–86), Sir Horace Rumbold (1829–1913), Sir Patrick Reilly (*d*. 1999), Sir Paul Gore-Booth (1909–84) and journalists Honor Balfour (*d*. 2001), Geoffrey Dawson (1874–1944), Arthur Mann (1876–1972), Maurice Latey (1916–85), Sir Hugh Greene (1910–87, a future Director–General of the BBC), and William Clark (1916–85).

The holdings of politicians' personal papers form the largest category of modern political material. The diaries, personal correspondence, pencilled notes of conversations, drafts of speeches and articles, photographs and printed ephemera are the documentary record of lives lived which will inform not only present but subsequent generations. Many provide a personal perspective on historic events such as Asquith's letter to his young confidante Sylvia Stanley following his resignation as Prime Minister in December 1916, or Lady Franklin's urgent request to Disraeli in January 1850 that a search be made for the ships of Sir John Franklin's Arctic expedition. The diplomat Sir Eyre Crowe, head of the Foreign Office in the early 1920s, wrote warm, affectionate letters to his wife and children; those written while he was in Paris to attend the Peace Conference in 1919 are among the most descriptive. Some collections include intriguing objects such as the ivory carriage passes to Constitution Hill Gate and Horse Guards belonging to Lord Bryce whose career as lawyer, academic, politician and diplomat was both distinguished and varied; locks of hair, pressed flowers, and even the odd ceremonial dagger.

The fact that the major collections can be consulted alongside the papers of minor political figures and individuals with no public role helps to produce a more rounded view of the past than if the holdings were made up solely of the papers of the major decision-makers. This is not only true in the study of British politics and society. The United Nations Career Records Project (UNCRP), begun in Oxford in 1989 and still open for acquisitions, consists mainly of the recollections of former British employees of the United Nations who worked in the Specialized Agencies such as UNESCO, UNICEF and the Food and Agriculture Organisation (FAO). The contributors' diaries and letters provide a window both into the everyday life of the host countries and the past experiences of the UN officials and their families.

Most of the contributions to UNCRP consist of only a box or two, but the project also attracted two large-scale acquisitions: the papers of Sidney Dell, an economist who spent more than 40 years in the UN, and brother of Edmund Dell, the former Labour Cabinet minister and Founder Chairman of Channel 4 Television, whose diaries were already in the Library; and those of George Ivan Smith, an Australian by birth (and pioneer of Australian radio broadcasting) who worked on the documentary series 'This Modern Age' before joining the UN in 1947. His later postings included the Directorship of the London United Nations Information Centre and several missions to the Middle East and Africa, often accompanying the then Secretary-General, Dag Hammarskjöld. Smith's investigations into the death of Hammarskjöld in a plane crash in the Congo in 1961 lasted into the mid-1980s and form one of the many interesting aspects of the collection.

Over the years politicians from all three major British political parties have placed their personal papers in the care of the Bodleian and they continue to do so. In 1978 the holdings of Conservative politicians were supplemented by the arrival, on deposit, of the Conservative Party Archive. Readers studying the history of the Labour Party have access to much of the Labour Party archives in microform. Twentieth-century records of the Cabinet and various cabinet committees of the Conservative and Labour governments are also available on microform.

Many of the researchers using the Bodleian's modern political collections are interested in a particular topic or set of topics rather than in the life of one person, and have no need to work through a collection from beginning to end, however enticing the prospect might at times seem. Over the years the Library has built on the existing strengths of its holdings to provide excellent coverage of a wide range of topics including most aspects of overseas and domestic policy, with foreign relations, war, overseas expansion and administration featuring largely in the former category, and housing, education, social reform, the economy, and women's suffrage and rights being major aspects of the latter. Among the countries particularly well represented in the collections are the United States, Ireland, India, South Africa and Egypt, but this list is by no means exhaustive. Coverage of the two World Wars is extensive, as in many other repositories, but the holdings relating to the 1956 Suez crisis are exceptionally strong and include both correspondence and papers contemporary with the event and reflective accounts. The photostat of the Israeli copy of the Sèvres Agreement signed between Britain and Israel is believed to be unique in the UK, the British copy having been destroyed shortly after its signature on the orders of the then Prime Minister, Anthony Eden (MS. Eng. c. 6168).

The viewpoint in the collections is mainly that of Westminster and Whitehall but dissenting voices are represented too, most notably those of pacifists. Here again the range is wide, including not only the distinguished historian and peace campaigner E.P. Thompson but also the relatively unknown David Ansell, active in Oxford University's Anti-War Committee in the 1930s. Britain's links with the wider world are reflected in numerous runs of correspondence between British politicians, diplomats and journalists and their overseas counterparts. There are letters to Violet Milner, editor of the *National Review* and widow of Lord Milner, from correspondents as varied as the French statesman Georges Clemenceau and the legendary American broadcaster Ed Murrow, and this collection is by no means atypical. Among further examples are the papers of the distinguished journalist and international civil servant William Clark, which include the largest concentration of correspondence with US journalists and broadcasters in any Bodleian collection. The papers of Sir Walter Monckton, held on deposit from Balliol College, include material on the abdication of King Edward VIII, whom Monckton served as lawyer and confidant, and a large amount of correspondence, from the mid 1940s to the mid 1960s, with and concerning the Nawab of Hyderabad, to whom he acted as legal adviser.

Changes in the position of women in society are another well-documented theme in the modern political collections. Lady Clarendon, wife of the nineteenth-century Liberal politician, and Margot Asquith, wife of the twentieth-century Liberal Prime Minister, were both great diarists. They took a keen interest in their husbands' careers, articulating their support and writing accounts of the day's political events, the successes and setbacks their husbands experienced, as well as details of family life.

Neither Lady Clarendon nor Margot Asquith were feminists; indeed, the latter was positively hostile to the suffragettes, in part because of their attacks on Asquith, but the Library holds several collections generated by those who actively campaigned for women's political and economic rights, including those of Barbara Keen (later Lady Clark), the suffragette and *Guardian* journalist Evelyn Sharp, Edith Marvin, Lady Selborne (one of the few aristocratic Conservative supporters of women's suffrage) and Mrs Annan Bryce, Lord Bryce's sister-in-law, and her daughter Marjorie.

As we move further into the twentieth century women became eligible to stand for Parliament. Dame Irene (later Baroness) Ward, elected to Parliament in 1931, was one of the early campaigners for the equal pay of women. Barbara (later Baroness) Castle, who entered the House of Commons in 1945 as Labour MP for Blackburn and later served in the Wilson governments, was a fellow member of the campaign committee. The private papers of both are now in the Library.

The history collections, both printed and manuscript, have continued to grow through substantial purchases and generous gifts, many from Oxford historians. The widow of Sir Charles Harding Firth, Regius Professor of Modern History, gave in 1936 a substantial part of his library, including 24 volumes of printed portraits and caricatures illustrative of English history from *c.*1603 to *c.*1830, 20 of broadside ballads and poems from the mid-seventeenth to the early nineteenth century, and 84 of political tracts, mainly of the second half of the seventeenth century. With these came a collection of Firth's working papers. Among other collections of historians' papers are those of two Regius Professors of Modern History, H.H. Vaughan and H.W.C. Davis, of H.A.L. Fisher, of A.G. Little relating to the Franciscans in England, of E.A. Freeman on Roman history, of Sir William Napier on the Peninsular War and of Geoffrey Baskerville on the suppression of the monasteries. Further sources for historiographical research are the archives of the *English Historical Review* and *Past and Present*.

Topography and local history

The primary and secondary materials for national history are complemented by very rich collections on the antiquities, topography and local history of almost all areas of the United Kingdom and Ireland. British enthusiasm for antiquarian studies from the sixteenth century onwards is reflected not only in the works published by generations of antiquaries, but also in the manuscripts accumulated by them. As one would expect, material relating to the history of the University, City and County of Oxford looms large.

Of particular note among the printed books are the collections of Anthony Wood (1632–95), strong in Oxford pamphlets and newspapers and in books printed in Oxford or written by Oxford men; of Philip Bliss (1787–1857) and Percy Manning (d.1917). The manuscript collections of local antiquaries are numerous. The earliest are those of Brian Twyne (1579–1644) on the city and university. Henry Hinton, a local ironmonger (1749–1816) and James Hunt, a chemist (1795–1857) are typical of a host of men who sought to preserve information about the churches of Oxfordshire and Berkshire. An unusual survival are the rubbings they took of monumental brasses in both counties between 1795 and 1815 (MSS. Rubbings Phillipps-Robinson 587–861, 876–933). The Phillipps-Robinson collection includes almost one thousand antiquarian and topographical manuscripts, relating to all areas of the United Kingdom, collected by or compiled for Sir Thomas Phillipps (1792–1872), and a most interesting and comprehensive series of letters to him covering the period from 1809 to 1872. In more recent times Henry Minn (1870–1961) built up a photographic record of the streets and buildings of Oxford, while P.S. Spokes systematically took photographs of the 'listed' buildings of Berkshire. From the seventeenth to the twentieth centuries, the correspondence and personal papers of generations of members of the University bring to life its history with often startling immediacy. The manuscript diaries of Anthony Wood for 1657–95 and of Thomas Hearne for 1705–35 provide unusually detailed accounts of university and city affairs. Both have been published by the Oxford Historical Society (A. Clark, *Life and Times of Anthony Wood*, 5 volumes, 1891–1900; C.E. Doble, *Remarks and Collections of Thomas Hearne*, 11 volumes, 1885–1921).

Most of the antiquaries, from the seventeenth century onwards, collected charters and title deeds which came into the Bodleian with their manuscript collections. Anthony Wood collected a large number of medieval monastic deeds and rolls, among them many from Oseney Abbey. Several Oxford colleges have deposited their medieval muniments in the Bodleian. Notable among them are those of Christ Church, to a large extent made up of the archives of the monastic houses (among them Oseney Abbey, and the priories of St Frideswide's, Wallingford and Daventry) that were suppressed to endow Wolsey's Cardinal College. In the twentieth century these earlier collections were expanded and enhanced both by the acquisition of large accumulations of estate papers of local landowers and by purchase of court rolls of local manors as they came on the market in the 1920s and 1930s. Among the estate papers are those of the Bertie family, Earls of Abingdon, of the Norths of Wroxton and of the Harcourts of Nuneham Courtenay and Stanton Harcourt. Among the series of court rolls are those of the manors of Headington (13th–17th centuries), Cumnor (1419–1817), Ipsden (16th–18th centuries), and Beckley (1580–1662).

The bequest by Richard Gough (1735–1809) of his huge library of topographical and antiquarian books, prints and drawings ensured that the Library's printed holdings covered all the counties of England, Wales, Scotland and Ireland. The same breadth of interest is reflected in the collections of antiquarian manuscripts. In the seventeenth century, Roger Dodsworth and Nathaniel Johnston accumulated materials for a history of Yorkshire, William Dugdale for Warwickshire, John Aubrey for Wiltshire and Surrey, Elias Ashmole for Lichfield and for Berkshire. In the eighteenth century Browne Willis did the same for Buckinghamshire, John Bridges for Northamptonshire, Richard Frank and John Burton for Yorkshire, John Watson for Cheshire and Lancashire, Richard Furney for Gloucestershire, William Holman for Essex, Jeremiah Milles for Devon. Pre-eminent among the eighteenth-century antiquaries is William Stukeley (1687–1765) whose manuscripts were acquired through a succession of purchases and gifts between 1924 and 1973. The large collection of diaries, correspondence and notes on topography, antiquities (especially Avebury and Stonehenge) and coins bears witness both to his pioneering work as the father of scientific field archaeology and to his decidedly eccentric work on the Druids. In the nineteenth century John Blakeway made collections for the history of Shropshire, John Pike Jones for Cornwall and Devon, W.N. Clarke for Berkshire and James Ford for Suffolk. Manuscripts of all these, and many more too numerous to mention, are to be found in the Library's collections. Unusual among the twentieth-century collections are those of Andrew Clark, who not only worked extensively on the history of Oxford and of Essex, but also kept a remarkable record of the impact of the First World War on his Essex parish of Great Leighs, or as he put it of such 'echoes of the Great War as reached the rectory from outside', preserving official bulletins and leaflets, letters, postcards and newspaper cuttings (MSS. Eng. hist. e. 88–177c). In another lengthy series of volumes he collected, arranged by subject, indexed and extensively annotated newspaper cuttings from August 1914 to September 1919 (MSS. Eng. misc. e. 265–329).

Select bibliography

All deeds acquired before 1878 are calendared and indexed in W.H. Turner and H.O. Coxe, *Calendar of Charters and Rolls Preserved in the Bodleian Library* (Oxford: Clarendon Press, 1878). This calendar, with its continuation of thousands of handwritten slips, was published on 223 microfiches by Chadwyck-Healey in 1992 as *Calendars of Charters and Rolls in the Manuscript Collections of the Bodleian Library, University of Oxford. An Index of Persons in Oxfordshire Deeds Acquired by the Bodleian Library 1878–1963*, compiled by W.O. Hassall, was published by the Bodleian Library as volume 45 of the Oxfordshire Record Society in 1966.

Calendar of the Clarendon State Papers Preserved in the Bodleian Library, ed. O. Ogle, W.H. Bliss et al. (5 vols.; Oxford, 1869–1970).

The diaries of the antiquary Thomas Hearne (1678–1735) are edited in Oxford Historical Society, vols. 2, 7, 13, 34, 42, 43, 48, 50, 65, 67, 72 (1885–1918).

Diaries and other papers of the antiquary Anthony Wood (1632–95) are edited by A. Clark as *The Life and Times of Anthony Wood*, Oxford Historical Society, vols. 19, 21, 26, 30, 40 (1891–1900).

E.H. Cordeaux and D.H. Merry, *A Bibliography of Printed Works Relating to Oxfordshire* (Oxford: Oxford University Press, 1955). Supplementary volume published 1981 by the Clarendon Press for the Oxford Historical Society.

R.W. Hunt, 'List of Phillipps Manuscripts in the Bodleian Library', *Bodleian Library Record* 6/1 (1957), 348–69.

P.S. Spokes, *Summary Catalogue of Manuscripts in the Bodleian Library Relating to the City, County and University of Oxford: Accessions from 1916 to 1962* (Oxford: Clarendon Press, 1964).

E.H. Cordeaux and D.H. Merry, *A Bibliography of Printed Works Relating to the University of Oxford* (Oxford: Clarendon Press, 1968).

E.H. Cordeaux and D.H. Merry, *A Bibliography of Printed Works Relating to the City of Oxford* (Oxford: Clarendon Press, 1976).

Queens and Kings: An Exhibition of Manuscripts and Charters Connected with the Monarchs of Britain (Oxford: Bodleian Library, 1977).

Ian Green, 'The Publication of Clarendon's Autobiography and the Acquisition of his Papers by the Bodleian Library', *Bodleian Library Record*, 10/6 (1982) 349–67.

Town and Gown: Eight Hundred Years of Oxford Life [exhibition catalogue] (Oxford: Bodleian Library, 1982).

Elias Ashmole 1617–1692: The Founder of the Ashmolean Museum and his World [exhibition catalogue] (Oxford: Bodleian Library, 1983).

The Douce Legacy [exhibition catalogue] (Oxford: Bodleian Library, 1984).

Helen Langley, 'The Woolton Papers', *Bodleian Library Record*, 11/5 (1984), 320–37.

The Medieval University of Oxford [exhibition catalogue] (Oxford: Bodleian Library, 1984).

Stanley Gillam, 'Thomas Hearne's Library', *Bodleian Library Record*, 12/1 (1985), 52–64.

Frances Henderson, "'Posterity to Judge" – John Rushworth and his "Historicall Collections'", *Bodleian Library Record*, 15/4 (1996), 247–59.

Helen Langley, *Modern Political Papers in the Bodleian Library* (Oxford: Bodleian Library, 1996).

Civil War: The Great Rebellion in Charles I's Three Kingdoms 1638–1653 [exhibition catalogue] (Oxford: Bodleian Library, 1999).

Napoleon and the Invasion of Britain [exhibition catalogue] (Oxford: Bodleian Library, 2003).

Benjamin Disraeli, Earl of Beaconsfield: Scenes from an Extraordinary Life, ed. Helen Langley (Oxford: Bodleian Library, 2003).

5. English Literature and Language

It is one of the ironies of the development of the Bodleian's diverse and, in many areas, unparalleled literary collections that the Library's founder always doubted if English books (that is, books in the vernacular) merited inclusion in the library or its catalogues. Sir Thomas Bodley was no lover of the perceived 'friuolitie' of literature. Of the 5,000 or so books listed in the 1605 catalogue only about 170 are in English, and of these only three are works of literature: a 1561 edition of Chaucer, Lydgate's *Fall of Princes*, and Puttenham's *The Art of English Poesie*. When a second catalogue was published in 1620, seven years after Bodley's death, there were a few more literary works but nothing by Jonson, Marlowe or Shakespeare.

Yet it was Bodley's own 1610 agreement with the Stationers' Company which ensured that, as the century progressed, the Library's holdings of printed works of English literature were transformed from frivolous 'baggage bookes' into one of the Bodleian's greatest strengths: a richness of provision that was augmented by Robert Burton's 1640 bequest (which included works by the famous names of Elizabethan literature which Bodley had earlier rejected) and, in subsequent years, by a variety of purchases and donations relating to the seventeenth century, such as the collections of Richard Rawlinson and Edmund Malone, described below.

This pattern of acquisition – of printed material coming freely to the Library through the provision of successive Copyright Acts, supplemented by purchases and gifts – has, broadly speaking, been preserved since 1610 and has to a great degree determined the scope and nature of the Bodleian's literary holdings. In the Bodleian as a library of legal deposit, researchers in the modern, printed field can expect to find all the canonical and many of the uncanonical texts, together with works of criticism and other essential secondary sources. But in the past, following in the decorous footsteps of Sir Thomas Bodley and his University, where the study of English literature has been on the syllabus for little more than a century, the Library was much more selective in its copyright uptake, so that lacunae in the printed holdings have been – and continue to be – filled by purchase and by gift: the means by which the Library has acquired its manuscripts and non-copyright materials.

For the purposes of this guide, the following paragraphs offer a brief summary of selected holdings, beginning with the earliest manuscripts written in the medieval period, and ending with the heterogeneous productions of the twenty-first century.

However, the history of the Bodleian's collections is important in its own right and accounts such as W.D. Macray's *Annals of the Bodleian Library* (1890), Edmund Craster's *History of the Bodleian Library 1845–1945* (1952) and Ian Philip's *The Bodleian Library in the Seventeenth and Eighteenth Centuries* (1983) provide indispensable information about collections and collectors, like the eccentric Francis Douce whose extraordinarily eclectic bequest of 1834 remains one of the outstanding benefactions to the Library; while for detailed descriptions the reader is referred throughout to the Bodleian's own catalogues, in both printed and electronic form.

English literature to the fifteenth century

The great collections of medieval manuscripts include fine examples of Anglo-Saxon and Middle English. Among the most renowned are 'The Caedmon Manuscript' of the Anglo-Saxon paraphrases in alliterative verse of parts of *Genesis*, *Exodus* and *Daniel* (MS. Junius 11); 'The Ormulum', Middle English homilies on the Gospels (MS. Junius i); the miscellany of Middle English poetry, made in Scotland, which includes the unique copy of King James I of Scotland's poem *The Kingis Quair* (MS. Arch. Selden. B. 24); the unique surviving copy of *The Lay of Havelock the Dane*, which appears at the end of what is claimed to be the earliest surviving manuscript of the *South English Legendary* (MS. Laud Misc. 108) and 'The Vernon Manuscript', the largest surviving anthology of Middle English verse, given around 1677 by Colonel Edward Vernon of Trinity College, whose presentation inscription proudly proclaims that he had been a dashing cavalier (MS. Eng. poet. a. 1).

Although early editions of the classics and of the Bible predominate in the Library's collection of incunables, Francis Douce's collection is especially rich in literature in vernacular languages, such as romances and fables, many with woodcut illustrations. Examples of works in English include a copy of the first printed English translation of Aesop's Fables (Westminster, 1484; Arch. G d. 13 (4)), and three copies of the *Faits d'armes* of Christine de Pisan ([Westminster], 1489; Douce 180, S. Seld. d. 13 and Arch. G d. 16), both works translated and printed by William Caxton.

The sixteenth and seventeenth centuries

The core of the Bodleian's holdings for the sixteenth and seventeenth centuries was formed by the original agreement with the Stationers' Company, which in 1662 became a statutory obligation to deliver books to the Library. As the seat of Royalist government during the Civil War, Oxford also had a wider, historical connection with the period, which is reflected in the breadth and depth of its collections for the time. Robert Burton's bequest of printed books has already been referred to, but the largest gift of literary manuscripts came to the Library in the eighteenth century after the death of Richard Rawlinson in 1755. This consisted of 254 manuscripts, most of which were poetical miscellanies, including the now-infamous Shakespeare attribution: 'Shall I die, shall I fly' (MS. Rawl. poet. 160, fol. 8^v) although the most important Shakespearean collection of first and early printed editions, including the famous Quartos, was given to the Library in 1821, by the brother of the scholar Edmund Malone (1741–1812). The great bequest of Francis Douce (1757–1834), which features so frequently in this guide, included a major collection of materials all too often overlooked by others: poems, songs and ballads, as well as drama. Later acquisitions relating to the literature of the sixteenth and seventeenth centuries have included George Thorn-Drury's printed collection of minor poets of the Restoration period; Bent Juel-Jensen's gift of Michael Drayton books; E.J.M. Buxton's gift of his collections of works by Sir Philip Sidney, Samuel Daniel and Charles Cotton; and the purchase in 1971 of the only surviving complete autograph of the poet John Donne, 'A Letter to the Lady Cary' (MS. Eng. poet. d. 197).

The eighteenth and nineteenth centuries

The most important holdings of this period are centred on two poets: Percy Bysshe Shelley (sent down from Oxford in 1811) and Gerard Manley Hopkins. Shelley's manuscripts now rank among the finest of the Library's collections. Nine were given by Jane, Lady Shelley in 1893, together with a volume of his letters; while an incomparable series of twenty-eight of the poet's notebooks (now all published in facsimile by Garland), was given and bequeathed by Sir John Shelley-Rolls in 1926 and 1946.

In contrast to Shelley's well-publicised life and works, when Balliol graduate Hopkins died in 1889 he was unknown outside his small circle of family, friends and co-religionists. The author of only half a dozen published poems, his reputation is wholly posthumous and derives from the corpus of manuscripts which he gave into the keeping of the future Poet Laureate Robert Bridges, who began publishing them in 1912. The Bodleian was able to buy these manuscripts, together with Hopkins's personal papers and correspondence, from his great-nephew Leo Handley-Derry in 1953.

Other manuscript holdings range from single items – such as Jane Austen's *Volume the First* (MS. Don. e. 7), one of three notebooks in which she copied her earliest stories, beginning with 'Frederick and Elfrida', which she probably wrote in 1787 when she was twelve years old – to extensive collections of holograph works, correspondence, diaries and miscellaneous papers relating to Arthur Hugh Clough, James Thomson and 'Michael Field'.

Published literature of the nineteenth century is particularly well covered, with the copyright intake significantly supplemented by the libraries of private collectors. Arguably more significant for social historians than for students of English literature is Frank Pettingell's collection of 'penny dreadfuls'. The Dunston family's collection is particularly strong in editions of Browning, Butler, Byron, Pope, Scott, Stevenson and Tennyson. The collection of the novelist Sir Hugh Seymour Walpole consists of first editions of the works of English writers of fiction, poetry and *belles lettres* in the 1890s. University College deposited the Robert Ross Memorial collection of works by and about Oscar Wilde. The Bodleian itself has systematically built up a collection of Tauchnitz editions of British and American authors from the 1840s to the 1940s, of particular interest when, as was often the case, they were printed from proofs of the English edition.

The twentieth century

The Bodleian's modern manuscript holdings reflect the Library's interest in acquiring the papers of authors who have a connection with the City and the University of Oxford. The most significant collections in this respect are those of J.R.R. Tolkien, C.S. Lewis, Charles Williams and other members of the Inklings circle, while other Oxford-related authors include Brian Aldiss, Joyce Cary, Kenneth Grahame, T.E. Lawrence, Louis MacNeice, John Masefield and Barbara Pym. Because it is relatively unusual for large archives of twentieth-century material to have been preserved in the UK, there is also a wealth of literary material to be found in the Bodleian's general collections: important single manuscripts and groups of documents, such as W.H. Auden's juvenilia; letters and papers of Kingsley Amis, Philip Larkin and related Movement writers; and poems by T.S. Eliot, Thomas Hardy and W.B. Yeats.

The Library's collections of published twentieth-century literature have been enhanced by many gifts such as the library of Joyce Cary; John A. Hogan's remarkable collection of books and periodicals by and about Edgar Wallace; and Mrs. E.G.V. Gilliat's collection of presentation copies of works of the Sitwells, chiefly Edith, but also Osbert and Sacheverell.

(*See also* the chapters 'North America' and 'Australia and New Zealand' for treatment of literature in English from those countries.)

English language and linguistics

Materials for the study of the English language have also accumulated in the Library, for the most part as gifts from scholars working in the field. The earliest dictionary of the Anglo-Saxon language, compiled by Lawrence Nowell, Dean of Lichfield around 1550, came in John Selden's collection a century later (MS. Selden Supra 63). The philologist Francis Junius (1589–1677) was attracted to Oxford by the Bodleian's Anglo-Saxon collections, collections which he enhanced by his bequest of his books, manuscripts and working papers. John Fell, Bishop of Oxford, and Thomas Marshall, Rector of Lincoln College, made significant additions to the philological holdings later in the same century. In 1876 the executors of Joseph

Bosworth, Rawlinson Professor of Anglo-Saxon in the University, gave his books and manuscripts. These included his working papers for his Anglo-Saxon dictionary of 1838. They were followed twenty years later by the working notebooks of Thomas Hallam of Manchester, who had devoted much of his life to the study of English dialects. More recently, in 1967, T.W. Thompson's papers relating to Gypsies and Gypsy folklore, including a dictionary of Gypsy language in twenty-four notebooks, came by the bequest of their compiler. In 1972, the papers of Joseph Wright, Corpus Christi Professor of Comparative Philology, mainly concerning his *English Dialect Dictionary* (1896–1901), were transferred from the Taylor Institution. Correspondence of the great lexicographer Sir James Murray (1837–1915) was given by his grand-daughter Dr. Elizabeth Murray in 1994.

The Library also collects extensively in many other aspects of linguistics. The central Bodleian holds a broad range of scholarly publishing from many countries on general linguistics, applied linguistics and comparative philology. The Radcliffe Science Library and Hooke Library maintain collections in psycholinguistics, neurolinguistics and language disorders, while the Philosophy Library's holdings include coverage of the philosophy of language, rhetoric and logic. Linguistic material is strongly represented in the Bodleian's Oriental collections, including those at the Bodleian Japanese Library and the Indian Institute Library.

Select bibliography

Sir Philip Sidney 1554–1586 [exhibition catalogue] (Oxford: Bodleian Library, 1954).

English Literature in the Seventeenth Century [exhibition catalogue] (Oxford: Bodleian Library, 1957).

Carl J. Stratman, 'A Survey of the Bodleian Library's Holdings in the Field of English Printed Tragedy', *Bodleian Library Record*, 7/3 (1964),133–43.

William Shakespeare 1564–1964 [exhibition catalogue] (Oxford: Bodleian Library, 1964).

Margaret Crum, ed., *First-Line Index of English Poetry, 1500–1800, in Manuscripts of the Bodleian Library, Oxford* (2 vols.; Oxford: Clarendon Press, 1969).

P. Beal et al., *Index of English Literary Manuscripts* (Vol. 1– ; London & New York: Mansell, 1980–).

The Bodleian Shelley Manuscripts: A Facsimile Edition (23 vols.; New York and London: Garland, 1986–2002).

Sir Philip Sidney: Life, Death and Legend [exhibition catalogue] (Oxford: Bodleian Library, 1987).

Location Register of Twentieth-Century English Literary Manuscripts and Letters (2 vols.; London: The British Library, 1988).

T.E. Lawrence: The Legend and the Man [exhibition catalogue] (Oxford: Bodleian Library, 1988).

Gerard Manley Hopkins (1844–89) [exhibition catalogue] (Oxford: Bodleian Library, 1989).

B.C. Barker-Benfield, 'Hogg-Shelley Papers of 1810–12', *Bodleian Library Record*,14/1 (1991), 14–29.

Judith Priestman, 'Philip Larkin and the Bodleian Library', *Bodleian Library Record*, 14/1 (1991), 30–66.

Shelley's Guitar: A Bicentenary Exhibition (Oxford: Bodleian Library, 1992).

J.R.R. Tolkien: Life and Legend [exhibition catalogue] (Oxford: Bodleian Library, 1992).

Location Register of English Literary Manuscripts and Letters: Eighteenth and Nineteenth Centuries, ed. David C. Sutton (2 vols.; London: The British Library, 1995).

6. Children's Books

The Bodleian holds, and continues to augment, outstanding resources for the study of books for children. The largest body of this material is formed by the Opie Collection of Children's Literature. This major collection, acquired in 1988, is well-known to scholars the world over through the pioneering work of Iona and Peter Opie on nursery rhymes and the lore, language, and games of children. It covers all kinds of books for children from grammars to colouring books, battledores to nursery rhymes, stories to catechisms, books presented by Lewis Carroll and Queen Victoria, and one owned by the boy who was the inspiration for Christopher Robin; and ranges chronologically from the sixteenth to the twentieth centuries. The greatest strengths of the collection are its eighteenth- and nineteenth-century holdings, a lavish assemblage of books from the time when children were first offered reading and illustrative matter which appealed to and engaged with their imagination, and were not simply books of instruction. Books from the late nineteenth and first half of the twentieth centuries predominate numerically – a natural reflection of the ever expanding trade in this material. Because the collection began as a working library, when Iona and Peter Opie were compiling what was to become *The Oxford Dictionary of Nursery Rhymes*, it contains many books charting the textual history of these nonsense verses from their earliest appearance in print. However, Peter Opie soon decided that he would set no limits (other than the inevitable financial constraints) to the scope of his collecting, with the result that there will be something for all students of children's literature among its 20,000 volumes.

This one collection, however, is set in the context of the vast resources of a legal deposit library which, since about 1850, has received a copy of most children's books published in this country. The holdings of earlier material are substantial. Academic opinion in Oxford was understandably opposed to the acquisition of juvenilia in the seventeenth and eighteenth centuries, though some remarkable books seem to have slipped past the censorious notice of contemporary librarians. A notable example of this is *A play-book for children, to allure them to read as soon as they can speak plain* by J.G., dated 1694 (8° S 188(2) Art.). This book, the only known copy, is an extraordinary witness to that shift in sensibility which recognised that children would learn more easily, more effectively, and more enthusiastically if they were to have books which entertained and amused their imaginative capabilities. In 1693 John Locke had forcefully expressed this idea in his *Some Thoughts Concerning Education*, and the anonymous J.G. put it into practice. His little book must have been sent to the Library by the Stationers' Company and somehow escaped notice by being bound with five others; it did not appear in the printed catalogue of 1738.

While this was the exception for the university library, independent scholars and private collectors were not so exclusive, some indeed going out of their way to buy children's books for their own sake as part of the culture of the period to which they belonged, and the libraries of several such social historians have come to the Bodleian. The most important of these, containing a significant number of late eighteenth-century children's books, is the collection of Francis Douce (1757–1834). He was interested in nursery rhymes and bought some of the earliest published anthologies. Indeed, Iona and Peter Opie came to Oxford to consult these when they were researching 'Mother Goose', forging that link with the Library which eventually led to their books coming here.

The decision to accept all the books for children made available by copyright law led to a rich representation of the golden age of British children's books, from Lewis Carroll through Beatrix Potter and Kenneth Grahame to A.A. Milne, and also caused more attention to be directed at retrospective acquisition. In March 1882 the Library bought thirty eighteenth-century children's books which had belonged to an Isle of Wight family. The books, which cover a wide range of subjects, are all rare, and eleven of them seem to be unique. In the same year Brasenose College presented to the Library a hornbook which had been found when clearing ground in the college for new buildings. Dating from about 1620 it is the only known copy of the earliest surviving hornbook (Arch. A. f. 11). In the early twenty-first century children's books remain a significant part of the Library's antiquarian accessions.

Periodicals for children are well represented, with long runs of the major titles published in the nineteenth and early twentieth centuries. Children's comics, which flourished in the 1950s, 60s, and 70s, were only taken selectively, though there are runs of some of the most famous titles, such as *Beano*, *Eagle*, *Girl*, and *Bunty for Girls*. The Opie Collection has some runs and many sample issues. Children's annuals, on the other hand, have been acquired in larger numbers, and many of these contain characters from the comics from which they derive.

The limited, deluxe editions of some notable illustrators' works are a category of books which have not come to the Library by legal deposit. A fine run of those by Arthur Rackham has recently been acquired (with many other books illustrated by this artist) in the collection of Simon Castello. There are odd copies of similar books by Edmund Dulac, Kay Nielsen, and others in other collections. Original art-work for children's books is not well-represented in the Bodleian, with the notable and spectacular exception of J.R.R. Tolkien's drawings; a few examples of other artists' work are in the Opie Collection.

Foreign children's books have never been systematically collected by the Library;

however, there are sufficient numbers of Dutch, French and German books of the nineteenth century to make useful comparisons with books being published in this country. The Opie Collection has an extraordinary assemblage of foreign books in Western and Eastern languages, some deliberately acquired, some presented by contemporary authors. The early twentieth-century Russian illustrated books, both pre- and post-revolution, are of special interest.

The Library's manuscript collections contain much of interest to the student of children's books. Apart from such literary masterpieces as Jane Johnson's *A very pretty story* (MS. Don. d. 198) or Kenneth Grahame's letters to his son (MS. Eng. misc. d. 281) which formed the basis of *The Wind in the Willows*, there are many diaries and letters by and about children. The John Johnson Collection of Printed Ephemera also contains relevant material, including some toys and games which were very much part of the children's bookseller's stock in the late eighteenth and nineteenth centuries.

Select bibliography

Iona and Peter Opie, *Three Centuries of Nursery Rhymes and Poetry for Children* (2nd edn.; Oxford and London: Oxford University Press, 1977).

Children: An Exhibition to Mark the Year of the Child (Oxford: Bodleian Library, 1979).

Iona and Robert Opie, Brian Alderson, *The Treasures of Childhood: Books, Toys and Games From the Opie Collection* (London: Pavilion Books, 1989).

Early Children's Books in the Bodleian Library: An Exhibition (Oxford: Bodleian Library, 1995).

7. Theology

It has become a commonplace of Bodleian historiography that Sir Thomas Bodley designed his library from the outset as 'a bulwark of extreme Protestantism'. This view, first articulated by the Oxford antiquary Thomas Hearne, who was on the library staff from 1703 to 1716, has been modified in recent years. Nowadays the emphasis tends to be on the astonishing vision of the founder who collected books on subjects and in languages far beyond the curriculum of his University and indeed beyond the range of British scholarship in his day.

The first catalogues of the library nevertheless bear eloquent witness to the preponderance of theological works on its shelves in the first decades of the seventeenth century. In 1605 roughly 3,500 of the 8,700 catalogue entries refer to theological works. A handwritten catalogue of 1612 reveals that by then more than half of the books in the library were classified as theology. In his preface to the 1620 catalogue, Bodley's Librarian Thomas James made a veiled apology for the large number of theological works listed.

This preponderance undoubtedly reflects the interests of the first Librarian and of many of his contemporaries at the University. Bodley and James both came from staunchly Protestant families who had gone into voluntary exile during Mary Tudor's reign. James's major scholarly work was to compare the editions of the Latin Fathers printed in Rome and Paris with texts in English medieval manuscripts, in order to demonstrate what James believed to be deliberate distortions.

Of the 530 manuscripts listed in the 1605 catalogue, 365 are theological. During the century after the Norman Conquest, Britain's monastic and cathedral libraries were systematically stocked with standard texts by patristic and later theological writers, from Augustine and Gregory to Bernard of Clairvaux and Hugh of Saint-Victor. Biblical scholarship, often in the form of glossed books of the Bible of which many were imported from Paris, formed another major topic in the twelfth-century monastic libraries. Production standards were high, and many noble twelfth-century books survived the Dissolution. Such books formed the core of the Bodleian's manuscript collections in theology, starting with a large group given in 1602 by the Dean and Chapter of Exeter Cathedral. Those of known provenance are listed in Ker 1964 (*see Select bibliography*).

The manuscripts collected by Christopher, 1st Baron Hatton, almost entirely medieval, were bought by the Library in 1671. They are strong in theological works and include two major treasures: King Alfred's translation of Gregory the Great's *Liber Pastoralis* (MS. Hatton 20) and the earliest surviving manuscript of the *Rule of St. Benedict* (MS. Hatton 48).

Manuscripts of scholastic theology were produced in great numbers for university use from the thirteenth to the fifteenth centuries. College collections such as those of University College and New College (both now deposited on long-term loan at the Bodleian) are especially rich in such books, which may well have belonged to the same Oxford colleges since the Middle Ages. Medieval Oxford and its theology faculty were producing new works and commentaries, with major contributions especially from its Franciscan and Dominican convents. This period also produced many sermon-collections and manuals of pastoral theology: treatises on the virtues and vices, confessional handbooks, and digests of theological topics. In 1984–5, the Bodleian held an exhibition on *Wyclif and His Followers*, to mark the 600th anniversary of the death of Oxford's most controversial theologian.

The Bodleian, though a post-medieval foundation, also acquired many medieval scholastic and other theological manuscripts, from both England and the Continent: for example, those from Italy which arrived in 1817 with the purchase of the Canonici manuscripts. The Canonici manuscripts include distinct subsections of MSS. Canonici Latin Biblical and Latin Patristic. The Hamilton Collection, given in 1857 and deriving from the monastic libraries of Erfurt, is especially rich in late medieval German manuscripts of Latin sermons. From 1887 onwards, miscellaneous new accessions of papyri, medieval and later manuscripts were classified by language and subjects, including categories for Bibles, liturgies and theologies in both Latin and Greek.

The foundation stone of the Bodleian's Greek theological collections is an enormous volume of patristic and later Greek texts (MS. Auct. E. 1. 16) which starts with a synopsis of the *Thesaurus of Orthodoxy* by Niketas Choniates. It had been transcribed in France in 1553–4 for Queen Mary I, apparently to symbolise her revival of the Catholic faith; yet in 1601 it was given by Sir John Fortescue to Thomas Bodley's Protestant foundation. Greek theological texts form a large proportion of every collection of Greek manuscripts acquired by the Bodleian, from the Barocci collection of 1629 onwards. They include numerous biblical texts, from papyrus fragments and early uncial manuscripts to illuminated Byzantine gospel-books. Archbishop Laud's gifts of Greek manuscripts in the 1630s included 'The Laudian Acts' (MS. Laud Gr. 35), a bilingual copy in uncial script of *c*.600 AD which was almost certainly used by Bede for his two commentaries on the Acts of the Apostles. Codex Ebnerianus (MS. Auct. T. inf. 1. 10), an early twelfth-century New Testament, is illuminated with miniatures which form in themselves a source for the study of Byzantine liturgy. (*See also the chapter on Classical Studies.*)

Liturgical and devotional manuscripts provide the raw materials not only for the study of medieval forms of worship but also for religious music and iconography. For the liturgy of Anglo-Saxon England, the Bodleian has two primary sources in the Leofric Missal (MS. Bodl. 579) and the Winchester Troper (MS. Bodl. 775). Francis Douce's taste for fine illumination brought in manuscripts such as the Ormesby Psalter (MS. Douce 366), and many Flemish and French Books of Hours of the fifteenth century. Liturgical manuscripts in the Rawlinson, Gough and Canonici collections are classified together (MSS. Rawl. Liturg., MSS. Gough Liturg., MSS. Canon. Liturg.). Some miscellaneous liturgical manuscripts acquired before 1887 are shelfmarked simply as MSS. Liturg.

From the beginning the Library's printed collections were rich in the works of the Church Fathers, medieval schoolmen, Reformation (especially German) writers and contemporary controversialists, and in Bibles and liturgical works. The prominence of theology as a subject of study in the University and of controversy in the country at large ensured that the Bodleian continued to increase its stock of such works and of theological tracts and pamphlets. By 1840, when the original four-part classification (into Theology, Law, Medicine and Arts) was finally abandoned, books in the 'Th.' classification numbered some 11,000, while gifts and bequests of scholars' own collections (kept separately as named collections) had brought with them many thousands more. The bequest of Thomas Marshall, Rector of Lincoln College, in 1685 was substantially contemporary Protestant theology; that of Thomas Barlow, Bishop of Lincoln, in 1691 was strong in sixteenth-century theology and in Civil War theological tracts; that of Thomas Tanner, Bishop of St Asaph, in 1736 included many rare pamphlets of the Reformation period; that of Richard Rawlinson in 1755 was particularly strong in theological works of the sixteenth to eighteenth centuries. Even the great Gough bequest of 1809, best known as the foundation of the Bodleian's topographical collections, included much on ecclesiastical topography and over 200 printed service books of the English church before the Reformation.

Bulkeley Bandinel, Bodley's Librarian from 1813 to 1860, was particularly knowledgeable about early printing, and aimed to build up a representative collection of incunable Bibles. As a result, for example, out of nearly 100 editions of Latin Bibles printed in the fifteenth century, the Bodleian has 87. Other theological incunabula are spread across most of the Library's collections, and include large numbers of patristic texts (copies of more than 100 pre-1500 editions of the works of Augustine alone), much scholastic theology (copies of 13 of the 23 pre-1500 editions of Peter Lombard's *Sentences*, and more than 80 editions of the works of Thomas Aquinas); popular theology, such as the saints' lives which form the *Legenda aurea* of Jacobus de Voragine, of which the Bodleian has copies of nearly 50 incunable editions; devotional works, such as the *Imitatio Christi* of Thomas à Kempis (of which the Bodleian has more than 20 pre-1500 editions) and several *sacre rappresentazioni* (in Italian) intended for the edification of their readers; and a fine collection of liturgical books, including copies of many rare missals and books of hours. The Douce Collection, for example, contains many saints' lives, sermons and preachers' manuals.

Throughout the nineteenth and twentieth centuries the strength of the theological collections and of theological studies and disputes within the University ensured their continued growth, through legal deposit, gifts and purchases. These acquisitions include a group of 170 works by and about the New England divines, Cotton Mather (1663–1728) and Increase Mather (1639–1723); an important collection of Latin and German tracts by the German Reformers, especially Luther (Tract. Luth.); a comprehensive collection of German, Dutch and Scandinavian academic dissertations of the seventeeth to mid-nineteenth centuries (Diss.); fine liturgical books and Bibles in the Douce Collection; many editions of the Psalms and works relating to the Quakers among the books of Philip Bliss; English theological tracts of the Civil War and Interregnum in Elias Ashmole's library; pre-1850 Bibles in all languages and Books of Common Prayer; interesting works relating to the Congregational church and sermons printed in the provinces from Mansfield College; a collection of about 80 works by and about the Danish philosopher and theologian Søren Aabye Kierkegaard (1813–55), and the rare survival of the Marlborough Vicar's Library, the bulk of it assembled by William White (1604–78), who had been a master at Magdalen College School.

As in so many other subjects, the manuscript collections of the early modern and modern periods grew alongside the printed collections and reflect their strengths. Particularly numerous are manuscripts of seventeenth-century theology and church history. Most important papers on the history of the Anglican Church are to be found in the Tanner Collection. Thomas Tanner (1674–1735) bought the papers of Archbishop William Sancroft (1617–93) from Sancroft's executors. They include many volumes of official papers relating to dioceses in the Province of Canterbury, as well as a long series of the Archbishop's own notebooks and several of Richard Holdsworth, Master of Emmanuel College, Cambridge (1590–1649).

Among the many collections of seventeenth-century manuscript sermons are five large volumes of notes of John Warner, Bishop of Rochester (1581–1666) (MSS. Eng. th. b. 4–8) and an unusual survival of twenty notebooks of Thomas Aldersey, who matriculated at Brasenose College in 1653, containing his notes of sermons he heard preached in Oxford, 1653–5, London, 1661, and Cheshire, 1667–89 (MSS. Don. e. 155–6, f. 38–50). Two famous volumes of sermons – the 'Merton' and 'Dowden' manuscripts of the sermons of John Donne – were given by E.S. de Beer in 1960 (MSS. Eng. th. c. 71 and e.102).

The Rawlinson Collection contains (MSS. Rawl. E) over 200 volumes of seventeenth- and eighteenth-century sermons, many by nonconformists and non-jurors and (in MSS. Rawl. D) the papers of several eminent non-jurors, among them Richard Rawlinson himself (1690–1755), Thomas Hearne (1678–1735), John Fitzwilliam (d.1699), Henry Gandy (1649–1734), George Hickes (1642–1715), Lawrence Howell (1664?–1720) and Nathaniel Spinckes (1653–1727). Twenty-five volumes of the correspondence and papers of another non-juror, Thomas Brett (1667–1744) were purchased in 1933, while in the mid-nineteenth century the Library bought a collection of 360 published non-juror sermons for five guineas and some 300 volumes of non-juror tracts.

Much is to be learned about the eighteenth-century church from the sermons (MSS. Eng. th. e. 72–100) and the diaries (MSS. Eng. misc. f. 103–72) of James Woodforde (1740–1803), Curate of Castle Cary and Ansford in Somerset and from 1774 Rector of Weston Longeville in Norfolk, and from the papers of Edmund Gibson, Bishop of London (1669–1748). The collections of nineteenth-century clergymen are too numerous to list, but outstanding among them are those of Samuel Wilberforce, Bishop of Oxford and of Winchester and of his brother R.I. Wilberforce; of Mark Pattison, Rector of Lincoln College; and of Henry, Cardinal Manning. Probably the most eccentric Anglican clergyman whose manuscripts are to be found in the Bodleian is Robert Stephen Hawker (1803–75), who was Vicar of Morwenstow in Cornwall from 1834.

The present scope of the Bodleian's collecting of printed works embraces biblical studies (including texts, theology, commentaries, criticism and hermeneutics); Early Church Fathers (including texts, translations and criticism); doctrinal theology; the history and practice of all significant Christian churches; and texts by Christian theological writers over the centuries. Material relating to broad subject areas such as church and society, science and religion, and the philosophy of religion, is also collected.

Select bibliography

P. Glorieux, *Répertoire des maîtres en théologie de Paris au XIIIe siècle* (2 vols., Paris 1933–4). Lists many continental theologians – Aquinas, Bonaventure, etc. – whose works were being imported.

C. Kirchberger, 'Bodleian Manuscripts Relating to the Spiritual Life, 1500–1750', *Bodleian Library Record*, 3/31 (1951), 155–64.

Liturgical Manuscripts and Printed Books [exhibition catalogue] (Oxford: Bodleian Library, 1952).

The Bodleian's Latin liturgical manuscripts are catalogued together by class of manuscript (Mass Books, Office Books, etc.) in an unpublished typescript by S. J. P. van Dijk (6 vols. in 7 parts, 1957–60), held on open shelves in Duke Humfrey's Library at R. 6.152.

N. R. Ker, *Medieval Libraries of Great Britain: A List of Surviving Books* (2nd edn.; London: Royal Historical Society, 1964), with *Supplement* by A.G. Watson (London: Royal Historical Society, 1987).

Typologie des sources du moyen âge occidental (Turnhout, 1972–). A good introduction to the different categories of books in this mass of material is to be found in various volumes of the series.

Archbishop Laud: Commemorative Exhibition (Oxford: Bodleian Library, 1973).

The Benedictines and the Book 480–1980 [exhibition catalogue] (Oxford: Bodleian Library, 1980; corrected repr. 1982).

English Hymns and Hymnbooks [exhibition catalogue] (Oxford: Bodleian Library, 1981).

The History of the University of Oxford, vols. 1–2 (eds. J. I. Catto and R. Evans; Oxford: Oxford University Press, 1984, 1992) and the chapters on 'Theology and Theologians'.

Wyclif and His Followers [exhibition catalogue] (Oxford: Bodleian Library, 1984).

A Continental Shelf: Books across Europe from Ptolemy to Don Quixote [exhibition catalogue] (Oxford: Bodleian Library, 1994), 32–61.

R. Sharpe, *A Handlist of the Latin Writers of Great Britain and Ireland Before 1540* ([Turnhout], 1997). For medieval British authors, often with lists of manuscripts for unpublished texts.

The Garden, the Ark and the Tower: Biblical Metaphors of Knowledge in Early Modern Europe [exhibition catalogue] (Oxford: Bodleian Library, 1998).

A card index of iconographic subjects, with colour slides of many examples, is available in the Filmstrips / Slides library.

8. Philosophy

Medieval manuscript sources and incunabula

No single collection of medieval manuscripts at the Bodleian is devoted exclusively to philosophy. Although numerous, the manuscripts of philosophical texts are dispersed across many collections, and are best retrieved by a search for authors' names in the general indexes. Searches by first words can be made in an unpublished source by G.E. Mohan (*see Select bibliography*). The general range of authors and texts is surveyed in *Repertorium edierter Texte...* (*see Select bibliography*). Besides those texts recognisable as philosophy in today's terms, manuscripts in the fields of natural philosophy and grammar are also fruitful sources for the understanding of medieval thought.

Oxford's most important manuscript of classical philosophy is the Clarke Plato (MS. E.D. Clarke 39), the oldest surviving manuscript for about half of Plato's dialogues, which was acquired by the University in 1809: it was written in Constantinople in AD 895. Philosophical texts from ancient Greece and Byzantium are naturally represented by copies amongst the Bodleian's Greek manuscripts, though scarcely any of these had reached Britain before the seventeenth century. The Bodleian also holds the oldest surviving manuscript of the *Discourses* of Epictetus (MS. Auct. T. 4. 13), a twelfth-century text acquired in 1820.

In the early Latin West, echoes of Greek philosophy were available through encyclopaedists such as Martianus Capella, from whom the Bodleian owns two important manuscripts from ninth-century France: a copy of the text itself with gloss (MS. Laud Lat. 118), and a manuscript of the commentary by Johannes Scotus Erigena (MS. Auct. T. 2. 19). Manuscripts of Latin classical and Late Antique philosophers remained accessible, some texts more common than others. Boethius' *De consolatione philosophiae* was transcribed with its Carolingian gloss in a superb manuscript made at Canterbury in the late tenth century (MS. Auct. F. 1. 15, part 1). In the twelfth century William of Malmesbury searched successfully for the works of Cicero: the Library has his copy of the *De officiis* (MS. Rawl. G. 139). Philosophical study in twelfth-century Ireland is witnessed by a manuscript which includes Calcidius' Latin translation of Plato's *Timaeus* and extensive excerpts from Erigena's *Periphyseon* (MS. Auct. F. 3. 15).

Latin translations of Aristotle, made either directly from the Greek or via the Arabic, were becoming available from the twelfth century. A collection of early Aristotelian translations, including parts of the *Metaphysics* and *Ethics*, was at St Albans Abbey by the thirteenth century (MS. Selden Supra 24). At the universities from the thirteenth to the fifteenth century, Aristotle's texts and the many commentaries on them provided both the content and the logical tools for philosophical study to progress. The patterns of university exercises and debate have left their mark in the many surviving manuscripts of *Quaestiones*, *Quodlibetica* and the like from Oxford and other universities. Oxford itself was producing philosophers of European stature, such as Roger Bacon, Walter Burley and William of Ockham.

In Renaissance Italy, scholars could regain access to ancient philosophical texts in the original Greek. Humfrey, Duke of Gloucester was the dedicatee of new Latin translations of both Plato's *Republic* and Aristotle's *Politics*. Whilst his own copies of these texts no longer survive in Oxford, the influence of his books and of his encouragement of humanistic scholarship is perceptible, for example in a manuscript of Leonardo Bruni's translation of Aristotle's *Ethics* and *Politics* written by an English scribe in 1452 (New College MS. 228). Manuscripts of Aristotelian translations and commentaries are listed in Lacombe, Lohr and Kristeller (*see Select bibliography*). Later Bodleian accessions of Italian manuscripts include a copy of Marsilio Ficino's commentary on Plato's *Symposium* with Ficino's own autograph corrections (MS. Canon. Class. Lat. 156), one of the many humanistic manuscripts bought in 1817 from the Canonici Collection of Venice.

Ancient and medieval philosophy is well represented among the incunable collections. Of the ancients the Library has, for example, approaching 50 incunable editions of the works of Aristotle, and copies of nearly half the pre-1500 printed editions of the works of Plato. Medieval scholastic philosophy is represented by authors such as Duns Scotus and William of Ockham.

Post-medieval and modern collections

In the field of early modern philosophy, the Library's outstanding collection is that of John Locke (1632–1704). The manuscripts (for the most part bought from the Earl of Lovelace in 1947) include journals, notebooks, correspondence and early drafts of *An Essay Concerning Humane Understanding*. In 1978 Paul Mellon presented his Locke collection which consists of a large part of the 'King moiety' of Locke's library and other books and manuscripts, with the result that the Bodleian now holds over 800 volumes owned by Locke, including all those with the location 'Oak Spring' in Harrison and Laslett's *The Library of John Locke* (*see Select bibliography*).

The Bodleian's modern philosophy holdings reflect the development of the study of philosophy in the University. Until the foundation of the School of Philosophy, Politics and Economics (PPE) in 1920, philosophy was only studied as part of the

Literae Humaniores School, with a syllabus that was, until the early nineteenth century, focussed on ancient philosophy and logic, as were Bodleian acquisitions. In the 1830s modern philosophy began to be studied, initially only as a means of illuminating the ancient texts, but gradually, under the influence of Oxford philosophers like F.H. Bradley and T.H. Green, as a subject in its own right.

From the nineteenth century, the library of Thomas Fowler (1832–1904), Wykeham Professor of Logic, is now held in the Philosophy Library. The collection combines rare and antiquarian material with the standard journals and textbooks of the period. Fowler was a noted authority on Sir Francis Bacon and on the history of logic, and these books were the tools of his trade. There are a number of late fifteenth- and early sixteenth-century volumes from the Aldine Press. The texts of Bacon's writings include first editions of *Sylva Sylvarum* and *Opuscula varia posthuma*. Other rare books of interest include John Milton's *Artis logicae plenior institutio* of 1672, and *The Game of Logic* by Lewis Carroll (1887), with the original counters and an inscription to Fowler by the author.

The chief significance of the Fowler collection, however, is as a surviving working library, ancient and modern, of one of the major figures of Victorian Oxford. Beyond Fowler's own research interests, the only modern philosophical texts included are those which were finding reluctant acceptance in the Oxford teaching syllabus of the late nineteenth century as adjuncts to the ancient philosophy course. The Fowler Collection is complemented by another turn-of-the-century collection of philosophy books, those of Shadwell Holloway Hodgson, a friend of Fowler and first President of the Aristotelian Society. Bequeathed to Corpus Christi College, the majority are on loan to the Philosophy Library. The collection is strong in nineteenth-century Continental philosophy, and demonstrates the extent to which new ideas were transforming the Oxford philosophy scene.

The Bodleian's acquisitions responded to these developments throughout the nineteenth century and on into the twentieth, with an increase both in purchases of philosophical works published abroad and of British philosophy acquired through legal deposit. The Library also houses papers of the Positivist Richard Congreve (1818–99); of H.H. Joachim (1868–1938), Wykeham Professor of Logic; and of the moral philosopher H.A. Prichard (1871–1947). In 1967 it acquired by gift the typescript of Wittgenstein's *Tractatus logico-philosophicus* from which the German text was probably published in 1921 (MS. German d. 6), and in 1969 purchased an early manuscript of the *Tractatus* (MS. German d. 7). The Library holds the papers of the philosopher of history R.G. Collingwood (1889–1943), which are on deposit from the family.

The period following the Second World War was one in which Oxford philosophers, and even a branch of philosophy known as 'Oxford Philosophy', or ordinary-language philosophy, were pre-eminent. From that period the Bodleian holds some papers of the analytical philosopher J.L. Austin (1911–60), including his notes for his lecture series 'Words and Deeds', and papers of the logician A.N. Prior (1914–69). Further insights into this period may be found in the Jowett Society minute-books for 1920–59 (MSS. Top. Oxon. d. 359/1–3; printed papers at G.A. Oxon 4° 603), the minute-books of the Oxford University Philosophical Society from 1898 to 1971 (MSS. Top. Oxon. e. 369/1–2; Eng. misc. d. 937), and those of the Origen Society, 1904–29 and 1933–59 (MSS. Top. Oxon. d. 374/1–4, 6–10). The Philosophy Library houses some further papers of J.L. Austin, as well as manuscript material relating to the American philosophers W.V. Quine (1908–2000) and Saul Kripke (1940–), and the Oxford professors H.H. Price (1899–1985) and Gilbert Ryle (1900–76), although the majority of Ryle's papers are held at Linacre College.

The extensive archive of Sir Isaiah Berlin (1909–97) was given to the Bodleian by the Isaiah Berlin Literary Trust in 1999. It includes a wide range of correspondence, academic, literary and personal papers. A detailed catalogue, due to be completed in 2004, is being made available online (*see Select bibliography*). The study of the philosophy of science also expanded greatly in the post-war period, and holdings were built up at the Radcliffe Science Library.

In recent years the scope of acquisitions has widened to include electronic journals and databases, a video collection of contemporary philosophers and the digitisation of primary resources with, for example, the inclusion of the Wittgenstein manuscripts in the Bergen electronic edition.

Select bibliography

G.E. Mohan, *Incipits of Philosophical Writings in Latin of the XIIIth–XVth Centuries* [enlargement from microfilm of the original at St Bonaventure University, N.Y., n.d., bound in 4 vols.]. Held in Duke Humfrey's Library at R.5.497/1–4.

G. Lacombe et al., *Aristoteles Latinus* (Corpus Philosophorum Medii Aevi; vol.I, Rome, 1939; vol. II, incl. Suppl., Cambridge, 1955; Suppl. Altera, ed. L. Minio-Paluello, Bruges & Paris, 1961).

Philip Long, *A Summary Catalogue of the Lovelace Collection of the Papers of John Locke in the Bodleian Library* (Oxford Bibliographical Society Publications, n.s.8; Oxford, 1959).

P.O. Kristeller et al., *Catalogus translationum et commentariorum: Medieval and Renaissance Latin Translations and Commentaries: Annotated Lists and Guides* (Washington, D.C., 1960–).

Philip Long, 'The Mellon Donation of Additional Manuscripts of John Locke from the Lovelace Collection', *Bodleian Library Record*, 7/4 (1964), 185–93.

C.H. Lohr, *Medieval Latin Aristotle Commentaries* (successive articles in *Traditio*, 23–30 (1967–74)), and *Latin Aristotle Commentaries II, Renaissance Authors* (Corpus Philosophorum Medii Aevi, Subsidia 6; Florence, 1988), with III, *Index Initiorum – Index Finium* (Subsidia 10; Florence, 1995).

Duke Humfrey and English Humanism in the Fifteenth Century [exhibition catalogue] (Oxford: Bodleian Library, 1970).

John Harrison and Peter Laslett, *The Library of John Locke* (2nd ed.; Oxford: Clarendon Press, 1971).

H.A.S. Schankula, 'A Summary Catalogue of the Philosophical Manuscript Papers of John Locke', *Bodleian Library Record*, 9/1 (1973), 24–35; and 'Additions and Corrections', *BLR* 9/2 (1974), 81–2.

Alfredo Sammut, *Unfredo duca di Gloucester e gli umanisti italiani* (Medioevo e Umanesimo, 41; Padova: Antenore, 1980).

Repertorium edierter Texte des Mittelalters aus dem Bereich der Philosophie und angrenzender Gebiete, eds. R. Schönberger & B. Kible (Berlin, 1994).

Information on the archive of Sir Isaiah Berlin can be found at: http://berlin.wolf.ox.ac.uk/information/berlin_papers.html

9. Social Sciences

Formally defined, the literature of the social science disciplines (economics, psychology, sociology, political science and anthropology) occupies little more than the most recent quarter of the Bodleian Library's 400 years. Nevertheless, these youthful sciences are rich in the scope and volume of their works and the Bodleian collections reflect the full breadth and development of our knowledge about our own societies and behaviour. Also represented in the collections are some of the personalities who have contributed to social science thought over the past 100 years, or those, like the politicians and government economists, who have tried to implement findings and influence its debates.

What one can expect in the way of special and unique social science collections in the Bodleian is largely determined by its long history, its status as a legal deposit library, its relationship to the research and teaching practices of the University, and its role within the research community at large. These factors have given rise to a complex and distributed collection, particularly with respect to the relative demarcations and collection policies of different parts of the Bodleian. The Bodleian Library of Commonwealth and African Studies at Rhodes House (Sub-Saharan Africa and Commonwealth collections), Vere Harmsworth Library (United States studies), the Bodleian Japanese Library, the Chinese Studies Library, the Indian Institute Library and the Oriental Institute Library are all examples of libraries that collect a wealth of material of interest to the social sciences but which have a specific focus upon one geolinguistic area. In the central Bodleian there is also a considerable degree of area and language specialisation, with substantial collections of Slavonic, Latin American, and Oriental publications, all similarly of great interest to social scientists researching and teaching both within and beyond those linguistic and geographic boundaries.

In the collections organised by subject rather than area, one can expect to find legal material in the Bodleian Law Library (*see pp. 68–74*) and certain subjects conventionally subsumed under standard definitions of the social sciences (especially psychology) in the Radcliffe Science Library (*see pp. 88–97*). The collections for Oxford's core social science disciplines of economics, political science, international relations, sociology and gender studies, though, are primarily housed in the central Bodleian, and this chapter focuses principally on the particular strengths of material in these collections. Like the disciplines themselves, the central Bodleian social science collections are mainly Anglo-Saxon in emphasis but also contain substantial collections in other major European languages. Taken as a whole this material constitutes a comprehensive intellectual record of the development of the social science disciplines in the languages represented. Along with the monograph and journal publications (both deposited and purchased), it is also possible to find a wealth of archival material which has been placed in the care of the Library and which offers unique primary material for social scientists and historians alike. Finally, the collection includes a substantial official papers section as a result of its many years of legal deposit privilege.

Economics

As the oldest and most established of the social science disciplines, economics has enjoyed a long and productive history in Oxford, which has been home to such eminent economists as the Nobel Prize winners Sir John Hicks, Sir James Mirrlees and Amartya Sen, as well as one of the pioneers of the discipline, Nassau William Senior. A two-volume first edition of Adam Smith's *An Inquiry into the Nature and Causes of the Wealth of Nations* (1776) provides a marker as to the chronological beginning of the Bodleian's collections, although a separate and distinctive discipline of 'political economy' did not emerge until the nineteenth century. Adam Smith was a graduate of Oxford, and contemporary translations of and later reactions to his work give an understanding of its impact. First editions of works by other political economy pioneers include those of David Ricardo, John Stuart Mill, Nassau William Senior, Frederic Bastiat and Jean-Baptiste Say which, along with reactions to their works and published letters, enhance our understanding of the beginnings of economics as a social science discipline and of the development of economic theory in the nineteenth century.

The Bodleian's Department of Special Collections and Western Manuscripts is home to a wealth of personal correspondence from eminent British economists. Nassau William Senior (1790–1864) was the first holder of the Drummond Chair of Political Economy at Oxford, working within the Oxford-Dublin tradition of supply and demand economics. Facsimiles of Senior's journals are also held in the collection. Senior's successor to the Drummond Chair was William Forster Lloyd (1795–1852), credited with independently introducing the concept of diminishing marginal utility and connecting demand to value. The papers and correspondence of other notable economists include those of another Drummond Professor, J.E. Thorold Rogers (1823–90), said to have been 'one of the most indefatigable searchers for the facts of everyday life ever known in England'; two memoranda 'On the Financial Situation' (1915–16) from John Maynard Keynes; correspondence between the colonial historian Lionel George Curtis and the two economists Henry Vincent Hodson (1906–99) and Thomas Jones (1870–1955); correspondence of Alexander

Nove (1915–1994) with Michael Kaser relating to Soviet economics; the diaries of barrister and economist Wolseley Partridge Emerton (*b.*1843) from 1863–1915; and correspondence between Professor Gilbert Murray and the economist John Atkinson Hobson (1858–1940). The Library also holds an extensive collection of papers and correspondence belonging to the economist and United Nations official Sidney Dell (1918–1990), and to the philanthropic Secretary of the Share and Loan Department of the London Stock Exchange Sir Henry Burdett (1847–1920). Burdett's papers include correspondence and papers relating not only to the Stock Exchange but also to *Burdett's Official Intelligence* (which ran from 1880 to 1933 when it became *The Stock Exchange Official Intelligence*, now subsumed within *The Stock Exchange Official Year-Book*). Other primary materials for economists include official publications (*see below*) and research material, in both printed and microfilm format, distributed throughout the collection. A notable series on microfilm, *Business and Financial Papers, 1780–1939* (1992–), contains selections from titles in the Bodleian and the British Library's Newspaper Library at Colindale.

Politics and International Relations

Oxford is perhaps more famous for its politician graduates than its contributions to political science. Pelham, Pitt the Elder, Canning, Peel, Gladstone, Attlee, Macmillan, Eden, Wilson, Heath, Thatcher, and most recently Tony Blair head an impressive cast of Oxford graduates who have reached the very highest political spheres.

The collections of the central Bodleian reflect Oxford's academic strengths in combining legal deposit and unique British material with very strong foreign language and area studies holdings. The Slavonic and East European collections are amongst the most extensive in the country and possess material (including official publications) relating to Russia and the former USSR, Poland, the Czech and Slovak Republics, Hungary, the former Yugoslavia, Romania and Bulgaria. Similarly, a Latin American collection provides material of social interest relating to the Hispanic speaking South American countries. Other foreign language strengths include – in Europe – material on the political system of Italy, as well as French and German political works. For Asia, there is material on the politics of modern China (including many newspapers of record) in the central Bodleian; on Japan at the Bodleian Japanese Library; and on the Indian subcontinent at the Indian Institute Library.

The archival strengths of the Bodleian's political science collections lie in British politics and British political history. In 1978 the Library became home to the Conservative Party Archive (CPA), complementing its existing collections of modern political papers to create an archival collection of significant importance to both political scholars and political historians alike. The CPA consists of the records

II. The Benefactors' Register

Bodley provided an impressive volume in which all
substantial gifts to his library were to be recorded.
It was kept on display in the reading room to
encourage further benefactions. The enamelled
plaque in the centre of the binding bears Bodley's
coat of arms and motto.

Given by the Founder in 1604
Library Records b. 903, front cover
See p. 16

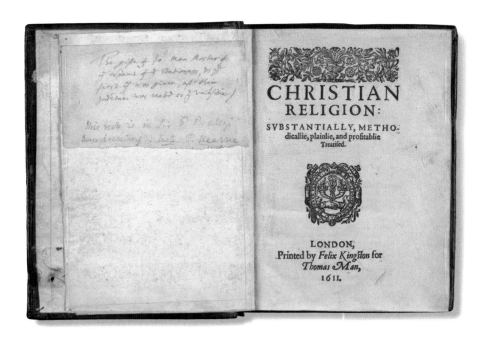

III. Thomas Cartwright, *Christian religion:*
substantially, methodicallie, plainlie and profitablie
*treatised***, 1611**

Sir Thomas Bodley's note on the fly-leaf attests
that this was the first book received by the
Bodleian under the agreement with the Stationers'
Company.

Acquired in 1611
4º R 34 Th, title-page
See p. 20

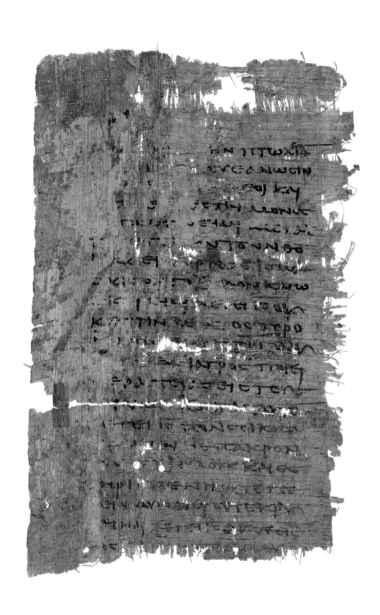

IV. Sayings of Jesus

A single leaf from a papyrus codex of the third
century AD contains the 'Sayings of Jesus',
identified from a parallel Coptic version as part of
the Gospel of St Thomas.

Given by the Egypt Exploration Fund in 1900
MS. Gr. th. e. 7(P)
See p. 26

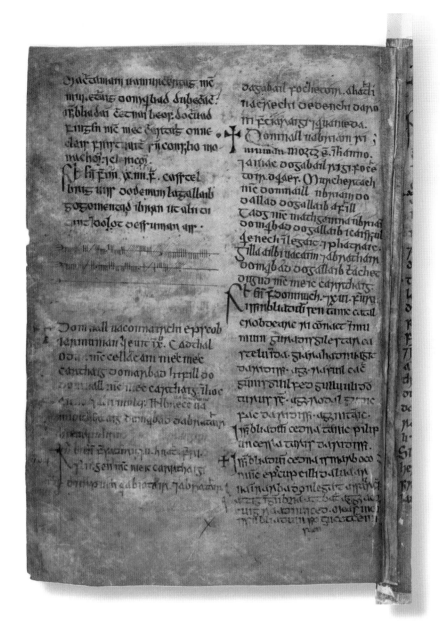

V. Annals of Inisfallen

The oldest surviving manuscript of any Irish
historical text, the 'Annals of Inisfallen' were
compiled around 1092 and continuously updated to
the end of the fourteenth century at the island
monastery of Inisfallen in the Lake of Killarney.

Bequeathed by Richard Rawlinson in 1755
MS. Rawl. B. 503, fol. 40v
See p. 32

I declar yt ye Title of King was forc't upon
mee & yt it was very much contrary to my opinion
when I was proclaim'd.   For ye Satisfaction of
the world I doe declare that ye late King told me that
Hee was never married to my Mother.
Haveing declar'd this I hope yt ye King who is now
will not let my Children Suffer on this Accoual. And to
this I put my hand this fifteenth day of July
1685.   Monmouth

Declar'd by Himselfe & Sign'd in the presence of us.

                    Fran: Ellis.
                    Tho: Batherby
                    Tho: Tenison
                    Geo: Hooper

VI. The Duke of Monmouth's acknowledgement of his illegitimacy

Condemned to death after the failure of the 1685 rebellion against James II, the Duke of Monmouth, who had claimed the throne as the son of Charles II, signed this poignant acknowledgement of his illegitimacy on the morning of his execution, 15 July 1685.

Bequeathed by Richard Rawlinson in 1755
MS. Rawl. A. 139B, fol. 8
See p. 32

VII. Harold Macmillan, letter to Lady Waverley

Written on the morning of Macmillan's speech to the Conservative Party Conference, 12 December 1961. It includes a comparison between the role of an ageing Prime Minister and an oak tree in whose shade young roots flourish, adding that Lloyd George had been in this respect better than Churchill.

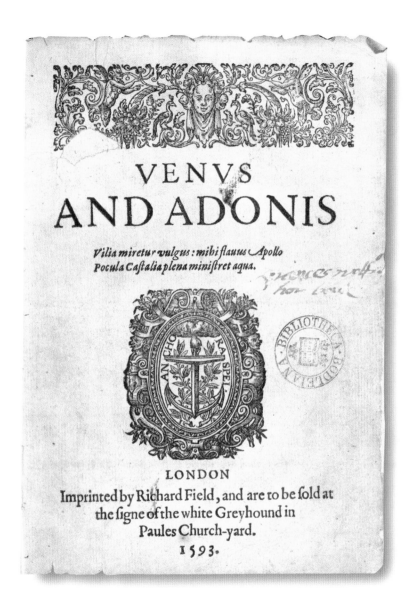

VENVS
AND ADONIS

Vilia miretur vulgus: mihi flauus Apollo
Pocula Castalia plena ministret aqua.

LONDON

Imprinted by Richard Field, and are to be sold at
the signe of the white Greyhound in
Paules Church-yard.

1593.

VIII. William Shakespeare, *Venus and Adonis*

The only known copy of the first of Shakespeare's
works to be printed, by Richard Field in London in
1593. It is from the collection of Edmund Malone,
one of the finest editors of Shakespeare. An earlier
owner, Frances Wolfreston, has inscribed the title-
page; she is the earliest collector of Shakespeare's
works of whom we are aware.

Given by Malone's brother, Lord Sunderlin, in 1821
Arch. G. e. 31(2), title-page
See p. 44

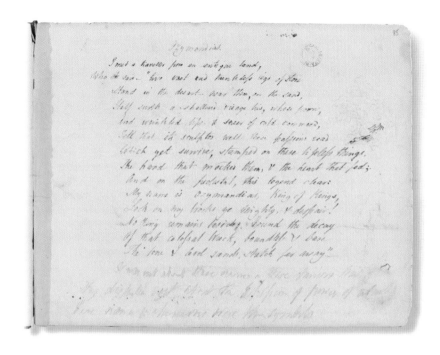

IX. Percy Bysshe Shelley, *Ozymandias*

Intermediate fair copy of Shelley's sonnet *Ozymandias*, which was first published in *The Examiner* on 11 January 1818.

Given by Jane, Lady Shelley in 1893
MS. Shelley e. 4, fol. 85r
See p. 44

thought a bit + then he said "There is just one thing I can do, + its your only chance. We are coming to a long tunnel, + on the other side of the tunnel is a thick wood. I will put on all speed while we are running through the tunnel, + as soon as we are through I will "slow up" for a few seconds, + you must jump off + run into the wood + hide yourself before the other engine gets through the tunnel, + then I will go on at full speed + they will continue to chase me, thinking you are still on the train."

Next moment they shot into the tunnel, + the engine-driver piled on more coals, + the sparks flew, + the train rushed + roared + rattled through the tunnel, + at last they shot out into the moonlight on the other side, + then the engine-driver put on his brakes hard + the train slowed down to almost a walking pace + the Toad got down on the step + the engine-driver said "now jump!" and the Toad jumped, + rolled down the embankment + scrambled into the wood + hid himself.

Then he peeped out + saw the train get up speed again + go off very fast. And presently the other engine came roaring + whistling out of the tunnel, in hot pursuit, with the policemen waving their revolvers + shouting "Stop, Stop, Stop!!!" Then the Toad had a good laugh — for the first time since he was put into prison.

But it was now very late, + dark, + cold, + here he was in a wild wood, with no money + no friends. And little animals peeped out of their holes + pointed at him + made fun of him; + a fox came skinking by, + said "Hullo washerwoman! how's the washing business doing?" and sniggered. And the Toad looked for a stone to throw at him, + couldn't find one, which made him sad. Presently he came to a hollow tree, full of dry leaves; + there he curled himself up as comfortably as he could, + slept till the morning.

In my next letter I will try to tell you the Adventures of the Toad + the Bargee; + about the Gipsy, + how the Toad went into Horse-dealing.

Ever your affectionate
Daddy

X. Kenneth Grahame, letter to his son, 1905

Kenneth Grahame's letters about the adventures of Mr Toad, sent to his son Alastair, whose nickname was 'Mouse', formed the basis of *The Wind in the Willows*, published in 1908.

Given by Mrs Elspeth Grahame in 1943
MS. Eng. misc. d. 281, fols 7v-8r
See p. 45

XI. *Eagle*, No.2, 21 April 1950

Eagle was created in 1950 with almost missionary zeal by Marcus Morris, an Anglican clergyman who feared the malign influence on boys of other comics, particularly those from the United States. Dan Dare, pilot of the future, was a powerful force for good.

Received by legal deposit in 1950
Per. 2529 c. 77
See p. 49

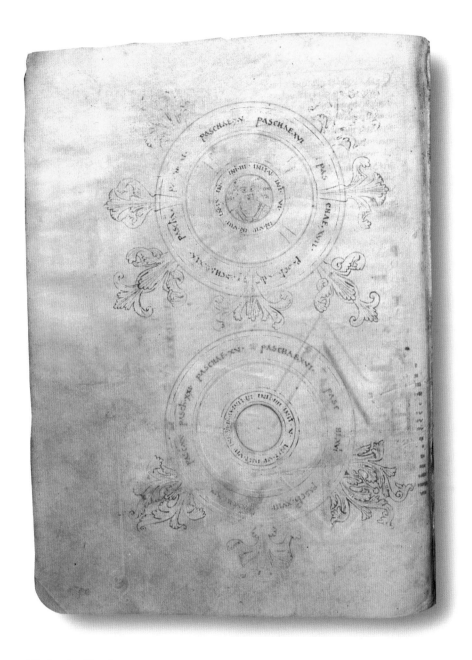

XII. The Leofric Missal

A primary source for studies of the liturgy in
Anglo-Saxon England, the 'Leofric Missal'
contains a ninth-century Continental sacramentary
to which a calendar and computistical tables were
added in mid-tenth century England. It was given
to Exeter Cathedral by Leofric, Bishop of Exeter
from 1046 to 1072.

Given by the Dean and Chapter of Exeter in 1602
MS. Bodl. 579, fol. 50v
See p. 53

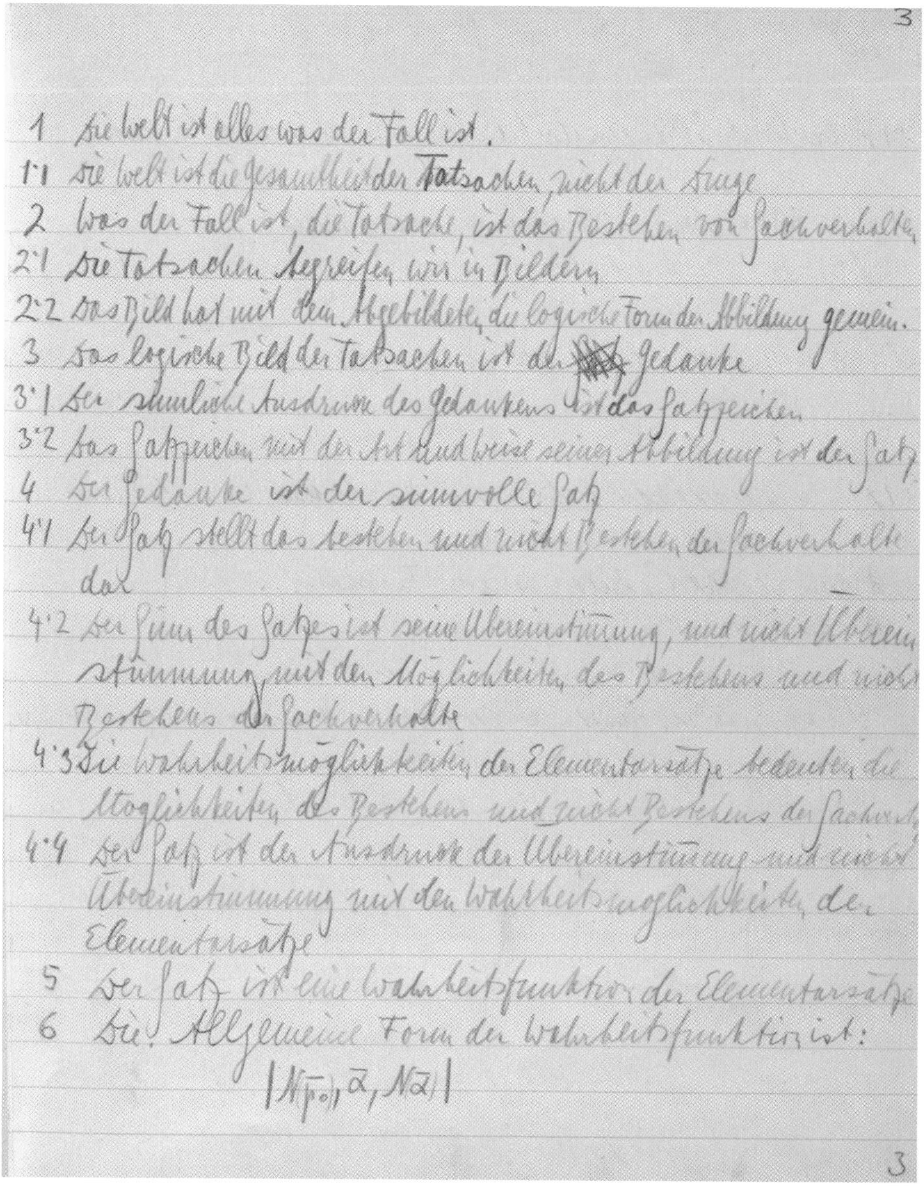
3
1 Die Welt ist alles was der Fall ist.
1·1 Die Welt ist die Gesamtheit der Tatsachen, nicht der Dinge
2 Was der Fall ist, die Tatsache, ist das Bestehen von Sachverhalten
2·1 Die Tatsachen begreifen wir in Bildern
2·2 Das Bild hat mit dem Abgebildeten die logische Form der Abbildung gemein.
3 Das logische Bild der Tatsachen ist der Gedanke
3·1 Der sinnliche Ausdruck des Gedankens ist das Satzzeichen
3·2 Das Satzzeichen mit der Art und Weise seiner Abbildung ist der Satz
4 Der Gedanke ist der sinnvolle Satz
4·1 Der Satz stellt das Bestehen und Nicht Bestehen der Sachverhalte dar
4·2 Der Sinn des Satzes ist seine Übereinstimmung, und nicht Übereinstimmung mit den Möglichkeiten des Bestehens und nicht Bestehens der Sachverhalte
4·3 Die Wahrheitsmöglichkeiten der Elementarsätze bedeuten die Möglichkeiten des Bestehens und nicht Bestehens der Sachverhalte
4·4 Der Satz ist der Ausdruck der Übereinstimmung und nicht Übereinstimmung mit den Wahrheitsmöglichkeiten der Elementarsätze
5 Der Satz ist eine Wahrheitsfunktion der Elementarsätze
6 Die allgemeine Form der Wahrheitsfunktion ist:
$|N(\bar{p}), \bar{\alpha}, N\bar{\alpha}|$
3

XIII. Ludwig Wittgenstein, *Logisch-philosophische Abhandlung*
Holograph pencil manuscript of Wittgenstein's ground-breaking *Logisch-philosophische Abhandlung*, *c.* 1918, published in 1921.

Purchased with the help of the Pilgrim Trust in 1969
MS. German d. 7, fol. 3r
See pp. 59, 100

XIV. Women's suffrage postcard

Postcard (*c.* 1902-05) satirising the aspirations of the Suffrage movement and reflecting the nineteenth-century craze for Phrenology. This science, dating from 1796, attempted to determine personality traits by feeling the bumps in the head. Here, the head of the notorious criminal Charles Peace (1832-1879) is contrasted with that of Sir Arthur Balfour who, although not antagonistic to the principle of Women's Suffrage, did little to further the cause. Margaret Thatcher came to power some 80 years later in 1979.

XV. Magna Carta

This original 1217 re-issue of the great charter of 1215, as revised by the Council of the infant King Henry III, was the copy sent for safe-keeping to St Peter's Abbey, Gloucester.

Bequeathed by Richard Furney, Archdeacon of Surrey, in 1753
MS. Ch. Gloucs. 8
See p. 68

XVI. Gratian, *Decretum*

Compiled about 1140, the *Decretum* became the
basic text on which masters of canon law lectured
and commented. This early printed version was
produced by Gutenberg's collaborator, Peter
Schoeffer, at Mainz in 1472. The historiated
miniature on the first page shows Christ,
surrounded by a pope, a cardinal, a king and a
courtier.

See p. 69

XVII. The Gough Map

The earliest map of Great Britain to include roads, the 'Gough Map' dates from around 1360. It shows the routes and distances between towns in red.

Bequeathed by Richard Gough in 1809
MS. Gough Gen. Top. 16
See p. 77

of the Party's central organisation. It also holds the papers of Sir Keith Joseph, the 1922 Committee and the Whips' Office, and a library of published Party material (including a large collection of General Election posters dating from 1909).

Some of the other political institutions and groups represented in the Bodleian's collection have a distinctly Oxford and Oxfordshire focus, including reports from the Campaign for Nuclear Disarmament in Oxford (1985–1993), minutes and accounts of the Oxfordshire branch of the Fabian Society (1895–1916), and minutes of the Oxford Constituency Labour Party, North Ward (1948–68). Also in the archives are a number of polling books and associated election papers from across the country, for example a 1713 poll book from the Sussex elections, a canvass book from the 1784 Yorkshire elections, and correspondence and papers relating to Abingdon borough parliamentary elections (1768–80). At an international level, the Bodleian houses the records of the Royal Institute of International Affairs, Chatham House (1906–60), and since 1989 it has been home to the United Nations Career Records Project (UNCRP), a record of contributions (contemporaneous papers, memoirs and interviews) from workers in the field, peacekeeping forces and administrative staff, as well as material from national representatives to the UN and from members of non-governmental organisations involved in UN work.

Alongside the papers of nineteenth- and twentieth-century politicians (*see pp. 34–7*), the Library holds papers of several political scientists, among them the correspondence (1949–57) between Alastair Buchan, Professor of International Relations at Oxford, and William Clark; the correspondence and papers of historian and political scientist Philip Maynard Williams (including papers on the formation of the SDP and correspondence with Shirley Williams and Roy Jenkins); and correspondence (1945–48) between the political scientist William James Millar Mackenzie and the 3rd Earl of Selborne. There are also extensive papers and correspondence belonging to Gilbert Murray and Alfred Zimmern, two Oxford professors who were involved in the establishment of the League of Nations in 1919. Finally, not to be missed are the examples of satirical cartoons and other political ephemera in the John Johnson Collection (*see pp. 163–5*).

Sociology, Social Work, Social Policy and Gender Studies

The Bodleian holds a number of works and manuscripts of interest to sociologists as well as to the more specialised disciplines of social work, social policy and gender studies. The historical and intellectual development of sociology is perhaps one of the more complicated to pin down. One can, though, cite numerous formative and rare works in the collection such as Herbert Spencer's extensive (and ultimately highly ambitious) multi-volume work *Descriptive Sociology, or, Groups of Sociological Facts* (published in its original form from 1873–1934 in 15 volumes). Also of particular note, when considering the development of the discipline, are the papers of Karl

Mannheim (relating to the Society for the Protection of Science and Learning (*see below*)), the American sociologist Lewis Mumford (letters to Alfred Zimmern), and papers by Sir Claus Moser (Professor of Social Statistics) relating to his work on the UN Statistics Commission (1960–1992).

The Department of Special Collections and Western Manuscripts similarly holds papers of social reformers who have influenced social policy and also has listings for two social workers, Sir Wyndham Deedes (knight, soldier, social worker, and Zionist) and Mary Augusta Ward (*née* Arnold, novelist under the name of Mrs Humphrey Ward, and social worker). The papers of Wyndham Deedes relate specifically to the Co-ordinating Committee for Refugees, whilst Mary Ward's notebook includes the minutes of the 'Oxford Lectures for Ladies' (1873–76).

The archival evidence of Oxfordshire's historical association with women's rights groups continues with the papers of the Association for the Education of Women in Oxford (1878–1920) and the letters of Lady Frances Balfour (churchwoman, suffragist and author) from 1890 to 1929. A significant gender and social history collection on microfilm (drawn from original publications held in the Bodleian) is *Women Advising Women* (Marlborough: Adam Matthew, 1992–), comprising advice books, manuals, almanacs, and journals from 1625 to 1837. A companion collection for men (again using the Bodleian's resources) is *Masculinity: Men Defining Men and Gentlemen, 1560–1918* (Adam Matthew, 2000–) ; and for both sexes *Sex and Sexuality, 1640–1940: Literary, Medical and Sociological Perspectives* (Adam Matthew, 1998–). Using sources from both the Bodleian and the Wellcome Institute, this collection consists of advice books reflecting the sexual attitudes of the time and some of the more unusual social historical aspects of human sexuality.

The Society for the Protection of Science and Learning Archive

The Bodleian is home to a large body of archival material relating to the Society for the Protection of Science and Learning, which will have particular interest for social scientists as many of the founders, supporters, and beneficiaries of the Society were from disciplines such as economics, sociology, and political science. The Society was founded in 1933 as the Academic Assistance Council and was formed to 'assist scholars and scientists who, on the grounds of religion, race, or opinion, were unable to continue their work in their own country'. At the time, this was mostly to combat Nazi persecution. In 1958 the bulk of the archive was deposited at the Bodleian (for the use of the Society's principal founder, Lord Beveridge). It consists of administrative records, personal case files of refugees assisted by the Society, and case papers of refugees dealt with by the Society since 1945. Notable refugees include Harro Bernardelli, Moritz Bonn, Fritz Kroner and Theodor Plaut in economics (with testimonials from J.M. Keynes and F. von Hayek), and Norbert Elias, Hugo Fischer and Ernst Kohn-Bramstedt in sociology.

Official publications

Official publications play a key part in the research activities of many social scientists. Across the Bodleian's collections one can find the official publications of nations and organisations throughout the world, whilst within the central Bodleian the Library has substantial holdings of official publications from the United Kingdom, from Eastern and Western Europe, and from many international organisations.

The holdings of British official publications in the Bodleian are matched only by those of the other copyright libraries in the United Kingdom. The legal deposit intake is used in part as the basis for the *United Kingdom Official Publications* database (UKOP) and the *Catalogue of British Official Publications not Published by the Stationery Office* (COBOP). It includes British Parliamentary papers (House of Lords and House of Commons papers from 1801, eighteenth-century Sessional Papers, and more recently the papers of the devolved assemblies); non-Parliamentary papers (including those of agencies, authorities, boards, departments and inspectorates published by the Stationery Office); and Republic of Ireland Parliamentary papers. A complete run of the UK census, beginning in 1801, is also available.

Foreign and international papers include the official journals and gazettes of many European countries, while the Bodleian has also been a depository for United Nations publications since 1950. A substantially complete collection of League of Nations documents is also held. There are long runs of documents from other international organisations including the International Labour Organisation (from 1938), the International Civil Aviation Organisation (from 1951), the World Trade Organisation, the International Monetary Fund (from 1955), the Council of Europe, the Western European Union, the OECD (from 1951), and UNESCO (from the 1950s). The European Documentation Centre at the Bodleian Law Library is a depository library for European Union official publications in all subjects. The Radcliffe Science Library selectively acquires material issued by the International Atomic Energy Agency, the World Health Organisation, the Food and Agriculture Organisation and the European Space Agency. There are also substantial holdings of official publications at the Bodleian Library of Commonwealth and African Studies, the Vere Harmsworth Library and the Indian Institute Library (*see pp. 157–60, 152–55 and 138 respectively*).

Select bibliography

R.P. Sturges, *Economists' Papers 1750–1950: A Guide to Archive and Other Manuscript Sources for the History of British and Irish Economic Thought* (London: Macmillan, 1975).

Nicholas Baldwin, *The Society for the Protection of Science and Learning Archive* (Oxford: Bodleian Library, 1988).

10. Law

Early law in the Bodleian

At Oxford and other medieval universities, the higher faculties of civil and canon law produced a regular demand for standard texts: the fundamental works of the *Corpus iuris civilis*, transmitting Roman law (Justinian's *Digestum*, *Codex*, *Institutiones* and *Novellae*); and the collections of papal decrees which formed the *Corpus iuris canonici*, from the twelfth-century *Decretum* collected by Gratian to the *Decretals* of Gregory IX (1234) and the *Liber sextus*, *Constitutiones Clementinae*, *Extravagantes Johannis XXII* and *Extravagantes communes* of his successors. Around these, in the thirteenth and fourteenth centuries, there built up layers of commentary, whether as marginal glosses or as separate volumes. Scholars such as Azo and Accursius in civil law, and the canonists Bernardus de Botone of Parma and Johannes Andreas, produced commentaries which achieved their own status as the standard *glossa ordinaria* around the primary texts. Manuscripts of civil and canon law survive as the physical relics of the university courses, both in the Bodleian (with imports from other universities such as Bologna) and especially in the college libraries, where some law books have remained since the Middle Ages.

Alongside the inheritance of Roman law in Latin, the laws and statutes of individual countries might be in Latin or the vernacular: in Irish, the Brehon laws (MSS. Rawl. B. 502, 487, 506); in Welsh, the Laws of Hywel Dda (Jesus College MS. 57). Collections on English law compiled in the thirteenth century include 'Bracton' in Latin (MSS. Bodl. 170, 344) and 'Britton' in Anglo-Norman (MS. Rawl. C. 898). The Statutes of England might be transmitted in Latin, French and/or Middle English (MS. Rawl. C. 612B, MS. Hatton 10). Registers of writs, usually in smaller format, provided formulary collections of varying materials for practical use.

For ecclesiastical law (in Latin), the Bodleian's earliest manuscript is a three-volume set of the canons of several early councils, written in Italy in uncial script of the late sixth or early seventh century (MSS. e Mus. 100–102). A complex volume of church canons compiled in France in the ninth century was imported into Anglo-Saxon England (MS. Hatton 42). Later collections include the *Constitutiones provinciales* of successive archbishops of Canterbury (MS. Wood empt. 23), and the legatine constitutions of cardinals Otto and Ottobuono of 1237 and 1268 (MS. Ashmole 1146).

Jurisprudence, as one of the four faculties of the University at the beginning of the seventeenth century, was one of the four classes into which the acquisitions of Bodley's new library were arranged. The early book collecting efforts of Sir Thomas Bodley, Thomas James and their agents concentrated on civil and canon law. The first printed catalogue (1605) contains a separate index to the commentaries on Justinian's works (of which the library now holds nearly fifty pre-1500 editions), while English law material in the catalogue is insignificant. In canon law, 13 incunable editions of Gratian's *Decretum* are contained in the collections, along with copies of 18 editions of the *Constitutions* of Pope Clement V, and 19 of the *Liber sextus Decretalium* of Pope Boniface VIII. The Library also possesses copies of editions of legal works and handbooks, including the copies of all three incunable editions of William Durand the Elder's standard reference book, the *Speculum iudiciale*, and the *Apparatus notularum* of Petrus de Unzola (Vicenza, 1490). The Library's collections also contain numerous printed editions of the statutes of Italian cities, such as those of Milan (1480) and Venice (1492).

Several of the rare book collections contain significant accumulations of English and foreign legal works, among them those of the jurist John Selden (1584–1654), in whose donation the books are arranged by the four faculties of the University; of Chief Justice Sir Edward Coke (1552–1634) in the Holkham collection; of Gerhard Meerman (*d.*1771); and of Robert Warden Lee (1868–1958), Rhodes Professor of Roman-Dutch Law at Oxford. Most of the legal works given by Richard Rawlinson (1690–1755) are in the 'Jur.' classification.

The post-medieval manuscript holdings include a range of precedent books, formularies, reports of cases, year books, manuals for justices of the peace and lawyers' notebooks from the sixteenth, seventeenth and eighteenth centuries. Correspondence of eminent lawyers of the nineteenth and twentieth centuries and papers relating to a host of legal issues are to be found in many of the collections of modern papers, notably in those of Sir John Dodson (1780–1858), judge in the Prerogative Court of Canterbury; Sir Jonathan Frederick Pollock (1783–1870), Lord Chief Baron of the Court of Exchequer; Ernest Murray Pollock, 1st Viscount Hanworth (1861–1935), Master of the Rolls; Walter, 1st Viscount Monckton (1891–1965); and A.L. Goodhart (1891–1978).

Until Blackstone lectured on common law in 1753, only civil law was taught in Oxford and the law collections in the Bodleian and in college libraries reflect this. Attempts to establish a reading room for law in 1857 failed and from 1867 the Codrington Library at All Souls was the principal law library in the University. A separate Bodleian law reading room was created in the Examination Schools in 1923. It was soon moved to the ground floor of the Radcliffe Camera and then to the first floor of the Old Library.

The Bodleian Law Library

The development of the current collection of modern law material dates from the establishment of a purpose-built Law Library in the early 1960s. The majority (70,000 volumes) of the Bodleian Library's post-1850 law holdings were transferred to the new St Cross Building in 1964. They were gathered together from the law reading room in the central Bodleian, the Bodleian stacks, and, in the case of legislation from Commonwealth countries, from other sections of the Library. With the addition of newly purchased foreign law materials, the initial stock of the Bodleian Law Library was 90–100,000 volumes. The extensive purchasing policy was continued during the next few years in order to build up holdings of materials especially from the United States and Commonwealth countries and to supplement holdings from Continental Europe. The concept of the Bodleian Law Library is that it serves as both a student taught course facility and a modern research library.

The establishment of the Bodleian Law Library was the opportunity to bring together all the Bodleian's law holdings and to establish firm demarcations where materials might arguably be appropriate to another subject. Antiquarian legal material – both English and Continental European works, with some exceptions – remains in the central Bodleian for consultation with other historical materials, as does canon law, although ecclesiastical law is in the Bodleian Law Library. Modern works on Continental European legal history may be in either the central Bodleian or the Bodleian Law Library. There is a fine distinction between American constitutional law, which is the responsibility of the Bodleian Law Library, and the political and social dimensions of American constitution and government collected by the Vere Harmsworth Library. Law in non-Roman and non-Cyrillic scripts is generally accommodated in the section of the Bodleian Library most appropriate for the jurisdiction, in particular the Indian Institute Library and the Bodleian Japanese Library. However, a small collection of modern Islamic law on international commercial subjects was started in the Bodleian Law Library in 2000. With that exception, the 1964 demarcations have remained intact.

Collection criteria have changed since 1964 due to a variety of external and internal factors, including varying legal deposit arrangements, changes in the curriculum (especially in postgraduate taught courses), changes in areas of research interest within the Law Faculty and amongst law postgraduate students, and not least new developments within the law, *e.g.* EC/EU law, environmental law, employment law, and the increasing tendency for regulation in many departments of daily life. Material on criminology was transferred to the Bodleian Law Library soon after it opened, and grants for the acquisition of material on European Community law and the law of the early member states were received in 1966–67.

Current strengths

Thanks to legal deposit, holdings of British and Irish legal materials are very strong. For materials from other jurisdictions the Bodleian Law Library currently concentrates on academically important materials from common law countries, especially the USA, Australia, Canada, New Zealand, South Africa and, to a lesser extent, other Commonwealth and former Commonwealth countries; and on European countries, especially France, Germany, Austria, Italy, Spain, but also Russia and the countries of Eastern Europe. Holdings of source materials – legislation and law reports – are strong for these countries, supplemented by a good range of journals, monographs and law reform reports. Selection has concentrated on books and journals dealing with constitutional and administrative law, contract, tort, family law, and labour law, reflecting the special interests of members of the Law Faculty. Collections of European Union law, criminology and jurisprudence are also currently maintained. Public international law and many subjects with an international perspective, *e.g.* international commercial arbitration, intellectual property and environmental law, are also well represented in the stock. Continuing to reflect local interests, commercial law in its widest interpretation has been added to the areas of purchase during the 1990s. Fewer books on Roman law are being acquired than in the past. Material in scripts other than Roman and Cyrillic is rarely purchased. Reductions in funding during the 1980s and 1990s has led to an inability to keep up with law report series, journals and books in as many jurisdictions or subjects as hitherto.

The greatest strength of the collection is for the jurisdictions of the British Isles, England and Wales, Scotland, Ireland (pre- and post-1922, North and South), the Channel Islands and the Isle of Man, built up from legal deposit and some purchasing. Although many of the pre-1850 publications remained in the central Bodleian, several thousand volumes were transferred to the new Bodleian Law Library. Consequently there are some anomalies in present day location, an obvious example being that most of the legally significant editions of Blackstone's *Commentaries* are in the central Bodleian rather than in the Bodleian Law Library.

In addition to the modern sets of British public general acts, the Bodleian Law Library has several compilations of acts in printings from the early to mid-sixteenth century onward, including acts passed during the Commonwealth period, which are normally held by libraries, if at all, in *Acts and Ordinances of the Interregnum 1642–60* (HMSO, 1911). Local, personal and private acts were not included in compilations or sets of public acts and the Bodleian Law Library has separate collections of local and personal acts from about 1780 and private acts from about 1727. Many annual volumes of local, personal and private acts for the earlier years of these periods are incomplete, although some individual acts are held in specialist local history collections in the central Bodleian. Where acts are held as individual items they have been separately catalogued and can be found through the OLIS online catalogue. Where they are bound into complete annual volumes, there is an open entry in the catalogue for the series and individual acts may be traced through the published indexes.

It is a feature of legal textbook publishing that a book which establishes a good reputation is updated and republished in revised editions. Many of the standard English legal texts are in their fiftieth or later edition, and were first published in the early decades of the nineteenth century. One of the Bodleian Law Library's strengths is its excellent runs of old editions of textbooks. They facilitate the work of the researcher and the writers of new editions and of modern textbooks tracing the development of the law.

The Bodleian Law Library was intended to be a library for modern legal research. Since the Bodleian's pre-1964 law holdings were strong on European and Commonwealth legal materials and the Oxford Law Faculty approached its research and teaching from a comparative perspective, efforts in the early years of the Bodleian Law Library concentrated on building up its American law holdings as well as supplementing Commonwealth and European law. Eastern European specialists on the Library staff during its first twenty years and in the Law Faculty ensured select collections from the USSR and some Eastern Bloc countries.

Acquisition of primary legal source materials – legislation and law reports – was greatly assisted until the 1970s and 1980s by the deposit of legislation, especially by Commonwealth countries. Despite the gradual decline in deposit, often following independence, a large proportion of the holdings for each jurisdiction consists of legislation, subordinate legislation and law reports. For Australia, Canada and the USA in particular, legislation is held for some of the states and provinces as well as for the federal jurisdiction.

Special collections

The Bodleian Law Library holds the law books from the library of Charles Viner (1678–1756), the compiler of *Viner's Abridgement* (23 vols., 1742–53) and the founder by bequest of the Vinerian Chair. He was fortunate that the fame of his benefaction was ensured by the appointment of Sir William Blackstone as its first holder. The Chair still exists today. Viner also left his library to the Radcliffe Library at the University. Its collections were incorporated within the Bodleian in 1860. The Viner books were sorted and handlisted in 1913 and all but a few non-law books were moved to their present home in the Bodleian Law Library in 1964. The collection today consists of 542 volumes and provides an interesting example of a mid-eighteenth century lawyer's library. It was very much a working collection supporting the compilation of the *Abridgement* and many volumes are annotated in Viner's hand. Among the more interesting items bibliographically are a good selection of single year *Year Books* from the sixteenth century printed by Richard Tottell plus two by John Wight, and a remarkably full collection of law reports in the best text editions available up to 1750. The best items among 145 legal texts are Staunford's *Pleas of the Crown* (Tottell, 1560), Littleton's *Tenures* (Tottell, 1579) in French, and Bracton's *De legibus* (1640). The main digests and abridgements of the period are well represented, including two early editions of Brooke, but most are heavily annotated or have parts missing which implies that they were used extensively. There are a number of miscellaneous items, both legal and non-legal, including a fine *Leges Wallicae* (1730), an edition of Zouch on Roman law and, most curiously, Scheffer's *History of Lapland* (1674). Viner's manuscripts, for the most part transcripts and notes for the *Abridgement*, are held in the Department of Special Collections and Western Manuscripts.

The Kahn-Freund Collection contains approximately 1,250 books and pamphlets on labour law and industrial relations from the personal library of Sir Otto Kahn-Freund (1900–1979), former Professor of Comparative Law in the University. This augments the holdings of a subject in which the Bodleian Law Library has traditionally been strong, in particular supplying pamphlet and foreign language items not found in the general collections. The collection covers a wide range of countries including both civil and common law jurisdictions.

The Bodleian Law Library has a collection of at least 15,000 dissertations presented to continental European universities over a period of more than 100 years to *c.*1991. These are the dissertations relating to law extracted from the very much larger holdings of foreign dissertations elsewhere in the Bodleian. Their subject matter is very wide, including foreign law, comparative studies and international law. Foreign law dissertations are an under-used source, partly because some are not yet catalogued on OLIS, and partly because they are a little known type of literature in most common law countries. Although of variable quality, the collection contains many items which were later the basis of standard treatises.

The library has attempted to build up a reasonably broad collection on the legal status of indigenous peoples, in keeping with the Law Faculty's tradition of comparative law research. Most of the purchases are textbooks and concentrate on native legal rights in Australia and Canada, and to a lesser extent the USA. There is also some coverage of relevant laws in other Commonwealth jurisdictions. Examples of recent acquisitions include books covering the *Mabo* decision by the High Court of Australia (1992) concerning Aboriginal land tenure, and materials covering the rights of the Inuit people in Canada. The subject of native rights in international law is also covered, especially in relation to self-determination.

Select bibliography

J. F. von Schulte, *Die Geschichte der Quellen und Literatur des Canonischen Rechts von Gratian bis auf die Gegenwart* (3 vols., Stuttgart, 1875–80).

S. Kuttner, *Repertorium der Kanonistik (1140–1234): Prodromus corporis glossarum*, I (Studi e testi 71; Vatican City, 1937).

P.B. Carter, 'The New Bodleian Law Library at Oxford', *Journal of the Society of Public Teachers of Law*, n.s. 8 (December 1964), 80–5.

Councils & Synods with Other Documents Relating to the English Church, I, *A.D. 871–1204*, eds. D. Whitelock et al (2 vols.; Oxford: Clarendon Press, 1981), and II, *A.D. 1205–1313*, eds. F. M. Powicke & C. R. Cheney (2 vols.; Oxford: Clarendon Press, 1964).

F.H. Lawson, *The Oxford Law School 1850–1965* (Oxford: Clarendon Press, 1968), 178–83.

E. de Haas and G. D. G. Hall, eds., *Early Registers of Writs*. (Selden Society 87; London: Quaritch, 1970).

G. R. Dolezalek & H. van de Wouw, *Verzeichnis der Handschriften zum römischen Recht bis 1600* (4 vols.; Frankfurt am Main, 1972). Lists manuscripts of civil law.

S.A. Lush, 'The Bodleian Law Library, Oxford', *The Law Librarian*, 7/2 (August 1976), 19–21.

Blackstone and Oxford: An Exhibition Held at the Bodleian Library, Oxford on the Occasion of the Bicentenary of Sir William Blackstone 1723–1780 (Oxford: Bodleian Library, 1980).

R.G. Logan, 'Law Libraries in Oxford', *The Law Librarian*, 20/2, (August 1989), 49–54.

R.G. Logan, 'The Viner Collection at the Bodleian Law Library', *The Law Librarian*, 23/2 (June 1992), 93–6.

S. L'Engle and R. Gibbs, *Illuminating the Law* [exhibition catalogue] (London & Turnhout, 2001). A guide to the types and physical appearance of both civil and canon law manuscripts, albeit based on Cambridge collections.

11. Geography and Maps

The diverse nature of geography as an academic discipline, exemplified in the description of geographers as 'jacks of all trades and masters of none', is broadly reflected in the provision of material within the Bodleian. The Geography and Map Reading Room (with its comprehensive collection of gazetteers, atlases, and guide books, around 6,000 key reference works and journal titles on open shelves) is the natural focus for those studying geography, cartography and travel. But provision is by no means limited to this one reading room. Standard works on political geography are included on the open shelves of the PPE reading room in the New Bodleian. Those interested in physical geography will find material in the Radcliffe Science Library, while geography of the Commonwealth is covered in the collections of the Bodleian Library of Commonwealth and African Studies at Rhodes House and that of the United States in the Vere Harmsworth Library. Much material on the geography of Asia is held by the Indian Institute Library, the Bodleian Japanese Library, and the Department of Oriental Collections in the central Bodleian. The study of geography as an academic discipline started in Oxford in 1899 when, with the help of the Royal Geographical Society, the School of Geography was established. The University remains a major centre for geographical, meteorological and environmental research, supported by library materials in both the Bodleian and the School of Geography and the Environment.

The Geography and Map Reading Room houses a comprehensive card catalogue of around 250,000 records arranged alphabetically by country, continent and ocean; within each section there are up to thirty subdivisions based upon compass points and subject headings identifying material ranging from town plans to air navigation charts. The catalogue provides access to a collection of maps of all parts of the globe and beyond, with topographic and thematic maps dating from medieval times to the present day. The Bodleian holds one of the world's principal cartographic collections, amounting to some 1,200,000 maps and 20,000 atlases alongside rapidly growing numbers of CD-ROMs, digital datasets and cartographic software. As a result of legal deposit, one of the great strengths of the collection is its almost complete run of Ordnance Survey maps, which are all the more important since a significant part of the Ordnance Survey's own collection was destroyed in the Second World War. They are matched by a fine series of Admiralty charts from 1800 onwards.

Mapping produced by overseas national surveys is also readily accessible, ranging from the commonly available Western European and North American output – for example French, Swedish and American medium–scale topographic series – to more recently released Eastern European material. Political changes in Eastern Europe brought on to the market in the early 1990s topographical maps previously withheld from circulation in the West for security reasons. With the help of the Friends of the Bodleian, complete series of maps of the 1970s and 1980s of Eastern Germany, Czechoslovakia, Poland and Hungary were bought, with later additions from Albania, Bulgaria, Romania and the former USSR. The Library was also able to acquire Soviet–produced maps for much of the rest of the world, for example some countries where late twentieth–century mapping was particularly difficult to obtain, such as China and the Middle East. It is the intention of the collection to hold mapping at a scale of 1:100,000 or greater for all of the world, and this has already been achieved for a considerable proportion of the Earth's land surface, in particular Europe, much of Africa, North America, Australasia, the Indian subcontinent and most island nations. Overseas thematic material is purchased to meet demand, with particular strengths in geological, land utilisation and transport mapping. In 2002, major acquisitions were complete topographic coverage at a scale of 1:50,000 of Finland, Norway and Poland, and at 1:100,000 for Papua New Guinea. Geological maps at 1:50,000 for most of Spain were also acquired, as were administrative maps of all Vietnam's provinces.

From its foundation the Bodleian acquired atlases and books relating to travel and navigation. Many are in the collections of Francis Douce, Richard Gough, the Earls of Leicester at Holkham, Martin Lister, John Locke, Sir Henry Savile and John Selden. Its holdings contain numerous examples of early cartography, ranging from town plans such as the *Civitatis Orbis Terrarum* of Georg Braun and Francis Hogenberg, published in six folio volumes between 1572 and 1618, through navigational charts like L. J. Waghenaer's *Mariners Mirrour* of 1588, to celestial charts like Johannes Hevelius's *Selenographia sive lunae descriptio* of 1647. Geographical and cartographic material among the incunabula in the Library's collections includes the journey of Bernhard von Breydenbach to the Holy Land (a work which was in effect the earliest printed travel guide) in its first Latin edition of 1486 (Douce 223 and S.Seld. d.9), its Dutch edition of 1488 (Auct. 6Q 5.21) and its second German edition of the same year (Auct. 5Q 5.43). Ptolemy's *Cosmography* is particularly well represented, with copies of all six of the pre–1500 Latin editions being found in the Bodleian. An unusual survival in the Broxbourne Collection is a single-sheet map of Europe, printed *c.*1494, for the use of pilgrims travelling through Germany to Rome (Broxb. 95.24(1)).

Many of the county maps published in Britain in the late eighteenth century came into the Library through legal deposit. The published maps and charts of the Ordnance Survey and Hydrographic Office, which from 1800 followed the same route into the Bodleian, together with Richard Gough's bequest of his magnificent cartographic and topographic collection in 1809, prompted further extensive purchases of British and foreign maps which were a feature of the early years of the nineteenth century.

By far the most important cartographic collection to be acquired in recent years, the Todhunter Allen Collection, ranks alongside and complements Gough's. The generous gift of Mr and Mrs H. M. Allen, it filled many gaps in the Library's already strong holdings and illustrates three centuries of the cartography of the British Isles, from Christopher Saxton to the early twentieth century. It includes 113 county atlases of England and Wales dated between 1617 and 1855, with many variant states and editions of the maps of individual counties. Its remarkable run of county maps of the late eighteenth and early nineteenth centuries contains fine examples of the work of the eminent cartographers Christopher and John Greenwood and Andrew Bryant. From the same period are rare thematic maps of canals, roads and railways.

The most famous single map in the Bodleian is undoubtedly the 'Gough Map' of *c.*1360, regarded as the earliest surviving road map of Great Britain (MS. Gough Gen. Top. 16). With east at the top of the map, the outline of the islands is recognisable, settlements are marked with drawings of individual buildings and the distances between them given in Roman numerals. Rivalling the Gough Map in its importance to the history of map-making is the Arabic *Book of Curiosities* (MS. Arab. c. 90), composed towards the end of the eleventh century and containing 17 maps, most of them unique. This was purchased in 2002 (*see also p. 130*).

The Western manuscript collections also include a number of early portolans (navigational charts of sea-coasts and harbours), the majority from the sixteenth century, and of the Mediterranean, the Aegean and the European Atlantic coasts (*e.g.* MSS. Canon. Ital. 140–144). The Douce collection includes a fine portolan atlas produced in Venice *c.*1400 (MS. Douce 390) and a map of the Holy Land designed for pilgrims in the second half of the fourteenth century (MS. Douce 389). Numerous manuscript estate maps and plans have been acquired over the centuries, the best known being the very detailed 1635 map of the manors of Laxton and Kneesall in Nottinghamshire (Maps MS. C17:48(9)), with an accompanying terrier of 1635, and surveys and plans of 1727 and 1732 (MS. Top. Notts. c. 2). Other notable individual maps include the 1644 map of the Civil War fortifications of Oxford (MS. Top. Oxon. b. 167), the Agas 1578 map of Oxford and Hamond's 1592 map of Cambridge. Many of the items in Dr. A. B. Emden's gift in 1946 of over 500 printed and manuscript maps, principally of Continental Europe and dated before 1770, originated in the collection of Philippe Buache (1700–73), who held the post of *'premier géographe du Roi'*. It includes twenty–two maps drawn by Buache himself.

While continuing to acquire atlases and sheet maps in traditional format, the Library is collecting an increasing amount of cartographic material as CD-ROMs and digital datasets. Ordnance Survey mapping is now deposited in digital format and the Geography and Map Reading Room provides facilities for work with Geographical Information Systems. A site licence for *MapInfo Professional* enables educational users to create customised maps for academic purposes. The *Digimap* service, bringing digital Ordnance Survey map data to the desktop, was launched in January 2000 after a two-year trial at the Bodleian. Oxford University is now one of over seventy-five higher education institutions which have an agreement with the Ordnance Survey for the provision of datasets to those currently teaching, researching or studying there.

Select Bibliography

E.J.S. Parsons, *The Map of Great Britain Circa A.D. 1360 Known as the Gough Map* (Oxford: Bodleian Library, 1958, repr. 1996).

E.M. Rodger, 'An Eighteenth-Century Collection of Maps Connected with Philippe Buache', *Bodleian Library Record*, 7/2 (1963), 96–106.

Notable Accessions: Guide to an Exhibition Held in 1958 (Oxford: Bodleian Library, 1958).

Cartographic Treasures in the Bodleian Library (Oxford: Bodleian Library, 1975).

N. N. James, *List of Estate Maps and Plans in the Bodleian Library, 1586–1849* (typescript, 1979).

Catalogue of an Exhibition of Ordnance Survey Material from the Map Collection to Commemorate the Bicentenary of the Ordnance Survey (Oxford: Bodleian Library, 1991).

N. James, *A List of Ordnance Survey District Special and Tourist Maps 1861–1939* (Maplist 1; Oxford: Bodleian Library, 1993).

N. James, *A List of Ordnance Survey Catalogues, Publication Reports & Other Publications* (Maplist 2; Oxford: Bodleian Library, 1993).

A Continental Shelf: Books Across Europe [exhibition catalogue] (Oxford: Bodleian Library, 1994), section 1.

All at Sea: The Story of Navigational Charts: An Exhibition to Celebrate Two Hundred Years of the Hydrographic Office (Oxford: Bodleian Library, 1995).

P. Dryburgh, 'The Todhunter-Allen Collection: A Little-Known Treasure Trove', *Mercator's World*, 2/1 (1997), 52–5.

O. Loiseaux, ed., *World Directory of Map Collections* (4th edn., IFLA Publications 92/93; Munich: K.G. Saur, 2000), 425–6.

N. Millea, 'The Bodleian Library, Oxford, United Kingdom', *Cartographic Perspectives*, 37 (2000), 88–90.

N. Millea, 'The Development of Map Collections in Oxford', *Bulletin of the Society of Cartographers*, 34/1 (2000), 33–35.

British Cartographic Society, *A Directory of UK Map Collections*, 4th edn; www.cartography.org.uk/Pages/Publicat/UKDirect.html .

Street Mapping: An A to Z of Urban Cartography [exhibition catalogue] (Oxford: Bodleian Library, 2003).

E. Edson and E. Savage-Smith, *Medieval Views of the Cosmos* (Oxford: Bodleian Library, 2004).

12. Music

The Bodleian's music collections include (in 2003) about 500,000 items of printed music, 45,000 books and periodicals, 3,500 manuscripts and 1,000 microfilms, making it the second largest music research library in the country after that of the British Library. Although British music, aided by legal deposit, naturally forms the core of the collections, it also has abundant foreign material of many nations and periods, and the whole forms a rich general resource as well as having certain outstanding specialist strengths. The provisions of legal deposit in Great Britain, however, do not extend to sound recordings, and most of the recordings in the Bodleian have been acquired as adjuncts to printed material. The Library does not otherwise actively collect sound recordings with the exception of those of local interest; the main collection of recordings in Oxford will be found in the Music Faculty Library.

Before the final decades of the eighteenth century the Bodleian possessed very little music. Although some books on the subject entered the Library in the early days under the terms of Sir Thomas Bodley's 1610 agreement with the Stationers' Company, very little printed music was received until about 1780. The Library's copy of *Parthenia* (1613) is a rare exception. A series of court cases in the 1770s, confirming that intellectual copyright could subsist in items other than printed books, seems to have been the catalyst behind the regular influx of music under legal deposit which then started. What did accumulate in the first two centuries were manuscripts of both medieval liturgical books and treatises on music, mostly acquired as part of donated general collections. The first large specifically musical donation came in 1801 with the bequest of manuscript and printed music from Osborne Wight, Fellow of New College. This really laid the foundations of the Bodleian's music manuscript collections, containing as it did much seventeenth- and eighteenth-century English music, including autographs of Purcell, Greene and Boyce, as well as printed editions of Handel and others. Apart from legal deposit material, the nineteenth century saw only one other substantial addition, the transfer to the Bodleian in 1885 of the collection which had been built up in the Music School of the University from 1627 to the end of the eighteenth century, with its rich accumulation of both manuscript and printed music. Important new foreign books on music were regularly purchased, but no current printed music. The purchase of such material began only in the twentieth century, and more particularly after World War II, since when steady purchase of both new and antiquarian material has enabled a well-rounded collection to be formed.

By contrast, in the last three decades of the twentieth century the Library has been exceptionally fortunate in the acquisition of several major music collections. The Harding Collection, received by bequest from Walter Harding of Chicago in 1975, impressively strengthened the library's resources in the fields of English secular music and English and foreign opera scores, as well as making it the major holder of American nineteenth- and twentieth-century song material on this side of the Atlantic. The M. Deneke Mendelssohn Collection, acquired mostly by donation directly or indirectly from descendants of the composer, made the Bodleian a leading centre for Mendelssohn research. With the closure of St. Michael's College, Tenbury, in 1985, its famous music library, largely formed by the college's founder Sir Frederick Ouseley (1825–1889), essentially found a new home in the Bodleian – the manuscripts by donation, and such printed music and treatises as were not already in the Bodleian by purchase. A further addition came with the transfer between 1995 and 1997 of the manuscripts and early printed music held by the Music Faculty Library. Most recently, the acquisition by bequest of 2,400 items from the collection of the late Alan Tyson, with its copious holdings of first and early editions, especially of composers of the Viennese Classical School, has greatly enriched an area in which the Library's holdings were hitherto very modest.

Manuscripts

The Bodleian has substantial holdings of liturgical musical manuscripts; amongst the earliest are the 'Leofric Missal' (MS. Bodl. 579), a ninth-century French Sacramentary supplemented in tenth-century England, and two eleventh-century tropers, the Winchester Troper (MS. Bodl. 775) and the Heidenheim Troper (MS. Selden Supra 127). The medieval polyphony includes many fragments recovered from bindings, as well as the famous source of fifteenth-century music by Dufay and others in MS. Canon.Misc. 213, and an anthology of fifteenth-century English carols, including the 'Agincourt Song' (MS. Arch. Selden B. 26). Outside the Western church tradition, there are also important sources of Byzantine chant of the eleventh to nineteenth centuries. In the field of music theory the Bodleian has numerous sources of both ancient Greek and medieval Latin theory, as well as important sources for Hebrew, Arabic and Persian writings on music.

Major sources of mid-sixteenth-century English music are the pre-Reformation Forrest-Heather partbooks (MSS. Mus. Sch. E. 376–381), with Latin masses by John Taverner, John Marbeck and others, and the early Reformation manuscripts of the Wanley partbooks (MSS. Mus. Sch. E. 420–422), whilst the later part of the century is represented by the Sadler partbooks of 1585 (MSS. Mus. e.1–5), and numerous sets in the Tenbury Collection. One of the most famous and ample sources of seventeenth-century English church music is the so-called Batten Organ Book (MS. Tenbury 791). Seventeenth-century instrumental consort music is a prominent feature of the Music School Collection, and includes volumes of autograph music by William Lawes – probably the earliest substantial corpus of identifiable autographs from any composer.

From this time onwards, examples of the hands of most significant British composers will be found in the collections, including John Wilson, Henry Purcell and John Blow in the seventeenth; William Croft, John Eccles, Handel, Maurice Greene, William Boyce (including his complete court odes), William and Philip Hayes, and Samuel Wesley in the eighteenth; and Balfe, Bishop, Cowen, Horsley, Sterndale Bennett, Sullivan, and Stainer in the nineteenth. The world's most famous choral work, Handel's *Messiah*, is represented here by the composer's conducting score, used at the first and all subsequent performances directed by him (MSS. Tenbury 346–347).

In the twentieth century the policy of encouraging the donation of British composers' manuscripts has resulted in the accumulation of substantial collections of the manuscripts of Hubert Parry, Basil Harwood, Percy Sherwood, George Butterworth, Ernest Farrar, Gerald Finzi, Roger Fiske, Robin Milford, Ernest Walker, Alfred Hale, Howard Ferguson, Christobel Marillier, Bruce Montgomery and Clifton Parker, as well as isolated manuscripts of Bax, Delius, Elgar, Holst, Howells, Rubbra, Smythe, Vaughan Williams, Walton, Maxwell Davies and others. In a special category is the collection of Oxford B.Mus. and D.Mus. exercises, which from the nineteenth century onwards were required to be deposited by successful supplicants for those degrees, though a few eighteenth-century examples are also to be found in the collection, the earliest being that of John Isum (1713).

Manuscripts from continental Europe are naturally fewer in quantity, but include important examples of Italian and German music from the seventeenth to the nineteenth century. Important sources of early seventeenth-century Italian monody are to be found in MSS. Tenbury 1018–1019, while a batch of manuscripts of late seventeenth-century German vocal music by Samuel Capricornus, Sebastian Knüpfer, Johann Philipp Krieger, Johann Scheller and others, is a surprising find in the Music School Collection (MSS. Mus. Sch. C. 28–31, 43). These, together with much of the other German and Italian music in the Music School Collection, may have been collected during a Grand Tour by the Marquis of Tavistock in 1697–99. The Tenbury Collection also includes the only sources of Johann Pachelbel's sacred music, apparently autograph (MSS. Tenbury 1208–09, 1256, 1311), and a fine collection of copies of Italian opera and cantata scores from the eighteenth and early nineteenth centuries, as well as autograph manuscripts of Galuppi (MS. Tenbury 619) and Cimarosa (MS. Tenbury 1047).

The Bodleian has examples of the autograph manuscripts of many of the major continental composers from the classical period onwards – Haydn, Mozart,

Beethoven, Schubert, Schumann, Chopin, Liszt, Brahms, Wolf and Reger included. Though many are small works, exceptions include Schubert's Grand Duo (D 812), Chopin's Fourth Ballade, and a copyist's score of Beethoven's Seventh Symphony, corrected on almost every page by the composer. But it is the Library's Mendelssohn collection which constitutes its major resource in the field of continental nineteenth-century music, and makes it one of the main centres for research on the composer and his circle. The wide range of autograph manuscripts is complemented by much of the composer's music library and a great array of personal papers – letters both to and from the composer, diaries, drawing books, portraits and albums. The main M. Deneke Mendelssohn Collection is complemented by Mendelssohn letters and other items received in 1987 as part of the archive of the Horsley family, who were some of Mendelssohn's closest English friends. Thanks in particular to the Heritage Lottery Fund and the Friends of the Bodleian, the Library was able to celebrate its quatercentenary in 2002 by acquiring at auction a further major treasure in the form of the final autograph score of the *Hebrides* Overture.

Printed music

Although British printed music only began to be received regularly under legal deposit from about 1780, the Library has an abundance of earlier material from the sixteenth century onwards, thanks mainly to donations over the centuries. Additions have been and continue to be made on a modest scale by purchase. The sixteenth- and seventeenth-century material is also complemented by the published microfilm sets of *Short-Title Catalogue* (STC) and *Wing* books, which include the music publications of the period. The receipt of music under legal deposit remained rather haphazard in its coverage until the early part of the twentieth century, but from the 1920s onward the British collection is reasonably comprehensive at least so far as the traditional forms of music publications are concerned. In the last decade or so, the increasing amount of 'published-on-demand' material now available, which is not on the whole received under legal deposit, has again reduced the comprehensiveness, even though the more important examples of this type of material are purchased so far as funds allow.

The Bodleian has never rejected the popular music of the day receivable under legal deposit, and in consequence has very large collections from the days of the Victorian and Edwardian music hall song through to the latest rock music albums. In addition, part of the Harding Collection has provided not only further music hall songs, but about 100,000 American songs and popular piano pieces from *c*.1800 to 1950. Much of this latter collection is organised topically, with subjects ranging from the American Civil War to presidential campaign songs, railroads and waterfalls. With its many pictorial covers, it offers a valuable resource not only to musicians but to social historians and those in search of illustrative material.

The early sixteenth-century foreign music imprints offer scope for a survey of the infancy of music printing, including one example of Ottaviano Petrucci's printing by triple impression (*Motetti libro quarto*, Venice, 1505), and the remarkable woodcut publication of Andrea Antico (*Missarum liber quindecim*, Rome, 1516), as well as some of the earliest Italian madrigal prints from the 1530s. The outstanding seventeenth-century resource is the collection of over 80 editions of Italian instrumental music by Cazzati, Torelli and others, in the Music School Collection; it includes several *unica*. Other countries are less well represented before about 1680, though there are some notable individual items. The German holdings have recently been complemented by over 100 fine facsimile reprints of sixteenth- and seventeenth-century sources from Cornetto-Verlag. French opera holdings from Lully onwards are very extensive, thanks in particular to the Harding Collection, and operatic material in general is a great strength of the music collections. French and German eighteenth-century chamber and keyboard music is well represented (again complemented by facsimile editions from Minkoff, Fuzeau and others), whilst the Harding Collection includes a fine collection of French song books from *c.* 1700 to the early twentieth century.

Owing in large part to the Tyson bequest the Bodleian now has excellent holdings of first and early editions of the Viennese Classical School, including about 400 editions of Beethoven, 350 of Schubert, 200 of Haydn and 100 of Mozart. The nineteenth-century holdings in general are strong, with particularly fine collections of Berlioz, Chopin and Mendelssohn. With twentieth-century composers the policy has been to collect the major international figures fairly comprehensively, and to have a good representative collection of many others of note. There is a wide geographical spread, with Eastern Europe and the United States strongly represented, whilst stylistically the music ranges from Boulez to Chinese revolutionary operas to Broadway musicals. Areas of growing present-day interest, such as music by women composers (both contemporary and historical) are also well catered for. Printed folk music collections from all over the world together with associated literature are abundant, with Eastern Europe being particularly well represented. Current accessions policy for new publications is to maintain comprehensive collections of composers' collected editions and other scholarly *Denkmäler*, to purchase extensively worthwhile facsimiles and other new editions of older music, and as wide a range of contemporary (including popular) music as funds will permit.

Music literature

Legal deposit material combined with donated and purchased items (including microfilm) provides a fairly comprehensive collection of British writings on music. The foreign holdings cover much of the important source material, either in originals or reprints, starting with a fine copy of Gafurius's *Theoricum opus musice discipline*

(Naples, 1480). The periodical holdings are exceptionally strong, with complete or substantial sets of many important European and American journals. Holdings of approximately 1,200 titles of current and non-current journals are recorded in the *British Union Catalogue of Music Periodicals* (2nd ed., Aldershot, 1998). The Bodleian, in addition to housing copies of all Oxford doctoral theses, also has many European theses on music from *c.* 1900 onwards, and a small collection of microfilms of American theses, chiefly of the period 1957–1964.

Microfilm collections

In addition to keeping consultation copies of films of much of its own older music manuscript collections, the Bodleian has purchased many of the commercial microfilm sets of music manuscripts held in other British libraries, including those of the British Library, National Library of Scotland, Cambridge University Library, Fitzwilliam Museum, Rowe Music Library, Royal College of Music, and the Gerald Coke Collection. Amongst other microfilms are substantial accumulations of source material relating to J.S. Bach's keyboard music, Mozart and Beethoven.

Local music collections

The records of many local music societies, both town and gown, are housed in the Bodleian. There is also an extensive collection of local concert programmes and posters, dating back to the early Holywell Music Room concerts of the 1760s. It is still added to, and is complemented by a collection of CDs of local interest.

Programmes

The opera programmes collected by the founding editor of *Opera* magazine, Harold Rosenthal, form a substantial resource. Dating from the 1930s onwards, many also have associated press cuttings with them. Although predominantly British, there is also a fair representation of foreign productions, particularly festivals. Other sets of concert and opera programmes in the library stem from major institutions such as the BBC, and the Aldeburgh and Glyndebourne festivals, as well as from personal donations. A recent acquisition is a large collection of *c.*1,000 London concert programmes from the 1870s to the 1930s, assembled by the critic F. Gilbert Webb, including many substantial runs from the principal concert organisations. Various miscellaneous nineteenth- and twentieth-century programmes will also be found in the John Johnson Collection of Printed Ephemera.

Song index

A unique resource is the Harding First-Line Song Index, on *c.* 80,000 cards, which provides a near-comprehensive analytical index to songs in English songbooks, song sheets, plays and operas for the period 1600–1800, together with a less comprehensive one for the period 1801–1850. Song sources both with and without the music are included.

Select bibliography

R. Hake, *Catalogue of Music Belonging to the Music School.* (MS, 1854). Held in Music Reading Room at MUS.AC.2.

E.H. Fellowes, *The Catalogue of Manuscripts in the Library of St. Michael's College Tenbury* (Paris, 1934; 2nd ed., Brighton, 1981).

A.Hughes, *Medieval Polyphony in the Bodleian Library* (Oxford: Bodleian Library, 1951).

D. Stevens, '17th-Century Italian Instrumental Music in the Bodleian Library', *Acta Musicologica*, 26 (1954), 67–74.

English Music [exhibition catalogue] (Oxford: Bodleian Library, 1955).

D. Stevens, 'Unique Italian Instrumental Music in the Bodleian Library', *Collectanea historiae musicae*, 2 (1957), 401–12.

M. Crum, 'A 17th-Century Collection of Music Belonging to Thomas Hamond, a Suffolk Landowner', *Bodleian Library Record*, 6/1 (1957), 373–86.

S.J.P. Van Dijk, *Handlist of the Latin Liturgical Manuscripts in the Bodleian Library Oxford* [unpublished typescript, 1957–60]. Held in Duke Humfrey's Library at R. 6. 152.

RISM: Répertoire international des sources musicales (Munich and Kassel, 1960–).

N.G. Wilson and D.I. Stefanovic, *Manuscripts of Byzantine Chant in Oxford* (Oxford: Bodleian Library, 1963).

M. Crum, 'Early Lists of the Oxford Music School Collection', *Music & Letters*, 48 (1967), 23–34.

M. Crum, 'Working Papers of Twentieth-Century British Composers', *Bodleian Library Record*, 8/2 (1968), 101–3.

M. Crum, *Felix Mendelssohn Bartholdy* (Bodleian Picture Book; Oxford: Bodleian Library, 1972).

P. Ward Jones, 'Music at the Bodleian', *Brio*, 10/2 (1973), 1–3.

D.W. Krummel, 'A Musical Bibliomaniac', *Musical Times*, 115 (1974), 301–2. (On Walter Harding.)

J. Geil, 'American Sheet Music in the Walter N.H. Harding Collection at the Bodleian Library, Oxford University', *Notes*, 34 (1977/78), 805–13.

William Boyce, 1711–1779 [exhibition catalogue] (Oxford: Bodleian Library, 1979).

M. Crum and P. Ward Jones, *Catalogue of the Mendelssohn Papers in the Bodleian Library, Oxford* (3 vols.; Tutzing, 1980–89).

Musical Anniversaries 1985: Thirteen Composers from Tallis to Berg [exhibition catalogue] (Oxford: Bodleian Library, 1985).

W. Shaw, 'Sir Frederick Ouseley and his Collection', *Brio*, 27/2 (1990), 45–7.

P. Ward Jones, 'The Fate of the Music Collections of St Michael's College, Tenbury', *Brio*, 27/2 (1990), 48–9.

R. Flotzinger, *Choralhandschriften österreichischer Provenienz in der Bodleian Library Oxford.* (Vienna, 1991).

Mozart: A Bicentenary Loan Exhibition (Oxford: Bodleian Library, 1991).

J. Craig-McFeely, 'Fragments of English Lute Music, ii: Oxford Libraries', *The Lute*, 33 (1993), 34–54.

P. Wollny, 'A Collection of Seventeenth-Century Vocal Music at the Bodleian Library', *Schütz-Jahrbuch*, 15 (1993), 77–108.

P. Holman, 'Original Sets of Parts of Restoration Concerted Music at Oxford: A Preliminary Catalogue', in: *Performing the Music of Henry Purcell*, ed. M. Burden (Oxford: Clarendon Press, 1996), 265–71.

Mendelssohn: an Exhibition to Celebrate the Life of Felix Mendelssohn Bartholdy (1809–1847) (Oxford: Bodleian Library, 1997).

P. Ward Jones and D. Burrows, 'An Inventory of Mid-Eighteenth-Century Oxford Musical Hands', *Royal Musical Association Research Chronicle*, 35 (2002), 61–139.

13. Science, Technology and Medicine

The early collections

The Bodleian's present-day holdings in the fields of science, technology and medicine are the aggregation of three major collections of scientific material, owing their origins respectively to the three great Oxford names of Thomas Bodley, Elias Ashmole and John Radcliffe.

The foundation collection, catalogued by Thomas James, includes perhaps 500 works on mathematics, astronomy, physics and medicine (including commentaries on Aristotle, Hippocrates and Galen). The medical works were (and are) in their own section but those on mathematics, astronomy and physics found a permanent home with the Arts, since the higher part of the Seven Liberal Arts, the Quadrivium, comprised arithmetic, geometry, astronomy and music – the study of music requiring the application of mathematics – and the Arts degree examination required a knowledge of natural philosophy (broadly, physics).

It is not surprising that among the earliest acquisitions of the Bodleian Library are scientific books, since Thomas Bodley's circle included men with scientific interests. One such was Thomas Allen, of Gloucester Hall (now Worcester College). Allen collected assiduously manuscripts dispersed by the closure of religious houses in the Oxford region and beyond. He bequeathed his manuscripts to his friend and former pupil Kenelm Digby, and they form more than half of Digby's collection of 238 manuscripts received by the Library in 1634. These manuscripts have been described as a unique record of medieval science. They include, for example, the earliest weather record known, for Oxford and Lincoln in 1337–1344 (MS. Digby 176, fol.4).

Large donations came from Archbishop Laud (in 1640) and John Selden (in 1659). Laud's collection is notably strong in mathematics and astronomy, including, for example, most of the Greek mathematicians translated into Arabic. With Selden's bequest, augmented by the gift of his executors, the Bodleian received a wealth of scientific works in one of the great personal libraries of the age, numbering about 8,000 printed books.

Other acquisitions from the seventeenth century include 120 mathematical and astronomical works donated by Thomas Twyne (in 1612) and Thomas Wotton's donation of Tycho Brahe's *Astronomiae instaurandae mechanica* of 1598 with extra pages by the author. At the end of the century, in 1697, the Library purchased from the collection of Edward Bernard, Savilian Professor of Astronomy, again strong in astronomy and mathematics. After almost a hundred years of existence, the special scientific strengths of the Bodleian at the end of the seventeenth century, therefore, were in mathematics and astronomy and in the whole range of medieval science.

We must now turn to the second great Oxford figure mentioned at the beginning of this chapter. Elias Ashmole was the fortunate inheritor of the collection of rarities built up by the Tradescants, John senior and junior, but beyond that he was a voracious collector of books and manuscripts in the fields of alchemy and astrology. Among Ashmole's personal collection was the library of William Lilly 'the English Merlin'. Ashmole bestowed his entire collection – curiosities, coins, portraits, books and manuscripts – on the University, thus creating the Ashmolean Museum in 1683.

The chief scientific components of the Ashmolean's library collection, as it developed, were three. First came Ashmole's personal collection of books and manuscripts, or rather such of it as had not been destroyed in a disastrous fire in the Inner Temple. This included papers of the mathematician and astrologer John Dee (1527–1608), and of the astrologer Simon Forman (1552–1611). Then came over 1,400 works, mainly medical and scientific, from Martin Lister (1638–1712), the first British conchologist. The Chemical Library, created in 1683 for the use of Robert Plot, first Professor of Chemistry, and his students, and originally housed next to the basement Chemical Laboratory in the original Ashmolean building, was the third component. All this eventually came to the Bodleian, in 1860.

Another University collection now in the Bodleian, the Savile Library, was built up from 1619 by successive Savilian Readers and Professors in Geometry and Astronomy, including Sir Christopher Wren. In this collection the Bodleian eventually (1884) acquired an outstanding collection of sixteenth- and seventeenth-century mathematical and astronomical works, including in its scope applications such as optics and harmonics as well as pure mathematics. The Savile Library also includes the notebooks of Savilian Professor Stephen Rigaud, while his collection of 840 eighteenth-century mathematical and astronomical books came to the Bodleian separately.

The eighteenth and nineteenth centuries

Two important groups of scientific material were acquired by the Bodleian in the late eighteenth and early nineteenth centuries. Section C of the Rawlinson manuscripts, received in 1755 from Richard Rawlinson, includes many medical manuscripts, both medieval and later. The large miscellaneous section of the Canonici manuscripts, a collection made by the Venetian Matteo Luigi Canonici (1727–c. 1806), includes manuscripts in medicine, astronomy and alchemy. A loan of £2,000 was contributed by the Radcliffe Trustees towards the cost of the purchase of the Canonici material in Venice in 1817. The Trustees were already making a huge contribution to the future scientific and medical collections of the Bodleian Library, in the foundation and development of the Radcliffe Library.

John Radcliffe (1652?–1714) was a highly respected and very wealthy physician, who among other charitable bequests set up by his last will an Oxford library independent of the Bodleian. It opened, on an adjoining site, in the building now known as the Radcliffe Camera, in 1749. After sixty somewhat inauspicious years, the standing and significance of the Radcliffe Library were transformed by the appointment of George Williams, Regius and Sherardian Professor of Botany, as Librarian. He prevailed upon Radcliffe's Trustees to turn their eclectic and moribund library into a lively, expansive institution that specialised in medicine and natural history.

Williams took over a library containing few scientific books. However, the donation of Richard Frewin (1681?–1761) – a polymath who turned from the successful practice of medicine to become Camden Professor of Ancient History – contains medical books and an interesting volume of pressings of medicinal plants with annotations. Likewise, the material presented by James Gibbs (1682–1754), architect of the Radcliffe Camera, contains mathematical books. In the next 25 years, Williams prepared, and his successor John Kidd printed, a catalogue of the scientific works in the Radcliffe Library, and from this Williams's own contribution can be assessed. There were, at this stage, few periodicals. Almost half the books were concerned with medicine, anatomy or physiology. Two-thirds of the remainder were botanical or zoological, and the residue dealt with mineralogy and geology, chemistry, and 'voyages and travels'. Between a third and a half of the books were newly published, and another third had been published in the previous century. Almost a quarter, however, were from the sixteenth and seventeenth centuries: the oldest material was principally medical.

In retrospect, the great contribution of Williams and his successor Kidd (who, however, had to be much more parsimonious in library expenditure after 1841) is seen as the acquisition of the lavishly decorated flora and fauna produced at the time. Perhaps the most notable of these, and the one of which Williams was seemingly proudest (and justly so), is the *Oiseaux dorés* of Audebert and Veillot (Paris, 1802), which is one of twelve copies with the text printed in gold, but uniquely includes in manuscript a third unpublished volume.

The middle years of the nineteenth century saw a realignment of science teaching, libraries and museums in Oxford. The Honours School of Natural Science was begun in 1850, and under the leadership of Henry Wentworth Acland, Regius Professor of Medicine, a new centre for science teaching was opened in 1860 as the New Museum or University Museum in Parks Road. The museum proper contained geological, mineralogical and other specimens formerly housed in the Clarendon Building annexe to the Ashmolean Museum; there were lecture rooms; there was accommodation for ten Departments (future University departments): Astronomy, Geometry (later Mathematics), Experimental Physics, Chemistry, Mineralogy, Geology, Zoology, Anatomy, Physiology and Medicine; and, most importantly in this context, the Radcliffe Library was moved from the Radcliffe Camera to the first-floor front of the new building.

The detail of the organisation of the Museum is far from incidental to this account. Acland also held the office of Radcliffe Librarian from 1851 to 1899. In that post he pursued a threefold policy. First, he selected acquisitions for their utility in supporting teaching, learning and research, not for their beauty or rarity; second, he believed that specimens and the books which described and illustrated them should be available for use side by side; and third, he believed in the University getting value for money, deploring wasteful duplication. Though he met with limited success in his third aim, from that point on the Radcliffe Library's purchasing policy has been related to the teaching and research needs of the University, and so the history of the purchased part of the present science, technology and medicine collection is to a large extent a reflection of the history of science teaching and research in Oxford University since 1861.

Thus, Acland's own research interests as Regius Professor of Medicine were represented by a new Radcliffe Library section of Comparative National Health (i.e. public health) developed in 1872–3 'to elucidate the progress of Sanitary Laws in all countries'. Similarly, in the following year Acland began to meet demand for library provision from ethnologists – a need which gathered momentum from the University's acquisition ten years later of the Pitt Rivers ethnological collection and the opening of the Pitt Rivers Museum as an annexe to the University Museum. By 1895, Acland was telling the Radcliffe Trustees: 'Anthropology [is] now becoming the highest department of Biology ... the special educational duties of the British Empire and of Oxford ... compel me increasingly to spend largely on your behalf for this Department'. Acland's own pamphlet collection is in the Radcliffe Science Library. His personal correspondence, presented to the Bodleian in 1926, is in the care of the Department of Special Collections and Western Manuscripts. Papers relating to his Radcliffe Librarianship (and to some extent, his Regius Chair of Medicine) survive in Radcliffe Records, the Radcliffe Library archive.

From 1845 to 1881 Bodleian purchasing policy eschewed the scientific (and the first fifteen years of this period coincided with a swingeing cut in Radcliffe purchasing, with serious effects on the strength of the collection), except for what was received by legal deposit. However, the science, technology and medicine collections were built up in another way, for a further effect of the building of the University Museum was the relocation of the books and manuscripts from the Ashmolean Museum to the Bodleian.

E.W.B. Nicholson (Bodley's Librarian 1882–1912) made a special contribution to the science, technology and medicine collections by his assiduity in collecting the full range of scientific, technical and medical material available by deposit arrangements. He greatly increased the amount of material acquired under the Copyright Acts, and he widened the range of European printed doctoral theses deposited by their awarding institutions. In 1881, the ten Prussian universities and the University of Strasbourg were depositing, but Nicholson widened the scope of the scheme to include all German, Scandinavian, Dutch and Swiss universities, and the sixteen academies of the University of France. This was to lead to many tens of thousands of scientific theses being obtained. Its usefulness to the University's science teaching and research must be doubted; however, for posterity it has provided a huge and neglected resource.

Thanks to Williams's vision, Acland's purposefulness and Nicholson's perfectionism, Oxford has an exceptional collection of nineteenth-century scientific literature (with its weakness, if there is one, in the coverage of the period 1845 to 1860). An illustration of the strength of the collection is that of the one million or so nineteenth-century scientific papers recorded in the exhaustive *Royal Society Catalogue of Scientific Papers*, half a million are available in Oxford.

The twentieth century to the Second World War

In the twentieth century, collection development in the field of science, technology and medicine was affected by several factors: a change in the relative importance of books and periodicals; an exponential growth in the literature; the diversification of science; and the impact of geopolitical events on the ability to collect. These trends were all apparent in the first quarter of the twentieth century. W. Hatchett Jackson (Radcliffe Librarian 1900–1924) reflected that Acland had considered appropriate an equal division between spending on books and periodicals, whereas he, Jackson, needed to spend a much higher proportion on periodicals, with the result that the coverage of books was narrower than previously, and certainly narrower than he would have wished.

Jackson was also faced with the emergence of new taught subjects, for which library provision needed to be made. Departments of Forestry and Pathology were established in 1905 and an Agriculture Laboratory was opened a year later; Engineering Science was taught from 1908; a Diploma in Ophthalmology was taught from 1910; Organic Chemistry got its own laboratory in 1915 and Pharmacology joined it in 1917; the Biochemistry Department was founded in 1920. All this meant a collection broader in scope but shallower in depth. Deficits in the periodicals collection caused by the interruption of trade in the First World War were made up. Far more serious was the rising price of German periodicals in the post-war period. From 1917, Oxford D.Phil. theses were deposited with the Bodleian. (The Radcliffe Science Library now has well over 15,000 in the fields of science and medicine, together with some Oxford M.Sc. dissertations.)

Three significant acquisitions in the first quarter of the twentieth century, however, were the Richardson correspondence, the Tylor collection, and the Wilson bequest. Richard Richardson (1663–1741) was a botanist and antiquary, in correspondence with others of like interests. His letters were secured at auction for the Radcliffe Trustees in 1916, and because of their mixed botanical and antiquarian interest were deposited in the Bodleian. The books of Sir Edward Burnett Tylor (1832–1917), first Professor in Anthropology, were presented to the Radcliffe Library in 1917: partly monographs and partly a collection of offprints and pamphlets, but all on a wide range of anthropological subjects, particularly linguistic. These are kept in the Radcliffe Science Library even though many of them are concerned with cultural anthropology and are thus beyond the normal scope of that library's anthropological collections (*i.e.* biological and physical anthropology). The bequest of Charles Joseph Wilson led to 470 of his ornithological volumes coming into the Radcliffe Library's collections in 1925–6, adding particularly to the ornithological literature of the English counties.

On Hatchett Jackson's death in 1924, the future of the Radcliffe Library was reviewed, in the light of its rising cost and the continuing wastefulness of duplication between the Bodleian and Radcliffe Libraries. In 1927, the Radcliffe Trustees presented their library premises and their contents to the University. The Radcliffe Library became a 'dependent' library of the Bodleian, under the new name of Radcliffe Science Library. The almost immediate benefit was an increase in spending on foreign periodicals (only to be cut back in the early 1930s). Following a University inquiry into library provision, the Radcliffe Science Library building was doubled in size, and the post-1883 scientific stock of the Bodleian and the RSL was deduplicated and merged at the RSL. However, the period which followed cannot be characterised as a successful period for collection development in science, technology and medicine.

Once again, the development of new teaching and research outstripped the ability to provide library resources. Lord Nuffield's benefaction set up seven new medical departments (Anaesthetics, Clinical Biochemistry, Clinical Medicine, Obstetrics and Gynaecology, Orthopaedic Surgery, Pathology and Bacteriology, and Surgery). That meant an increase in medical research and teaching, but no library funding to go with it. In this pre-war period the premier UK scientific library was that of the Science Museum, South Kensington, which made strenuous efforts to collect periodicals from around the world by whatever means possible.

The post-war period

In 1940, the Bodleian Curators determined that essential scientific works should be exempted from a general injunction not to purchase from enemy countries. However, even after the Second World War it was difficult to acquire German periodicals. Regrettably, German works reprinted by the Custodian of Alien Property in

Washington were not collected to a great extent in wartime. The 1950s and 1960s, by contrast, were a period of expansion for the Radcliffe Science Library's collections, and from 400 periodical subscriptions in 1901 a figure five times as great had been reached by 1981. Russian journals were taken, particularly in chemistry and physics, both in the original language and in cover-to-cover English translations.

Fluctuations in the strength of the pound, pressure on University funding, and rising periodical prices have subsequently meant a sharp decline in the number of periodical subscriptions, and similarly a reduction in the number of foreign monographs purchased. Once again, the opening and closure of scientific departments has led to changes in the range of material bought. The Departments of Agricultural Science, Botany and Forestry were merged into a single Plant Sciences department in 1985 and agriculture ceased to be taught.

At the present day, the Radcliffe Science Library supports the teaching, learning and research of three academic divisions of the University. For Life and Environmental Sciences, biochemistry and biology, physical and biological anthropology, and physical geography and geomorphology are supported. For Medical Sciences the subjects covered are clinical medicine, human anatomy, physiology, pathology, pharmacology and psychology. Thirdly, for Physical and Mathematical Sciences the RSL supports work in mathematics, computing science, statistics, physics, chemistry, materials, engineering and earth sciences. All this is reflected in purchasing policy and in the choice of legal deposit material for the reading room shelves.

The legal deposit privilege also means that British scholarly material in scientific subjects not studied in the University is obtained: dentistry, veterinary medicine and agriculture are the best examples of this. The world of industrial technology as distinct from engineering science is well represented. (It should be noted that some technologies were traditionally classified by the Bodleian as 'Arts and Trades' and that their literature has not been moved to the Radcliffe Science Library: examples are metallurgy, textile manufacture and paper, print and paint technologies, which are housed in the central Bodleian.)

A wide range of popular works is received, reflecting the wider adoption (and sometimes debasement) of scientific ideas. Since the 1970s, self-help works in popular psychology have boomed. The greatest increase, however, has been in textbooks and commercially-produced manuals for computer hardware and software, to the extent that they now comprise at least a third of the scientific copyright intake.

Lastly, British official publications are received in the areas of science, technology and medicine. These include medical publications from the Department of Health and local health trusts, vital statistics from the Office of National Statistics and reports issued by research institutes, including declassified reports from the laboratories at Harwell, Culham and Daresbury. The complete range of British Standards is received.

Beyond the scope of legal deposit, but still in the area of official publications, selective acquisitions are made from the publications of the International Atomic Energy Agency, the World Health Organisation, the Food and Agriculture Organisation and the European Space Agency.

Since the 1970s, working papers of contemporary scientists have been collected by the Department of Special Collections and Western Manuscripts, with the assistance of the Contemporary Scientific Archives Centre (founded at Oxford in 1973). The papers of over thirty scientists are now held, including those of Dorothy Hodgkin and Sir Rudolf Peierls. Complementary material has been obtained as well: while the working papers of Christopher Strachey are held by the Department of Special Collections and Western Manuscripts, the Radcliffe Science Library has his collection of programming manuals. Earlier collections of scientific papers include those of the chemist Frederick Soddy (1877–1956) and of Mary Somerville (1780–1872), the latter deposited by Somerville College; while the archive of the British Association for the Advancement of Science spans the nineteenth and twentieth centuries.

The Hardy Collection in the Radcliffe Science Library consists of offprints collected by the mathematician G.H. Hardy (1877–1947). There is a similar, extensive, collection amassed by Sir Wilfrid Le Gros Clark (1895–1971) on anatomy, physiology, physical anthropology and primatology, and smaller collections on theoretical chemistry by C.A. Coulson (1910–1974) and on herpes viruses, infectious mononucleosis, hypertension and other medical topics by the physician Bent Juel-Jensen. The materials for Austin Seckersen's unpublished *Encyclopaedia of Medical Eponyms* are held, as are W.E. Van Heyningen's offprints of papers on bacterial toxins collected 1946–79, and papers relating to malaria and its eradication collected by C. Garrett-Jones while working as an entomologist for the World Health Organisation. There is an uncatalogued collection of materials on coconuts, deposited by Reginald Child, author of a standard work on that subject.

Another class of material which should be mentioned consists of papers (chiefly minutes and accounts of meetings) relating to the University's scientific and medical societies: the Oxford University Junior Scientific Club and its successor the Oxford University Scientific Society; the Oxford Medical Club; the Osler Society; and the Oxford Mathematical and Physical Society.

Other important scientific, technical and medical collections are held elsewhere in the University: in medical sciences at the library of the Department of Physiology; in life and environmental sciences at the Plant Sciences Library, successor to the library (founded 1621) of the Botanic Garden, the Alexander (ornithological) Library of the Department of Zoology, and the library of the University Museum of Natural History; and in mathematical and physical sciences by the astrophysical collections of the Department of Physics, and the libraries of the Departments of Engineering Science and Earth Sciences. Departments also hold materials relating to the history of Oxford science.

The present state of the Radcliffe Science Library collections is (in 2003) as follows: about 350,000 monographs, about 30,000 serial titles, about 4,500 live periodical titles. This places the Radcliffe Science Library among the world's top ten specialist scientific, technical and medical libraries. Of the 4,500 current periodicals, 3,500 come by legal deposit and about 1,000 are purchased. Of the 3,500 legal deposit titles, about 1,500 are from the core of most-cited journals. The remainder are the more esoteric scholarly journals, the proceedings of local natural history and geology societies, trade journals and professional associations' newsletters, the serial publications of international and national government organisations and quangos, popularising magazines, enthusiasts' and hobby publications, and controversial literature from pressure groups. Like the scientific literature itself, some 60% of the RSL's periodicals acquisitions fall within the biomedical and biological sciences.

Taking the usefulness of the current periodicals as a measure, and treating the University's collections as a single whole for purposes of comparison, Oxford's collection is second among UK universities to Cambridge, followed by the Imperial College / Science Museum group of libraries and Leeds University Library. Oxford takes half of the 5,550 'core' or most-cited scientific periodicals and six out of seven of these are at the RSL. Monograph acquisitions have been a declining proportion of the totality of science acquisitions since the late nineteenth century, and today monograph purchases take up only about one-tenth of the budget. Legal deposit scientific monographs number about 10,000 a year. Of these, about one-third are specialist works and textbooks, about one-third are relatively scholarly but outside the scope of the University's teaching, and the remainder are non-scholarly, popularising, recreational, or children's books.

Select bibliography

W. Hatchett Jackson, 'The Radcliffe Library', in: J.B. Nias, *Dr John Radcliffe : A Sketch of his Life* (Oxford: Clarendon Press, 1918).

Exhibition of Scientific MSS. and Printed Books at the Bodleian Library (Oxford: University Press, [1926]).

R.T. Gunther, 'The Ashmole Printed Books', *Bodleian Quarterly Record*, vol. 6/68 (1930), 193–5.

R.T. Gunther, 'The Chemical Library of the University', *Bodleian Quarterly Record*, vol. 6/68 (1930), 201–3.

Bibliotheca Radcliviana, 1749–1949 : Catalogue of an Exhibition … . (Oxford : Bodleian Library, 1949).

Doctrina Arabum : Science and Philosophy in Medieval Islam & their Transmission to Europe. (Oxford: Bodleian Library, 1981).

Dennis F. Shaw, *Oxford University Science Libraries : A Guide* (Oxford: Bodleian Library, 1981).

Ivor Guest, *Dr. John Radcliffe and his Trust* (London: Radcliffe Trust, 1991).

Katherine D. Watson, *Sources for the History of Science in Oxford* (Oxford : Modern History Faculty, University of Oxford, 1994).

Women & Natural History : Artists, Collectors, Patrons, Scientists: An Exhibition in association with the Society for the History of Natural History at the Bodleian Library, Oxford (Oxford : Bodleian Library, 1996).

For collection-level descriptions of the papers of contemporary Oxford scientists, see: www.archiveshub.ac.uk, and use 'advanced search' facility with 'contemporary scientists' in the full text search and 'Bodleian' in the repository.

14. German Studies

The Bodleian has important collections of German books in most academic disciplines, the strengths of which reflect both the influence of German scholarship on Oxford studies and the vagaries of the Library's own history. It has been estimated that there are in the Library in the region of 102,000 pre-1900 books from the German-speaking area of Europe (compared with *c.*500,000 from the United Kingdom, about 60,000 from France and 31,000 from Italy).

In the years between its foundation in 1602 and the outbreak of the Civil War, the Bodleian systematically bought books from Continental Europe, for the most part through London booksellers, but also through agents who travelled extensively abroad buying books which both pre-dated 1602 and kept the collections up to date with current publications. As a boy, Thomas Bodley had spent the years of Mary Tudor's reign in exile in Germany and Switzerland and his purchases for the Library reflect his knowledge of, and interest in, those countries. The regulations governing the Library after his death in 1613 required its Curators to meet within a week of the arrival of the spring and autumn catalogues of the Frankfurt Book Fair in order to select books for purchase – an arrangement which ensured that German books continued to figure prominently in its collections.

The Library's income was much reduced by the disturbances of the Civil War and its purchasing of foreign materials diminished until the 1680s. It is interesting to note that when expenditure increased, the Curators again looked to Germany for assistance with book selection, in 1684 ordering that they should regularly be shown the *Acta eruditorum*, a German learned periodical which contained reviews and summaries of recent publications.

Acquisition of German as of all foreign books dropped again in the course of the eighteenth century, but picked up early in the nineteenth, which witnessed a steady growth through both purchase and gift. This development was signalled by the purchase in 1818 of an important collection of some 2,500 Lutheran tracts, subsequently added to, and giving the Library the largest holding of such publications in Britain. Around 1826 several series of German learned periodicals of the eighteenth and early nineteenth centuries were acquired. Beginning in 1827, the Library purchased a series of large collections of foreign academic dissertations, eventually totalling about 50,000 items, some dating from as early as the 1650s and most of them originating from German universities.

The purchase in 1824 of books from the library of the Dutch scholar and jurist Gerard Meerman and of his son Johan included useful additions to the Bodleian's holdings of eighteenth-century German theology and legal studies. Richard Gough's bequest of 1809, while overwhelmingly English, added many important volumes of Germanic literature and German topography. The great collector Francis Douce (1757–1834) bought a substantial number of books in vernacular languages, usefully complementing the Bodleian's more traditionally academic purchases with materials of popular culture like books of fables, lives of saints, manuals for preachers and editions of the Dance of Death. The Library's great collection of incunables includes about 1,950 editions printed in the German-speaking area before 1500, and many more of German provenance.

From the 1840s onwards, after the foundation of the Taylor Institution Library, collecting for the study of German language and literature was no longer concentrated at the Bodleian, but German books continued to be bought for the general collections both directly from booksellers in Germany and through the Oxford booksellers, Parker. Acquisitions were interrupted by the First World War and severely hampered by exchange, import and export restrictions during the inter-war years. An unusual donation came from the Military Censor in 1919: a large collection of mainly German books and pamphlets seized from postal packages during the war as enemy propaganda. Among more traditional German acquisitions of the twentieth century were the collections of D. B. Monro (chiefly German books on Homeric studies) given by his friends in 1905. The acquisition of German university theses, begun by purchase in the 1820s and continued through exchange agreements, still brings many doctoral dissertations into the Library.

Collecting became more extensive after the Second World War, covering publications from all German-speaking countries including the German Democratic Republic. There has been a strong emphasis on published sources and secondary works for the history of Germanophone Europe from the mediaeval period to its contemporary politics and society. They include major microfilm series on, for example, the Third Reich, the Nazi Party and the Nuremberg tribunals, and extensive – though not comprehensive – sets of parliamentary proceedings. Coverage extends to regional and local history, and special attention has been devoted since 1989 to acquiring source material on the German Democratic Republic appearing in the aftermath of German reunification, as well as secondary literature on *die Wende*.

Major donations since 1945 include those of P. S. Allen (mainly relating to his work as editor of Erasmus, *Opus epistolarum*) bequeathed by his widow in 1953 (Allen Collection); and of Nathaniel Micklem, presented in 1946 and augmented by similar collections from Richard Gutteridge. The Gutteridge-Micklem

Collection is a unique assembly of material (books, periodicals, pamphlets, documents and ephemera) relating to the struggles, known as the *Kirchenkampf,* between the Nazi regime and the German churches in the years before the Second World War.

The Library's foremost collection of medieval manuscripts of German provenance (but mostly containing Latin, not German vernacular, texts) is that given by Archbishop Laud. These manuscripts came in large part from the libraries of St Kylian, Würzburg; St. Mary, Eberbach; and the Carthusian house at Mainz, all of which had suffered depredations as a result of the disturbances of the Thirty Years' War. The Laudian manuscripts include the 'Paradisus animae intelligentis', a collection of sermons from the Erfurt Dominicans containing the oldest sermons of Meister Eckhart (Middle Rhine, *c.*1330) (MS. Laud Misc. 479); and 'Der Heiligen Leben', the Middle High German prose legendary (Nürnberg, shortly before 1400) (MS. Laud Misc. 443).

The most important of the Bodleian's constituent collections for the study of medieval German is the Junius Collection, given to the University by the pioneering seventeenth-century philologist Francis Junius. This consists both of the manuscripts Junius collected, and of his transcripts from manuscripts elsewhere. They include the Bodleian's single most important medieval German manuscript, the so-called 'Murbach Hymnal' (MS. Junius 25), a collection of early texts from the eighth and ninth centuries, including the Latin-Old High German interlinear Murbach hymns, and the Old High German glossaries known as Junius A, B, and C. Other manuscripts of interest to medieval Germanists are scattered throughout the collections, not least in MSS. Lyell, which include several important manuscripts from German and Austrian monastic libraries, and in MSS. Douce, one of the Library's most important collections of illuminated manuscripts. The Bodleian has one great treasure of Ottonian manuscript illumination, the early eleventh-century Sacramentary from the abbey of Reichenau (MS. Canon. Liturg. 319).

The most important modern Western manuscripts in the German language are undoubtedly those of Franz Kafka, which came to the Bodleian through deposit and gift. The Bodleian also holds the manuscript and a typescript with manuscript additions of Ludwig Wittgenstein's *Logisch-philosophische Abhandlung* (MSS. German d. 6 and d. 7) and a large collection of microfilms and photocopies of Wittgenstein papers held elsewhere in Austria and England. For the nineteenth century, the M. Deneke Mendelssohn Collection contains a wealth of the composer's correspondence as well as diaries, accounts and, of course, music scores. An *album amicorum* of Goethe, presented to St George Cromie, a member of Goethe's household, and containing inscriptions by Goethe and many of his friends in Weimar, was given to the Bodleian with a similar volume of Cromie's own, in 1942 (MSS. German c. 13, d. 5). In the general Western manuscript collections, many travel diaries of English men and women include accounts of visits to Germany in the eighteenth, nineteenth and twentieth centuries, while the strong holdings of diplomatic papers, from the nineteenth to the twentieth centuries, provide much evidence for studies of Anglo-German relations.

The Library also has important Yiddish collections, which are described in the chapter on the Near and Middle East (*p. 123*).

Select bibliography

E. Sievers, *Die Murbacher Hymnen* (Halle, 1874).

Robert Priebsch, *Deutsche Handschriften in England* I (Erlangen: Fr. Junge, 1896), 143–87.

J.M.S. Pasley, 'Franz Kafka MSS: Description and Select Inedita', *Modern Language Review*, 57 (1962), 53–9.

R.W. Hunt, introduction to the revised edition of H.O. Coxe, *Bodleian Library, Quarto Catalogues II, Laudian Manuscripts* (Oxford: Clarendon Press, 1973), especially pp. xxiii–xxvi.

Otto Pächt and J.J.G. Alexander, *Illuminated Manuscripts in the Bodleian Library Oxford I: German, Dutch, Flemish, French and Spanish Schools* (Oxford: Clarendon Press, 1973), 1–15.

Michael A. Pegg, *A Catalogue of German Reformation Pamphlets 1516–1546 in Libraries of Great Britain and Ireland* (Baden-Baden: Koerner, 1973).

D.M. Sutherland, 'Early editions of Goethe, Schiller and Wagner', *Bodleian Library Record*, 9/1 (1973), 40–64.

Catalogue of the Kafka Centenary Exhibition [by Sir Malcolm Pasley] (Oxford: Bodleian Library, 1983).

Der Kirchenkampf: the Gutteridge-Micklem Collection at the Bodleian Library, Oxford (London etc.: Saur Microfilm Edition, 1988) [with introduction by Catherine Blundell and Judi Vernau; 'The Creation of the Micklem-Gutteridge Collection' by Richard Gutteridge].

Bettina Wagner, 'Bodleian Incunables From Bavarian Monasteries', *Bodleian Library Record*, 15/2 (1995), 90–107.

Nigel F. Palmer, *Zisterzienser und ihre Bücher. Die mittelalterliche Bibliotheksgeschichte von Kloster Eberbach im Rheingau unter besonderer Berücksichtigung der in Oxford und London aufbewahrten Handschriften* (Regensburg: Schnell u. Steiner, 1998).

E.G. Stanley, 'The Sources of Junius's Learning as Revealed in the Junius Manuscripts in the Bodleian Library', in Rolf H. Bremmer Jr, ed., *Franciscus Junius F.F. and His Circle* (Amsterdam and Atlanta, Ga.: Rodopi, 1998), 159–76.

Handbuch deutscher historischer Buchbestände in Europa. Band 10: A Guide to Collections of Books Printed in German-Speaking Countries Before 1901 … Held in Libraries in Great Britain and Ireland (Hildesheim: Olms-Weidmann, 2000), 268–303. A very detailed and fully-referenced account of the Bodleian's older German printed holdings.

15. French Studies

The Library of the Taylor Institution holds the University's principal research collections on modern European languages and literature. The Bodleian nevertheless has significant holdings of French books (in the region of 60,000 printed before 1900, including over 800 incunabula) which reflect its long history and the Europe-wide interests of its founder and benefactors. From 1576 Sir Thomas Bodley spent much of his four years abroad travelling in France and once he entered the diplomatic service of Elizabeth I, he went on a brief, confidential mission to France in 1588. In the summer of 1602 one of his agents, John Bill, was buying books for him in Paris. In the introduction to the 1620 catalogue of the Library's holdings, the Librarian, Thomas James, drew attention to the large numbers of foreign books – French, Italian and Spanish – that it contained.

The foremost monument of medieval French literary culture in the Bodleian is the earliest surviving manuscript of *La Chanson de Roland*, the greatest of the epic poems known as *chansons de geste*. Written in Anglo-Norman, it was almost certainly penned in England and was bequeathed to the Bodleian by Sir Kenelm Digby in 1634 (MS. Digby 23, part 2). The Bodleian's collections also include other important medieval textual witnesses, especially in the Anglo-Norman field. MS. Douce 6, a thirteenth-century manuscript, contains (amongst other texts) the longest surviving fragment of Thomas's *Tristan*, whilst MS. Fr. d. 16, also of the thirteenth century, contains two fragments of Thomas's *Tristan*, partly overlapping with the Douce text. The only complete text of the Anglo-Norman *Les enfaunces de Jesu Christ* survives in a manuscript of the first quarter of the fourteenth century (MS. Selden Supra 38), accompanied by the earliest and longest English series of miniatures depicting the Apocryphal Infancy miracles. Outstanding among the bi- and tri-lingual manuscripts from England is MS. Digby 86, a late thirteenth-century miscellany from Worcestershire containing texts in French, Latin and English, several of them unique.

The Bodleian is rich in illuminated manuscripts from France and French Flanders (with texts in either Latin or French). The two most important examples had both arrived in the Library within one or two years of its foundation: the verse Alexander romance illuminated by Jehan de Grise and assistants between 1338 and 1344, perhaps in Tournai (MS. Bodl. 264, part 1), and one volume of a three-part Latin

Bible moralisée produced in Paris, perhaps in the mid-1230s (MS. Bodl. 270b), the other parts surviving in Paris and London. Of the Library's constituent collections, the richest in this field, particularly for the fourteenth and fifteenth centuries, is that of Francis Douce (1757–1834), who acquired many of his manuscripts as a result of the dispersal of famous libraries on the Continent, such as those of L.J. Gaignat, P.A. Crevenna, and the Duc de la Vallière. Douce's French treasures include a composite early fourteenth-century manuscript containing five illuminated French texts, amongst them a *chansonnier* (MS. Douce 308); a de-luxe late fifteenth-century manuscript of *Le Roman de la Rose*, with illumination attributed to Robinet Testard (MS. Douce 195); and two Burgundian manuscripts from the second half of the fifteenth century illustrated in grisaille, one a volume of Jean Miélot's *Miracles de Nostre Dame* made for Duke Philip the Good (MS. Douce 374), the other a collection of moral and religious treatises made for Margaret of York, wife of Duke Charles the Bold (MS. Douce 365).

The acquisition of French books and manuscripts continued steadily throughout the centuries. The large number of French manuscripts in the bequest of Richard Rawlinson (1690–1755) reflects that great collector's travels on the Continent. One of the most interesting gifts of a single manuscript in the eighteenth century was a beautifully written and illuminated chronicle, the *Mirouer historial abregie de la France* made for Charles d'Anjou, Count of Maine between 1443 and 1461 and given by the Earl of Radnor in 1767 (MS. Bodl. 968). The huge bequest of Richard Gough in 1809 included sixteen folio volumes of some 2,000 coloured drawings of monuments in the churches of France, made by François-Roger de Gaignières and presented to Louis XIV in 1711 (MSS. Gough drawings - Gaignières). They are part of a larger series, the bulk of which survives in the Bibilothèque Nationale. Exactly how Richard Gough acquired 16 of the 25 volumes lost from that series between 1779 and 1784 is not clear. Their importance as a record of church monuments which have since been damaged or lost is incalculable.

With Douce's library came a fine collection of works of lighter French fiction of the seventeenth and eighteenth centuries. Captain Montagu Montagu's collection, received in 1863, included many editions of Boileau and La Fontaine. French books of all sorts came into the Library among the larger acquisitions of the twentieth century – John Johnson's collection of writing masters' copy books included many from France, while the vast collection of Walter Harding included, alongside French songbooks and opera from 1700 onwards, interesting chapbooks, jestbooks and plays.

Robert Shackleton (1919–86), Bodley's Librarian and Marshal Foch Professor of French Literature, bequeathed his comprehensive collection of books by and about the political philosopher Charles de Secondat, Baron de Montesquieu (1689–1755). Among the one thousand volumes are early editions of virtually all Montesquieu's works. At the end of the eighteenth century, interest in France and

French politics was reflected in the high price (£104) paid for Maraldi and Cassini's *Atlas de France*, and in the purchase of a set of the *Moniteur* from 1789 to 1800. In 1925 Lord Curzon bequeathed his collection of some 330 works on Napoleon, many relating to Napoleon's captivity on St Helena, and with it the furniture of the Empire Room in Carlton House Terrace in which it was stored. It includes a magnificent set of 39 folio volumes, grangerised editions of Holland Rose, *Life of Napoleon* (1902), Lord Rosebery, *Napoleon the Last Phase* (1900) and A.M. Broadley, *Napoleon in Caricature* (1911), enhanced with thousands of engraved portraits and views, contemporary caricatures and broadsides, autograph letters and original drawings (Curzon b. 2–40).

Although the Library rarely purchased fine bindings for their own sake, it has acquired several splendid examples of French binding through the generosity of its Friends, among them two royal ones presented by J.H. Burn in 1923–4: Ambrose Paré, *La manière de traicter les playes* (1551), bound for Henri III and *L'office de la semaine sainte* (1674), bound in red morocco with the arms of Maria Theresa of Austria, wife of Louis XIV. The Buchanan Collection includes many interesting bindings embellished with the arms of great French collectors.

French publishing, as represented in the central Bodleian's post-1900 collections, spans most fields of the humanities and social sciences, with the exception of those subjects (most notably literature, language and art history) for which other libraries in the University have primary responsibility. Particular strengths of the Bodleian include French regional history and culture, as exemplified by the extensive series of *inventaires sommaires*, in which French Departmental archives publish their local records of all kinds. These have been collected continuously since the nineteenth century and therefore constitute a major resource. Also abundant are the annals of learned societies which, like the *inventaires sommaires*, provide cover over several centuries of French social and cultural history. The Bodleian's French-language holdings in philosophy (both primary and secondary sources), classical studies (in the form of both texts in translation and critical literature), theology and religious studies are worthy of note, as are social and economic studies of France and the French-speaking world. The history of the book has long been a special collecting area for the Bodleian in all languages, and French scholarship is prolific in this field. A special effort was made soon after the Second World War to acquire French wartime publications. Of particular note from this period are the university theses published in Paris, which were acquired almost in their entirety.

Select bibliography

C. Samaran, *La Chanson de Roland. Reproduction phototypique du manuscrit Digby 23 de la Bodleian Library d'Oxford* (Roxburghe Club, 182; Paris, 1932).

Otto Pächt and J.J.G. Alexander, *Illuminated Manuscripts in the Bodleian Library Oxford. I: German, Dutch, Flemish, French and Spanish Schools* (Oxford: Clarendon Press, 1966), 32–68.

The Douce Legacy: An Exhibition to Commemorate the 150th Anniversary of the Bequest of Francis Douce (1757–1834) (Oxford: Bodleian Library, 1984).

David H. Thomas, *A Checklist of Editions of Major French Authors in Oxford Libraries 1526–1800* (Oxford: Voltaire Foundation, 1986).

Giles Barber, 'Francis Douce and Popular French Literature', *Bodleian Library Record*, 14/5 (1993), 397–428.

Giles Barber, 'Iure et Merito: French Prize Books of the Seventeenth Century', *Bodleian Library Record*, 15/5–6 (1996), 383–407.

French Livres d'Artiste in Oxford University Collections [exhibition catalogue] (Oxford: Bodleian Library, 1996).

Giles Barber, 'Acquiring Enlightenment: Oxford and the Encyclopédie', in *The Culture of the Book: Essays […] in honour of Wallace Kirsop* (Melbourne: Bibliographical Society of Australia and New Zealand, 1999), 232–44.

Ruth J. Dean, *Anglo-Norman Literature: A Guide to Texts and Manuscripts* (London: Anglo-Norman Text Society, 1999).

Giles Barber, 'Voltaire et Oxford' in *Voltaire en Europe: hommage à Christiane Mervaux* (Oxford: Voltaire Foundation, 2000), 3–11.

16. Italian Studies

The University's major collecting in European languages, linguistics and literatures (except English) has been concentrated outside the Bodleian since the foundation of the Taylor Institution in the 1840s, but the Library nevertheless has significant accumulations of Italian books (in the region of 31,000 printed before 1900) which reflect its long history. Two of the very few books which survive from Sir Thomas Bodley's private library are works by Boccaccio: *Corbaccio* (1569) and *Vita di Dante* (1544). John Bill, a leading London bookseller, visited Rome, Venice and nine other towns in northern Italy buying books for Bodley's new library in 1602, and a collection of Italian books, presented by Sir Michael Dormer in 1603, was among the earliest gifts. John Glanville of Balliol College presented more in 1614. In the 1630s and early 1640s, the Library's accounts record several payments to the bookseller Robert Martin for 'books out of Italy'.

In the mid-nineteenth century the Italian collections were augmented by four important acquisitions. Between 1838 and 1843, Sir George Bowyer, author of *Dissertation on the Statutes of the Cities of Italy* (1838), gave seventy-eight volumes of the statutes of Italian cities, chiefly of the seventeenth and eighteenth centuries. In 1846 a collection of 1,426 volumes on Italian topography, antiquities and art formed by George C. Scott was bought from his brother. In 1852 the Library purchased from Count Alessandro Mortara his collection of 1,400 books, rich in rare sixteenth-century editions of Italian authors, including early editions of Ariosto, Boccaccio, Dante and Tasso. In 1863 a considerable number of editions of Petrarch came in the bequest of Captain Montagu Montagu. Occasional purchases of single rarities were made when Bulkeley Bandinel was Bodley's Librarian, among them the 1532 Ferrara edition of Ariosto's *Orlando Furioso*, and Thomas Bodley's copy of Boccaccio's *Corbaccio*.

In the 1920s and 1930s the Bodleian's foreign collecting was not on a large scale. After the Second World War, however, more plentiful resources were channelled in this direction. In the early post-war years great emphasis was placed on acquiring foreign wartime publications which were, for the most part, lacking from libraries in their countries of origin. For a period after 1945 the Bodleian was ahead of the British Museum Library in acquiring Italian-language materials, at least in the field of that country's social, cultural and political history which was – and still is – one of the Library's principal areas of strength. Its national and international significance has been notably reinforced by gifts from Denis Mack Smith, historian of the Italian Risorgimento and the fascist regime in Italy, whose extensive personal library has been coming to the Bodleian in instalments since 1987.

One of the principal acquisitions of special collections of Italian books during the twentieth century came as gifts from the Dante scholar Paget Toynbee. His donations began in 1912 with numerous sixteenth-century editions of Boccaccio, for the most part printed at Florence or Venice, and continued with works printed at Italian presses such as those of Aldus and Giunta, as well as numerous incunable editions of the works of Dante and Petrarch. His later gifts included many editions and translations of Dante, and commentaries on his writings and general Italian literature of the sixteenth to twentieth centuries, alongside Toynbee's own working papers on Dante. In 1918 the miscellaneous collections of the Reverend Colonel Robert Finch, bequeathed to the university in 1830, were divided between appropriate institutions. Some 3,500 volumes, mainly of Italian topography, came to the Bodleian. The Bodleian's share of Finch's monetary bequest was from 1941 allocated to the purchase of pre-1800 books of Italian interest. Purchases in 1953 from the library of the Earl of Leicester at Holkham Hall in Norfolk included five hundred sixteenth-century Italian books, in a wide range of subjects. A substantial collection of books printed by Giovanni Mardersteig at the Officina Bodoni in Montagnola and Verona between 1923 and 1977 was purchased in 1990 from the library of John Ryder. Another feature of the Italian holdings is the collection of so-called 'bank books', lavishly published in limited editions by Italian banks for distribution to shareholders and valued customers and therefore not readily available elsewhere. These cover a wide range of subjects and constitute a publishing phenomenon in their own right. Fine press books published by the Edizioni dell'Elefante in Rome came to the Bodleian in the form of an exhibition mounted by the publisher in 1987.

Amongst the Bodleian's rich collections of illuminated manuscripts, those from Italy are second only to those from the British Isles. By far the most important single group of them is part of the great collection of the Venetian Matteo Luigi Canonici (1727–c.1806). Canonici was a Jesuit who had devoted himself to collecting after the suppression of the order in parts of Italy in 1773. The majority of his manuscripts are from Northern Italy and of these a considerable proportion come from the Veneto. The Bodleian purchased the greater part of Canonici's collection in 1817, the largest single purchase of manuscripts ever made by the Library. Chiefly of the fifteenth century, they include works of Boccaccio, Dante and Petrarch, translations of Latin classical and patristic texts, legendaries and books of devotion, many of them fine examples of Italian humanist illumination. The Canonici manuscripts include such treasures as the copy of the *Notitia Dignitatum* (a handbook of officials of the late Roman Empire) made in 1436 for Pietro Donato, Bishop of Padua (MS. Canon.

Misc. 378), and the illustrated manuscript of Boccaccio's *Il Filocolo* made in 1463–4 for Lodovico III Gonzaga, Marquess of Mantua (MS. Canon. Ital. 85).

Of the Italian medieval manuscripts from other sources, a few belonged to the fifteenth-century University Library and have returned by a variety of routes. These include not only survivors from the gifts of Duke Humfrey of Gloucester, but also manuscripts acquired by John Tiptoft, Earl of Worcester, very probably during his stay in Padua in *c.*1459–61. Important Italian manuscripts are also to be found in the collections of Sir Kenelm Digby (1603–65), Richard Rawlinson (1689–1755), Jacques Philippe D'Orville (1696–1751), E.D. Clarke (1769–1822) and Francis Douce (1757–1834). Of the manuscripts bequeathed by Douce, those made in Italy form only a small proportion, but they include such important illuminated treasures as the Hours of Eleonora Gonzaga (MS. Douce 29). At several points in the second half of the twentieth century the Bodleian acquired Italian manuscripts from the library of the Earl of Leicester, collected by Thomas Coke in Italy on the Grand Tour in 1717–18: they include illuminated copies of Dante and Boccaccio (MSS. Holkham. misc. 48 and 49 respectively).

In the general Western manuscript collections are to be found an assortment of travel journals and of diplomatic papers relating to Italy. The largest group of nineteenth-century Italian papers is the correspondence of Thomas Ward, Baron Ward of the Austrian Empire, a jockey who went from Yorkshire to join the household of Charles Louis of Bourbon and rose in the Duke's service to become in 1847 chief minister of Parma. The late nineteenth and early twentieth centuries are represented in the papers of Count Pietro Antonelli, diplomat and explorer, mainly concerning his embassies to Ethiopia, Eritrea and Brazil. They are supplemented by papers of his brother, Cardinal Giacomo Antonelli. Also of interest are the diaries and correspondence of the author Linda Villari (*d.* 1915), wife of the Italian historian Pasquale Villari.

Select bibliography

A. Mortara, *Catalogo dei manoscritti italiani che sotto la denominazione di Codici Canoniciani Italiani si conservano nella Biblioteca Bodleiana a Oxford* (Oxford, 1864).

Italian Illuminated Manuscripts from 1400 to 1550 [exhibition catalogue] (Oxford: Bodleian Library, 1948).

Duke Humfrey and English Humanism in the Fifteenth Century [exhibition catalogue] (Oxford: Bodleian Library, 1970).

Otto Pächt and J.J.G. Alexander, *Illuminated Manuscripts in the Bodleian Library, Oxford. 2: Italian School* (Oxford: Clarendon Press, 1970).

Alfonso Sammut, *Unfredo duca di Gloucester e gli umanisti italiani* (Medioevo e Umanesimo, 41; Padova: Antenore, 1980).

Autographs of Italian Humanists [exhibition catalogue] (Oxford: Bodleian Library, 1974).

A.C. de la Mare, 'Further Italian Illuminated Manuscripts in the Bodleian Library', in: *La Miniatura Italiana tra Gotico e Rinascimento*, I (Florence: Olschki, 1985), 127–54.

Amanda J. Peters, *Italian Studies Periodicals in the Bodleian Library* (Oxford: Bodleian Library, 1986).

A.J. Fairbank and R.W. Hunt, *Humanistic Script of the Fifteenth and Sixteenth Centuries* (Bodleian Picture Books, new series, 2; Oxford: Bodleian Library, 1993).

The Department of Special Collections and Western Manuscripts also houses important scholarly resources (available for consultation on application) for the study of Italian humanistic script. These include J. Wardrop's albums of photographs, and A. Fairbank's and A.C. de la Mare's collection of facsimiles. The index which accompanies the latter contains valuable unpublished information about manuscripts in Oxford and beyond.

17. Hispanic Studies

At the time of the refoundation of the University Library by Sir Thomas Bodley, England was engaged in a bitter military and ideological struggle with Habsburg Spain, Portugal and the Indies: a struggle that did not end until 1604, two years after the Library's opening. Partly as a result, the Bodleian's Hispanic collections got off to a spectacular start, with the library of a Portuguese bishop seized as a prize of war. In 1596 the Earl of Essex, returning from the sack of Cadiz, landed at Faro in the Algarve and quartered himself in the bishop's palace. While he was there, he removed the 252 volumes which comprised the bishop's library (now known as the Mascarenhas Collection after the incumbent), and subsequently passed them on to his friend Bodley. This was, in fact, the earliest recorded donation of a complete collection of books to the new library. Other books also came to the Bodleian as a result of the expedition.

The works thus acquired were Hispanic more by origin than by content, consisting principally of works of Roman Catholic theology in Latin. The donation seems to have alerted Bodley to the importance of having a selection of books produced by and concerning what was then seen as England's greatest enemy: the Roman Catholic Church, and its chief supporter, Habsburg Spain, which at that time included Portugal and the Indies. Bodley (and his first Librarian, the fiercely Puritan polemicist Thomas James) saw the new library as a centre of Protestant learning, and the English answer to the great Catholic libraries of Europe. The Librarian was therefore anxious to acquire new copies of the index of works condemned by the Spanish Inquisition with a view to using it as a desiderata list. An annotated 1629 example of the *Index* (published under the authority of Bishop Mascarenhas, in his capacity as Inquisitor-General) is held in Duke Humfrey's Library (B 21.20(2)Th).

After the peace treaty was signed in 1604, Bodley decided to send his own representative to Spain. In 1604 John Bill, a London bookseller, went to Seville on Bodley's behalf in search of books. He was able to arrange for a considerable consignment of Spanish books to be sent to Oxford, including one of only two extant copies of the first edition (1605) of Cervantes' *Don Quixote* (4° C 31 Art.).

Between 1600 and 1660 the Library received from three different sources the five Mexican codices now known as the Codex Bodley, Codex Laud, Codex Mendoza,

Codex Selden and the Selden Roll. These were for many years, and may still be, the most important group of such codices held by any library in the world. John Selden was a man of extraordinarily wide learning by the standards of his time, and seems to have been one of the first Englishmen to interest himself in Mexican civilisation. In addition to the three Mexican codices his library (of some 8,000 volumes) includes some early printing from New Spain (once again, principally theological). Two works bound together, both printed in Mexico by Pedro Ocharte in 1567, form an example: the *Doctrina christiana en lengua castellana y çapoteca* by Pedro de Feria, and the Dominican primer *Hore Beate Marie Virginis* (4° F3 Th. Seld.). All this material came to enrich the Library's collections and helped to raise the Bodleian to preeminence as a repository of early Mexican records.

During the remainder of the seventeenth century (and virtually the whole of the eighteenth) the Bodleian's Hispanic holdings remained in a state of suspended animation. The mid-nineteenth century, however, witnessed a renaissance in the collection of Spanish, Portuguese and Latin American materials. 1848 saw the opening of the second major Oxford library to collect Hispanic materials: that of the Taylor Institution, established following the bequest of Sir Robert Taylor for the teaching of modern European languages and literatures. The first teacher of Spanish took up his post in 1858, and over the next century the Taylor Institution Library came to acquire a representative selection of Spanish and Portuguese linguistics and literature. Indigenous languages of Latin America, together with works in any language on history or the social sciences, remained the responsibility of the Bodleian, but all literary works in Spanish or Portuguese were henceforth regarded as falling within the purview of the Taylorian.

The Bodleian had been collecting in the area of literature (notably at the sale of Robert Southey's books shortly after the poet's death). It is hardly surprising, though, that when George Ticknor, a notable authority on the Hispanic world, passed though Oxford in 1838, he had pronounced the Bodleian 'miserably deficient in Spanish literature'. Bulkeley Bandinel, Bodley's Librarian from 1813 to 1860, had tried to remedy the matter by purchasing more Spanish books, though once again mainly in the field of theology. To him we owe the *Mozarabic Breviary* and the famous Complutensian Polyglot Bible, both published at the command of Cardinal Jiménez de Cisneros, the Archbishop of Toledo (known to English readers as Ximenes). After the foundation of the Taylorian, the Bodleian was obviously determined to show its eminence in what it did collect: in 1843 the Library purchased for £8 a copy, wanting two leaves, of a grammar of the Milkayak and Alentiak languages by Luis de Valdivia, printed in Lima in 1607 (Arch. B. f. 43). By an extraordinary coincidence two leaves from this work were discovered between the pages of a Mexican book in Harvard University Library: they proved to be the very leaves wanting from the Bodleian copy, and – thanks to Harvard's generosity – are now back in their original place.

The general Western manuscript collections include many from medieval Spain, some finely illuminated, others of importance as texts, such as those relating to Alfonso of Castile and his court, and the early translations of Hispano-Arabic scientific treatises (for example MS. Bodl. 463, a manuscript which contains eleven texts translated into Latin, written in Spain *c.*1400 and which has been in Oxford since the mid-fifteenth century). The collection of J.P.R. Lyell includes, as well as medieval Spanish manuscripts, many historical documents and tracts relating to early modern Spain. Diaries of British travellers and papers of British diplomats and soldiers in Spain and Portugal survive in several of the collections. Although the earliest is William Wey's account of his pilgrimage to Santiago de Compostela around 1470 (MS. Bodl. 565), the majority date from the nineteenth century. They include letters and despatches of General Charles William Doyle while aiding the insurgents in Spain from 1808 to 1815 (MSS. North c. 13–15 and d. 64–5), papers of General Sir William Napier (1785–1860) relating to his service in and *History* of the Peninsular War, despatches of the 2nd Baron Howden as Minister Plenipotentiary in Madrid from 1850 to 1858, and the correspondence of the diplomat Sir John Crampton (1805–86). The most substantial series of diplomatic correspondence relating to Spain and Latin America in the nineteenth century are in the papers of the 4th Earl of Clarendon, Minister Plenipotentiary in Madrid in the 1830s and Foreign Secretary in the 1850s. One of the most unusual relics in the Bodleian collections is a fragment of cloth from the battle standard of Francisco Pizarro during his campaigns against the Inca Empire in the 1530s. It was cut from the flag in 1856 and presented to the British Minister in Colombia, who sent it on to Clarendon (MS. Res. f. 19).

The library received other Hispanic donations, like that of Edward King, Viscount Kingsborough, who presented to the Bodleian a coloured copy of his own magnificent though uncompleted *Antiquities of Mexico*, printed on vellum. In 1870, the Library acquired another of its Latin American treasures: the collection of Mexican pamphlets put together by Henry Ward Poole in Mexico City in 1861. This was after the suppression of the monasteries and convents, but before the French invasion of the 1862: the ideal time, in fact, to make such a collection. The forty-one volumes consist of nearly 1,500 pamphlets, dating from 1754 to 1841 (though the majority relate to the years 1820–1827, the decisive years for the establishment of the Mexican state). This collection alone makes the Library one of the major centres for the study of Mexican Independence pamphlets in general, and the works of José Joaquín Fernández de Lizardi in particular.

It was around this time that the Bodleian began collecting, as it does today, the important works published in the Hispanic world on all non-literary topics. Though the Copyright Act was amended too late for the Bodleian to acquire all the Ackermann publications of the 1820s and earlier, a great deal of time and money was spent in making up for the deficiency. Some effort seems to have been made in the Hispanic and Latin American area. In 1894 we have a note from the

Foreign Department of Parker's (the booksellers) to the then Librarian, E.W.B. Nicholson, referring to 'a list of about 30 books printed in S. America' which they had previously sent, and apologising for the high price of Errázuriz's 1881–1882 work *Seis años de la historia de Chile*: it was 34 shillings for a two-volume set. Similarly, an examination of the pre-1920 catalogue will show the strivings on the part of the Library's staff towards ensuring that the Bodleian holdings of materials published in the nineteenth century in Spanish and Portuguese were up to the standard found in other British universities.

In the early twentieth century most of the Bodleian's current acquisitions in the Hispanic area came not by purchase but by gift and exchange, from government departments, universities, banks and other similar institutions. Contact was made with most of the major libraries of Latin America, and profitable exchange agreements were reached with more than a dozen of them, as well as with similar Spanish and Portuguese institutions. In 1963 it was estimated that the Library held some 8,000 volumes from South and Central America alone, almost all in the fields of history, archaeology and social sciences.

In 1964 the Bodleian's Hispanic acquisitions were revolutionised, first by the setting up (with the financial aid of the Ford Foundation) of the Latin American Centre at St Antony's College, and secondly by the increased funding received by the University from the Parry Fund for Latin American Studies. The Centre rapidly built up its own small library, and also started a union catalogue of Latin American material in Oxford libraries, while the Bodleian's Latin American acquisitions also increased thanks to the additional funding.

The Bodleian and the Taylor Institution Libraries aim to collect extensively in the field of Spanish and Portuguese materials, and also wherever possible to make up previous deficiencies in the Hispanic field, caused by earlier lack of interest or lack of funds. Both libraries pay particular attention to those subject areas in which the University chooses to teach and research, though conversely most of the teaching and research is concentrated into those areas in which the libraries themselves are strong. An example is the case of the Mexican pamphlet collection: a previous Bodley's Librarian has commended the work of his predecessor H.O. Coxe, who was Librarian from 1860 to 1882: '[he] was ahead of his age and, as a University Librarian should, was leading opinion and assembling research material which future generations would value more highly than his own'. Over the last fifteen years more than 30,000 volumes from Spain, Portugal and Latin America have been added to the Library's collections, plus a considerable assortment of microfiches, CDs and tapes. In the same period, the Taylorian and other libraries have added more than 20,000 titles.

Select bibliography

Hispanic Manuscripts and Books before 1700 [exhibition catalogue] (Oxford: Bodleian Library, 1962).

A.R. Bonner, 'Mexican Pamphlets in the Bodleian Library', *Bodleian Library Record*, 8/4 (1970), 205–13.

Mexican Pictorial Manuscripts. (Bodleian Picture Books, special series 4; Oxford: Bodleian Library, 1972).

Colin Steele and Michael Costeloe (eds.), *Independent Mexico: A Collection of Mexican Pamphlets in the Bodleian Library* (London: Mansell, 1973).

Europeans in Latin America: Humboldt to Hudson [exhibition catalogue] (Oxford: Bodleian Library, 1980).

Spain in the Bodleian [exhibition catalogue] (Oxford: Bodleian Library, 1986).

18. Russia and
Eastern Europe

The Bodleian's collections of material from and dealing with Russia, the former USSR and Eastern Europe are probably the third largest in Britain after those at the British Library and the School of Slavonic and East European Studies (University College London). Taken together with other holdings in Oxford, notably those at the Taylor Institution Library and St Antony's College Russian and Eurasian Studies Centre, they form the largest concentration of resources in this field outside London.

The Bodleian has acquired printed and other material relating to Russia and Eastern Europe ever since the refoundation of the university library by Sir Thomas Bodley at the beginning of the seventeenth century. Acquisition was sporadic and unsystematic until at least the early years of the twentieth century, however. A small number of Russian books reached the library by donation and bequest during the seventeenth century, some publications of the Russian Imperial Academy of Sciences during the eighteenth, and several important collections (described below) during the nineteenth. Regular receipt of some scholarly series and journals from Russia and Eastern Europe began in the late eighteenth century, but much of the Bodleian's very rich holdings of this type is the result of later retrospective acquisition. Some effort was made in the years after 1918 to acquire publications from the new states of Eastern Europe, and some important antiquarian material was obtained from the USSR during the same period. Following the recommendations of the Scarbrough Report in 1947 (confirmed by the Hayter Report of 1961), Oxford was designated as a centre for Slavonic and East European studies, and acquisition was much expanded with the help of special grants.

Publications of a scholarly standard relating to Russia and all East European countries are now acquired as extensively as funds permit in the following main subjects: history (including local, cultural and economic history); politics and government; historical geography; bibliography, libraries, archives and publishing; and general works of reference. More selective acquisition is made in sociology; statistics and demography; economics; fine arts and music; philosophy; religion; law (at the Bodleian Law Library); and Oriental studies. The Bodleian does not in principle collect material in Slavonic or other East European linguistic or literary studies (except, for historical reasons, Hungarian), leaving this responsibility to the Taylor Institution Library. First priority is given to obtaining adequate coverage of newly published titles, but older material has been widely acquired by donation, exchange and purchase, including many important items and sets in microform, especially of historical documents and publications. There is much contemporary documentation of current events throughout the area from the early years of the Cold War onwards, including longs runs of press summaries from several British embassies in Eastern Europe; many of the Radio Free Europe and Radio Liberty report series; and the broadcast monitoring reports of the BBC and (in the 1990s) the US Foreign Broadcast Information Service. Efforts are made to collect by similar criteria from all countries in the area, in all the published vernacular languages. Scholarly publishing in Western languages relating to the area is also acquired extensively, and the process of legal deposit ensures the near-comprehensive acquisition of relevant British books and journals.

Holdings relating to Russia and Eastern Europe are estimated (in 2003) at around 190,000 book titles in European languages, with a further 25,000 in the non-European languages of the former USSR. Periodicals and other serials published in the countries concerned amount to over 2,000 current and about 5,000 discontinued titles. Between one-third and one-half of this stock falls within the broad field of historical studies. A widening range of online electronic data services bearing on Russian and East European studies is accessible through the Bodleian and other libraries in the University.

Russia and the former USSR

Holdings of pre-nineteenth-century Russian books and manuscripts are very miscellaneous in provenance and character, although they do include some important items. The library has the microfilm series *Sixteenth and Seventeenth Century Russian Books*, and is receiving the companion series *Eighteenth Century Russian Books*. From the mid-nineteenth century, complete or near-complete runs of most Russian historical and general cultural journals and of academy and learned society series are held. (They are complemented by others at the Taylor Institution Library.) Scholarly monographs on Russian history and related topics are very well represented from about the same point; and the donation of the historian Nikolai Dejevsky in 1996 gave the Bodleian the leading UK collection on Russian medieval history. Holdings of Russian official publications from the pre-1917 period are numerous but by no means comprehensive; among other items, proceedings of the Duma and State Council, treaty series, some statistics, and the major legislative collections (the latter at the Bodleian Law Library) are present. Russian bibliography, archaeology, geography and religion are other subjects well covered by nineteenth- and early twentieth-century holdings. Religion in particular is strengthened by the Birkbeck Collection of nearly 300 volumes on the Russian Church, which also contains an Ostrog Bible. Another interesting collection is of newspaper issues and satirical journals from the years 1904–1906. The Library also holds in photocopy many of the papers of Charles Sydney Gibbes (1876–1963), English tutor to the last Tsarevich.

A special effort has been made to obtain publications from 1917 and the immediate post-Revolutionary years, but holdings are still patchy, although many of the major scholarly journals are well represented. Russian émigré publications of academic value were acquired fairly extensively from the 1920s onwards. Between the two world wars the scope of selection expanded although some subjects, such as economics, planning, law and music, still received relatively little attention. Selection was again enlarged from the late 1940s onwards as described above. Long runs of several major Soviet newspapers were maintained on microfilm until the mid-1990s. Until the end of the Soviet period special attention was given to Communist Party documents and other official materials, and to published collections of *samizdat* material. Since then particular emphasis has been placed on obtaining published work which draws on, or reproduces, archival and other material not accessible during the Soviet era. The Library has also formed one of the largest collections in the UK of specimen issues and short runs of the 'parallel press' from the late 1980s and early 1990s.

Material from the non-Russian republics of the former USSR is largely of post-1945 origin, with the exception of that from the Baltic States (*see section below*). Publications in Ukrainian (including scholarly émigré publications), Belorussian and Moldavian have been collected since the 1950s under similar criteria to those in Russian. The Library is exceptionally rich in works on the Caucasus region, especially Georgia. These are described in the chapter on Near and Middle Eastern Studies.

Baltic States

For the period up to 1918, holdings published in the Baltic area are somewhat miscellaneous in character, but include some substantial sets of publications such as those of the Lettische Literaerische Gesellschaft (from 1830), the Gelehrte Estnische Gesellschaft (from 1846) and the University of Dorpat (from 1893). There are over 450 titles published in the area before 1920, among them about 40 Vilnius books from the sixteenth and seventeenth centuries. From the interwar period of independence (1918–40) some official publications of all three countries are held, including good coverage of Latvian and Estonian statistical material; series from Tartu and Riga; and some titles from Vilnius (then in Poland) in Polish. From the late 1950s onwards, coverage has been similar to that for the rest of the former USSR.

Poland

An outstanding element in the Bodleian's Polish holdings is the Libri Polonici collection, formerly the library of the historian Józef Łukaszewicz (1799–1873), which contains many rare items. It consists of over 1,700 titles, about 800 of them in Polish, published between the early sixteenth and early nineteenth centuries, most of them with a bearing on Polish history, culture and religion. From the nineteenth century to 1945, holdings of Polish publications are uneven, although learned society and academy publications are present in long runs (including most wartime publications of the Polish Academy), along with many scholarly monographs, especially in history, and a certain number of official publications, including statistics. Selection expanded after the Second World War, to reach its present scope in the early 1960s. The collection was further strengthened by the donation of *c.* 1,000 volumes of Polonica in 1983 by Dr Maria Danilewicz-Zielińska. The Library has an extensive collection of Polish Parliamentary papers, and long runs of major newspapers are held up to the late 1990s. Unofficial and clandestine publications of the 1980s are extensively covered (partly in reproductions). Holdings of Polish publishing in the UK since the early years of the Second World War are close to comprehensive, and émigré works from other countries have also been acquired.

Czech and Slovak Republics

The library has a few mediaeval manuscripts and some early printed books from Bohemia. There is a notably wide range of Czech and German-language serials from the early nineteenth (and in a few cases the eighteenth) century onwards. The publications of the main learned societies, academies, museums and universities are well covered from the nineteenth century, as is scholarly monographic literature in history, bibliography and music. Holdings relating to Czech and Slovak history, politics and society from 1918 onwards are probably the foremost in the UK. They include much material from the former Comenius Library at the University of Lancaster, transferred in 1983, and strongly feature Tomáš Masaryk and Edvard Beneš. Post-war publications in both Czech and Slovak have been acquired very widely, including Parliamentary papers and long runs of major newspapers (maintained until the late 1990s). Special attention has been devoted to the period 1967–1970, and there is near-exhaustive coverage of Czechoslovak émigré publishing between 1968 and 1989.

Hungary

Hungarian printed books from the seventeenth century onwards are held. The special collection known as the Libri Hungarici contains 416 volumes published largely between 1700 and 1830, with Latin ecclesiastical history and topography well represented. Coverage up to the early twentieth century is not extensive, although some academy series are present and the main bibliographical and legal series are held in full, as well as Parliamentary papers for the period 1920–1944. Efforts have been made since 1970 to fill the more important gaps in holdings of historical writing, and selection of post-1945 works did not reach its present scope until that point. It now includes a representative amount of classical and modern Hungarian literature as well as the subjects listed in the introduction to this chapter. The Bodleian holds much of the library and many of the papers of the historian C.A. Macartney, dealing largely with the history and politics of Hungary, the Habsburg Empire and the Danube Basin. There is also a collection of press-cuttings and typescripts on events in Hungary between 1945 and 1960.

Yugoslavia and successor states

Holdings of pre-twentieth-century publications from the countries formerly comprising Yugoslavia are scanty, although a few South Slavonic manuscripts and early printed books have reached the library by a variety of routes. Croatian and Serbian academy series are held from the second half of the nineteenth century onwards, and some other scholarly journals from that period and the early twentieth century. There is some historical literature and statistical material from the period between the two world wars. Post-1945 (and particularly post-1960) publishing from all the Yugoslav republics and their independent successors is well covered and includes large numbers of scholarly series. Special attention has been paid to representing all viewpoints on the breakup of the federation since the early 1990s.

Romania

The very small number of pre-nineteenth-century books and manuscripts from Romania includes a notable fifteenth-century illuminated Gospel manuscript from Moldavia (MS. Canon. Gr. 122). A few university and academy series begin in the late nineteenth and early twentieth centuries, but apart from these and a small number of scholarly journals, coverage of the inter-war period is thin. From the 1960s onwards, acquisition has been on the wide basis described above, and until the mid-1990s included Parliamentary papers and long runs of major newspapers.

Bulgaria

Serial publications of Sofia University, and statistical and legislative series, begin in the late nineteenth and early twentieth centuries, and the various series published by the Bulgarian Academy of Sciences mostly somewhat later. There has been considerable retrospective acquisition of scholarly works on Bulgarian history published from the late nineteenth century onwards. Post-1945 monographs and serials are well represented, especially from 1970 onwards.

Albania

There are a small number of books from the first years of Albanian independence (1912–39) and – in Italian – from the subsequent period of Italian occupation. The Library has aimed at a generous coverage of the limited range of Albanian scholarly literature published from the 1960s onwards, as well as acquiring official and political documentation. The emphasis is on history and political events.

Select bibliography

P.A. Syrku, 'Zametki o slavianskikh i russkikh rukopisiakh v Bodleian Library v Oksforde', *Izviestiia Otdieleniia russkago iazyka i slovesnosti Imperatorskoi akademii nauk*, 7/4 (1902), 325–49; and 12/4 (1907), 87–140.

J.D.A. Barnicot, 'The Slavonic Manuscripts in the Bodleian', *Bodleian Library Record*, 1/2 (1938), 30–33.

J.D.A. Barnicot and J.S.G. Simmons, 'Some Unrecorded Early-Printed Slavonic Books in English Libraries', *Oxford Slavonic Papers*, 2 (1952), 98–118.

J.S.G. Simmons and B.O. Unbegaun, 'Slavonic Manuscript Vocabularies in the Bodleian Library', *Oxford Slavonic Papers*, 2 (1952), 119–127.

M. Tadin, 'Glagolitic Manuscripts in the Bodleian Library, Oxford', *Oxford Slavonic Papers*, 4 (1953), 151–8; and 5 (1954), 133–44.

J.S.G. Simmons, 'Slavonic Books in Oxford Libraries', *Solanus*, 2 (1967), 6–10.

V.M. Du Feu and J.S.G. Simmons, 'Early Russian Abcedaria in Oxford and London', *Oxford Slavonic Papers*, n.s.3 (1970), 119–33.

R. Auty, 'Sixteenth-Century Croatian Glagolitic Books in the Bodleian Library', *Oxford Slavonic Papers*, n.s.11 (1978), 130–5.

R.J.W. Evans, 'Hungarica in the Bodleian: A Historical Sketch', *Bodleian Library Record*, 9/6 (1978), 333–45.

Janet M. Hartley, *Guide to Documents and Manuscripts in the United Kingdom relating to Russia and the Soviet Union* (London: Mansell, 1987), 345–58.

Ralph Cleminson, *A Union Catalogue of Cyrillic Manuscripts in British and Irish Collections* (London: School of Slavonic & East European Studies, 1988), 218–306.

Russian Books from the Bodleian's Pre-1920 Catalogue (Oxford: Bodleian Library, 1990).

Zofia Florczak, 'Libri Polonici, a Special Collection in the Bodleian Library', *Bodleian Library Record*, 14/3 (1992), 207–27.

Polonica from the Bodleian's Pre-1920 Catalogue (Oxford: Bodleian Library, 1994).

Ralph Cleminson et al., *Cyrillic Books Printed before 1701 in British and Irish Collections: A Union Catalogue* (London: The British Library, 2001).

19. Near and Middle East

Hebrew, Yiddish, Aramaic and Ancient Egyptian collections

Hebrew

In what is known as a triangle of Hebrew collections, comprising London, Oxford and Cambridge, there exists the world's richest treasure of Hebrew manuscripts and printed books. In this context the Bodleian possesses what is probably still the most important collection of Hebrew manuscripts in the world as well as an extraordinarily rich collection of Hebrew printed books. Unusually, the interest in Hebrew books stems directly from the founder of the Library, Sir Thomas Bodley.

At first sight, it may seem odd that such a substantial collection of Jewish books should have been started around 1600, when officially at least there were no Jews in England. However, Bodley was an accomplished linguist who knew the classical and modern languages 'but Hebrew particularly, the parent of all the others'. It is astonishing how many Hebrew books are listed in the first catalogue of the library (1605) with 58 of them given their titles in Hebrew script; they are overwhelmingly from Venice, where Hebrew printing was then in its prime. Bodley took a detailed personal interest in them, and at the end of the catalogue a page largely in Latin shows his own indignant corrections of some misprints in Hebrew.

After Bodley's death the Library continued to enrich the Hebrew collections. In 1692 it purchased the collections of Dr Robert Huntington and Professor Edward Pococke, the Regius Professor of Hebrew. Among the 212 Hebrew manuscripts bought from Huntington is the *Mishneh Torah* of Maimonides (1135–1204) with the author's signature (MS. Huntington 80), attesting that the text had been corrected against his original. This manuscript is supremely important both for historical reasons and for the accuracy of its text. Huntington bought it while acting as chaplain to the English merchants in Aleppo.

In 1829 the Bodleian bought the Oppenheimer Library, thought to be the most important and magnificent Hebraica collection ever accumulated. Rabbi David ben Abraham Oppenheimer (1664–1736) was the Chief Rabbi of Prague, and devoted more than half a century to building up his library. A bibliophile from his early youth, he went on long journeys to obtain rare manuscripts with a view to subsidising their publication. The collection, which comprises 780 manuscripts and 4,220 printed books in Hebrew, Yiddish and Aramaic, is particularly famous for its early printed Hebrew and Yiddish books, many of which are the only surviving copies known. Oppenheimer specialised in collecting books printed on parchment, and commissioned printers to produce copies on parchment especially for his collection.

During the second half of the nineteenth century, the Library had the good fortune to have on its staff two of the greatest Hebraists of their time, Dr Moritz Steinschneider (1816–1907) and Dr Adolf Neubauer (1831–1907). Their great catalogues of, respectively, Hebrew printed books and manuscripts in the Bodleian remain standard works for the study of Hebraica. All the Hebrew manuscripts have been microfilmed by the Institute for Microfilmed Hebrew Manuscripts in Jerusalem, and staff of the Institute contributed significantly to the *Supplement of Addenda* to Volume I of Neubauer's catalogue, published in 1994 (*see Select bibliography*). Further significant collections of Hebrew manuscripts were added in 1848, 1890 and 1981, while many incunabula were acquired in Victorian times. The Library continues to select and acquire hundreds of the latest Hebrew and Yiddish books from Israel (and to a lesser extent elsewhere) every year. Consequently there is an unbroken tradition of collecting Hebrew books from Bodley's time to the present. The situation described in the *Annals of the Bodleian Library* for 1829 – that the collection is 'never without several foreign visitors engaged in its examination' – still applies. The great Hebrew collection appears to have been amassed by following a middle way between the courses of, on the one hand, collecting everything available and, on the other, forming merely a selection of material in the various subjects. By modern standards it was relatively easy to acquire Hebrew books in the early days of the Library, particularly from the major centres of Hebrew printing such as Venice and, later, Amsterdam. Works from centres such as Cracow and Salonica were also acquired.

As we have already seen in the case of Huntington's activities in Aleppo, Oxford alumni were often able to direct Hebrew collections to the Bodleian. In the case of the bequest of John Selden in 1654, however, only 'such Rabbinical and Talmudical printed books as were not already in the Library' were brought from London to Oxford. Before his impeachment in 1640, Archbishop Laud took pains to send the Library four consignments of manuscripts, in all nearly 1,300, many of which are in Hebrew and cognate languages.

By no means all collections came from alumni. Matteo Luigi Canonici, a Venetian Jesuit, had originally intended his collection of manuscripts for the Jesuits' college at Venice. But as the Society of Jesus remained suppressed at the time of his death in 1805 and he died intestate, the bulk of his manuscripts were purchased by the Bodleian in 1817, up to then the largest single purchase ever made by the Library. The collection contains over 110 valuable Hebrew manuscripts, chiefly on vellum. The purchase in 1829 of the Oppenheimer Library has been described above. In 1848, also at Hamburg, another collection of Hebrew manuscripts was purchased. This was the library of Heimann Joseph Michael, numbering 862 volumes and nearly 1,300 separate works. He was the author of an encyclopaedic work on medieval Jewish scholars, reprinted as recently as 1965, and corresponded in a lively and attractive Hebrew with the Jewish scholars of his own time.

The most recent acquisition of Hebrew manuscripts of major international importance was the purchase of fragments from the Cairo Genizah, beginning in 1890. A genizah is usually a room attached to a synagogue used for storing texts which were worn out and had become unusable; in this case the genizah was in the attic of the Ezra synagogue in Old Cairo. An enormous number, over 200,000, of fragments in Hebrew, Judaeo-Arabic and Yiddish were kept there, which are now somewhat chaotically dispersed in over 25 public and private libraries in many countries. Cambridge, with over 150,000 fragments, has the majority of them, while 25,000 are in New York, 10,000 in Manchester, and 5,000 each in the British Library and the Bodleian. Other collections are in Russia, Israel and elsewhere.

Yiddish

Yiddish, which seems to be a tenth-century combination of medieval German city dialects written in Hebrew script, became the spoken language of most Jews over a vast area of Europe and beyond. In writing, it had an inferior status to Hebrew and was chiefly used to address women, children and males ignorant of Hebrew; significantly, the first book printed in Yiddish (Cracow, 1534) is a translation of difficult phrases in biblical Hebrew. For the same reason, early books in Yiddish were badly printed and ephemeral, and so have survived if at all in very few copies. One of the few bibliophiles to collect these objects systematically was Rabbi David Oppenheimer (see above) so that the Bodleian finds itself with a very important collection of early Yiddish printed books, in many cases holding the only surviving copy.

Later, because of its proletarian status, Yiddish was the natural choice of language for the propagation of socialism. The donation of the library of the US daily Yiddish newspaper *Morning Freiheit*, founded in 1922 by the Jewish section of the American Communist Party, gave the Bodleian an extensive representation of the rich Socialist literature of the later nineteenth century and the first half of the twentieth. This was a totally loyal Stalinist mouthpiece, a viewpoint which is apparent in its library. However, since such organs are dying out (like the language itself), the Bodleian is unlikely to be able to add significantly to the collection in future.

Aramaic

Aramaic features prominently in the works described above as Hebrew, partly because they are similar languages and authors change from one to the other even in mid-sentence. The Bodleian possesses a unique series of documents in Aramaic written on leather; nothing definite is known of their origin, but they were acquired by the Bodleian in 1943–4. They are undated, but belong somewhere in the fifth century B.C.

Egyptian and Coptic

The Bodleian has a small but interesting collection of over one hundred Egyptian papyri containing texts in all three written forms of the Egyptian language: hieroglyphic, hieratic and demotic. The Egyptian papyri are among the earliest written records in the Library. The oldest, a marriage contract, bears the date 527 B.C. A notable group within the collection is represented by fifteen funerary papyri. In addition there are a number of ritual texts and a handful of mummy wrappings. Some of the funerary papyri formed part of the bequest of the antiquary Francis Douce (1757–1834), making them the Library's first Egyptian accessions. Later in the nineteenth century papyri were purchased from, and given by, Archibald Henry Sayce (1845–1933), professor of Assyriology at Oxford, and the Rev. Greville John Chester (1831–92). In 1912 the Rev. Vivian Eccles Skrine gave a small group of papyri of which several are funerary compositions. The large number of fragments of burnt papyri, mostly demotic, found by Flinders Petrie in 1884 at Tanis, form another component of the collection. They were given to the Library in 1918 by the Egypt Exploration Fund.

The Coptic language made its first appearance in the Bodleian in the seventeenth century when 23 manuscripts came in 1685 as part of the bequest of Thomas Marshall, Rector of Lincoln College and Dean of Gloucester. A further 29 were received in 1693 with the purchase of Robert Huntington's Oriental manuscripts. These manuscripts are mainly biblical and liturgical, with a number of lexicographical and grammatical works. The most famous Coptic manuscript in the Library is the so-called Codex Brucianus (MS. Bruce 96), a papyrus codex containing Gnostic compositions, which James Bruce had bought in Upper Egypt around 1769, and which was purchased by the Bodleian, with the rest of his collection of manuscripts, in 1843. In 1885 the Delegates of the Clarendon Press deposited in the Bodleian the Coptic portion of the library of the Coptic scholar Charles Godfrey Woide, which they had purchased on his death in 1790. Five volumes of this library contain Sahidic fragments dating from as early as the seventh century. The remainder of Woide's collection contains his correspondence, transcripts and collations. Another scholar whose manuscripts found their way into the Library, this time via the Radcliffe Trustees, was the German Paul Ernst Jablonski (1693–1757); five volumes of his were deposited by the Trustees in 1894.

As with the Egyptian papyri, miscellaneous Coptic fragments were acquired from Professor Sayce and the Rev. G.J. Chester towards the end of the nineteenth century, and through the former's bequest of 1933. In 1908 the Library took possession of the whole of the find made during the excavations at Deir el-Bala'izah by Flinders

Petrie in the previous year. This collection, dating from the sixth to eighth centuries, represents the remains of the library and charter-room of the Coptic monastery of St Apollo at Deir el-Bala'izah in Egypt's Western Desert. It is estimated that the material contains fragments of over 3,000 texts – the Bible, liturgies, homilies, lives of the saints as well as taxation receipts and monastic accounts.

The Library's first Coptic acquisitions are described by J. Uri (1787) in his catalogue of the Bodleian's Oriental manuscripts. Woide's Sahidic fragments were catalogued by Henry Hyvernat in 1887. The catalogue remains in manuscript and is available to readers in the Oriental Reading Room. The collection of Coptic texts from Deir el-Bala'izah was edited by Paul E. Kahle and published in 1954.

The Bodleian's holdings of Egyptian and Coptic-related printed material is fairly modest, especially when compared with the richness of the library of the nearby Griffith Institute, which boasts 20,000 volumes on Egypt and the ancient Near East. But the Bodleian has many early European works on the Egyptian and Coptic languages and currently acquires books and a number of serials relating to all periods of the language and literature of Egypt, including text editions.

The Christian Orient

Armenian

Although the Armenian collections were not systematically developed until the mid-twentieth century, Armenian materials were collected from the seventeenth century and the Bodleian has amassed significant holdings relating to Armenian culture, religion, history, literature (particularly classical Armenian literature), art and archaeology, along with good coverage of Soviet Armenia. Efforts are also made to ensure that the literature of the Armenian diaspora (particularly in Lebanon and Iran) is properly represented. Attention is now focussed on building up the collections of the post-Soviet period.

The earliest Armenian donations were the manuscripts presented by Archbishop Laud in 1635. Other early acquisitions of manuscripts include some from Thomas Marshall in 1685, from Edward Pococke in 1692 and Narcissus Marsh in 1713. The real expansion of the collection came with the librarianship of Nicholson in the late nineteenth century, who acquired among other items an antiphonary of 1296 (MS. Arm. f. 22), the earliest dated Armenian manuscript held by the Library. By 1918, 124 Armenian manuscripts were held and some 18 manuscripts have been acquired since then but the collection remains essentially a modest one.

The earlier Armenian printed books are scattered among twelve or more of the famous collections acquired by the Library, such as the Selden (acquired 1659), Marshall (acquired 1685) and Douce (acquired 1834) collections. Archbishop Laud's 1636 benefaction included an Armenian printed book, the Venice Psalter of 1587. The earliest record of the purchase of an Armenian printed book is in 1673, when the Amsterdam editions of the Bible of 1666 and 1673 were acquired. Among the Armenian printed items in the Pococke collection, which had been acquired in 1693, a hitherto unknown edition of the Psalms was discovered in 1969. It was printed in New Julfa, Iran in 1638 – the only known copy of the first book to be printed in Iran. In 1707, when visiting Oxford, Archbishop Thomas Vanandetsi presented to the Library a collection of Armenian works printed at his Amsterdam press. Many of the nineteenth-century books came from the collection of S.C. Malan, donated to the Indian Institute Library in 1883. During the early part of the twentieth century, the acquisition of Armenian books remained slow and sporadic. In the 1950s and 1960s efforts were made to fill some of the gaps, and many of the publications of the Mechitarists of Venice and Vienna were purchased at this time. Between 1965 and 1992 specialist staff enabled exchanges to be set up with the principal libraries in Soviet Armenia and at that time about 200 publications were acquired annually. After a decade when collecting activity was dormant, acquisitions activity has been resumed, with the aim of developing a representative collection to support the University's Armenian studies programme, and filling gaps in the historic collections as far as possible.

Georgian

The nucleus of the Library's rich holdings of Georgian books and manuscripts is the Wardrop Collection, formed by Sir Oliver Wardrop, consular official and Georgian scholar, and his sister Marjory, a notable Georgian scholar in her own right. After Marjory's early death in 1909, the Marjory Wardrop Fund was founded for the encouragement of Georgian studies and from 1910, through this fund, the Bodleian became the beneficiary of all Marjory's papers, books and manuscripts. These were supplemented by further donations from Sir Oliver until his death in 1948. In this way the library has become the major European repository of Georgian material outside Russia. Most of the Wardrop manuscripts are from the eighteenth century or later, and in addition to important literary, ecclesiastical, historical and legal texts include the extensive personal papers, correspondence and photographs of the Wardrops, dating roughly from the late 1880s to the late 1940s. Both brother and sister were enthusiastic correspondents and Marjory maintained contact in Georgian with many of Georgia's leading writers, poets and scholars of the time. Non-Wardrop Georgian manuscripts include a valuable *menologion* (Lives of the Saints) copied in Jerusalem in 1038–40 (MS. Georg. b. 1). The Georgian printed books collection comprises books in Georgian, including many rare early editions, and titles relating to Georgian and Caucasian studies in other languages, and gives outstanding coverage in both categories up to 1917. It has since been added to selectively, especially 1960–1990, when an exchange programme was in effect. Today the collection is enhanced intermittently but steadily.

Ethiopic

The collection of Ethiopian manuscripts in the Bodleian now contains some 130 items. As the number of such texts in European collections, public and private, is very considerable, the Bodleian's holdings are not, with the exception of one group, particularly outstanding. A period of study at the Escorial caused 'that full-blooded but unveracious Scot, James Bruce' (to quote Craster) to begin collecting Abyssinian manuscripts. His collection of 25 Ethiopic manuscripts is both artistically and textually out of the ordinary; Ullendorff describes them as 'fine volumes' and one is a rare text of Enoch. The collection was purchased in 1843. In 2002, an unusual illustrated seventeenth-century manuscript of a Marian text, *Arganona weddase* ('Harp of Praise') (MS. Aeth. e. 28), was added to the collection.

Syriac

There is a vast literature in Syriac, enlarged by many translations from Greek. As early as 1864, when the main catalogue for Syriac manuscripts was printed, the Bodleian possessed 205 codices. As many of these contain several items the number of works is much larger; there have also been later additions. Most of the manuscripts arrived in the Library as donations, often from the same sources, such as Laud and Huntington, as the Hebrew manuscripts. Syriac has also given rise to two other bodies of literature. Karshuni is the Arabic language written in Syriac script. Mandaean is a development of Syriac used chiefly for magical texts of which, in the Drower Collection, the Bodleian Library is the world's foremost repository.

Islamic collections

Manuscripts

The opening of the Bodleian Library at the beginning of the seventeenth century coincided with a period of increasing scholarly interest in Oriental studies in England and Europe. Arabic studies in particular were cultivated for a variety of reasons, and Oxford University, with its newly refurbished library, played a major role in this intellectual trend. By the second decade of the eighteenth century the Library already possessed over 1,500 Arabic manuscripts, together with a smaller number in Persian and Turkish. These foundation collections remain the centrepiece of the Bodleian's Arabic and Islamic resources. They comprise manuscripts as opposed to printed books: it was to be some two centuries before printing with moveable type became widespread in the Near East.

In 1602, when the Bodleian opened, it already numbered among its holdings a manuscript of the Koran, and a Persian and a Turkish manuscript were received by gift in the same year. The Library's founder was keen to encourage the acquisition of Near Eastern manuscripts and to this end he approached Paul Pindar, consul of the English merchants in Aleppo, Syria. Pindar's efforts on behalf of the Library were only modestly successful, however, and at the time of Bodley's death in 1613, Arabic and Islamic holdings remained fairly insubstantial.

Matters improved considerably when William Laud, as Chancellor of the University, lent his patronage to the acquisition of Oriental materials for the Library and the promotion of Oriental studies within the University. Among the several donations Laud made to the Library between 1635 and 1640 there were some 147 Arabic and 74 Persian and Turkish manuscripts. The Laudian Oriental collection, though somewhat eclectic, includes representatives of most branches of traditional Islamic scholarship, and even an illustrated Persian manuscript, something of a rarity in Europe at that time. In 1640 the Library received the small collection of Oriental manuscripts of Sir Kenelm Digby, and over 150 manuscripts in Arabic, Persian and Turkish came into the Library in 1659 with the bequest of John Selden. In 1678 the library bought the collection of the Orientalist Thomas Greaves and his brother John. John Greaves was Professor of Geometry at Gresham College and was later the Savilian Professor of Astronomy at Oxford. He was thoroughly conversant with the Islamic tradition of astronomy and spent time in Constantinople and Egypt pursuing his antiquarian and astronomical interests. In addition to collecting Arabic and Persian manuscripts for himself, Greaves also played a significant part in obtaining manuscripts for the Library on behalf of Laud. He was interested in Persian as well as Arabic and compiled a Persian grammar. Among his Persian manuscripts are the star tables of Ulugh Beg and an illustrated copy of the poetical romance *Yusuf u Zulaykha* by the poet Jami (MS. Greaves 1).

In 1692 the Bodleian purchased the magnificent collection of Oriental manuscripts belonging to Edward Pococke. Pococke (1604–91), who was the first incumbent of the Laudian Chair of Arabic at Oxford, spent five years in Aleppo as chaplain to the Levant Company and a further three years in Constantinople. He was the leading Arabist of his time in England and a discerning collector. His collection of over 400 volumes is largely Arabic but includes some one hundred Hebrew and a handful of both Persian and Turkish manuscripts. It is strong in the areas of history, philology, literature and philosophy. Among the treasures of his collection are the *Book of Roger* by al-Idrisi (dated 1553) (MS. Pococke 375), with its attractive world and regional maps, and the charmingly illustrated animal fables of Bidpai, copied in Syria in 1354 (MS. Pococke 400). In the same year as the Pococke purchase was made, the small collection of Arabic and Persian manuscripts of Thomas Hyde was acquired. Hyde, in addition to his academic appointments, held the post of Bodley's Librarian from 1665 until 1701, and clearly encouraged the acquisition of Oriental material for the Bodleian. Another important collection was acquired in 1693 when the Library bought the Near Eastern manuscripts of Robert Huntington (1637–1701). Huntington, a fellow of Merton College, had lived

XVIII. Mendelssohn, 'Hebrides' Overture

The final autograph score of Mendelssohn's 'Hebrides' Overture, with many revisions, written in London in 1832.

Purchased with the aid of the Heritage Lottery Fund in 2002
MS. M. Deneke Mendelssohn d.71, fol. 13r
See p. 83

XIX. 'Yankee Doodle'

English song sheet with the probable first music
edition of 'Yankee Doodle'. One of only three
known copies (and the only one in the UK), and
one of *c.* 5,000 eighteenth-century song sheets in
the Harding Collection.

Bequeathed by Walter Harding in 1973
Harding Mus. G. 70(3)
See p. 83

Pectoralia

Aqua pector. destillat.

℞ fol. Meliss. Month. Ling. Cerv. hod. broß. ā. M iiij. fl. Lamij
malv. famb. ā. M iiij. rad. symph. loß. limac. nund. loß.
alb. ovor. lbj. lact. vaccin. lbxv. vini Canar. lbij. destilla

W͞m Hoggersson ℞ pil. Styrac. ℥ij. f. pil. 24. cap. j. alt͞n. noct. urgent.
lact. afin. tostae.

S͞r Isaac Newton ℞ Linct: comm. ℥iiij.
fang. ℞ ag. lact. ℥ij. Prothor. ℥ß. Conf. Frac. ℥j. f. h.
℞ chel. Magy. ret ♄ Jacob. pil. ā. ℥ß. in chart: 4
lac. afin. ℞ ag. lact. ℥ijß. proth. ℥ß. syr. cap. ♃ dð mocou ā.
℥iiij. ℥ß. haust.
℞ Linct: com. ℥iiij.

M͞r Wyndham ℞ fol. bolon. Tußilag. ā. ℥j. fl. roriв. ℥ß. olib. craßo ♃ ℥j.
ol. anisi gtt. 8. f. ♃ craßo.
℞ olib. Succin. alb. ā. ℥ß. sp. Diatrag. frig. ℥ß. f. ♃ in chart. xxiiij.
℞ syr. ō moc. bals. ā. ℥iij. ag. limac. ℥ij.

XX. Dr Radcliffe's Prescription Book

Remedies for chest ailments recorded by Dr John
Radcliffe's steward, *c.* 1700, including his
prescription for Isaac Newton.

Purchased by the Radcliffe Library in 1902
Radcliffe Records A.3, p. 107
See p. 90

XXI. Franz Kafka, *Die Verwandlung*

One of the notebooks of Franz Kafka contains his famous short story *Die Verwandlung (Metamorphosis)*, written in November and December 1912 and published in 1915.

Deposited in 1969, and bequeathed by Gertrude Kaufmann in 1972 and Marianna Steiner in 2001
MS. Kafka 18A, fol. 1r
See p. 100

par amistiez bel sire la nos dunt.
que uos aidez de roll' le barun.
q uen rere guarde troner le pousui.
B en serat fait li quens guenes respunt.
puis se baiserent es uis 7 es mentuns.

A pres munt un paien climorins.
cler en riant a guenelun l'ad dit.
tenez mun heline unches meillor ne ui.
Si nos aidez de roll' li marchis.
par quel mesure le pousui hunir.
ben serat fait guenes respundit.
puis se baiserent es bûches 7 es uis. Aoi.

A tant uint la reine bramimunde
Jo uos aim mult sire dist ele al cunte.
car mult uos p̃set mi sire 7 tuit si hume.
a uostre feme enueierai dous nusches.
B ien iad or matices 7 iacunces.
e les ualent mielz q tut l'aueir de rume.
u re empere si bones ne uit unches.
I lles ad p̃set en sa boete les buret. Aoi.

I reis apelet maldüit sun tresorer.
l'aueir carlun est il apareilliez.
e oil respunt oil sire asez bien.
.V ii. c. cameilz d'or 7 argent cargiez.
e .xx. hostages des plus gentilz desuz cel. Aoi.

M arsilies l'anc guen par l'espalle.
Si ha dit mult par es ber e sage.
par cele lei que uos tenez plus salue

XXII. *La Chanson de Roland*

The earliest surviving manuscript of *La Chanson de Roland*, the greatest of the epic poems known as *chansons de geste*, was written in Anglo-Norman, almost certainly in England, around the second quarter of the twelfth century.

Given by Sir Kenelm Digby in 1634
MS. Digby 23, Part 2, fol.12r
See p. 102

XXIII. Giovanni Boccaccio, *Il Filocolo*

This manuscript of Boccaccio's vernacular romance
was written by Andreas de Laude in 1463-4 for
Lodovico III Gonzaga, Marquess of Mantua,
whose arms are in the centre of the border below
the miniature.

*From the library of Matteo Luigi Canonici, purchased
in 1817*
MS. Canon. Ital. 85, fol. 114v
See p. 108

XXIV. Miguel Cervantes, *El ingenioso hidalgo*
Don Quixote de la Mancha

This rare first edition (Madrid, 1605) of *Don Quixote* was one of over 400 books and manuscripts, many in French, Italian and Spanish, bought through the London bookseller, John Bill, with the Earl of Southampton's gift of £100.

Purchased in 1605
4º C 31 Art, title-page
See p. 110

XXV. Codex Laud

Codex Laud, one of three Mexican screenfolds in the Bodleian, depicts deities and the 260-day calendrical cycle called *tonalpohualli*, with appropriate rituals and offerings used in divination .

Given by William Laud, Archbishop of Canterbury, in 1636

MS. Laud Misc. 678, p. 9

See p. 110

XXVI. Moldavian Gospels

The oldest illuminated Moldavian manuscript, written in Bulgarian Church Slavonic at the monastery of Neamţ in 1429 for Princess Marina, wife of Prince Alexander the Good of Moldavia. A parallel text in Greek was added some 200 years later. The opening page of St Mark's Gospel is shown here.

From the library of Matteo Luigi Canonici, purchased in 1817
MS. Canon. Gr. 122, fols. 89v–90r
See p. 119

XXVII. Isaac ben Solomon ibn Sahula,
Meshal ha-Kadmoni

This Hebrew work, written in Spain in 1281, was intended to displace light literature such as *Kalila and Dimna* and the *Voyages of Sinbad the Sailor*. The illustrations here depict two seers addressing two kings.

From the library of Rabbi David Oppenheimer, purchased in 1829
MS. Oppenheimer 154, fols. 44b-45a
See p. 121

XXVIII. Gospels in Armenian

The verso of the first leaf contains a miniature of
the Last Judgement, with Christ enthroned. The
scales of justice are attended by an angel and several
demons. The miniature on the facing page
represents a nativity scene. The manuscript is dated
1596.

Purchased in 1972
MS. Arm. d. 25, fols. 1v-2r
See pp. 125, 175

XXIX. The Assemblies of Al-Hariri

Illustration accompanying the 46th Assembly, in which the protagonist meets with a schoolmaster instructing his pupils in the open air. The manuscript is dated 1337; its miniatures are fine examples of the book art of the Mamluke period.

From the collection of Narcissus Marsh, Archbishop of Armagh, bequeathed in 1713
MS. Marsh 458, fol. 116a
See pp. 129, 176

XXX. Nevai, *Alexander's Wall*

Mystics discoursing in a Turkish garden. The
volume is one of five forming the 'Quintet' of the
celebrated Central Asian poet and statesman. The
miniatures are in the Herat style. The set is dated
1485.

Given in 1859
MS. Elliott 339, fol. 95b
See pp. 129, 176

XXXI. Atasāhsrikāprajnāpāramitā

One of only three manuscripts that can be
identified as having come from the great Buddhist
monastic university of Nālandā in Bihar, India.
This eleventh-century Sanskrit Buddhist palm leaf
manuscript is written in fine Kutila script and has a
cycle of 18 miniatures illustrating scenes from the
life of the Buddha and various Buddhist deities.
These miniatures represent the high point of art
from the Pala dynasty.

Purchased in 1900
MS. Sansk. a. 7(R), fols. 187v, 188r
See pp. 136-7, 177

XXXII. Buddhist canonical texts

This eighteenth-century traditional Thai folding
book on *khoi* paper with ten paired paintings of
Buddhist scenes is an example of the finest quality
Thai art. The Pali text, written in *Kham*
compressed script, is from the Buddhist canon but
the paintings illustrate the *jataka* or birth tale of
the Buddha as Prince Janaka.

Probably purchased in the Gibson Craig sale, 1888
MS. Pali a. 27(R), fols. 14-15
See pp. 139, 178

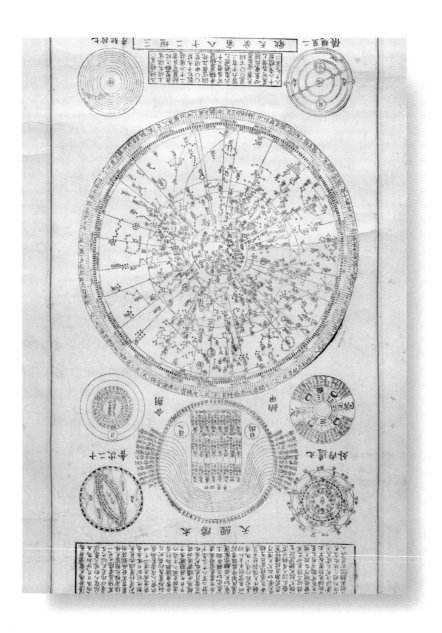

XXXIII. Chinese maps of the Earth and the Heavens

The maps *(Huang yu di tu kao, Tong hua jing wei tu kao)*, which are of unknown date, are presented as a pair of hanging scrolls, each having a map in the centre with text at top and bottom. They have an ephemeral quality, and appear to have been produced for the popular market, which would account for their rarity. They are possibly unique survivals.

Given by George White, East India merchant, in 1684
Sinica 123/1
See p. 141

and travelled in the Near East. His collection of over 600 volumes, which contains many rare and early items, includes a number of works of Christian content in Arabic, Coptic and Syriac, which reflect his interest in the Eastern Churches. His collection also includes over 200 Hebrew manuscripts. One of the many items worthy of mention is an illustrated twelfth-century manuscript on weaponry commissioned by Saladin for his own library (MS. Huntington 264).

In 1714 the Library received by bequest over 700 manuscripts belonging to Narcissus Marsh, Archbishop of Armagh and a fellow of Exeter College. This splendid addition to the Bodleian's holdings further consolidated the Library's position as the leading repository of Arabic and Islamic manuscripts in the country. Noteworthy among the Marsh manuscripts is the Arabic version of the *Conics* of the Greek geometer Apollonius of Perga (MS. Marsh 667). Dated 1070, this manuscript was used by the astronomer Edmund Halley for his 1710 edition of Apollonius's work. Another remarkable item is al-Sufi's *Book of Fixed Stars*, with its striking illustrations of the constellations. The manuscript bears a date equivalent to 1009, but appears to have been copied about 150 years later (MS. Marsh 144). In addition to astronomical and mathematical works the Marsh Collection contains many historical, literary, medical and philological manuscripts. It also contains two illustrated sixteenth-century Persian manuscripts (MSS. Marsh 431, 517).

By the end of the seventeenth century interest in Arabic studies had declined and during the eighteenth century few acquisitions were made after the Marsh bequest. At the end of the eighteenth century there were still fewer than 200 Persian manuscripts at the Bodleian but this figure increased dramatically during the following century when the Library acquired the magnificent collections of Sir William and Sir Gore Ouseley. Sir Gore went to India as a young man in 1787 for purposes of trade and whilst he was there began to learn Persian and collect manuscripts, both for himself and for his elder brother William. Sir Gore had an eye for illuminated and illustrated manuscripts, a taste which he was able to indulge during his embassy to Persia in the years 1810–14. William accompanied his brother on the mission and was able to enhance his own collection of several hundred Persian manuscripts which he had assembled in London. The Library purchased this collection in 1843, and in 1859 – through the donation of J.B. Elliott – it was joined by Sir Gore's, uniting the two Ouseley collections under the same roof. One of the many notable items is the fifteenth-century manuscript of Omar Khayyam's *Ruba'iyyat* on which the English poet Edward Fitzgerald based his famous composition of the same name (MS. Ouseley 140). Undoubtedly the most magnificent illustrated Persian manuscript is a copy of the poet Firdawsi's *Shah-namah*, copied at Shiraz in the 1430s (MS. Ouseley Add. 176). The work of the artists of the Indian Mughal courts is well represented in the Ouseley/Elliott collections and is referred to in the chapter on South Asia.

Although the Bodleian's Turkish manuscripts are fewer in number and generally less striking than their Arabic and Persian counterparts, they nonetheless include materials potentially important for research in Turkish language, literature and history. Outstanding in terms of artistic merit are the four magnificent volumes of the *Hamseh* ('Quintet') of the Central Asian poet Nevai (MSS. Elliott 287, 317, 339, 408). The manuscripts were copied in 1485 and one of the miniatures has been attributed to the master-painter Bihzad. An important manuscript in the genre of narrative literature is the *Bahtiyar-name* ('History of the Ten Viziers'), dated 1435 and written in Uighur script (MS. Huntington 598).

Other scholars and collectors whose Islamic manuscripts are now in the Bodleian are George Sale (*d.* 1736), the English translator of the Koran; James Fraser of the East India Company (*d.* 1754); the Scottish explorer James Bruce (1730–94); and General Alexander Walker, political resident in Baroda. The Bruce manuscripts were purchased in 1843 whilst the Walker manuscripts were presented in 1845. The Fraser and Sale collections were deposited in the Library by the Radcliffe Trustees in 1872. An interesting Arabic acquisition of the early nineteenth century is the seven-volume set of the *Arabian Nights* that Edward Wortley Montague had brought from Egypt, purchased by the Library in 1802 (MSS. Bodl. Or. 550–6). In 1878 and 1884 the Library acquired its first Arabic papyri from Egypt. The initial acquisitions were supplemented by later purchases that brought the number of pieces up to its present tally of over 90. The papyri are datable to the period from the eighth to the tenth century.

There were no large-scale accessions of Islamic manuscripts during the twentieth century, but a number of interesting items were acquired such as the illustrated Arabic version of the *Materia Medica* of Dioscorides bequeathed to the Library by Sir William Osler, Professor of Medicine, in 1926 (MS. Arab. d. 138). During the 1970s a substantial number of Turkish manuscripts was purchased, chiefly of literary and historical interest. In 2002 the Library was able to add to its Islamic scientific and cartographic holdings by purchasing – with the financial support of the Heritage Lottery Fund, the National Art Collections Fund, the Friends of the Bodleian and others – the remarkable, unique and newly discovered *Book of Curiosities*, a late twelfth- or early thirteenth-century Arabic manuscript containing a series of rare maps and astronomical diagrams (MS. Arab. c. 90). The Bodleian's holdings of Arabic manuscripts now (2003) stands at some 2,350 whilst the Persian manuscripts number 2,530 and the Turkish 480. Although these figures are not nearly as high as those of the British Library, or of several libraries in Europe, the Bodleian collections make up in quality for what they may lack in quantity. There are particular strengths in fields such as Arabic science, mathematics and medicine, and Persian illuminated and illustrated manuscripts form another outstanding group.

Printed books and other materials

The first book printed with Arabic moveable type bears the imprint Fano, 1514 (the Library has a copy (Vet. Or. f. Arab. 1)), and several first editions of Arabic works were printed in Europe rather than the Near East, notably by the Italian Medici Press at the end of the sixteenth century. The Bodleian is fortunate to have a number of their productions, as well as a comprehensive collection of books published by English and European Orientalists from the seventeenth century onwards. A printing press for Arabic type was first officially established in Constantinople by İbrahim Müteferrika, who printed a series of seventeen works between 1729 and 1742. The Library has originals of all but one of these. Among the collection referenced 'Elliott printed', the Library has a number of early printed items from India, mostly works of classical Persian literature printed lithographically in Bombay and Calcutta in the period 1825–1855. In 1870 a collection of 74 Arabic works (in some 150 volumes), printed at the government press at Boulak, Cairo, was given to the Library by the Khedive Ismail of Egypt through his son Prince Hassan, who was an undergraduate at the University. Among the earlier printed material is a selection of books printed lithographically in Fez, Morocco, at the end of the nineteenth and the beginning of the twentieth century. The Library's small collection of *Karamanlidika* (Turkish-language books printed in Greek characters) is also of some interest.

Today the Bodleian continues to collect scholarly books published in the Near East in Arabic, Persian and Turkish. Emphasis is laid on acquiring critical editions of texts composed during the classical period of Islamic civilisation, thereby building on the foundations of the manuscript resources. But modern studies are not neglected. Particularly in the case of Persian and Turkish materials, important works by established literary figures are collected in addition to significant works of modern history, economics, sociology and the arts (cinema and music). The present size (in 2003) of the printed collections is: Arabic 16,000 titles, Persian 6,500, and Turkish 17,500. The figure for Turkish includes works in Ottoman (a significant number) and other languages in the Turkic family. The Library also currently receives Western-language books and periodicals covering most aspects of the history and culture of the Islamic world. In the area of non-book materials, in 1994–5 the Library purchased microfilms, through the Library of Congress in Washington, of select manuscripts in the collections of St Catherine's Monastery on Mount Sinai and the Greek and Armenian Patriarchates in Jerusalem. Since 1988 the Bodleian has been the sole European repository of the Iranian Oral History Collection. The Collection, which is based at Harvard University's Center for Middle Eastern Studies, consists of taped interviews and transcripts with over one hundred politicians and other individuals who played significant roles in the political history of Iran during the period from the 1920s to the 1970s.

Central Asia

The Bodleian's holdings of manuscripts in the Eastern Turkish literary language of Central Asia known as Chagatay are referred to in the section on the Islamic collections, as is the Library's single example of a manuscript in Uighur script. Apart from these few, but important, manuscript items, the Central Asian collections consist exclusively of printed material. The development of Central Asian studies was closely linked to the expansion of the Russian Empire, which by the nineteenth century included large parts of Transcaucasia and Central Asia. Studies on the languages, literatures and history of the various peoples under Russian control began to appear in St Petersburg (the Imperial Academy of Sciences) and later in several Muslim cultural centres such as Kazan and Tashkent. The Library is fortunate to possess a number of these early productions. Following the 1917 Revolution in Russia, many languages in the region, which until then had existed only as spoken dialects, were promoted to literary status. Publications began in a whole range of 'new', mainly Turkic languages, for which, from the 1940s, modified versions of the Cyrillic alphabet were used. The Bodleian is one of only a small number of British libraries to have collected actively in this area.

From the period before the Second World War the Library has a selection of Central Asian items, for example a grammar of Turkmen (Ashkhabad, 1929) and a novel in Azerbaijani (Baku, 1938). During the 1960s the acquisition of Turkic-language and Tajik publications was put on a firmer basis, and from then until the break-up of the Soviet Union at the beginning of the 1990s the Library was successful in obtaining a considerable quantity of literary and linguistic monographs and journals in a large number of languages. The Library has publications in the following languages, arranged here in order of the size of their holdings: Azeri, Uzbek, Kazakh, Tajik, Turkmen, Kirgiz, Tatar, Bashkir, Chuvash, Uighur and Ossetian (an Iranian language). 'Uighur' includes publications from Kazakhstan, in Cyrillic script, and from the People's Republic of China, printed in a modified form of the Arabic script. There are smaller numbers of publications in miscellaneous other Turkic languages including Altai, Balkar, Crimean Tatar, Gagauz, Karachay, Karaim, Karakalpak, Khakass, Kipchak, Koibal, Kumyk, Nogay, Tuva and Yakut. The total number of titles in all these languages, and including Western-language related works (mainly Russian), is in the region of 10,000.

Select bibliography

Hebrew and Yiddish

M. Steinschneider, *Catalogus Librorum Hebraeorum in Bibliotheca Bodleiana* (Berolini: Friedlaender, 1852–1860).

A. Neubauer and A.E. Cowley, *Catalogue of the Hebrew Manuscripts in the Bodleian Library and in the College Libraries of Oxford* (2 vols. Catalogi Codd. MSS. Bibliothecae Bodleianae pars xii; Oxford: Clarendon Press, 1886–1906, repr. 1994).

A.E. Cowley, *A Concise Catalogue of the Hebrew Printed Books in the Bodleian Library* (Oxford: Clarendon Press, 1929).

A.E. Cowley, 'Additional Geniza Fragments' [*i.e.* fragments not recorded in A. Neubauer's *Catalogue*]. Unpublished typescript *c.* 1950, held in the Oriental Reading Room.

M. Lutzky, *Catalogue of Yiddish Printed Books (Until the Year 1800) Held in the Bodleian Library, Oxford and in the British Museum* (New York, 1954).

S. Brisman, 'A History and Guide to Judaic Bibliography', *Bibliographica Judaica*, 7 (1977), 36–73, 275–85.

M. Beit-Arié and R.A. May, *Catalogue of the Hebrew Manuscripts in the Bodleian Library: Supplement of Addenda and Corrigenda to Vol. I (A. Neubauer's Catalogue)* (Oxford: Clarendon Press, 1994).

B. Richler, *Guide to Hebrew Manuscript Collections* (Jerusalem: Israel Academy of Sciences and Humanities, 1994).

Aramaic

G.R. Driver, *Aramaic Documents of the Fifth Century B.C.* (Oxford: Clarendon Press, 1957).

B. Porten, *Textbook of Aramaic Documents from Ancient Egypt, Newly Copied, Edited and Translated into Hebrew and English* (Winona Lake, 1986–).

Egyptian and Coptic

Colin Wakefield, 'The Egyptian Papyri in the Bodleian Library', *Bodleian Library Record*, 14/1 (1991), 94–97.

Marc Coenen, 'The Egyptian Funerary Papyri in the Bodleian Library'. *Bodleian Library Record*, 16/6 (1999), 450–469.

Armenian

Sukias Baronian and F.C. Conybeare, *Catalogue of the Armenian Manuscripts in the Bodleian Library* (Oxford, 1918).

Vrej Nersessian, *Catalogue of Early Armenian Books 1512–1850* (London: The British Library, 1980).

Georgian

Gregory Peradze, 'Georgian Manuscripts in England'. *Georgica*, 1/1 (1935), 80–88.

D. M. Lang, 'Georgian Studies in Oxford'. *Oxford Slavonic Papers*, 6 (1955), 115–43.

David Barrett, *Catalogue of the Wardrop Collection and of other Georgian Books and Manuscripts in the Bodleian Library* ([Oxford]: Published for the Marjory Wardrop Fund by Oxford University Press, 1973).

Nino Wardrop, 'Oliver, Marjory and Georgia'. *Bodleian Library Record*, 14/6 (1994), 501–523.

Peter Nasmyth, *The Wardrops : A Legacy of Britain in Georgia* [exhibition catalogue] (Tbilisi : British Council, 1998).

Ethiopic

A. Dillmann, *Catalogus Codicum Manuscriptorum Bibliothecae Bodleianae Oxoniensis, pars vii. Codices Aethiopici* (Oxford, 1848).

E. Ullendorff, *Catalogue of Ethiopian Manuscripts in the Bodleian Library, vol. II.* (Catalogi Codd. MSS. Bibliothecae Bodleianae, pars vii; Oxford: Clarendon Press, 1951).

Syriac

Robert Payne Smith, *Catalogi Codicum Manuscriptorum Bibliothecae Bodleianae pars vi, Codices Syriacos, Carshunicos, Mendaeos, complectens* (Oxford, 1864).

Islamic collections

J. Uri, *Bibliothecae Bodleianae Codicum Manuscriptorum Orientalium Catalogus pars prima* (Oxford: Clarendon Press, 1787).

A. Nicoll, *Catalogi Codicum Manuscriptorum Orientalium Bibliothecae Bodleianae pars secunda, Arabicos complectens* (Oxford: University Press, 1835).

E. Sachau, H. Ethé and A.F.L. Beeston, *Catalogue of the Persian, Turkish, Hindûstâni and Pushtû Manuscripts in the Bodleian Library* (Oxford: Clarendon Press, 1889–1954).

The Persian Art of the Book [exhibition catalogue] (Oxford: Bodleian Library, 1972).

Doctrina Arabum: Science and Philosophy in Medieval Islam and Their Transmission to Europe [exhibition catalogue] (Oxford: Bodleian Library, 1981).

Michael Daly, 'Karamanlidika in the Bodleian'. *Bodleian Library Record*, 12/1 (1985), 65–72.

The Turkish Legacy [exhibition catalogue] (Oxford: Bodleian Library, 1988).

Colin Wakefield, 'Arabic Manuscripts in the Bodleian Library: The Seventeenth-Century Collections', in: G.A. Russell, ed., *The 'Arabick' Interest of the Natural Philosophers in Seventeenth-Century England* (Leiden: Brill, 1994), 128–46.

Jeremy Johns and Emilie Savage-Smith, 'The *Book of Curiosities*: a newly discovered series of Islamic maps'. *Imago Mundi*, 55 (2003), 7-24.

20. South, South East and Inner Asia

South Asia

The Bodleian's collection of materials from and about South Asia and Tibet forms one of the five largest resources in the UK. The Bodleian has one of the most important collections of Mughal paintings in the world and is the repository of some 8,700 Sanskrit manuscripts, the largest known collection outside the Indian sub-continent. The printed book collection contains (in 2003) over 110,000 volumes and grows by approximately 2,000 volumes per year. The Library subscribes to over 300 current serial titles and holds about 300 discontinued titles.

The Library acquires publications relating to South Asian and Tibetan and Himalayan studies, as extensively as funds permit, both in the general humanities and social sciences, regardless of the language or of place of publication. The collection covers the history and culture of these regions from pre-history to the present day. The fields of language, literature, religion, history and politics are particularly strongly represented. Responsibility for the South Asian research collections is shared between a number of locations within the Bodleian. The bulk of the printed collection is held on open access at the Indian Institute Library on the central site and all manuscripts are read in the Oriental Reading Room, also on the central site. Responsibility for Sri Lankan materials is shared with the Bodleian Library of Commonwealth and African Studies at Rhodes House. Oxford's major collection of books on South Asian painting, textiles and crafts is found in the Eastern Art collection at the Sackler Library. Indian legislation, law reports, and text books on Indian law are kept at the Bodleian Law Library. The Bodleian Law Library also has a basic collection of law reports for Pakistan and a small collection on the laws of Sri Lanka and Burma.

Manuscripts

Since the earliest years of its refoundation by Sir Thomas Bodley, the Bodleian has acquired manuscripts relating to South Asia. The first South Asian acquisitions came to the library in a series of gifts from Archbishop William Laud between 1635 and 1640 and consist of a Telegu almanac for the year 1632 A.D. (MS. Laud Or. Rolls e. 1) and a set of 18 *Rāgamālā* paintings illustrating the mood and sentiment behind the traditional forms of Indian music (MS. Laud Or. 149).

The collection continued to grow through the eighteenth and nineteenth centuries with a number of purchases and gifts. A collection of Mughal paintings came as part of the bequest of the antiquary and bibliophile Francis Douce in 1834 and the Library's holdings were augmented in 1859 by Mughal paintings and other fine manuscripts from the collection of the diplomat Sir Gore Ouseley. The outstanding item from Sir Gore's collection is the *Bahāristān* manuscript of 1595 (MS. Elliott 254), which was prepared for the Emperor Akbar and illustrated by leading artists of the time.

When the Indian Institute Library came under Bodleian management in 1927, the Bodleian acquired, as part of the library's collection of manuscripts, a set of III Kālighat paintings. These formed part of the original collection of materials given to the library by its founder, Sir Monier Monier-Williams in 1883. Little regarded at the time of their acquisition, they have since come to be recognised as important examples of this nineteenth-century Bengali school of bazaar painting. H.J. Stooke lists 109 of them in his article of 1946 (*see Select bibliography*).

The Bodleian's collection of Sanskrit manuscripts and books undoubtedly owes much of its strength and depth to Colonel Boden's foundation of a Sanskrit Chair in 1827, making this the oldest chair of Sanskrit in Britain. The University's early interest in the study of Sanskrit and classical India gave rise to many opportunities for the Bodleian to build up its Sanskrit collection. The first Boden Professor, Horace Wilson, who was appointed in 1832, sold his considerable personal library of 627 manuscripts to the Bodleian in 1842. In 1845 Sir William Walker presented the Library with some 100 Sanskrit manuscripts (with a few in Gujarati and Hindi), which had been collected by his father, General Alexander Walker, while political resident in Baroda. In 1849, a further 160 manuscripts were purchased from Dr. W.H. Mill, Regius Professor of Hebrew at Cambridge, which he had collected whilst he was Principal of Bishop's College Calcutta. These three collections led Professor Max Müller in 1856 to describe the Bodleian's Sanskrit manuscript holdings as the second best in Europe, surpassed only by those of the East India Company.

The three foundation collections were particularly strong in seventeenth- and eighteenth-century manuscripts written on paper, but in the years following their arrival at the Library the Bodleian was able to acquire some very early manuscripts written on palm-leaves and birch bark. E.W.B Nicholson, then Bodley's Librarian, made a significant addition to the collection with a purchase made 'on a passing call at Mr. Quaritch's shop' in 1898. His find was a fifth century A.D. Buddhist manuscript (MS. Sansk. c. 17) consisting of portions of works on medicine and divination and written on fifty long strips of birch bark. This manuscript has come to be known as the Bower Manuscript, named after the Lieutenant H. Bower who had disinterred it from a buried city in Chinese Turkestan. Another notable Buddhist Sanskrit manuscript, this time on palm-leaf, was purchased from Dr. A.F.R. Hoernle in 1900. This philosophical text, known as the *Astasāhasrikāprajñāpāramitā*

(MS. Sansk. a. 7(R)), is one of only three manuscripts known to survived from the great Indian Buddhist monastic University of Nālandā. Dated in the fifteenth year of the reign of King Ramapala (*c*.1097), it is illustrated with eighteen miniatures of the life of Buddha, which represent the high point of Pāla dynasty art. Dr. Hoernle in 1902 also donated to the library an early Indian mathematical manuscript (MS. Sansk. d. 14) written on birch bark. Known as the *Bakhshālī* manuscript, after the village north of Peshawar where it was unearthed by a peasant in 1881, and dating from the tenth to twelfth century A.D., this work has played an important part in debates over the development of Indian mathematics.

In 1909 the largest single collection of Sanskrit manuscripts ever to come to the Bodleian was donated by the Prime Minister of Nepal, the Maharajah Sir Chandra Shum Shere. Numbering over six thousand manuscripts, it more than doubled the Library's collection of unique Sanskrit texts and covers every branch of Sanskrit literature. Cataloguing of the Chandra Shum Shere collection is still in progress, with three volumes so far published.

In 1927 the Library's Sanskrit manuscript collection was further enriched when the Indian Institute Library came under Bodleian management. The Indian Institute Library manuscript collection consisted, in addition to a small number of manuscripts purchased in 1886, of collections presented by Sir Monier Monier-Williams, the Rev. S.C. Malan and Major J.S. Law. Sir Monier's collection contained a valuable series of Jaina manuscripts procured in 1877–1878. The Indian Institute collections were catalogued by A. B. Keith in 1903, but this publication does not include the 368 texts, mainly in Sanskrit, which were acquired by Sir Marc Aurel Stein during his visits to Kashmir between 1888 and 1905. This collection, which includes some rare birch bark items, was handed over as a deposit to the Curators of the Indian Institute in 1911 and was bequeathed to the Indian Institute in his will. A handlist of the items was published in the *Journal of the Royal Asiatic Society* in 1912. Another manuscript from the Indian Institute collection, the nineteenth-century *Śikṣāpattrī* (MS. Ind. Inst. Sansk. 72) was identified by the scholar Raymond Williams in 1981 as the copy given by Lord Swaminarayan to Sir John Malcolm, the Governor of Bombay in 1830. It has since become an object of veneration for approximately a million Swaminarayan Hindus, who come to the Bodleian from all over the world to have *darshan* (a religious viewing) of a text believed to represent the embodiment of their founder, Lord Swaminarayan. The popular appeal of this text for British Hindus was recognized in 2001 by a grant from the New Opportunities Fund to digitise the manuscript and place it online.

The Bodleian has also collected manuscripts in other Indic languages, though holdings are small in relation to the Sanskrit collections, with some 200 Hindi manuscripts and with just over 100 manuscripts in Tamil, Prakrit, Marathi, and Pali respectively.

Printed books

As with the manuscript collection, so the printed book collection represents an amalgamation of the Bodleian's holdings and those of Sir Monier Monier-Williams' Indian Institute. The fields of language, literature, religion, history and politics are particularly strongly represented and the Library actively acquires current publications in these subject areas from South and South-East Asia, China, Japan, Tibet, Europe and the USA. The collection contains many early editions of Indological works, some with manuscript additions by the editors and authors. Although the holdings of other Indic languages are less substantial than those for Sanskrit, Prakrit and Pali, the Hindi collection is worthy of special mention. Comprising some 1,900 titles, it is built on a core of 250 or so nineteenth-century Hindi books donated by the publisher Naval Kishore of Lucknow to the Indian Institute at the time of its foundation in the 1880s. These represented the current productions of this famous press and, combined with a large selection of the output of nineteenth-century mission presses as well as other indigenous presses, constitute an important resource for research. The Library has a substantial collection of official publications, numbering some 16,000 volumes, dating from the nineteenth century to the present day, and adds approximately 280 titles to the official publications collection each year.

Tibet

The acquisition of the Bodleian's first major Tibetan manuscript collection goes back to 1806, when the library bought some Tibetan manuscripts from Captain Samuel Turner, who had been sent by Warren Hastings on a mission to the Panchen Lama in 1785. A more substantial collection of some 207 works in 118 items was purchased in 1885 from Dr. Emil Schlagintweit. He and his brothers, Adolph and Robert, had collected these manuscripts in the Indian Himalayas between 1855 and 1858. One of the most important items in the collection is a history of Ladakh, the *rGyal rabs gsal ba'i me long* (MS. Tibet. c.7), in pursuit of which Hermann Schlagintweit had negotiated with the ex-king of Ladakh, 'Jigs-med rNam-rgyal in 1856.

The other significant Tibetan collection to reach the Bodleian at this period came as a result of the Younghusband Expedition, which in 1904 forced its way into Lhasa to counter an imagined threat from the north. Lieut.-Col. Austin Waddell, who accompanied the mission as medical officer, managed to acquire a large collection of Tibetan material. These manuscripts and xylographs were then arbitrarily divided and presented by the government of India to the British Museum Library, the India Office Library, Cambridge University Library and the Bodleian, which received some 131 volumes. A number of important manuscript sets were split up in the process. The Bodleian, for instance, owns two volumes of the Shel-dkar manuscript *bKa'-'gyur*, which were prepared in the monastery of Shel-dkar in Southern Tibet in 1712 (MS. Tibet. a.15 (R) , MS. Tibet. a.23 (R)), the British Library has 102 volumes and the remaining seven are missing. This manuscript has attracted considerable scholarly attention because of the part it plays in the history of the transmission of the Tibetan canon.

Acquisition of titles on Tibetan and Himalayan studies received a considerable impetus in the year 2000, when the Bodleian received a collection of around 4,000 academic books, manuscripts and papers, which had belonged to the Oxford Tibetologist, the late Dr. Michael Aris. The Michael Aris Trust for Tibetan and Himalayan Studies also funded a five-year post for a specialist librarian to build up the Tibetan and Himalayan collections, and raised a substantial sum of money for acquisition of books, journals and multimedia publications in this subject area. The bequest in 2001 of the papers of the Tibetologist Hugh Richardson further strengthened resources for the study of modern Tibetan history.

South East Asia

While manuscripts in South East Asian languages were among the earliest gifts to the Library from Archbishop Laud in the seventeenth century, and significant efforts were made to build up the book collections between 1960 and the 1990s, the South East Asian collection remains patchy, but with some good concentrations of printed material, and some important manuscripts, mainly among those donated to the Library by its great benefactors of the seventeenth to nineteenth centuries, Laud, Narcissus Marsh, Edward Pococke and Francis Douce. The most significant manuscript collections are those in Burmese or Burmese script (over 30), Javanese (15), Malay (21) and Thai (12), whereas for books, Vietnamese is strongest after Burmese and Thai, and there are relatively few printed items in Cambodian, Lao and Malay.

Historically, the holdings of Burmese printed books were negligible and largely held in the Indian Institute. For a short period in the 1970s, Aung San Suu Kyi joined the staff in an advisory capacity and through her initiative a fair number of modern publications were acquired. Subsequently, generous donations of printed books, in bulk, were received from the Universities Central Library in Rangoon. There was some activity in collecting printed Thai material prior to 1939. In the 1970s and 1980s, a modest collection of modern publications and reprints of historical texts, royal chronicles and modern fiction in Thai was assembled. Collecting of Vietnamese language printed material began in the 1980s, initially of materials from South Vietnam. Later North Vietnamese publications were acquired in some volume, but the collection is now in need of updating.

Coverage of the discovery and colonisation of the Dutch East Indies includes many works in Dutch and English from the seventeenth century onwards, and much material on the society, culture and languages of the area's indigenous peoples.

Select bibliography

South Asia

Theodor Aufrecht, Moriz Winternitz and A.B. Keith, *Codices Sanscriticos complectens. Catalogue of Sanscrit Manuscripts in the Bodleian Library* (2 vols. Oxford: Clarendon Press, 1864–1905).

A. Hoernle, 'On the Bakhshālī Manuscript', *Verhandlungen des VII Internationalen Orientalisten Congresses, Arische Section*, 1888, 127–47.

A.B. Keith, *A Catalogue of the Sanskrit and Prākrit MSS. in the Indian Institute Library Oxford* (Oxford: Clarendon Press, 1903).

A.B. Keith, *Catalogue of Prākrit Manuscripts in the Bodleian Library* (Oxford: Clarendon Press, 1911).

G.L. Clauson, 'Catalogue of the Stein Collection of Sanskrit MSS. from Kashmir', *Journal of the Royal Asiatic Society*, July 1912, [587]–627.

E. Conzé, 'Remarks on a Pāla Manuscript in the Bodleian Library', *Oriental Art*, 1 (1948), 9–12.

H. Stooke, 'Kālighat Paintings in Oxford', *Indian Art and Letters*, n.s.20 (1946), 71–3.

H. Stooke, 'An XI Century Illuminated Palm Leaf MS', *Oriental Art*, 1 (1948), 5–8.

Herbert J. Stooke, and K. Khandalavala, *The Laud Rāgamālā Miniatures: A Study in Indian Painting and Music* (Oxford: Bruno Cassirer, 1953).

Jonathan Katz (gen. ed.), *A Descriptive Catalogue of the Sanskrit and Other Indian Manuscripts of the Chandra Shum Shere Collection in the Bodleian Library* (Oxford: Clarendon Press, 1984– [in progress]). For details of published volumes see: www.bodley.ox.ac.uk/dept/oriental/

Jonathan Katz, 'The Vyasa Indian Manuscripts', *Bodleian Library Record*, 15/1 (1994), 33–7.

Andrew Topsfield, *Indian Paintings From Oxford Collections* (Oxford: Ashmolean Museum in association with the Bodleian Library, 1994).

Takao Hayashi, *The Bakhshālī Manuscript: An Ancient Indian Mathematical Treatise* (Groningen: Egbert Forsten, 1995).

J. Filliozat, 'Survey of the Pāli Manuscript Collection in the Bodleian Library, Oxford', *Journal of the Pali Text Society*, 24 (1998), 1–80.

Tibet

Michael Aris, 'A Note on the Resources for Tibetan Studies at Oxford', *Bodleian Library Record*, 10/6 (1982), 368–75.

South East Asia

R. Greentree and E.W.B. Nicholson, *Catalogue of Malay Manuscripts and Manuscripts Relating to the Malay Language in the Bodleian Library* (Oxford, 1910).

Pe Maung Tin, 'Burma MSS in the Bodleian Library Oxford', *Journal of the Burma Research Society*, 15/2 (1925), [145]–147.

M.C. Ricklefs and P. Voorhoeve, *Indonesian Manuscripts in Great Britain: A Catalogue of Manuscripts in Indonesian Languages in British Public Collections.* (Oxford, 1977.)

21. East Asia

China

It is a testimony to the perceptiveness of Sir Thomas Bodley that at a time when most of his contemporaries were collecting Chinese books for their cabinets of curiosities, he was adding them to his newly formed library, having personally inscribed the earliest datable acquisition, part of a popular edition of the Confucian *Si shu* ('The Four Books') (Sinica 2), in the year 1604. These works had been bought from overseas Chinese communities in South East Asia by Dutch East India Company merchants, and were split up and sold in Amsterdam in the opening years of the seventeenth century. As the century progressed, in addition to the works that Bodley and his agents had themselves acquired, other Chinese works that reached Europe at this time arrived with the bequests of Laud (1635), Selden (1659), Thurston (1661) and Marsh (1771), with the result that the Bodleian now holds as many as a quarter of all the extant Chinese books that arrived in Europe in the seventeenth century.

For a number of reasons, the importance of this corpus is inversely proportionate to its size – fewer than 90 titles in 170 volumes. It contains a number of unique surviving printed editions, among them chapters 11 and 12 of the version of the *San guo zhi zhuan* ('Romance of the Three Kingdoms') (Sinica 46) printed in Jianyang by Yu Xiangdou in 1592, of which other chapters are held in Cambridge University Library, the Württembergische Landesbibliothek and the British Library, a good example of how these early European imports are now scattered across the Continent. The editions are mostly the products of the late Ming printing industry in Jianyang and Jinling (Nanking), and together with other examples in both Europe and the Far East enable the intricate pattern of commercial printing, publishing and book illustration in this period to be pieced together. Among the books from Laud is the well-known manuscript rutter, or manual of compass directions *Shun feng xiang song* ('Favourable Winds in Escort') (MS. Laud Or. 145) which may have been derived from accounts of the voyages of the great Ming Dynasty navigator Zheng He (1371–1433). Another notable accession of this period is the Jesuit missionary Giulio Aleni's *Tian zhu jiang sheng chu xiang jing jie* ('Illustrated Life of Christ') (Sinica 60) of 1637, a particularly fine copy printed on heavy gold-flecked paper and bearing Portuguese manuscript notes on the cover.

The provenance of the seventeenth-century acquisitions is itself of interest. The three Dutch inscriptions of 1603 on the cover of another of the unique surviving copies, the *Er shi si xiao* ('Tales of the Twenty-four Filial Exemplars') (Sinica 35) are particularly illuminating as well as extremely early, referring to 'a little Chinese box, various sea-shells, and two sheets of white Chinese paper', the other curiosities which presumably formed the job lot at the Amsterdam sale.

It was to be at least two centuries before there was anyone in Oxford capable of reading the acquisitions made by Bodley and his immediate successors, and the eighteenth century is notable only for its near total absence of Chinese accessions at a time of increasing intercourse with East Asia. During this time however the scholar, antiquary and bibliophile Francis Douce was beginning to form the stupendous collection that he was to bequeath to the Library in 1834, which contains a small number of Chinese printed works of the utmost interest and rarity, among them the 1735 edition of *Shi xue* ('On Perception') (Douce Chin.b.2), a work by Nian Xiyao on Western perspective that he had learned from the Jesuit painter and architect Giuseppe Castiglione. Also part of the Douce legacy is one of the very few surviving copies of the so-called 'Red Decree' of 1716 (Sinica 3762), a large handbill from the Kangxi emperor, written in Latin, Chinese and Manchu and printed in red, that was handed to all Westerners passing through the port of Canton, enquiring of the whereabouts of two emissaries that he had despatched to the papal court and who had failed to return.

When the nineteenth-century Protestant missionaries began to take an interest in the civilisation of their prospective converts, the nature and quality of the Chinese collections began to change markedly, and it was only when the Library began to acquire their increasingly systematic collections that scholarly Sinological enquiry in Oxford could be sustained. In 1876, the year in which the missionary and scholar James Legge (whose critical translations of the *Chinese Classics* and other texts are still used as standard reference today) became the University's first Professor of Chinese, Joseph Edkins published his catalogue of the Library's Chinese collection. Although it contained only 299 items, it included such large-scale editions as the Ming dynasty encyclopaedia *San cai tu hui* (Sinica 180), which had come with the collection sold to the Library by the missionary Edwin Evans in 1858, and a complete set of the fine 1871 Canton reprint of the Qing dynasty imperial edition of the *Shi san jing zhu shu* ('The Thirteen Confucian Classics with Commentary') (Sinica 364).

Alexander Wylie, another missionary and scholar, sold his Chinese books to the Library in 1882. His *Notes on Chinese Literature* (Shanghae, 1867), an outstanding work which was a major revelation to Western scholars of the nature and extent of Chinese bibliography, and which even today is not without its uses, was based largely on these books, the acquisition of which doubled the collections in quantity and even more in quality. Thus by the late nineteenth century, although the collections were still soundly classical in subject, with the acquisition of Wylie's books it was possible to speak of a broadly-based Chinese collection in the modern sense rather than a miscellany of individual objects of curiosity, important as the bibliographical rarities of the seventeenth and eighteenth centuries undoubtedly are.

Most of the small collections of Chinese books that passed into the Library during the nineteenth century included at least a few doctrinal works in Chinese by the missionaries themselves, but towards the end of the century, under circumstances that are not entirely clear, the Library acquired two large collections of missionary publications, the contents of the great International Exhibitions at Philadelphia in 1876 and London in 1884, so that there is now a corpus of some 2,000 such works representing at least 1,500 different titles. The collection is comparatively rich in tracts published during the first half of the century, of which the earliest is Robert Morrison's *Shen dao lun shu jiu shi zong shuo zhen ben* (Sinica 2672), a tract on redemption printed from blocks believed to have been cut in Canton in 1811. The missionary works have an interest which goes far beyond their value as expositions of Christian doctrine: some are written in local dialects, others provide glimpses of the popular Chinese religious and social customs which the missionaries encountered in the course of their work; all illustrate the process whereby traditional Chinese block-printing was gradually superseded by Western typography as the missionaries strove to circumvent local prohibitions and improve the efficiency of their publishing. The modern Chinese periodical press, which from the beginning was largely concerned with secular knowledge, also originated with the Protestant missionaries; altogether over twenty such periodicals are found in the collections, starting with a single offprint from William Milne's *Cha shi su mei yue tong ji zhuan* printed in Malacca in 1819 (Sinica 1268), and extending in some cases to complete runs. The Chinese Protestant missionary publications of the nineteenth century therefore constitute a special collection whose importance is increasingly recognised, and which is scarcely matched elsewhere.

Standing apart from anything that had been acquired hitherto, and ranking with the finest and most generous gifts in the Library's history, is the aristocratic collection that had been put together in Peking by Sir Edmund Backhouse in the early twentieth century as the Qing Dynasty gave way to the Republic. Unlike the Protestant missionary collections, palpably financed on a shoestring, the Backhouse Collection proclaims the resources of the scion of a Darlington banker collecting in courtly circles in Peking at a time of dynastic upheaval. It was received in stages between 1913 and 1922, and for a short time constituted the principal repository of fine Chinese editions outside the Far East. Even now, much of its content is unique in the West and exemplifies the art of Chinese printing in all its variety. For example, the 'three dynasty' edition of the *Song shu* ('History of the Liu Song Dynasty') (Backhouse 392), whose oldest blocks were cut in the Southern Song, can be laid side by side with the Nanking *Guozijian* edition that superseded it in the Ming (Backhouse 468); the Tang Dynasty encyclopaedia *Tai ping yu lan* ('Imperial Survey of the Taiping Period')

(Backhouse 534), though printed mostly from blocks cut in 1573, contains sections from the rare bronze moveable type edition of 1574. Private printing is represented by Mao Jin's Jiguge edition of *Tang ren si ji* ('Four Collections of Tang Poets') (Backhouse 477), while an early printing of the 1713 Palace edition of *Zhu zi quan shu* ('Complete Works of Zhu Xi') (Backhouse 69) demonstrates the visual and textual perfection of the official publishing of the Qing. Unlike many of the traditional Chinese books that European libraries acquired in previous generations, the Backhouse Collection was never rebound in Western style, so that it also constitutes an excellent resource for the study of the Chinese book as an object.

In common with other European libraries, the Bodleian was slow to respond to the flowering of Chinese commercial publishing in first half of the twentieth century, and although a number of important acquisitions were made during that period, many opportunities were lost. But in response to the increased demands resulting from the rapid expansion of Oriental studies in the years following the Second World War, the Library employed a professional Sinologist for the first time, and with regular and steadily increasing funding, the Chinese collection began to assume its present status as one of the largest and most rapidly expanding in Europe. This process was greatly assisted by a grant made to the University in 1948 following the recommendations of the Scarbrough Interdepartmental Commission of Enquiry on Oriental, Slavonic, East European and African Studies.

As is well known, it is a characteristically Chinese mode of publishing, no less in modern times than traditionally, to gather many works together and print them simultaneously in collectanea, or *congshu*. Also aided by Scarbrough funds, Professor Homer Dubs collected over 300 of the traditional *congshu* for the Faculty Library, as it was then called (now the Institute for Chinese Studies Library), which for the most part did not duplicate the existing Bodleian holdings, with which they were formally if not physically integrated in 1994. Continuing this tradition, and thus providing an extremely comprehensive coverage of traditional textual sources, through the generous gift of the National Palace Museum in Taipei the Library acquired the complete *Si ku quan shu* ('Imperial Manuscript Library') reproduction (Chin.d.5565), published in 1,500 volumes in 1986, and later, with the help of the Friends of the Bodleian and a General Board grant, the complementary *Si ku quan shu cun mu congshu* (Chin.d.10950) published in 1,200 volumes in 1997 – works which at the time were not deemed worthy of inclusion in the *Si ku* library but are now of the utmost rarity and scholarly value. Also presented in the form of *congshu* were the large sets of photo-lithographic reproductions of Chinese *difangzhi* ('local histories' or 'gazetteers') which began to appear in Taiwan from the 1960s. In response to the growing recognition of the value of these texts as historical sources of the first importance, the Library has made strenuous efforts to acquire them all. Recent manuscript additions have included a collection of about 1,350 examples of Daoist ritual texts produced by the Yao of South-West China.

In accordance with the needs of the Faculty of Oriental Studies, the Library had traditionally focussed on materials relating to the study of traditional China at the expense of the contemporary period and the modern social sciences; but the benefaction of Sir Run Run Shaw in 1993, and further funding from the Leverhulme Trust from 2002, have enabled regular funding to be made available to the Library to expand significantly its coverage of these areas. Thus, for example, the Library's holdings of traditional gazetteers have been augmented with their post-1949 equivalents, of which some 5,000 have been acquired to date; reproductions have been obtained of the important twentieth-century newspapers of record from all parts of China; and there are current subscriptions to some 750 Chinese periodicals, including where possible the social science editions of the journals of all China's universities and other higher educational establishments. The collection is now one of the most significant and fastest-growing in Europe.

Japan

The Bodleian houses the main research collection for Japanese studies in the University of Oxford. In 1993, a new building of the Nissan Institute was constructed in the precincts of St Antony's College, to which the Bodleian's extensive holdings on Japan were transferred. Combining with the residual collection of the Nissan Institute Library, the Bodleian Japanese Library (BJL) was created and opened to readers as the University's principal collections relating to Japan. The Japanese-language collections held in the BJL are probably the third largest in Britain after those at Cambridge University Library and the School of Oriental and African Studies (University of London). The BJL currently (2003) possesses about 81,300 printed books in Japanese, together with 19,000 volumes in European languages relating to Japan. In addition the Library holds approximately 600 serial titles, over 1,000 titles of antiquarian works, about 100 manuscripts, maps, microforms, and a small number of sound recordings and video tapes.

The BJL acquires material in support of teaching and research undertaken by Oxford specialists in Japanese, in both the general humanities and the social sciences, regardless of the language in which this is expressed or of place of publication. The collection covers the history and culture of Japan from the dawn of her civilization to the present day. The areas not covered are the natural and applied sciences, and law (except constitutional law), which are held by the Radcliffe Science Library and the Bodleian Law Library respectively.

The fields of literature, religion, history and politics are strongly represented. The collection of Japanese local histories is probably the foremost such collection outside Japan. Acquisition of Japanese official publications is selective, since the British Library receives this material under official exchange arrangements with the National Diet Library in Tokyo. First priority is given to securing adequate coverage of newly published titles, but steps have also been taken to fill gaps in holdings following the expansion of the spectrum of teaching and research, and scholarly standard works have been acquired by retrospective purchase whenever possible. Works in Western languages are extensively acquired. Works relating to Japanese arts are housed in the Eastern Art Library. Those Japanese-language works which relate to the study of China and Korea are housed in the central Bodleian.

The Bodleian's historical collections in Japanese are small. Nevertheless, the Library holds some unique treasures acquired in the early years of its foundation. The first known accession of Japanese printed material was three volumes of *Saga-bon* (Saga Press edition) (Nipponica 131–133), presented to the Library in November 1629 by Robert Viney, rector of Barnack, who studied at Oxford in 1621–25. The term *Saga-bon* refers to a group of luxury editions of Japanese literary works printed by Hon'ami Kōetsu's press at Saga, Kyoto, c.1608–15. The Bodleian's copies are texts of the Kanze school of Nō play. While a special place is accorded to *Saga-bon* in the fields of fine printing and production of *kanamajiri* books printed with movable type, the next acquisition, *Kirishitan-ban*, is similarly unique and significant in the history of Japanese printing.

Various kinds of missionary literature of the Jesuit Mission Press in Japan, collectively known as *Kirishitan-ban*, were produced from 1590 until the expulsion of the missionaries from Japan in 1614. The press used both Japanese and European typefaces, of both wood and metal. Many of these books were destroyed when the country was closed and the priests expelled. Today only 75 copies, including fragments, of 31 titles are known throughout the world. Thanks to its own long history the Bodleian is fortunate in possessing six of these rare titles, including *Sanctos no gosagueo no uchi nuqigaqi* (a Compendium of the Acts of the Saints), the first book printed from movable type in Japan, which came with the collection of John Selden received in 1659 (Arch.B.f.69).

The *shuinjō* (vermilion seal document) of 1613 was issued by Shōgun Tokugawa Ieyasu to grant the English Company trade privileges in Japan. The Bodleian's *shuinjō* is believed to be one of the two copies given to John Saris, the commander of the eighth voyage of the Company, for long presumed to be lost. The exact date of its acquisition by the Library is not known, but it was already included in the list of Bodleian manuscripts (Library Records e.337) which was probably compiled in 1680. Dated the 28th day of the 8th month of the 18th year of the Keichō (12 October 1613), the document, bearing Ieyasu's seal in vermilion, was issued to the captain of an English ship, to whom it grants privileges for trade in Japan and concomitant terms including jurisdiction rights in seven articles (MS. Jap.b 2).

Another interesting item illustrating aspects of the trading relationship with Japan in this period is the log-book of William Adams (1564–1620), *alias* Miura Anjin, the first Englishman known to have visited Japan, who helped in the negotiations between the Shōgun and Captain Saris. The log-book is of four voyages made by

Adams between 1614 and 1619 to Siam, Cochin China and Japan. It came to the Library as part of the bequest of Sir Henry Savile (MS. Savile 48).

The Bodleian has a rich collection of pre-1850 books in European languages dealing with Japan. This includes examples of the published correspondence of the Jesuit fathers, accounts of early travels to Japan in various published records of European voyages overseas, material relating to the East India Companies of England and Holland, and works of European explorers of the eighteenth and nineteenth centuries. The material vividly illustrates Europe's contacts with Japan from the sixteenth to the mid-nineteenth century.

As for material in Japanese, apart from the very early acquisitions it was but sparsely represented in the Library during this period. A few sporadic acquisitions were made from the libraries of Orientalists and others, including Alexander Wylie, F. Max Müller, S.C. Malan, and Sir Ernest Satow. Bodleian manuscripts in Japanese are few, numbering about 100 titles. Many of them were added to the stock by donation or purchase in the early years of the twentieth century when rare books were not too expensive to buy in Japan. The collection includes *Nara-ehon* (Nara picture books), for example a very decorative scroll of Urashima.

It was in the 1950s that acquisition of Japanese material was significantly increased and systematic acquisition started, when a major step in the development in the study of Japan in Oxford was taken. For the next thirty years, acquisition policy for Japanese books was followed fairly consistently; much emphasis was placed on the development of research collections in the humanities, reflecting the University's teaching and research programme. As research into the modern period has developed with the establishment of the Nissan Institute of Japanese Studies in 1979, the scope of selection has been extended to include the fields of modern history, politics, economics, and other social sciences. The Japan Library Group's co-operative acquisitions scheme, which flourished in the 1980s and early 1990s, allowed many seminal texts to be acquired. A video collection, originally set up in support of Social Anthropology courses, now holds over 160 titles, including a selection of Japanese films and recordings of Japanese television dramas and other programmes.

The Library has been significantly enhanced by the generosity of numerous individuals and institutions in Japan over many years. To name only a few, these include the National Diet Library, the Japan Foundation, the National Institute of Informatics (formerly NACSIS), the Historiographical Institute, Toyota City, and the Japanese Friends of the Bodleian.

Korea

Unlike the Bodleian's Chinese and Japanese collections which date from as early as the seventeenth century, the Korean collection was built up during the twentieth century, and is much more modest in size, coverage and depth. The earliest accessions, donated by Bishop Trollope, who first went to Korea in 1890, include two manuscripts, one of which is a painted representation of the funeral of Queen Dowager Chō in 1890 (MS. Asiat. Misc. a. 1(R)), along with a small number of eighteenth- and nineteenth-century printed Korean texts given in 1927.

The development of the modern printed collection started in the 1950s, and now (2003) amounts to some 10,000 volumes in Korean and European languages. Generally speaking the collection has focussed on the humanities, including Korean classical and modern literature and pre-modern history. A particular strength is modern local histories of provinces and major Korean cities, including places in North Korea. Histories of important banking institutions, corporations and companies as well as family records and genealogies are also acquired, as are Japanese publications relating to Korean studies. Much of the collection has been built up by active solicitation of donations, particularly of publications not commercially available, for example local histories and Korean university journals. Material published in North Korea is sparsely represented, but the collection contains a fair number of works relating to the history, governance and economy of North Korea published in Seoul and elsewhere.

Mongolia

The Bodleian has only a handful of Mongolian manuscripts. They include part of a primer of Mongolian conversation, dated 1787, a copy of a Buddhist canonical composition, comprising the Sanskrit text together with Tibetan and Mongolian versions, and letters and a volume of letters and papers in Mongolian, Bengali and Tibetan. Printed resources include works produced in China, Inner and Outer Mongolia and other areas with Mongolian-speaking populations, together with supporting material from a wide spectrum of Western and Eastern countries including Japan. The Library's earliest examples of Mongolian printing are a number of blockprints from the eighteenth century produced in Peking. They contain Buddhist Sutras, among them the Diamond Sutra and the Heart Sutra. Of the Library's two editions of the Heart Sutra, one was printed c. 1712. A small group of prints from the nineteenth century contain trilingual texts – Chinese, with Manchu and Mongolian translations. Mongolian is also found, with Chinese, in a number of essentially Manchu works. These items belong mostly to the famous Backhouse Collection. Another small group comprises blockprints from Peking of Mongolian translations of Tibetan Buddhist texts, with or without the original Tibetan. Several of the early Buddhist blockprints belonged formerly to the Rev. S.C. Malan, vicar of Broadwindsor, and were part of the Malan Library in the Indian Institute. The Indian Institute Library, it may be noted, possesses a copy of the 108-volume set of the Mongolian Kanjur (Delhi, 1973–9) which was reproduced from the Imperial Red edition of 1717–20.

With the spread of the Russian Empire in Central Asia in the nineteenth century the study of Mongolian in Russia and other European countries began to gather pace. Christian missionary activity led to the translation and publication of various parts of the Bible and the Library has editions published in St Petersburg (1819, 1827 etc.), London (1846) and Peking (1872). It also has many of the early grammars, dictionaries and studies published on the language and literature of the Mongols, which appeared in England, France, Germany, Russia and elsewhere. By far the largest component of the Bodleian's Mongolian collection is made up of books and journals in Khalkha Mongolian, the official language of the Mongolian Republic (the former Mongolian People's Republic), which makes use of a modified version of the Cyrillic alphabet. During the 1960s and the following two decades the Library made a concerted effort to acquire works of original literature in Khalkha Mongolian from Ulan Bator. From the same source it also obtained studies in Mongolian and Russian on Mongolian language(s) and literature. Publications in the two other main varieties of Mongolian (Buryat and Kalmuck) were also acquired; the Library has texts in, and studies on, both languages, published largely in Ulan Ude and Elista respectively. Since the 1980s Mongolian publications from the People's Republic of China have been acquired on a selective basis. These are printed in the traditional Uighur script and derive mostly from Huhehot. They number around one hundred titles.

The total number of Mongolian titles in the Library is perhaps in the region of 800. In addition to works in Mongolian this figure includes linguistic and literary studies in Western languages. Western-language books on the history, religion and culture of Mongolia are found scattered across the non-Oriental collections and are difficult to quantify. Compared with the British Library, the Bodleian has fewer manuscripts and blockprints, but overall its holdings constitute a useful resource for Mongolian studies.

Select bibliography

China

Joseph Edkins, *A Catalogue of Chinese Works in the Bodleian Library* (Oxford: Clarendon Press, 1876).

A.F.L. Beeston, 'The Earliest Donations of Chinese Books to the Bodleian', *Bodleian Library Record*, 4/6 (1953), 304–13.

David Helliwell, *A Catalogue of the Old Chinese Books in the Bodleian Library. Volume 1: The Backhouse Collection* (Oxford: Bodleian Library, 1983).

David Helliwell, *A Catalogue of the Old Chinese Books in the Bodleian Library. Volume 2: Alexander Wylie's Books* (Oxford: Bodleian Library, 1985).

David Helliwell, 'Two Collections of Nineteenth-Century Protestant Missionary Publications in Chinese in the Bodleian Library', *Chinese Culture*, 31/4 (1990), 21–38.

Japan

B.A. Nanjio, *A Catalogue of Japanese and Chinese Books and Manuscripts Lately Added to the Bodleian Library* (Oxford: Clarendon Press, 1881).

J.M. Bunn and A.D.S. Roberts, *A Union List of Japanese Local Histories in British Libraries* (Oxford: Bodleian Library, 1981).

I.K. Tytler, 'The Japanese Collections in the Bodleian Library', in *Japanese Studies: Papers Presented at a Colloquium at the School of Oriental and African Studies, University of London 14–16 September 1988* (British Library Occasional Papers, 11; London: The British Library, 1990), 113–22.

I.K. Tytler with D. Massarella, 'The Japonian Charters: the English and Dutch Shuinjo', *Monumenta Nipponica*, 45 (1990), 190–205.

Japan Encountered: From the 16th to the 19th Century [exhibition catalogue] (Oxford: Bodleian Library, 1991).

I.K. Tytler, *East Meets West: Original Records of Western Traders, Travellers, Missionaries and Diplomats to 1852. Part 1: The Log Book of William Adams (1564–1620) and Other Manuscript and Rare Printed Materials from the Bodleian Library, Oxford. A Listing and Guides to Part 1 of the Collection* (Marlborough: Adam Matthew, 1998).

K. Keta, 'Catalogue of Japanese Books of the Malan Collection in the Bodleian Library, Oxford: Literary Works and Dictionaries', *Bulletin of Graduate School of Humanities and Sciences, Ochanomizu University*, 22 (1998), 2–9 and 2–16.

K. Keta, 'A Catalogue of Japanese Books of the Malan Collection in the Bodleian Library, Oxford: Collection of Letters, Maxims, Miscellaneous Arts, Chinese Classics in Japanese and Others', *Bulletin of Graduate School of Humanities and Sciences, Ochanomizu University*, 23 (1999), 1–2 and 2–9.

K. Keta, 'The Moseley Collection in the Bodleian Library of Oxford University', *Japanese Literature*, 50(9) (2001), 29–39.

22. North America

United States

One of the complaints to the 1852 Royal Commission on Oxford University was that 'literature on the United States is almost wholly unrepresented' in the Bodleian's collections. This statement, not wholly accurate even then, is certainly far from the truth today, when the Vere Harmsworth Library in the Rothermere American Institute has as its aim the bringing together under one roof of 'the finest holdings in American history, politics and government outside North America'.

Many of the early items of Americana in the Bodleian came by donation. They include a copy of *The Whole Booke of Psalmes*, which was the first book to be printed in British North America (Cambridge, Mass., 1640), and several copies of John Eliot's translation of the Bible into the Indian language of Massachusetts (Cambridge, Mass., 1661). Also held is Eliot's translation of *The Practice of Piety* by Lewis Bayly, which was published as *Manitowampae pomantamoonk* in Cambridge, Mass. in 1665.

In the early nineteenth century the Library made a number of important purchases, including, in 1836, a collection of about 300 tracts relating to American affairs, the War of Independence and the Continental Congress; these are now included in the Godwyn Pamphlets. A similar collection, formerly in the possession of George Chalmers, author of *An Introduction to the History of the Revolt of the American Colonies* (Boston, Mass., 1845), was purchased in 1841. However, it was not until the twentieth century that the Library began to acquire substantial quantities of Americana in a systematic way, both by purchase and through legal deposit since a number of major US publishers with UK offices supply copies of their publications. Its collections on American history are now probably the strongest in the UK outside the British Library.

The Library's holdings on American political, social and economic history and conditions were transferred to Rhodes House Library after its opening in 1929, although the majority of works published before 1760 were retained in the central Bodleian, a division which has been maintained since. In the spring of 2001, the American materials held at Rhodes House were transferred again to the new purpose-built Vere Harmsworth Library in the Rothermere American Institute, where for the first time the majority of titles, other than those published before

1920, were placed on open shelves, thereby greatly increasing their accessibility to scholars.

The Vere Harmsworth Library is especially rich in holdings on the American Revolution, slavery and secession, the Progressive Era and the New Deal. In addition, it has good holdings on the history of the original thirteen colonies and on California, Illinois, New York and Pennsylvania, and generally attempts to acquire a representative coverage of state and local (especially city) history. Amongst the most important sets held is a complete collection of the Federal Writers' Program *Guides*, which were produced during the Depression through a job-creation programme for unemployed writers.

The printed collections are augmented by several important collections held on microcard. These include the set of *Early American Imprints, 1639–1800*, which is based on the titles recorded in Charles Evans' *American Bibliography*; the large collection of *Adams Papers* held by the Massachusetts Historical Society; and sets of *Travels in the Old South*, *Travels in the New South* and *Travels in the West and Southwest*.

The major US newspapers are held in paper, microform or CD-ROM. Newspapers from the eighteenth and early nineteenth centuries are held on microfilm in a set of *Early American Newspapers*; amongst the important nineteenth-century titles are the *Boston Daily Advertiser* (1836–1870), the *Richmond Enquirer* (1815–1867) and the Washington *National Intelligencer* (1800–1820).

Although the library has never been an official depository library, it nonetheless holds substantial numbers of US government documents. In particular, it has many publications of the Commission on Civil Rights, the State and Labor Departments, and an extensive set of the Census Bureau reports from the first census (1790) onwards. The series of published *Public Papers of the Presidents* is held in its entirety. The *American State Papers* are held, as are the *Debates and Proceedings*, the *Register of Debates*, the *Congressional Globe* and the *Congressional Record*. The Library also has a set of the *Journals of the Continental Congress* (1774–1789). Congressional committee publications have not been acquired systematically, although in recent years the Library has received several substantial donations of them; coverage is particularly good for the years 1950–1965. These holdings of government documents are supplemented by many important indexes and microform collections, including the *US Serial Set Index, 1789–1969*, the *Declassified Documents Catalog* and the *Congressional Research Service Major Studies and Issue Briefs*, together with some major non-official series such as Sibley's *The Congress of the United States, 1789–1989*.

The Vere Harmsworth Library also contains the books in the Aydelotte-Kieffer-Smith Collection. Funded by the American Association of Rhodes Scholars, and named after the first and second American Rhodes Scholarship secretaries and a former president of the Association, this collection of books on American life, history and culture is shelved within the main sequence of books, although the most recent acquisitions are displayed together as a browsing collection. The number of AKS books at the Vere Harmsworth Library totals approximately 1,100 at the time of writing (2003), while some of the older material is still held in the central Bodleian.

In 2002 the Vere Harmsworth Library received the Philip Davies Collection of American Election Campaign Ephemera. This extensive archive contains a wide range of campaign materials produced for national, state and local government elections in the US from the nineteenth century through to the present day; these include badges, posters, bumper stickers, leaflets and commemorative materials of all kinds. It is thought to be the largest collection of its kind in the country.

The Vere Harmsworth Library does not hold any manuscript material, but the library at Rhodes House retains a number of archival collections relating to the US. Of these the most substantial is the historic archive of the United Society for the Propagation of the Gospel. The oldest of the Anglican missionary societies, the SPG was founded in 1701, and the archive includes letters and reports from missionaries active in British North America up until the time of Independence. These papers, which include rudimentary censuses of many of the early settlements, are an important source for the early history of the US. The papers of the Anti-Slavery Society also contain considerable American material, including letters from American abolitionists such as Lewis Tappan, and the letters and papers relating to a US lecture tour by Sir John Harris, Secretary of the Anti-Slavery Society, in 1917. The papers of Lord Hailey include material from his official visits to the US during the Second World War, and some similar material can be found in the papers of Professor Herbert Nicholas.

The Western Manuscript collections in the central Bodleian contain much material relating to American history. They include papers relating to the early settlement of North America, for example in the collections of Sir John Bankes as Attorney-General in the 1630s and of John Locke in the last three decades of the seventeenth century. The papers of the North family include some of Lord North relating to trade with North America (transcripts of these are also held at Rhodes House). The modern political collections are a major source for studies of the United States and of Anglo-American relations in the nineteenth and twentieth centuries. They include papers of the diplomat Sir John Crampton, who was attached to the legation in Washington from 1845 to 1856, and correspondence of George, 4th Earl of Clarendon, Foreign Secretary three times between 1853 and 1870, both with British ambassadors in Washington and American ambassadors in London. The papers of James Bryce, author of *The American Commonwealth* and British ambassador to the US, 1907–1913, contain much correspondence and other material relating to the US, while, in the post-Second World War period, the papers of the journalist William Donaldson Clark (1916–85) and of A.L. Goodhart (1891–1978), Master of University College, are of particular interest. Besides these major collections, American material can be found in many smaller collections.

American literature is the responsibility of the central Bodleian. From the mid-nineteenth century many British editions of American works began to be received by legal deposit, at first in anthologies such as the *American Scrap Book and Magazine of United States Literature* (London, 1861–62). However, from the 1950s a major retrospective collecting policy was implemented with the aim of building up the holdings of works of major American authors such as Stephen Crane, Emily Dickinson, Robert Frost, Nathaniel Hawthorne, Herman Melville, Ezra Pound, Walt Whitman and Carlos Williams. During the 1970s this was extended to include coverage of many African-American and women writers, humorists, journalists and regional writers. Original editions of many earlier writers have been supplemented by the collection *American Fiction, 1774–1850* on microfilm and the microfiche collection *Black Literature, 1827–1940*.

A particular strength of the collections lies in American poetry, and especially contemporary poetry, which has been built up since the 1960s. Among the several hundred poets whose works have been collected are John Ashbery, Robert Bly and Allen Ginsberg. As part of this specialism, many small press, avant-garde and underground publications have been acquired, including over 400 American little magazines and literary periodicals, which mainly date from the 1960s onwards, although there are also some earlier titles. Again, these holdings have been augmented by microform sets of individual titles, such as *Blast: A Magazine of Proletarian Short Stories* (New York, 1933–34). Apart from that held at University College London, this is probably the most comprehensive such collection in the country.

Other areas in which the Library has strengths are American publishing and printing history, education, art and architecture, and cinema and photography. Coverage of all these tends to be split between the central Bodleian and the Vere Harmsworth Library. American law is covered by the Bodleian Law Library, although works on constitutional law and the Supreme Court may also be found at the Vere Harmsworth Library.

Canada

The Bodleian Library of Commonwealth and African Studies at Rhodes House holds some 12,000 monographs and pamphlets and approximately 250 current journals relating to Canada. Material received by legal deposit has been supplemented by the purchasing of new books published in Canada, the United States and elsewhere within the subject field. Government publications are a particular strength of the collection, many series having been presented since the 1920s. The library is a selective deposit for Canadian Federal government documents, and efforts have been made to acquire material retrospectively, with some series dating back to 1867 or even earlier. Where the originals are no longer available, selected titles have been obtained on microfilm. Provincial government documents are collected more selectively, but there are extensive holdings of Parliamentary *Journals* and *Debates*, although these are not always complete. A recent deposit of material from the Foreign and Commonwealth Office Library enabled the Library to fill in a number of gaps in its holdings of Provincial departmental annual reports.

The Library holds a number of early Canadian newspapers and gazettes on microfilm. These include *La Gazette du Québec* (1764–1817), the Toronto *Globe* (1844–1895), the *Montreal Gazette* (1785–1877), *Niagara Gleaner* (1817–1837), *The Nova Scotian* (1824–1870), the *Public Ledger and Newfoundland General Advertiser* (1827–1882), *Saskatchewan Herald* (1878–1900) and the *Upper Canada Gazette* (1793–1845).

The library's major manuscript holdings on Canada lie in the archive of the United Society for the Propagation of the Gospel. The Society was active in Canada from 1726 to 1940, and the archive contains correspondence, reports from missionaries, committee minutes and the Society's journal, annual reports, the Upper Canada Clergy Society papers (1836–45), and photographs. Subjects of especial interest for Canadian studies include Loyalist refugees from the United States in the 1780s, missions to the Indians, such as the Thompson River Indians in British Columbia (1860s–1880s) or the Church on the Prairies (1880–1930), and missions to the Chinese and Japanese in British Columbia in the late nineteenth and early twentieth centuries. There is an interesting file of correspondence with Michael Houdon, a French Canadian missionary, who accompanied Wolfe during his campaign in Canada in the Seven Years War, and who may have given him the crucial information about the path up the Heights of Abraham prior to the capture of Québec. Apart from the USPG collection, the library does not hold an extensive collection of manuscripts relating to Canada, although there are some items of interest. These include a *Journal of the most remarkable occurrences in the Province of Quebec from the appearance of the rebels in September 1775 until their retreat on the 6th May 1776*, probably written by Thomas Ainslie, and James McCullagh's *Journal relating to some experiences with the Indians of Naas River from 1883–1905*, which includes some fine coloured illustrations.

Canadian literature in English is covered by the central Bodleian and includes the works of many modern writers, among them Margaret Attwood, Robert Kroetsch and George Woodcock. The Taylor Institution Library covers Canadian authors writing in French. Canadian law can be found at the Bodleian Law Library. The holdings comprise basic legal material – statutes, law reports, periodicals and standard textbooks – together with some government publications from both the Federal government and the Provinces.

Select bibliography

John W. Raimo, *A Guide to Manuscripts Relating to America in Great Britain and Ireland* (London: Mansell, 1979).

Peter Snow, 'Bodley's US Printed Collections', *American Studies Library Group Newsletter*, 3 (April 1979), 12–14.

Peter Snow, *The United States: A Guide to Library Holdings in the UK* (Boston Spa: The British Library, 1982).

Judy Collingwood, *Canadian Studies in the United Kingdom and Ireland: A Guide to Resources* (3rd edn., Edinburgh: British Association for Canadian Studies, 1998).

23. Australia and New Zealand

For Australian and New Zealand studies the main categories of material held in the central Bodleian are reference books and bibliographies, material published before 1760, language and literature, little magazines, maps and music. Holdings of Australian and New Zealand literature are particularly strong, with a certain bias towards poetry. Amongst the Australian authors represented in the collection are Christopher Brennan, Rosemary Dobson, Geoffrey Dutton, David Forrest, Henry Lawson, Norman Lindsay, Henry Handel Richardson, Patrick White and Judith Wright. New Zealand is represented by, amongst others, Fleur Adcock, Katherine Mansfield and Ngaio Marsh. The Library's holdings of literary periodicals and little magazines include amongst their Australian and New Zealand titles *Arena: A Literary Magazine* (Wellington), *Australian Literary Studies* (St. Lucia), *Crucible* (Auckland), *Poetry: Quarterly of Australian and New Zealand Verse* (Adelaide), *Poetry Australia* (Sydney) and *Post Modern Writing* (Sydney).

Works published after 1760 on the political, economic and social history of Australia and New Zealand are held in the Bodleian Library of Commonwealth and African Studies at Rhodes House. Historical materials are well represented with early works on discovery and exploration, migration and settlement, and local history. Particular strengths of the collection include relations with the Aborigines and Maoris, demography, military history and biography.

Rhodes House has long runs of the *Sydney Morning Herald* and *New Zealand Herald*, and other shorter runs of some nineteenth century newspapers, including the *Port Phillip Herald* (1845–47), the Perth *Inquirer* (1840—47), *New Zealand Journal* (1841–49) and *New Zealand Gazette and Wellington Spectator* (1839–41).

Government publications are a particular strength of the collection. For Australia there are a few pre-Confederation publications, such as the *Journals and Printed Papers* of the Federal Council (1886–97), with the main series starting in 1901. Sets of *Debates*, *Parliamentary Papers*, annual departmental reports and census volumes all date back that far. State publications are similar in character, with some of the runs going back into the nineteenth century, although not all of them are complete. There are nineteenth-century censuses for most of the states. For New Zealand there are runs of annual departmental reports extending as far back as 1855; the set of Parliamentary *Debates* begins in 1854, and that of the House of Representatives *Journals* in 1855.

The inspirational nature of the collection was well expressed by Australian Prime Minister Bob Hawke who in his autobiography described how a visit to Rhodes House Library when a student led him to choose his research topic:

> There was a full set of Commonwealth Arbitration Reports, a complete set of Hansards, a complete set of the Convention debates and a complete set of the newspapers of the 1890s – the period of the Great Strike that had spawned arbitration. And there were all the relevant history books. It suddenly clicked! I'd study the Australian arbitration system – how wages were determined.

Although printed materials form the bulk of the collection, Rhodes House has a few manuscript collections relating to Australia and New Zealand. One of the most significant comprises the journals, letters, maps and watercolours of Charles Sturt's three expeditions of discovery into the interior of southern and central Australia in 1828–9, 1829–30 and 1844–6. However, the largest collection of manuscripts on Australia and New Zealand is contained within the historic archive of the United Society for the Propagation of the Gospel. The SPG was first active in New South Wales as early as 1793, and was sending missionaries to all of the Australian states by the late 1830s or early 1840s. Initially their efforts were directed towards the convicts, who were characterised as in 'a state more pitiful than that of the heathen'; later the Society attempted to evangelise the Aborigines too. Its first missionaries to New Zealand were appointed in 1840. The archive, held on deposit, contains correspondence and reports from missionaries in the field, committee minutes, journals and photographs.

Material on Australian and New Zealand law is held at the Bodleian Law Library. Sets of statutes are complete for the Commonwealth of Australia, and virtually complete for each state, with most of the runs dating back to the mid-nineteenth century. Other official material includes statutory regulations, law reform commission reports and constitutional documents at both federal and state level. The annual *Laws* of New Zealand is held from 1854 onwards.

Select bibliography

Valerie Bloomfield, *Resources for Australian and New Zealand Studies: A Guide to Library Holdings in the United Kingdom* (London: Australian Studies Centre and The British Library, 1986).

24. Sub-Saharan Africa

Although works on African literature and linguistics are held in the central Bodleian, and scientific and technical works in the Radcliffe Science Library, material for African studies is centred at the Bodleian Library of Commonwealth and African Studies at Rhodes House. This library was opened in 1929 when most works dealing with the political, economic and social history of sub-Saharan Africa and published since 1760 were transferred from the central Bodleian. Since then the library has continued to benefit from receiving the legal deposit copies of books and journals published in this country on African topics, which are supplemented by purchasing books published in Africa itself. The library now contains over 100,000 titles relating to Africa, and amongst these are many early editions of important works such as Mungo Park's *Travels in the Interior of Africa*, and Livingstone's *Narrative of an Expedition to the Zambezi*. Although all countries of sub-Saharan Africa are represented in the collection, the coverage of South Africa and Nigeria is especially strong, and the Library has a special responsibility for collecting on St. Helena.

The library also has extensive holdings of government documents, especially for the colonial period, from the former British territories in Africa. These include long runs of debates from the various forms of legislative assembly, of annual departmental reports and of government gazettes. The holdings of published census reports on Africa are amongst the most comprehensive in the country. Law is covered by the Bodleian Law Library, which contains legislation from Commonwealth countries in Africa, but not from Francophone Africa.

The library has not attempted to collect African newspapers comprehensively; rather, there are long runs of some of the continent's major newspaper titles, including the *Cape Times*, the *East African Standard*, and the *Herald* of Zimbabwe. These are supplemented by shorter runs of rare nineteenth- and early twentieth-century titles, such as the *Mafeking Mail* and *Ladysmith Lyre*.

From its opening in 1929 the library was envisaged as a library not just of books, but also of archival material. The Rhodes Trustees deposited the papers of Cecil Rhodes there, and within a few years these had been supplemented by the papers of some of his associates. These included papers relating to the Jameson Raid such as Bobby White's diary which he took with him on the Raid, and which was subsequently used by the Boers to implicate Rhodes in the plot. Other early acquisitions included the papers of Horace Waller who was David Livingstone's literary executor, and those of the Anti-Slavery and Aborigines Protection Society, which date back to the formation of the Committee on Slavery in 1823 and which the library continues to receive on a decennial basis. This collection contains letters from William Wilberforce and Thomas Clarkson amongst others, and associated with it are the papers of another leading campaigner against slavery, Sir Thomas Fowell Buxton.

However, it was principally through the work of the Oxford Colonial Records Project, established in 1963, that the manuscripts collection at Rhodes House was transformed into one of national and international importance for the study of British colonial history, which now comprises over 4,000 individual collections. The OCRP, which grew out of a number of preliminary discussions and pilot projects, set itself the task of collecting the private papers of colonial administrators, which would augment the official papers available at the Public Record Office. Approximately 13,000 former members of the Colonial Service were traced and approached, and many responded positively to the appeal. The range and variety of the papers collected was very wide. Former governors and district officers donated their papers, as did agriculturalists, teachers, doctors, settlers, engineers and surveyors. Donations varied considerably in size: some consisted of single items, others filled several trunks and packing cases. Many contained a great many personal letters home to their families, others had personal or work diaries, handing-over notes or other official reports and memoranda, and, in many cases, photograph albums. Many former officials produced unpublished memoirs of their service, and, on a lighter note, some of them also donated examples of colonial verse and amateur musicals. Within the first five years approximately 1,500 collections were acquired, including such major donations as the papers of Arthur Creech Jones, Colonial Secretary under Attlee, and of the Fabian Colonial Bureau, one of the principal pressure groups on colonial affairs from 1940 to 1964.

The OCRP was succeeded in 1977 by the Oxford Development Records Project. Whereas the former had focussed primarily on administrative and political history, the ODRP was specifically designed to widen the collecting policy to include the papers and recorded experiences of both officials and non-officials involved in the economic development of the former British dependencies in Africa. The majority of the papers collected were arranged into twelve groups, each of which dealt with a particular area of development, and each project resulted in one or more specially compiled reports on development, such as agriculture, education, health care and the role of women, which were based on the archival materials collected.

Since 1985 the work of the OCRP and the ODRP has been carried on directly by the library under the general title of Oxford Colonial Archives Project. OCAP continues to solicit documentary and, increasingly, visual material relating to the colonial and post-colonial history of all parts of the former British Empire with the exception of India, Pakistan and Bangladesh, as well as other aspects of British involvement in these countries, such as election monitoring or health care. Amongst the major collections made available during this period have been the papers of Lord Lugard, Sir George Farrar, Sir Roy Welensky, Michael Blundell and Elspeth Huxley. The centenary of the Anglo-Boer War of 1899–1902 saw the library acquire a number of interesting collections relating to the war, including siege diaries and journals from Ladysmith and Kimberley, and an unusual 'Flogging register', which records the punishments meted out by the British to their African servants and auxiliaries. Nor has more recent history been neglected. During the first fully democratic elections in South Africa in 1994 the library made a special effort to collect as many campaign materials as possible; these included manifestos, posters, badges, banners and cassette recordings as well as voter education materials, the aim being to reflect the style as well as the substance of the campaign.

Illustrative material acquired has included large number of photographs, but also some original art work. Notable in this category are the sketches and watercolours of Phoebe Somers (1902–1995), who was an art teacher in Kenya for a number of years and also travelled widely in other part of eastern and southern Africa, recording both the places, and more particularly, the people she saw. A similarly fine collection of original paintings and drawings, this time covering Nigeria, is contained in the papers of Charles Temple (1871–1929) who was Lieutenant Governor of Northern Nigeria 1914–1917.

The largest collection to come to the library during this period was the historic archive of the Society for the Propagation of the Gospel, which, having been founded in 1701, is the oldest of the Anglican missionary societies. This covers its work in Africa since the eighteenth century, and includes long series of letters and reports home from missionaries in the field as well as maps, photographs and a notable collection of glass lantern slides, some of which date back to the nineteenth century. The archive incorporates the papers of the former Universities' Mission to Central Africa which amalgamated with the SPG in 1965. This contains a number of important original watercolours by Charles Mellor who was a member of David Livingstone's party.

The SPG deposit also included a significant part of its library. This contains many scarce items, periodicals as well as books, which in many cases were printed on mission presses in the field. Amongst them is a copy of John Ogilby's *Africa* (1670) which contains a rare extra plate not found in the majority of copies (including the legal deposit copy held by the Bodleian).

Of almost equal size, but covering a much shorter time span, is the archive of the British Anti-Apartheid Movement, which was received in 1996 and which covers the entire history of the movement from the early Boycott Movement of 1959 through to the dissolution of the AAM in 1995. The AAM archive has also attracted other collections in its wake, making the library an important centre for the study of the liberation struggle in southern Africa. Papers in this group include those of the Namibia Support Committee and of Archbishop Trevor Huddleston, and the library also holds the papers of Michael Scott, who for many years was a leading participant in the campaign for Namibian independence. As with the SPG deposit, the acquisition of the AAM archive led to the library acquiring much rare printed material including pamphlets and runs of journals produced by anti-Apartheid movements from around the world, and similar materials produced by resistance and liberation movements located within southern Africa. It is also worthy of note that a good deal of material supportive of the Apartheid government and its policies was received, illustrating the fact that the library continues, as it has always done, to collect right across the political spectrum.

The Western Manuscript collections in the central Bodleian contain much material relating to Sub-Saharan Africa, especially to South Africa. Of outstanding importance are the papers of Alfred, Lord Milner, High Commissioner for South Africa from 1892 to 1905, and of his wife Violet. The papers of William Palmer, 2nd Earl of Selborne, Milner's successor as High Commissioner, and of Lionel Curtis and of the Round Table organisation of which he was a founder, also contain much of interest, as do many of the smaller collections.

Select bibliography

Louis B. Frewer, 'Rhodes House Library, its Function and Resources', *Bodleian Library Record*, 5/6 (1956), 318–332; and 'Addenda', *BLR*, 7/3 (1964), 144–148.

L.B. Frewer, *Manuscript Collections of Africana in Rhodes House Library Oxford* (Oxford: Rhodes House Library, 1968), and *Supplement* (1971).

W.S. Byrne, *Manuscript Collections (Africana and Non-Africana) in Rhodes House Library Oxford: Supplementary Accessions to the End of 1977.* (Oxford: Bodleian Library, 1978).

Patricia Pugh, 'The Oxford Colonial Records Project and the Oxford Development Records Project', *Journal of the Society of Archivists*, 6/2 (October 1978), 76–86.

Patricia Pugh, 'The Papers of Frederick Dealtry Lugard, Baron Lugard of Abinger (1858–1945)', *Bodleian Library Record*, 12/6 (1988), 478–488.

Patricia Pugh, 'The Papers of Dame Margery Perham', *Bodleian Library Record*, 13/2 (1989), 133–151.

C.E. Brown, *Manuscript Collections in Rhodes House Library Oxford: Accessions 1978–1994* (Oxford: Bodleian Library, 1996).

John Pinfold, 'Archives in Oxford relating to the South African War', *South African Historical Journal*, 41 (1999), 422–42.

South Africa in the Twentieth Century [exhibition catalogue] (Oxford: Bodleian Library, 2000).

25. Printed Ephemera

The John Johnson Collection

The John Johnson Collection is one of the largest, widest-ranging and most important collections of printed ephemera in Britain and, indeed, in the world. Collectors of what is now termed 'printed ephemera' had traditionally specialised in one or more specific areas: Samuel Pepys, for example, continued John Selden's collection of ballads and also collected *vulgaria*; John Bagford collected ballads, trade cards and title pages; Sir Ambrose Heal and Sarah Banks both specialised in trade cards. John Johnson was a pioneer in collecting across the whole spectrum of printing and social history. The term 'printed ephemera' was established, partly in response to Johnson's collection (and the contemporary collection of Bella C. Landauer at the New York Historical Society), by John Lewis through his seminal work, *Printed Ephemera* (1962).

John de Monins Johnson (1882–1956), C.B.E., Hon. D.Litt., was inspired to form his collection by his work as a papyrologist. It was while excavating ancient documents (he discovered a papyrus of Theocritus pre-dating by 900 years any previously known manuscript of the author) that he wondered what was being done to preserve our immediate paper heritage:

> Often I used to look over those dark and crumbling sites and wonder what could be done to treat the background of our own English civilization with the same minute care with which we scholars were treating the ancient.

Having returned from Egypt to Oxford, unfit for military service, at the beginning of the First World War, Johnson was employed by the Oxford University Press as Assistant Secretary to the Delegates of the Press. After the war he remained at the Press, becoming Printer to the University from 1925 until his retirement in 1946. The circumstances were ideal for the formation of his collection, which began at his home in Headington as potential illustrations for children's history books.

Realising that the material would increase in market value if it became desirable, Johnson did not advertise his nascent collection very widely. An article did, however, appear in the typographic journal *Signature*. With the help of his small circle of cognoscenti, booksellers and printers, Johnson's collection grew rapidly. It was transferred in 1931 to the former Bible Printers' Office at the Oxford

University Press (where it was called the Constance Meade Memorial Collection of Ephemeral Printing after one of Johnson's benefactors) and became the property of the University.

Johnson's collection was also enriched by material discarded from the Bodleian itself, which was passed to him by Strickland Gibson (the first Keeper of Printed Books) when, in 1938, a statute of the Library enabled the Curators to 'eliminate from the Library material of no literary or artistic value or of an ephemeral nature which it is not in the interests of the Library to include in the catalogue or preserve on the shelves.' Specifically included in the eliminations were 'illuminated texts, small calendars, and advertisements.'

When the collection came to the Bodleian in 1968, it was renamed The John Johnson Collection of Printed Ephemera. A major exhibition was held in 1971, the catalogue of which (*The John Johnson Collection, Catalogue of an Exhibition*) remains the standard work on the collection.

The John Johnson Collection numbers well over a million items, mostly but not exclusively British. It is in the organisation of the material that Johnson succeeded where so many had failed. Clearly, an item-by-item card catalogue was impractical for a collection of (mainly) single sheets. Johnson developed a self-filing system: differently coloured boxes and large folders for each major collecting area (Advertisements; Artists; Authors; Booktrade and Publishing History; Education; Entertainment; Political, Religious, Social and Economic History; Printing Processes; Private Presses; Transport; etc.). Additionally, some of the ephemera in the collection are kept by their form: Trade Cards, Tickets, Greetings Cards, etc. Within these broad categories are some 680 headings. The material was sorted and indexed by Johnson's assistant, Lilian Thrussell, *née* Gurden (who accompanied the Collection to its new home in the Bodleian) and by Elizabeth Fraser. In terms of preservation, Johnson was also ahead of his time. In contrast with many collectors who used albums, Johnson mounted the material, usually singly, on good-quality sheets of paper, which protected the items from direct handling.

When the collection came to the Bodleian, the priority was to enhance the finding aids by providing more detailed guides to the contents of the boxes. This work continues. Now, however, with the benefit of computer technology, an item-by-item catalogue is in preparation, using a tagged cataloguing format within the user-configurable German bibliographic database system *allegro-C*. This catalogue maximises the access points to this traditionally elusive material (often lacking title, author, date or imprint) and enables many strands of the Collection to be brought together, giving access by printer, engraver, artist, place, date, performer, tradesman, trade, product, subject of illustration, type of material, printing process, etc.

The collection also lends itself ideally to digitisation, which will further increase access by eventually enabling users (in the Library or elsewhere) to browse the material electronically in the order best suited to their research rather than in its physical sequence. Furthermore, digitisation makes the material available to a far wider user-group, without compromising the preservation of the original items for future generations. Digital projects already on the Internet are the Toyota Project (motor car and other transport ephemera); Ballads (all Bodleian ballad collections, including those in the John Johnson Collection); Political and Satirical Prints; Trade Cards; and Trades and Professions Prints. The *Backstage* cataloguing project has made it possible to catalogue the majority of the playbills and theatre programmes in the John Johnson Collection. Playbills and other eighteenth-century Entertainment Ephemera are being digitised for the Oxford Digital Library. An exhibition on the subject of trades (*A Nation of Shopkeepers: Trade Ephemera from 1654 to the 1860s in the John Johnson Collection*), was held from October to December 2001 and was the first Bodleian exhibition to be mounted on the Internet.

John Johnson collected retrospectively, believing that history should make its own unconscious selection of the past. The date of the earliest item of printed ephemera in the collection (pre-dated by some prints) is 1508. There are sixteenth- and seventeenth-century items, assembled into Wing and STC guardbooks and kept with Johnson's books. The collection is strong in the eighteenth century and stronger still in the nineteenth and early twentieth centuries. In addition to printed ephemera (mostly, but not exclusively, single sheets) there are artefacts. Johnson stopped collecting in most areas in 1939, realising that he could have filled rooms with the ephemera of the Second World War. When the collection came to the Bodleian it was decided to collect contemporaneously. The Bodleian remains one of the few libraries in England to collect current ephemera. Post-1960 material is kept in a separate sequence and sorted into categories analogous to those of John Johnson. The gap from 1940 to the late 1960s largely remains. Special categories within the modern sequence are Elections, Gallery Five (greetings cards and wrapping papers), the Stanbrook Abbey Press, the Tern Press, Oxford University Societies, the Millennium, and the Golden Jubilee (2002).

Pre-1960 accessions (by purchase or donation) are annotated and interfiled with the original collection. However, two large retrospective purchases since 1968, the Royal Printing Archive and the Bridgnorth Collection, have both been preserved as discrete collections within the John Johnson Collection. In 2002 the Mary Gardiner Collection of Card Games was acquired by donation.

Other ephemera collections in the Bodleian

Despite the 'eliminations' of the 1930s, the Bodleian's collections (other than the John Johnson Collection) remain a source of printed ephemera. While the classification system made it easy to identify for elimination whole areas of ephemeral material (advertising catalogues, postcards, calendars, childen's games, etc.), material within named collections (both printed and manuscript) was, of course, preserved. The ephemera that remain are, however, difficult to access as they are often uncatalogued. For the period 1475–1800, the *Short-Title Catalogue*, Wing, and the *Eighteenth Century Short-Title Catalogue* have identified much of this dispersed material. For Oxford ephemera, *A Bibliography of Printed Works relating to the City of Oxford* and the companion volumes for the county and university by E.H. Cordeaux and D.H. Merry are invaluable.

The principal Bodleian collections to include printed ephemera are: Douce and Douce adds., Firth, Wood, Gough and Gough adds., Malone adds. and Rawlinson. Ballads at the classification 2806 were also preserved. Another resource is the books themselves, frequently adorned with bookplates and booksellers' labels. Ephemera in manuscript collections can only be found by detailed reading of the catalogues, but such collections can provide a good resource of, for example, invitations, bill headings, menus and other personal memorabilia.

The Bodleian has recently acquired further collections rich in ephemera, for example the Dunston, Dew, Brister and Ryder collections. A checklist of ephemera dispersed among the Bodleian's collections is being compiled on the John Johnson Collection web page. Contributions from readers who come across ephemeral material are welcomed.

Select Bibliography

Holbrook Jackson, 'A Sanctuary of Printing: The Record Room at the University Press, Oxford', *Signature*, 1 (November 1935).

Desiderata for the Sanctuary of Printing (privately printed at the Curwen Press, 1937).

John Lewis, *Printed Ephemera* (Ipswich: W.S. Cowell, 1962).

The John Johnson Collection, Catalogue of an Exhibition (Oxford: Bodleian Library, 1971).

Maurice Rickards, *Collecting Printed Ephemera* (Oxford: Phaidon Christie's, 1988).

Michael Twyman, *Printing 1770–1970: An Illustrated History of its Development and Uses in England* (London: The British Library &c., 1998).

Maurice Rickards, ed. and completed by Michael Twyman, *The Encyclopedia of Ephemera* (London: The British Library, 2000)

A Nation of Shopkeepers: Trade Ephemera from 1654 to the 1860s in the John Johnson Collection (Oxford: Bodleian Library, 2001).

Napoleon and the Invasion of Britain [exhibition catalogue] (Oxford: Bodleian Library, 2003).

A list of the Main Subject Headings and information about the John Johnson Collection are available from the Librarian of the Collection and on the Internet (www.bodley.ox.ac.uk/johnson).

26. Pictorial Resources

The Sackler Library is the University's principal research library for the history of Western art and architecture; it now also houses the Eastern Art Library, which was built up within (and is still maintained by) the Bodleian's Oriental Collections department. Nevertheless, the Bodleian's collections form a rich repository of primary research materials for the history of art and architecture (principally – though not exclusively – in the field of the arts of the book), and in broader terms offer a vast range of pictorial and illustrative resources. The buildings housing the central Bodleian, though they lie outside the scope of this guide, are themselves major architectural monuments. The top floor of the Old Schools Quadrangle, now the Upper Reading Room, originally housed the University's collection of portraits, and can claim to have been the first public art gallery in Britain.

Europe

Medieval and Renaissance illuminated manuscripts

Of the Bodleian's rich collection of over 2,000 Western illuminated manuscripts, it is not surprising that British manuscripts constitute the largest single group. Many of the British manuscripts are survivors of the sixteenth-century Dissolution of the monasteries and their libraries, and were acquired by the Bodleian in the seventeenth and eighteenth centuries. Second in number are those from Italy; for these the most important source is the collection of the Venetian secularized Jesuit Matteo Luigi Canonici (1727–c.1806), the greater part of which was bought in 1817, the Bodleian's largest single purchase of manuscripts to date. For French and Flemish illuminated manuscripts, especially of the fourteenth and fifteenth centuries, the richest of the Library's constituent collections is that of Francis Douce (1757–1834), who acquired many of his manuscripts from sales of famous collectors' libraries on the continent of Europe. The largest single group of German illuminated manuscripts is that given by Archbishop William Laud (1573–1645), which came in large part from the libraries of St. Kylian's in Würzburg, St. Mary's in Eberbach, and the Carthusian house at Mainz, all of which suffered depredations in the Thirty Years' War. Beyond its large European and Byzantine collections, the Bodleian also contains a small but significant group of five

Mesoamerican illuminated manuscripts, all of which reached the Library in the seventeenth century, three of them in the collection of John Selden (1584–1654).

Later manuscripts

The most important manuscript collection for architectural and topographical studies came with Richard Gough's bequest to the Library in 1809. It comprises some 10,000 original drawings, plans, engravings and other views of buildings in all parts of Great Britain, chiefly dating from the seventeenth century to the end of the eighteenth. These are described in an itemised list, arranged by county, which is kept in Duke Humfrey's Library at R.Ref. 756. Details of later acquisitions of similar material have been added to this list.

Drawings and plans by a variety of architects are scattered throughout the Western manuscript collections. References to many of them are to be found in Howard Colvin, *A Biographical Dictionary of British Architects 1600–1840* (3rd edition, Yale, 1995). They include, for example, two volumes of notes and sketches by Thomas Rickman (1776–1841) for the third edition of his *An Attempt to Discriminate the Styles of Architecture in England* (MSS. Top. eccl. c. 3–4) and a large collection of his sketches of medieval architecture (Dep. b. 140). One of the seventy or so 'red books' of Humphry Repton (1752–1818) – elaborately illustrated reports of his commissions – survives in the Bodleian. In it he described and illustrated his proposals of 1806–7 for improvements to the house and grounds of John Fuller at Rose Hill, Sussex (MS. Top. Sussex d. 2). Two volumes of drawings in the Gough collection (MSS. Gough Drawings a. 4–5) contain about fifty plans for houses and gardens designed by Charles Bridgeman (*d.*1738). An intriguing little anonymous notebook of the late eighteenth or early nineteenth century contains designs for seats, lodges, rustic cottages, caves and hermitages (MS. Top. gen. g. 2).

A large collection of drawings, engravings and photographs of buildings in the city and university of Oxford, with similar material for towns and villages in Oxfordshire, Berkshire and Buckinghamshire, acquired from various sources at different times, is indexed on cards available in Duke Humfrey's Library. They include many drawings by, among others, J.C. Buckler (1793–1894), Frederick Mackenzie (1788?–1854), J.B. Malchair (d.1800) and J.C. Nattes (1765?–1822).

The extensive collections of antiquarian manuscripts include much pictorial material on the antiquities, buildings and landscape of Great Britain. Of particular importance are the drawings made by William Stukeley (1687–1765) 'the father of British archaeology', of various ancient British sites, especially those at Avebury and Stonehenge, many of which do not appear in his published works. The focus of the majority of the collections is ecclesiastical. Most of the volumes of church notes of antiquaries from the sixteenth to the twentieth centuries contain drawings of churches, monuments, stained glass and the like: for example those of Henry

Johnston compiled on tours around the West Riding in 1669–71 (MSS. Top. Yorks. c. 13–14); of Thomas Dingley c.1680 (MS. Top. gen. d. 19), reproduced in facsimile in Camden Society, series I, 94 (1867) and 97 (1868); and of Henry Hinton (1749–1816) and James Hunt (1795–1857) for Oxfordshire and Berkshire.

In the second half of the nineteenth century, the antiquaries' collections of drawings and engravings were enhanced with photographs, such as those in the collections of Professor J.O. Westwood (1805–93) on sculptured crosses; of his niece Emma Swann on fonts; of John Mitchinson on the architectural remains of religious houses in the late nineteenth century; of Henry Minn (1870–1961) on the buildings of Oxford; and of P.S. Spokes on 'listed' buildings in Berkshire, 1932–72.

The Library possesses some 2,000 rubbings of brasses in English churches. In addition to a general collection drawn from a number of sources, it holds two large collections built up by Sir Thomas Phillipps (1792–1872) and Major H.F. Owen Evans (d.1966). Details of all the brass rubbings in the Library are available in an annotated copy of Mill Stephenson, *A List of Monumental Brasses in the British Isles* (London, 1926; kept in Duke Humfrey's Library at R.6.366). Richard Gough's collection includes a large number of engravings and drawings (many by Jacob Schnebbelie (1762–92), John Carter (1748–1817) and James Basire (1730–1802)), assembled for a projected third edition of his *Sepulchral Monuments in Great Britain* (Gough Maps 221–8 and 228*). Gough also acquired, by means which remain obscure, sixteen volumes of drawings of royal and other monuments and tombs in France collected by François-Roger de Gaignières in the early eighteenth century (MSS. Gough drawings – Gaignières 1–16).

Journals of travels both in Great Britain and in Continental Europe exist in large numbers in the Western manuscript collections, and many of these contain drawings of buildings and views. The majority of collections of eighteenth- and nineteenth-century family papers include sketchbooks, though few of the sketches are as accomplished or as important as the many illustrations in the draft works of William Gilpin (1724–1804) in the Gilpin family papers or Mendelssohn's watercolours in the M. Deneke Mendelssohn Collection. Watercolours and drawings by J.R.R. Tolkien are preserved among his papers. Occasionally manuscripts collected as historical documents contain illustrations of considerable interest, such as the pencil sketches of Captain R.B. Hawley of the 89th Regiment which were enclosed in his letters from the Crimea in 1854–6 (MS. Crampton 90).

Heraldry

The antiquarian collections also contain a wealth of material for the study of heraldry. They include the papers of three heralds: Elias Ashmole, Windsor

Herald from 1660, Sir William Dugdale (1605–86), Garter King-of-Arms, and J.C. Brooke (1748–94), Somerset Herald, and provide many examples of rolls of arms, armorials, pedigrees and the like, many associated with heraldic visitations. Both heralds 'officially' and antiquaries 'unofficially' systematically recorded coats of arms in sepulchral monuments and stained glass, records which survive in their volumes of church notes. Those of the sixteenth to eighteenth centuries are of particular importance in recording features lost during Victorian renovations. Among the earliest are those of Robert Lee, Clarenceux King-of Arms, for his visitation of Oxfordshire in 1574–5 (MS. Wood D. 14). Ashmole's collections for Berkshire include the drawings he made during his visitation of the county in 1664–6 (MS. Ashmole 850). J.C. Brooke's manuscripts include a wide-ranging series of 'field books' for the period 1775–93 (MSS. Top. gen. e. 99–127). The tradition of making church notes was continued by generations of amateur antiquaries and gained fresh impetus with the growing interest in local history throughout the twentieth century. Two modern donations are particularly important for heraldic studies – those of William Harry Rylands (1847–1922), and of Major H.F.Owen Evans (d.1966).

The heraldic manuscripts collected by David Askew in the nineteenth century include an unusual survival of an heraldic painter's notebook, which contains notes and sketches for work at funerals, 1734–41 (MS. Eng. misc. f. 38). In the general collections is an interesting sketchbook (MS. Eng. misc. c. 115) of arms executed in stained glass c.1830–54 by Thomas Willement (1786–1871).

Illustrated printed books

Illustration can be broadly divided into two kinds: the practical (for example books of architectural design, anatomy, botany, and astronomy), and the decorative (enhancing the text or providing an alternative text for the illiterate). As a scholarly library the Bodleian has always been keen to acquire the former kind, though financial constraints have limited acquisition by purchase: books requiring large, high-quality and very accurate illustration are expensive. However, gifts, presentations, and legacies have often filled gaps in this area. Decorative illustration was not a priority for the Library for much of its history, but the collections of others coming in over the past four centuries have more than compensated for this lack of interest. Once legal deposit began to be more or less comprehensive (from about the middle of the nineteenth century), nearly all British illustrated books – from novels and children's books to medical textbooks – have been received, with the notable exception of the productions of private presses and *livres d'artiste*.

Practical illustration includes the woodcuts of plants in the copy of John Gerard's 1597 *Herball*, presented by the publisher; Hevelius' *Selenographia* (1643), with its beautiful copperplate illustrations of the moon, presented by the author;

Besler's *Hortus Eystettensis* (1613) and Dillenius' *Hortus Elthamensis* (1732); the woodcut views in the *Nuremberg Chronicle* (1493), and the hand-coloured panoramas of Breydenbach's *Peregrinatio* (1486). The splendid plate books of natural history produced in the nineteenth century, such as the bird books of Audubon and Gould, and the exquisite *Flora Graeca* (1806–40), though aimed at rich collectors, have found their way into the Library. Vesalius' *De humani corporis* (1543), with its haunting anatomical figures set in landscapes, Spaher's curious *An Exact Survey of the Microcosmus* (1670), with multiple layers of illustration, and George Stubbs's extraordinary *The Anatomy of the Horse* (1766), are characteristic medical and veterinary books. Architectural books range from Vitruvius in the fifteenth century to the Taylors' designs for shop-fronts in Regency towns. Decorative illustration ranges from the cheap, badly printed woodcuts in chapbooks and ballad sheets from the sixteenth to nineteenth centuries, to, at the other extreme, the fine art prints of artists' books. The Library's holdings of popular literature provide an extraordinary resource for research into popular prints.

Collections of fables and the Dance of Death have attracted distinguished artists such as Holbein and Rowlandson, and were produced for a popular market in editions with fine woodcuts by Bewick and Linnell, or in cheap formats with very crude cuts. Emblem books, popular among the educated in the sixteenth and seventeenth centuries, tended to remain at the upper end of the market and usually featured fine illustration. There are substantial works in print by artists ranging from Dürer to Blake to Sendak, and by the classic Victorian trio Caldecott, Crane, and Greenaway; a special collection is devoted to books illustrated by Arthur Rackham. The most enigmatic of all illustrated books, the *Hypnerotomachia Poliphili*, or *Strife of Love in a Dream*, published by Aldus in Venice in 1499, is present in several early editions. The revival of fine printing in the late nineteenth and early twentieth centuries is strongly represented with examples from the Kelmscott, Doves, and Golden Cockerel presses; and the Library continues to collect selectively in this field (in 2002 it acquired the latest Gehenna Press book, Ted Hughes's translation of the *Oresteia* with illustrations by Leonard Baskin). There is a small but significant number of *livres d'artiste* containing, for example, the work of Picasso, Braque, and de Chirico. Fifteenth-century blockbooks, telling biblical stories in pictures, often vividly coloured and accompanied by captions, are in certain respects the precursors of the twentieth-century children's comic, of which the Library has representative samples.

There are good holdings of that closely related genre, the how-to-draw-and-paint book, in the Library, particularly the nineteenth-century manuals for young people, and notably the myrioramas and their fellow teaching aids: finely engraved and coloured strips depicting a variety of landscape and groups of figures, which can be juxtaposed in every possible way to create the picture wanted by the drawing-master or his pupil.

Prints and printed ephemera

Although prints are not collected as such, the Library has a few significant collections of socio-historical interest. Approximately 1,200 political cartoons and caricatures relating to Napoleon are in the Curzon Collection; twenty-five albums of mainly British social and political satire are in the Firth Collection. Both these collections also contain portraits, historical scenes, topographical prints, and views. Some eighteen volumes and two boxes of portraits from the seventeenth to the nineteenth centuries are in the Montagu Collection. Mention should also be made of actual copperplates. There are some 2,000 in the Lister Collection, mainly plates made from drawings done to illustrate Martin Lister's *De cochleis* (1685); 400 in the Gough Collection, again mostly the plates for Richard Gough's *Sepulchral Monuments of Great Britain* (1786–99); and about 750 in the Rawlinson Collection, many purchased by weight by Richard Rawlinson, presumably to save them. These cover a large and miscellaneous subject field, but some are of great importance, particularly an early set of engravings for an apparently never-published book describing North America. Selected plates have been printed from in recent times.

The John Johnson Collection (on which see also the chapter on Printed Ephemera) contains much of art-historical interest and some material relating to architecture. There are boxes and folders relating to the work of individual illustrators and a catalogued sequence of artists' invitations, which includes invitations to exhibitions of such artists as Matisse and Picasso. The names index within the Johnson online catalogue increasingly provides access to the work of illustrators, engravers and the like across the collection (posters, advertisements, trade cards, etc.). The collection is also a major resource for the study of the history of design, especially through such media as advertisements, posters and book-jackets. Ephemera have been at the cutting edge of printing technology (for example in chromolithography and photo-reprographic processes) and provide insights into changes in graphic design. There are strong holdings of the ephemeral output of private presses, including work by such artists as Eric Gill and Charles Ricketts. Sections specifically of relevance to the study of architecture are: Housing and Town Planning, and Building Estates (including Garden Cities). There is also a small Art and Architecture section.

Photographs

Although the Bodleian does not have a photographic collection in the form of a concentrated, fully catalogued and indexed collection, the Library does hold tens of thousands of photographs (mainly prints and, to a lesser extent, glass plates, with a few daguerreotypes and ambrotypes), some by famous or notable photographers.

They are scattered throughout the numerous collections of manuscripts (the private papers of politicians, historians, theologians, writers, scientists, etc.); printed collections, including the first book published in this country illustrated with 'original' photographs, Fox Talbot's *The Pencil of Nature* (London, 1844–46); and ephemera (in the John Johnson Collection, see above). The subjects covered by the photographs are as wide-ranging as the collections in which they appear, but mostly fall within the following categories: family 'albums'; topographical and architectural views; historical events, for example Roger Fenton's photographs of the Crimean War published in 1855; portraits; art-photography by Julia Margaret Cameron and others; and photographs of works of art, including drawings and prints. Of particular importance are the photographs relating to the city and county of Oxford, notably the collections of Henry Minn, Percy Manning, George James Dew and Peter Spokes; and those relating to the University, its members, social life, buildings, and institutions, by Sarah Angelina Acland, James Edwin Thorold Rogers, Arthur Gray Butler and others.

The Bodleian has major holdings of publications on the history of photography and the work of leading photographers. Much of this comes from the purchase in 2000 of Dr. Mike Weaver's collection of 550 books and pamphlets (mainly American and continental European monographs and exhibition catalogues from the 1980s and 1990s), together with some important serial runs. It complements a high level of representation of twentieth-century British publishing in this field achieved through legal deposit.

Portraits

When the University Schools were completed in 1619, the top floor was designated part of the Bodleian. This, now the Upper Reading Room, was decorated just below ceiling level with a painted frieze of some 200 heads of learned men and one woman (Sappho) representing the great thinkers, theologians and world leaders from classical times onwards. Covered up during the Library restoration of 1830, the frieze was re-discovered in 1947 and restored in the 1950s and again in 2000. Sometime after the mid-seventeenth century the room developed into a picture gallery, the frieze possibly inspiring an initially haphazard accumulation of portraits of celebrated persons. This led to the acquisition by the Library of a collection of portraits which now exceeds 400 and which hangs in all parts of the central Bodleian, with some in other University buildings such as the Examination Schools. The first work of art acquired was appropriately the marble bust of Sir Thomas Bodley given by the Earl of Dorset in 1605. It now stands at the entrance to Duke Humfrey's Library opposite Le Sueur's fine bust of King Charles I, given by Archbishop Laud in 1636. Those which followed generally had an Oxford connection. Small groups were acquired, as in *c.*1670 when there arrived a series of imaginary portraits of Oxford college founders, mostly painted by Willem Sonmans; these now hang in Duke Humfrey's Library. In 1735 Humphrey Bartholomew presented eight portraits of celebrated doctors of medicine. A few years later Richard Rawlinson provided the Library with some 35 portraits of sitters ranging from Chaucer to himself.

Of particular interest is the series of portraits of Bodley's Librarians which runs, with a few gaps, from one of Thomas James (Librarian, 1600–20), attributed to Gilbert Jackson, to one of David Vaisey (Librarian, 1986–96) by Paul Brason, and includes portraits by Augustus John (of Sir Edmund Craster, Librarian, 1931–45) and Sir William Coldstream (of Robert Shackleton, Librarian, 1966–79). Two contrasting portraits of Sir Thomas Bodley are to be found in his library – a portrait in oils said to have been painted in Venice, c.1576–80, which was bought by the Bodleian in 1635, and an exquisite miniature painted by Nicholas Hilliard in 1598 and presented by Canon H.N. Ellacombe in 1897.

In recent years the portraits acquired by the Library have normally come as part of, or been associated with, manuscript or rare book collections, for example the miniatures and portraits in the Shelley collection. A couple of notable exceptions were the portrait of Ann Craster by Nathaniel Hone (1718–84), presented to mark her descendant Sir Edmund Craster's tenure of the Librarianship, and the half-length portrait in oils of Mendelssohn by Edward Magnus (1799–1872), presented by the Friends of the Bodleian in 1997. Another interesting miniature – of Byron in 1812 – was given by Lady Clementine Waring c.1960.

The Library also contains large collections of portrait engravings drawn from a variety of printed sources, chief amongst them being those in Montagu Illustrated. The important Hope and Sutherland collections of similar engravings formerly in the Library have been transferred to the Ashmolean Museum.

The Near and Middle East, Asia and Africa

Because of its long history the Bodleian has had unusual opportunities to acquire a wide range of material of pictorial and art historical interest, mainly manuscripts, produced in and relating to Asia and Africa. The Hebrew, Islamic and South Asian collections are particularly rich in fine illustrated manuscripts, but there are also many outstanding and important (though more isolated) examples in the Chinese and Japanese collections, and in those from the Christian Orient and Tibet, notwithstanding much smaller collections relating to South East Asia.

These unique primary sources are supported by a strong collection of secondary materials in European and vernacular languages held in the Eastern Art Library, which is recognised nationally as a significant research collection in its field. It covers all aspects of Asian and North African art, architecture and archaeology, including sculpture, painting, prints, ceramics, textiles, crafts, museum and exhibition catalogues, many from shows in Asia, and archaeological reports. Founded in 1962, since 1994 relevant materials acquired by the Bodleian under the legal deposit scheme have been integrated into the collection. The pre-Islamic Near East is excluded from its remit and is covered by other collections in the Sackler Library.

Hebrew collections

Although very far from all the Hebrew manuscripts in the Bodleian are illustrated, the three main schools are well represented. It is immediately striking that these schools did not develop in a vacuum but are influenced by the vernacular art of their countries of origin. Thus the Sephardic manuscripts reveal the influence of Islamic Spain in several respects. Most obvious is the use of 'carpet pages' which manifest the influence of Islamic design. Also their physical appearance and bindings are similar to their Islamic equivalents. They are also Spanish in lesser details; for instance, manuscripts produced in Castile sometimes use a castle as a motif. The Hebrew Biblical manuscripts of Benjamin Kennicott (1718–83), transferred to the Bodleian from the Radcliffe Library in 1872, include an outstanding example of Sephardic manuscript art in the 'Kennicott Bible', copied in 1476 (MS. Kennicott 1),

In a similar manner the Ashkenazic manuscripts, of which there are many in the Oppenheimer and Michael collections, have a distinctly 'Gothic' appearance in places, particularly in the architecture that they display. But it is the Hebrew manuscripts from Italy that most clearly demonstrate their country of origin. As those in the Canonici Collection were in fact assembled by an Italian Jesuit, it should not be surprising that the landscapes portrayed are manifestly of Italy, executed with delicacy and charm. For the illuminations in Hebrew manuscripts, a preliminary card index can be consulted upon request which lists the shelfmarks of each and the numbers of the folios which are illustrated, along with a brief description.

The Christian Orient

Some of the Syriac manuscripts are illustrated, in a style typical of the Eastern church, and there is a fine illuminated Coptic Gospels dated 1319 (MS. Marshall Or. 6). Among the Bodleian's modest collection of Ethiopic manuscripts are some interesting examples of Ethiopian painting, mainly of the seventeenth century, but including also a finely illustrated fifteenth-century Gospels (MS. Aeth. c. 2), along with some single sheet illustrations, in the Gondarene style. The Armenian manuscripts include an illuminated Gospels containing miniatures, including portraits of the Evangelists, which was produced in Julfa in 1596 (MS. Arm. d. 25). There are two illustrated manuscripts of the Georgian epic *The Man in the Panther Skin* by Shota Rustaveli, one of which, though incomplete, is of interest because of the quality of its miniatures (MS. Wardrop d. 27).

Islamic collections

The Bodleian's Islamic collections include many fine examples of Arabic and Persian manuscript ornamentation. Illumination is regularly found in Qur'ans as well as in manuscripts commissioned by wealthy patrons. There are illuminated Qur'ans from the Mamluk period, Safavid and Qajar Persia, and Ottoman and Indian examples. Among the scientific and technical Arabic manuscripts which contain illustrations are *The Book of Fixed Stars* by al-Sufi (1009) (MS. Marsh 144), Dioscorides's *Materia Medica* (1240) (MS. Arab. d. 138) and the *Automata* of al-Jazari (1486) (MS. Greaves 27). Two celebrated illustrated Mamluk literary manuscripts are the *Assemblies* of al-Hariri dated 1337 (MS. Marsh 458) and the *Kalilah wa-Dimnah* of 1354 (MS. Pococke 400). In addition might be mentioned the two manuscripts of al-Idrisi (MS. Greaves 42 and MS. Pococke 375) as well as other geographical works, including the Turkish manuscript of Piri Reis (MS. D'Orville 543), all illustrated with maps.

The Bodleian's Persian collection also includes many fine illustrated manuscripts representing the successive styles of Persian painting, from the fourteenth to the nineteenth century. Of the highest quality in terms of illumination as well as illustration is the *Shah-namah* of Firdawsi commissioned by Ibrahim Sultan (MS. Ouseley Add. 176). The manuscript dates from the period 1432–4 and is illustrated in the Shiraz style. Also from the Timurid period are the four volumes of Nevai's *Hamseh* ('Quintet'), dated 1485 (MSS. Elliott 287, 317, 339, 408), which represent the later Herat style. One of the miniatures in MS Marsh 517, an undated (but 1515–20) copy of the *Bustan* by the Persian poet Sa'di, bears an attribution to the master painter Bihzad. The style of the miniatures is that associated with Tabriz, the Safavid capital until 1548. From Mughal India there are illustrated codices and albums of pictures and calligraphy, including a seventeenth-century illustrated manuscript of al-Jazari's *Automata* (MS. Fraser 186). Of the highest quality is a copy of the poet Jami's *Abode of Spring* executed for the emperor Akbar in Lahore in 1595 (MS. Elliott 254). Among the albums and individual paintings is the haunting image of the dying 'Inayat Khan, painted in 1618 (MS. Ouseley Add. 171, fol. 4 verso). Turkish painting is not well represented in the collections though a manuscript of the *Sharafnamah*, a history of the Kurds dating from 1597 (MS. Elliott 332), contains twenty miniatures that are representative of the style.

Africa

The Bodleian Library of Commonwealth and African Studies at Rhodes House contains many original photographs, drawings, watercolours and other illustrative material in its manuscript collections relating to colonial history. Some of the most significant of these are referred to in the chapters on Sub-Saharan Africa,

Australasia and North America, but there are also a number of other items, including a set of five pencil sketches of Napoleon and Longwood House made by Captain Guy Rotton on St. Helena in 1821. The papers of the Anti-Apartheid Movement contain a bust of Nelson Mandela, and the Huddleston papers an oil painting of Huddleston when Bishop of Stepney.

South Asia

The Bodleian has an important collection of over 800 paintings in the Mughal style, and bazaar art is well represented by just over a hundred Kalighat paintings (see further in the chapter on South and South East Asia). Paper did not arrive in India until the thirteenth century and the use of vellum never developed because of religious objections to killing animals. The non-Islamic South Asian manuscript tradition, therefore, is based on palm-leaf manuscripts in the *pothī* format: thin strips of treated palm-leaf held together by string, which runs through holes cut in each of the leaves. Many manuscripts consist solely of palm-leaves but some do have loose wooden covers. Hinduism does not have a highly developed illustrative tradition and the Bodleian collection reflects this, with the majority of its Hindu texts being without illustration of any kind. The notable exceptions are some highly decorative eighteenth-century *Bhagavadgītās* and an *Adhyātmarāmāyana*, copied out on long rolls of thin, highly burnished paper, probably to be kept as amulets, conferring divine protection on their owners. Most of the illustrated texts in the collection are either Jain or Buddhist. Buddhist decoration runs from wooden manuscript covers painted with simple floral designs to eleventh- and twelfth-century manuscripts with finely detailed miniatures painted on the palm leaves and wooden covers. The finest illustrated manuscript in the collection is undoubtedly MS. Sansk. a. 7 (R), which contains miniatures of the Buddha's life painted during the high point of Pala art in the eleventh century.

Tibet

The Bodleian's Oriental Collections department houses at least three illuminated Tibetan manuscripts, which all represent texts from the Buddhist tradition. Illuminations usually show miniatures of deities, Buddhas and sometimes historical figures (for instance the sponsor of a text). Works that are illuminated throughout (i.e. on every page) are rare: normally the illuminations are found on the first few pages, sometimes also on the last page. This is true for the Bodleian's manuscripts, two of which (MS. Tib. a. 26 (R) + 27 (R)), from the late nineteenth - early twentieth century, form part of a Buddhist *sūtra* from the 'Perfection of Wisdom' section of the Tibetan Kanjur. The third one (MS. Tib. a. 24 (R)), dating from the late eighteenth century, represents volume one of a 33-volume set of the *rNying ma rgyud 'bum*, a collection of texts from the oldest of the four major schools of Tibetan Buddhism, the *rNying-ma-pa*. Apart from illuminated manuscripts the Tibetan collections include around 25 Tibetan *thangkas*, all on loan to the Ashmolean Museum, which are of relatively late date (eighteenth-nineteenth century) and reasonable quality.

South East Asia

Among the Library's Malay manuscripts is one of the oldest and most beautiful royal Malay letters, from the Sultan of Aceh to King James I (MS. Laud Or. Rolls b. 1). Javanese illustration is notably represented by a colourful divination almanac (MS. Jav. d. 2). There are a number of illustrated Burmese manuscripts, among them one from the nineteenth century containing a series of watercolours of Burmese life (MS. Burm. a. 5). A Thai religious manuscript (MS. Pali a. 27(R)), in folding format, has illustrations of animals and people painted in a provincial style.

China

Although the Library's collections of traditional Chinese books are not particularly rich in illustrated editions, there are nonetheless a number of outstanding examples. Two of these were acquired in recent years, the well-known *Lienüzhuan* ('Biographies of famous women') (Sinica 3738) printed in 1779 from blocks cut during the Wanli period of the Ming (1573–1620), and the *Shengxian xiangzan* ('Portraits and eulogies of Confucian worthies') (Sinica 3737) engraved in 1632. Of landscape illustration 'The Imperial progress to the southern provinces' (Backhouse 319), an imperial edition of 1766, and the *Ningxiangshi hongxue yinyuan tuji* ('Footprints of a wild goose in the snow') (Backhouse 139), the illustrated autobiography of the Manchu scholar-offical Lin Qing compiled and printed in 1849 by his secretaries, are both among the finest flowers of their period.

Japan

Bodleian illustrated manuscripts in Japanese are few, numbering some sixty titles. Many of them were acquired late in the nineteenth or early in the twentieth century, when rare books were still not too difficult nor too expensive to buy in Japan. Notable among these are a collection of *Nara-ehon* (Nara picture books), illuminated manuscripts in either book or scroll format from the seventeenth and eighteenth centuries, such as *Otogi zōshi*, a collection of medieval popular tales, and Urashima, one of the most ancient and popular Japanese legends. Those in bound book form have decorative covers. Some of these were produced as luxury volumes for daughters of a daimyō (feudal lord) as bridal gifts. A hand scroll of Hinazuru is a great rarity, thought to be the only existing text. Apart from *Nara-ehon*, the collection is miscellaneous in character. Included are over twenty titles donated from the collection of H. N. Moseley (1844–91), such as a very fine example of Baishō Tamate's picture books of *nō-kyōgen* illustrations (1858 or 1859), another rarity. The number of single-sheet woodblock prints is not many: the majority are pasted and made into albums. Many of the printed books of the Edo period in the collection, whether literary or non-literary, carry some form of illustrations.

Korea

The painted representation of the central part of the funeral procession of Queen Dowager Chō which took place in 1890, presented to the Library by Bishop Trollope in 1902, is one of only two Korean manuscripts held by the Library. The other contains illustrations of figures from China's legendary past.

Select bibliography

Medieval and Renaissance Illuminated Manuscripts

O. Pächt and J. J. G. Alexander, *Illuminated Manuscripts in the Bodleian Library Oxford. 1: German, Dutch, Flemish, French and Spanish Schools. 2: Italian School. 3: British, Irish, and Icelandic Schools* (Oxford, 1966–73); see also the *Concordance* of Bodleian shelf-marks for vols. 1–3 and addenda by B. C. Barker-Benfield (Oxford, 1974). For a small number of additions to Pächt and Alexander, see A. C. de la Mare, 'Further Italian Illuminated Manuscripts in the Bodleian Library', in *La Miniatura Italiana tra Gotico e Rinascimento, I. Atti del II Congresso di Storia della Miniatura Italiana, Cortona, 24–26 settembre 1982* (Florence, 1985), 127–54. The Byzantine illuminated manuscripts are described in the catalogue by I. Hutter, *Corpus der Byzantinischen Miniaturenhandschriften.* Vols. 1–3: Oxford Bodleian Library (Stuttgart, 1977–82). These catalogues include manuscripts with ornamental initials and decoration, as well as those with historiated initials and miniatures.

Full colour digital facsimiles of a small number of important manuscripts are available on the Early Manuscripts at Oxford University website (http://image.ox.ac.uk). Images of single pages accompany some of the entries in the online catalogue of all the Bodleian's Western medieval and Renaissance manuscripts: www.bodley.ox.ac.uk/dept/scwmss/wmss/online/online.htm .

The Library also sells 35mm colour filmstrip rolls of illuminated manuscripts, containing either images from an individual manuscript or selections from various manuscripts on a particular theme: see the catalogue *Colour Transparencies (35mm) Available from the Bodleian Library, Part I: Filmstrips* (Bodleian Library, 1983), with a *Supplement* (1988) and a *Second Appendix* (2001). Checklists based on this catalogue are available online at: www.bodley.ox.ac.uk/dept/scwmss/wmss/photos.htm#Filmstrips. Consultation copies of the filmstrips, together with an iconographic card index of the subjects illustrated in all the Bodleian's Western medieval and renaissance manuscripts, are housed within the Department of Special Collections and Western Manuscripts.

Published facsimiles of illuminated manuscripts, together with catalogues of other collections and monographs on the history of illumination, are kept on the open shelves of Duke Humfrey's Library, the main reading room for medieval and renaissance manuscripts.

Later Manuscripts

Drawings of Oxford by J.C. Buckler, 1811–27 (Bodleian Picture Book no. 3; Oxford: Bodleian Library, 1951).

P. Long, 'The Keiller Collection of Stukeley Papers', *Bodleian Library Record,* 5/5 (1956), 256–61.

Mary Clapinson, 'The Topographical Collections of Henry Hinton and James Hunt', *Oxoniensia,* 37 (1972), 215–220.

Alison Maguire and Howard Colvin, 'A Collection of Seventeenth Century Architectural Plans, MS. Rawlinson D 710', *Architectural History,* 35 (1992), 140–69; reprinted in association with the Bodleian Library (Oxford, 1992).

Annette Peach, '"San fedele alla mia Biondetta": A Portrait of Lord Byron formerly belonging to Lady Caroline Lamb', *Bodleian Library Record,* 14/4 (1993), 285–95.

Jerome Bertram, 'Calendar of Material Relating to Sepulchral Monuments in the Gough Collection, Bodleian Library' (10 fascicules, unpublished, 1997–2003). Kept in Duke Humfrey's Library at R.6.261.

Sir John Gardner Wilkinson: Traveller and Egyptologist 1797–1875 [exhibition catalogue] (Oxford: Bodleian Library, 1997).

Heraldry

Heraldry [exhibition catalogue] (Oxford: Bodleian Library, 1967).

Illustrated Printed Books

Catalogue of an Exhibition of Books on Medicine, Surgery and Physiology (Oxford: Bodleian Library, 1947).

Art and its Images: An Exhibition of Printed Books Containing Engraved Illustrations after Italian Painting (Oxford: Bodleian Library, 1975).

French livres d'artiste in Oxford University Collections [exhibition catalogue] (Oxford: Bodleian Library, 1996).

The Flora Graeca Story: Oxford's Finest Botanical Treasure [exhibition catalogue] (Oxford: Bodleian Library, 1999).

Alexandra Franklin, 'The Art of Illustration in Bodleian Broadside Ballads Before 1820', *Bodleian Library Record,* 17/5 (2002), 327–52.

The collection of broadside ballads is available in digital form at www.bodley.ox.ac.uk/ballads/

Prints and Printed Ephemera

Napoleon and the Invasion of Britain [exhibition catalogue] (Oxford: Bodleian Library, 2003).

The majority of the prints in the John Johnson collection are individually catalogued (see under Catalogue at www.bodley.ox.ac.uk/johnson/). Many are also digitised (political cartoons, trades and professions prints, etc.).

Photographs

C. W. Judge, *Oxford Past and Present* (Oxford: Oxford Illustrators Ltd, 1970).

Photography and the Printed Page in the Nineteenth Century: An Exhibition at the Bodleian Library (Oxford: Bodleian Library, 2001).

Portraits

Sections on prints, portraits, coins and art collections in Sir Edmund Craster, *History of the Bodleian Library 1845–1945* (*See General Bibliography*), 112–119, 222–225, 313–315.

Articles on the Upper Reading Room friezes by J. N. L. Myres in *Bodleian Library Record*, 3/30 (1950), 82–9; 4/1 (1952), 30–51; 5/6 (1956), 290–308, and by M. R. A. Bullard in *Bodleian Library Record*, 14/6 (1994), 461–500.

Catalogue of Portraits in the Bodleian Library, by Mrs. Reginald Lane Poole, revised and expanded by Kenneth Garlick (Oxford: Bodleian Library, 2004).

Hebrew Collections

Cecil Roth, *The Kennicott Bible* (Bodleian Picture Books, 11; Oxford: Bodleian Library, 1957).

Bezalel Narkiss, *Hebrew Illuminated Manuscripts in the British Isles: A Catalogue Raisonné* (Oxford: Published by the Oxford University Press for the Israel Academy of Sciences and Humanities and the British Academy, 1982).

Clare Moore, ed., *The Visual Dimension: Aspects of Jewish Art* (Boulder: Westview Press, 1993).

The Christian Orient

Edward Ullendorff, *Catalogue of Ethiopian Manuscripts in the Bodleian Library*, *II* (Catalogi codicum manuscriptorum bibliothecae Bodleianae ; pars 7; Oxford: Clarendon Press, 1951).

Islamic Collections

B. W. Robinson, *A Descriptive Catalogue of the Persian Paintings in the Bodleian Library* (Oxford: Clarendon Press, 1958).

Emmy Wellesz, *An Islamic Book of Constellations* (Bodleian Picture Books, 13; Oxford: Bodleian Library, 1965).

B. W. Robinson and Basil Gray, *The Persian Art of the Book: Catalogue of an Exhibition held at the Bodleian Library to mark the Sixth International Congress of Iranian Art and Archaeology* (Oxford: Bodleian Library, 1972).

Susan Skilliter, *Life in Istanbul 1588* (Bodleian Picture Books, 15; Oxford: Bodleian Library, 1977).

South and South East Asian Collections

Andrew Topsfield, *Indian Paintings from Oxford Collections* (Oxford: Ashmolean Museum in association with the Bodleian Library, 1994).

Annabel T. Gallop and Bernard Arps, *Golden Letters: Writing Traditions of Indonesia* (London: The British Library, 1991).

27. Bindings

Medieval manuscripts

An early ninth-century ivory book-cover of Christ in majesty (MS. Douce 176) is the earliest of a few continental treasure-bindings of ivory, enamel or metal in the Bodleian's collections. There are also a few blind-stamped Romanesque bindings. However, the Library's greatest wealth of medieval bindings lies in the large number of plainer examples, made in England between the eleventh and fifteenth centuries. The wooden boards of the earlier bindings are covered with tawed leather without decoration, whilst later ones have tanned leather decorated with blind stamps. Those of the Anglo-Saxon and early Norman periods were studied by Graham Pollard, with the use of X-ray photographs which are still available for consultation (MSS. Photogr. b. 5–6). Pollard's analysis of the four periods of early English binding – Anglo-Saxon, 'monastic', c.1230/50–1450, and late medieval – was based largely on Bodleian examples. In 1602, over eighty manuscripts were given by Exeter Cathedral to the Bodleian as a foundation gift; they were recovered around then with white leather, which however often conceals an earlier medieval structure. The Bodleian's collections of manuscripts and incunables also include important groups of German, Italian and Greek bindings of the medieval and Renaissance periods.

Incunabula

Many particularly fine blind-tooled pigskin and calf bindings, dating from the fifteenth and early sixteenth centuries, survive on incunabula in the Bodleian, the pigskin ones being almost exclusively from Germany, whereas the calf bindings come from throughout Europe. In addition, there are interesting examples of contemporary parchment binding. The comparatively large number of German blind-tooled bindings in the Library reflects the Bodleian's acquisition of its incunable collections, the majority of which came from German monastic libraries dispersed during the nineteenth century. These, and the bindings from Italy, France, England, Spain and the Low Countries, are described in detail for the Bodleian's new catalogue of incunabula.

Collections strong in fine bindings

Three of the rare book collections contain such a number of fine and historically interesting bindings as to suggest that their collectors were keen to acquire books for this reason. The three collectors were Francis Douce (1757–1834), T. R. Buchanan (1846–1911) and Albert Ehrman (1890–1969). Douce was concerned mainly with the contents of his books, but he liked to obtain a copy of a particular text with an interesting binding. These included not only elaborate blind- and gold-tooled bindings, particularly from France, but also beautifully embroidered pieces, such as the Bible presented by the Royal Printer, Christopher Barker, to Elizabeth I (Douce Bib. Eng. 1583 b.1). Buchanan's fine bindings come both from Continental Europe and also from Scotland, and date mainly from the sixteenth to the nineteenth centuries. The European bindings include plain morocco bindings bearing the arms of Jacques Auguste de Thou, an early collector of fanfare bindings, and modern French red morocco bindings from the Seillière Collection. The Scottish bindings are of the 'wheel' and 'herring-bone' styles. Ehrman, too, was a collector of interesting bindings: indeed, his Broxbourne Collection was described by the late Howard Nixon as one of the three great English twentieth-century collections of bookbindings. It consists of some 2,000 examples, on manuscripts and printed books, covering the period from the twelfth to the twentieth centuries, and is especially strong both in blind-tooled bindings from the fifteenth and sixteenth centuries, and in contemporary English and French bookbindings.

Materials for the study of binding history

The Bodleian is especially strong in materials for the study of the history of bookbinding. In addition to the books in the Douce collection, there is the collection of Douce bindings, a selection of loose covers, mainly of blind-tooled bindings and dating from the sixteenth century. The Rare Books Section also has in its care other material, including the collection of John Waynflete Carter (1905–75), consisting of more than 350 items illustrating the history of publishers' bindings during the nineteenth century; and the collection of Col. William E. Moss (1875–1953), consisting of photographs, rubbings, offprints and notes on Renaissance bindings, plus Mearne and Settle bindings. The Section's files also include a card index of bindings of interest in the Bodleian; a file of reproductions of binding rubbings and descriptions of bindings of interest in Oxford libraries, arranged by country and then chronologically; J. B. Oldham's collection of photographs of blind-tooled bindings; an index of names of binders, ornaments and notes on the bindings of books in the Bodleian; and a file of binding rubbings of armorial stamps, mainly English. There are also several boxes of material relating to binders and binding to be found in the John Johnson Collection of printed ephemera.

'Bound for Bodley'

Books were bound for the Bodleian from the very beginning. Initially, whilst Bodley was still alive, it is clear that he preferred to have the books bound in London, then sent up to Oxford. Two frequently-used styles of binding for these books are a plain limp parchment binding, and a plain calf binding with fillets. Gilt stamps were placed on the bindings of books given by several early donors: these stamps would usually display the coat of arms or the crest of the donor. After Bodley's death, books were increasingly sent out to Oxford binders: they were usually bound in a similar style to those books which Bodley had bound in London. The Library's archive holds a series of 'binders' books', recording books sent out of the Library to local binders for binding.

The next period when there was a discernible 'house' style for Bodleian bindings was at the end of the eighteenth century, in the years following the Library's bulk purchases of books at the sales of Maffeo Pinelli and Pietro Antonio Bolongaro-Crevenna in 1789. Many of the books purchased at these sales were first editions of the classics and were subsequently rebound for the Bodleian, usually in simple but elegant morocco bindings, by two German binders who had settled in London, Heinrich Walther and Christian Samuel Kalthoeber. The end-result was to make the Library's newly acquired books comparably bound with those in contemporary aristocratic collections. Thereafter, with the Bodleian buying incunabula in quantity at the sales of duplicates from the Royal Library in Munich, following the dispersal of German monastic collections, the Library had to resort to a somewhat less expensive style of binding for its mid-nineteenth-century acquisitions. Many of these were bound in a cheaper calf, but tooled in a way to imitate the blind-tooled bindings of the fifteenth century. Later in the century the style changed again, with many of the newer acquisitions of rare books then being bound in half dark blue or brown morocco, with dark blue or black cloth.

Gilt stamps were placed on the bindings of books given by several early donors: these stamps would usually display the coat of arms or the crest of the donor. In 1789 the Library had its own stamp engraved. It bore the University's coat of arms and was inscribed 'Bibliotheca Bodleiana'. It was probably made to be used on the elegant bindings of Walther and Kalthoeber. By the nineteenth century there seem to have been two sizes of stamp available, and the smaller one appears to have remained in use until at least the middle of the century.

Oriental bindings

The Bodleian's Oriental collections can show a wide variety of vernacular binding styles. There are some fine examples of binding among the early Hebrew printed books in the Oppenheimer collection. On the other hand, the Michael manuscripts were all rebound in the mid-nineteenth century. The manuscript known as the Kennicott Bible (MS. Kennicott 1) has a box binding, a very rare feature paralleled in only a handful of cases in other libraries. Many of the Ethiopian manuscripts are in European bindings but some are bound in the wooden boards characteristic of Ethiopia, with the spine uncovered, and a few also have leather satchels or carrying cases.

Many of the Library's older Islamic manuscripts have been rebound over the centuries, both in the Middle East and after they were brought to Europe. Both the al-Sufi and the *Kalilah wa-Dimnah* manuscripts mentioned in the chapter on Pictorial Resources are now bound in Ottoman bindings of the seventeenth century. Many manuscripts were bound or rebound in plain calf bindings in the Library in the nineteenth century. However contemporary examples do survive, such as the binding of MS. Huntington 2, an Arabic manuscript from Egypt dated 1478. Persian manuscripts may have lacquer-painted bindings. One spectacular example is the binding of MS. Greaves 1: gold and coloured designs of animals, birds, trees, flowers and clouds are painted onto dark green lacquer. The manuscript is dated 1569 and the binding is thought to be contemporary with it. Other such bindings were collected by Gore Ouseley in Persia between 1800 and 1812.

Wooden Tibetan book covers (*glegs shing*), usually plain boards, sometimes with carvings or paintings, represent artistic objects in their own right. For example, two manuscripts of a Buddhist sūtra from the late nineteenth or early twentieth century (MS. Tibet. A. 26 (R) + 27 (R)) are both kept between wooden covers with five layers of brocade on one side, covering the beginning and the end of the texts, which are set into the board.

Unlike many of the traditional Chinese books that European libraries acquired in previous generations, the Sinica and Backhouse Collections were never rebound in Western style, so that the Library possesses excellent resources for the study of the Chinese book as an object. In the Backhouse Collection there are a few Imperial editions of the Ming which retain their original *baobei* ('wrapped back') bindings of the early Ming (among them Backhouse 140), and many of the editions in this collection were repaired in the Liulichang in Peking before being despatched to Oxford, so that the collection also illustrates the traditional techniques of Chinese book restoration. The Bodleian Japanese Library possesses good examples of material in traditional Japanese format – scrolls, concertina and books in sewn bindings.

Select bibliography

Strickland Gibson, *Early Oxford Bindings* (Oxford Bibliographical Society Illustrated Monographs, 10; Oxford, 1903).

S. Gibson, 'Bookbindings in the Buchanan Collection', *Bodleian Library Record*, 2/16 (1941), 6–12.

'Elkanah Settle', *Bodleian Library Record*, 2/22 (1944), 92–3.

Gold-Tooled Bookbindings (Bodleian Picture Books 2; Oxford: Bodleian Library, 1951).

S. Gibson, 'Colonel William E. Moss', with 'The Moss Donation' [a list], *Bodleian Library Record*, 5/3 (1955), 156–66.

H.M. Nixon, *Broxbourne Library: Styles and Designs of Bookbindings from the Twelfth to the Twentieth Century* (London, 1956).

'The Carter Collection of Publishers' Bindings', *Bodleian Library Record*, 8/1 (1967), 5–6.

M.J. Sommerlad, *Scottish 'Wheel' and 'Herring-bone' Bindings in the Bodleian Library, Oxford* (Oxford Bibliographical Society Occasional Publications, 1; Oxford, 1967).

Fine Bindings 1500–1700 from Oxford Libraries [exhibition catalogue] (Oxford: Bodleian Library, 1968).

Graham Pollard, 'Describing Medieval Bookbindings', in: *Medieval Learning and Literature: Essays Presented to Richard William Hunt*, eds. J.J.G. Alexander & M.T. Gibson (Oxford, 1976), 50–65. See also Christopher Clarkson's revision of Pollard's work, 'Further Studies in Anglo-Saxon and Norman Bookbinding ...', in: *Roger Powell: The Compleat Binder*, ed. J. L. Sharpe (Bibliologia 14; Turnhout, 1996), 154–214.

The Douce Legacy: An Exhibition to Commemorate the 150th Anniversary of the Bequest of Francis Douce (Oxford: Bodleian Library, 1984).

Kristian Jensen, 'Heinrich Walther, Christian Samuel Kalthoeber and other London Binders', *Bibliothek und Wissenschaft*, 29 (1996), 292–311.

David Pearson, *Oxford Bookbinding 1500–1640, including a Supplement to Neil Ker's Fragments of Medieval Manuscripts used as Pastedowns in Oxford Bindings* (Oxford Bibliographical Society Publications, 3rd series, 3; Oxford, 2000).

A Catalogue of Books Printed in the Fifteenth Century now in the Bodleian Library, eds. Alan Coates et al. (forthcoming, Oxford, 2005).

28. Historical Bibliography and Book History

Resources for the study of historical bibliography and for the discipline which, perhaps under French influence, has evolved from it, namely the history of the printed book, have been well organised in the Bodleian for at least a century. Two factors have brought these resources together: material and method. The Library's wealth of material derives from its continuous acquisition of books, both newly published and older, from the date of its foundation in 1602 to the present time. The record of these acquisitions is, perhaps uniquely, to be found in a series of printed catalogues (*see Select bibliography*) and most recently on compact disc.

Material

Acquisition during the Library's earlier history gave, of course, no thought to creating a resource for historical bibliography as such; though an interest in book history can perhaps be inferred from the collection of John Selden (given in 1659), and more clearly from the bequests of Richard Rawlinson (1754) and Francis Douce (1834). The last-named very clearly reveals an interest in the historical diversity of the book both manuscript and printed.

   The basic material of historical bibliography has been provided by the flow of books, itself depending partly upon the financial resources (augmented by donation) available to the Bodleian, and partly upon the Library's exercise of the right of legal deposit, which it has had in various forms since Sir Thomas Bodley's agreement of 1610 with the Stationers' Company of London. One of the most important ingredients of bibliographical study is the physical evidence a book provides about itself. So many of the Bodleian's books were acquired at or near the time of their publication that their condition, though worn, is that of their period. An academic library cannot afford to embark on mass rebinding, as the British Museum did in the nineteenth century; fewer books are in what the late H.M. Nixon used to call 'swagger bindings', and the books in the Bodleian have remained in cleaner atmospheric conditions than their London-housed coevals. The late Gordon Ray, in a survey of nineteenth-century fiction, remarked both upon the wealth of the Bodleian's holdings (thanks, no doubt, to the enforcement of the Copyright Act), and upon the survival of so many novels in their original condition.

Many of the Bodleian's books have thus passed through a cycle of significance: acquired through the centuries for the sake of their content, they have survived in the Library to become documents in the history of the book.

Method

The discipline of historical bibliography, as it is now understood and practised, emerged in Britain towards the end of the nineteenth century. Its earliest achievements – which were international – lay in the establishment of a reliable chronology for the invention and spread of printing. The collections of British libraries had been greatly enriched by books dispersed from French libraries by the Revolution, and out of German and Austrian libraries by secularisation. These collections were exploited by scholars such as Henry Bradshaw in Cambridge and Robert Proctor in the Bodleian and the British Museum. Their researches are being continued in the Bodleian with the revision of the catalogue of incunabula.

The foundation in 1892 of the Bibliographical Society of London marked the establishment of historical bibliography as a serious academic discipline, as opposed to an amateur bibliophily. In addition to the investigation of early printing, founding members of the Society were preoccupied with the problems of the printing history and textual accuracy of the English drama (and particularly of Shakespeare), and with the technique of precise bibliographical description. Bodleian copies of the early drama were highly important in this research, while Falconer Madan, Bodley's Librarian from 1912 to 1919, made a major contribution to the establishment of standards of bibliographical description. Madan also compiled the definitive list of printing by the Oxford press; his own copies of his bibliography *Oxford Books*, in three volumes, 1895–1931, are deposited in the Library. His own library is not in the Bodleian, but the Library's collection of Oxford books is unrivalled, and has been strengthened by the deposit in 1980 of the Printer's Library from the University Press. Madan established the *Bodleian Quarterly Record* (later the *Bodleian Library Record*) in 1914. This was innovative among library journals in providing information about the Library and its staff, and scholarly articles about the collections, although the long lists of accessions and desiderata originally included were later dropped. The Oxford Bibliographical Society, founded in 1921, has always had a close relationship with the Library.

Upon the Library's quatercentenary, its resources for bibliography are thus founded on its historical collections. Access to these collections has been provided not only through the series of printed catalogues which began in 1605, but also by the Bodleian's contributions to the definitive records of British books covering the years 1475 to 1800. As is appropriate for a library whose holdings of British books can only be compared with those of the British Library, great care has been taken over the years to ensure that the *Short-Title Catalogue of English Books 1475–1640*, Donald Wing's *Short-Title Catalogue 1641–1700*, and the *Eighteenth Century Short-Title*

Catalogue should be fully comprehensive in their listing of books in the Bodleian. Annotated copies of the first two catalogues are held in the Library; in some cases, these copies have locations for books in Oxford libraries outside the Bodleian. More recently, the Library has been involved in the creation of the *Incunable Short-Title Catalogue* and has been making, with a view to publication, a catalogue of its own fifteenth-century books, paying particular attention to the texts appearing in these incunabula and to the provenance and annotations of Bodleian copies. The international importance of the Bodleian's early collections for the compilation of other national bibliographies has also been borne in mind; the *Pre-1920 Catalogue of Printed Books on CD-ROM* can be searched by place of publication.

In the last half-century, however, the increasing sophistication and complexity of bibliographical studies have made the Bodleian a magnet for donations of collections with overtly bibliographical themes. The largest is the Broxbourne Library formed by the late Albert Ehrman and given (in part) by John Ehrman in 1978. It is rich in early bookbindings, but perhaps the most significant element is the books that formed the material for Ehrman's book (with Graham Pollard) *The Distribution of Books by Catalogue* (1965).

Lesser collections of bibliographical importance include T.W. Hanson's materials for the study of the binding firm of Edwards of Halifax, and John Carter's collection of early bindings in cloth. The papers and books of John Ryder (1917–2001) are a valuable record of the work of an eminent book-designer; he also had a splendid collection of the books printed by Giovanni Mardersteig at the Officina Bodoni in Verona. The Donhead Collection of F.W. Dunston, given in 1981, was chiefly valuable to the Library as a reserve collection of English literature, but it contained a number of eighteenth- and nineteenth-century books in original boards. The enormous size and variety of the John Johnson Collection of Printed Ephemera (described more fully in a separate chapter) perhaps conceal its bibliographical resources. These can, however, be accessed through the printed guide or online.

The Bibliography Room

Early plans for the New Bodleian Library building designated a 'Bibliography Room' on the ground floor for instruction in historical bibliography, traditional printing techniques and textual criticism. The room was furnished with the Rev. C.H.O. Daniel's Albion Press (in the Library's possession since 1919) and other equipment, and courses were begun in 1949, mainly for postgraduate students in the English Faculty. Further equipment was added over the years, and the Bibliography Room remains an important centre for teaching historical methods to bibliographers and textual students. Many of the objects represent benefactions from individuals and institutions, and some items are of major historical importance. The contents include an original wooden press, rescued from a London printer in the 1920s by John

Johnson, Printer to the University; four nineteenth-century presses (three Albions, including the 'Daniel Press', and a Columbian); and several twentieth-century small desk top presses. There are examples of type moulds, punches, matrices, composing sticks, compositors' equipment, stereotypes and electrotypes, paper moulds, wood blocks and binders' tools. A full range of Caslon, Bell and Ancient Black types is held, and cases of a number of other type designs. The room also houses collections of illustrative materials to support the courses.

Select bibliography

The Bibliographical Society, 1892–1942: Studies in Retrospect (London: Bibliographical Society, 1945).

Herbert J. Davis, 'The Strickland Gibson Collection', *Bodleian Library Record*, 6/6 (1961), 645–64.

G. Pollard and A. Ehrman, *The Distribution of Books by Catalogue* (Cambridge: Roxburghe Club, 1965).

Fine Bindings 1500–1700 from Oxford Libraries [exhibition catalogue] (Oxford: Bodleian Library, 1968).

The Douce Legacy [exhibition catalogue] (Oxford: Bodleian Library, 1984).

Clive Hurst, 'The Dunston Collection', *Bodleian Library Record*, 12/3 (1986), 177–204.

Gordon N. Ray, *Books as a Way of Life: Essays* (New York: Grolier Club, Pierpont Morgan Library, 1988).

The Legacy of Democritus Junior: Robert Burton [exhibition catalogue] (Oxford: Bodleian Library, 1990).

Georgian R. Tashjian, David R. Tashjian and Brian J. Enright, *Richard Rawlinson: A Tercentenary Memorial* (Kalamazoo: Western Michigan University, 1990).

Nicholas K. Kiessling, *The Library of Anthony Wood* (Oxford Bibliographical Society Publications, 3rd Series, vol. 5; Oxford Bibliographical Society, 2002).

Julian Roberts, 'Falconer Madan', in *New Dictionary of National Biography* (forthcoming).

Early Bodleian catalogues

Thomas James, *Catalogus librorum Bibliothecae publicae quam* [...] *Thomas Bodleius* [...] *in Academia Oxoniensi nuper instituit* (Oxford, 1605; repr. in facsimile, Oxford, 1986).

Thomas James, *Catalogus universalis librorum in Bibliotheca Bodleiana* (Oxford, 1620).

John Rous, *Appendix ad Catalogum librorum in Bibliotheca Bodleiana, qui prodiit* [...] *1620* (Oxford, 1635).

Thomas Hyde, *Catalogus impressorum librorum in Bibliothecae Bodleianae* (Oxford, 1674).

Catalogus impressorum librorum Bibliothecae Bodleianae (2 vols.; Oxford, 1738).

Catalogus librorum impressorum Bibliothecae Bodleianae (3 vols.; Oxford, 1843).

See also G.W. Wheeler, *The Earliest Catalogues of the Bodleian Library* (Oxford: University Press, 1928); and Ian Philip, *The Bodleian Library in the Seventeenth and Eighteenth Centuries* (Oxford: Clarendon Press, 1983), 11–14, 31–33, 50–51, 87–90.

Works listed in the General Bibliography on pp. 12–15 should also be consulted.

Bodleian Shelfmarks
An Introduction

Full accounts of the shelfmarks and classification of the Bodleian printed book and Western manuscript collections to the end of the nineteenth century can be found in G.W. Wheeler, 'Bodleian Shelfmarks in Relation to Classification', *Bodleian Quarterly Record* I (1916), 280–92, 311–22, and R.W. Hunt, 'Historical Introduction', *Summary Catalogue of Western Manuscripts in the Bodleian* I (1953). The latter includes (pp. 1–66) a conspectus of shelfmarks then current.

Printed books

The original classification was according to the four main faculties of study in the University: Theology, Medicine, Jurisprudence/Law and Arts, with shelfmarks **Th.**, **Med., Jur.**, and **Art.** The books in each of the four subjects were divided by size into folios, quartos and octavos, and then arranged alphabetically under the first letter of the author's name. This classification produced shelfmarks in the form **B 3. 14 Th.** for folios, 8° **A 1 Th.** and 4° **S 1 Art.** It continued in general use from 1602 to the end of the eighteenth century, and on occasion for quartos and octavos to around 1824 and for folios to around 1840. From early in the eighteenth century the pressure of library growth led to many folios being 'classified' in accordance with available shelf-space rather than with the subject of the work.

The completion in 1640 of Selden End at the west end of Duke Humfrey's Library provided space not only for the books in Selden's bequest (the first special collection to be shelfmarked with the donor's name), but also for the housing of the general acquisitions. The latter were divided into the four faculties and shelfmarked accordingly, with the addition of BS. to indicate their location (*e.g.* 8° **A 12 Th. BS.**).

In the 1780s the Old Anatomy School on the first floor of the Schools was fitted out as a library room, and, as the first addition to be made to the seventeenth-century library building, was styled the 'Auctarium'. From 1789 its shelves were filled by removing from the existing collections early editions of the Bible, first and other fifteenth-century editions of the classics and texts of Greek and Latin authors annotated with scholia and marginalia. All were given the shelfmark **Auct.**, which remained in use until 1940.

XXXIV. *Urashima*

Japanese folktale of a journey to the submarine
otherworld. The oldest recorded versions are from
the eighth century. This is a fine work of *Narae-hon*
(Nara picture book) of the Kanbun period (1661-
72), mounted as a handscroll. Its conservation,
repair and mounting were carried out by Mr Philip
Meredith of the Far Eastern Conservation Centre
in Leiden, and were made possible by the generous
support of the Sumitomo Foundation.

Acquired in 1901
MS. Jap. c. 4
See pp. 146, 178

XXXV. Queen Cho's funeral
Detail of the funerary procession of the Korean
Queen Cho in 1890.

*Given by the Rev. M.N. Trollope, later Bishop of
Korea, in 1902*
MS. Asiat. Misc. a. 1 (R), detail
See pp. 148, 179

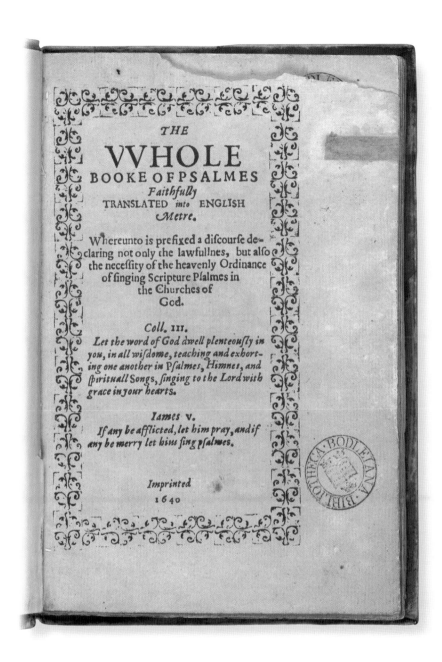

XXXVI. Bay Psalm Book, 1640

Published in Cambridge, Massachusetts, by
Puritans, this was the first book of any kind to be
printed in British North America. This copy is the
only one known outside the United States.

*Bequeathed by Thomas Tanner, Bishop of St Asaph,
in 1736*
Arch. G. e. 40, title-page
See p. 151

XXXVII. Phoebe Somers, 'Lamu Dhows'

Watercolour by Phoebe Somers (1902-95) of a
dhow off Lamu Island, Kenya, in 1969. She
worked as an art teacher in Kenya and Tanganyika
in the 1950s and 1960s and her papers include
many colourful sketches.

Purchased in 1969
MSS. Afr. S. 2162
See p. 161

XXXVIII. Anti-Apartheid poster

Poster produced by the National Union of
Metalworkers of South Africa on behalf of its
general secretary Moses Mayekiso, who was
arrested in 1986 and charged with high treason.
The poster is one of a large number in the Anti-
Apartheid Movement archive.

Given by the AAM Archives Committee in 1996
MSS. AAM
See pp. 161-2

XXXIX. Pantomime poster

Poster, probably for Oscar Barrett's 1889
production of *Aladdin* at the Crystal Palace.

John Johnson Collection
Posters, Theatrical. Crystal Palace
See p. 164

XL. The Douce Apocalypse

This superbly illustrated manuscript of the Apocalypse was made in Westminster for Prince Edward (shortly before his accession to the throne as King Edward I in 1272) and his wife Eleanor of Castile.

Bequeathed by Francis Douce in 1834
MS. Douce 180, p.42
See p. 167

XLI. Humphry Repton's 'Red Book'

Repton's design for improvements to the house and garden of John Fuller MP, at Rose Hill in Sussex, 1806-7.

Purchased in 1925
MS. Top. Sussex d. 2, fol. 20r
See p. 168

TOMBEAU *de marbre le troisième a droite dans la Chapelle de la Vierge dans l'Eglise de l'Abbaye de S* Denis. Il est du Roy* CHARLES VI. & d'ISABEL DE BAVIERE *Son espouse, derriere le Chapiteau du Roy est escrit.*

Icy gist le Roy Charles Sixiesme tres ame large et debonnaire fils du Roy Charles le quint qui regna 42 ans, un mois et six jours et trespassa le 21.º jour doctobre lan 1422 priés Dieu quen paradis Soit Son ame.

Derriere le Chapiteau de la Reine est escrit.

Cy gist la Royne Ysabel de Bavierre espouse du Roy Charles VI. et fille de tres puissant prince Estienne Duc de Bauiere et comte Palatin du Rin qui regna avec son dit espoux et trespassa lan 1435. le dernier jour de Septembre, priez Dieu pour elle.

XLII. Louis Boudan, The Tomb of Charles VI

Drawing by Louis Boudan, c. 1700, of the tomb of Charles VI of France and his wife Isabella of Bavaria in the church of the abbey of St Denis, from the collection of François Roger de Gaignières.

Bequeathed by Richard Gough in 1809
MS. Gough Drawings Gaignières 2, fol. 44r
See p. 169

MARTIN FROBISER MILES, EX DONO GVALTERI CHARLETON, M.D.

XLIII. Portrait of Sir Martin Frobisher

Cornelis Ketel's portrait of Sir Martin Frobisher
(?1535-1594) was commissioned by the Cathay
Company to commemorate his exploration of the
North West Passage in 1577.

Given by Walter Charleton MD in 1674
Lane Poole 50
See p. 173

**XLIV. Muhammad Shah with courtiers
by Bhupal Singh**

Muhammad Shah (1719-48) was an incompetent
statesman and general who suffered the humiliating
invasion and sack of Delhi by Nadir Shah of Persia
in 1739. He was, however, a devoted patron of
poetry, music and painting and this portrait
(*c.* 1730) is an example of the refined Mughal art
inspired by his patronage.

Bequeathed by Francis Douce in 1834
MS. Douce Or. a. 3, fol. 14
See p. 136

32

Typis præscripti OCHYLY naVis qua utrobiq̄ ualidis Remig
36 quorum uni Saltem 7 CHristiani eius Seruitio Astri
ti insubuerunt : Id Nauium Genús illorum Idiomate
CATTEGA, dicitur.

XLV. Picture book of life in Istanbul

The galley of the Ottoman High Admiral Uluc
Ali, with 36 oars manned by Christian slaves. On
internal evidence the manuscript can be dated to
1588, an early example of the kind.

Given in 1607
MS. Bodl. Or. 430, fol. 32r
See pp. 176, 181

XLVI. The Douce Ivory

This ivory panel of *c.* 800, representing at its centre the triumphant Christ trampling on a serpent and a lion, is set in the binding of a gospel lectionary of about the same date, written and decorated by nuns of the convent of Chelles near Paris.

Bequeathed by Francis Douce in 1834
MS. Douce 176, upper cover
See p. 182

XLVII. Paul Bonnet, binding for Honoré de Balzac, *Le chef d'œuvre inconnu* (Paris: Ambroise Vollard, 1931)

A binding created in 1944 by one of the greatest twentieth-century designer-bookbinders. Bonnet's inspiration here seems to have been the illustrations by Picasso rather than the text by Balzac.

From the collection of Albert Ehrman, given by his son John in 1978
Broxbourne 59.7, front cover
See p. 183

XLVIII. Tibetan book cover

A Mahayana Sutra from the 'Perfection of Wisdom' class of the Buddhist canon. Late nineteenth or early twentieth century (?). It is covered by five layers of brocade and set into the wooden book cover. Being the first page, it is written in gold on blue. The remaining pages are written on Tibetan paper in alternating lines of black and red. The illustrations show two different Buddhas: Candanaśrī on the left and Anantaujas on the right.

Bequeathed by W. Y. Evans-Wentz in 1965
MS. Tibet. a. 26 (R), upper wooden board
See pp. 177, 185

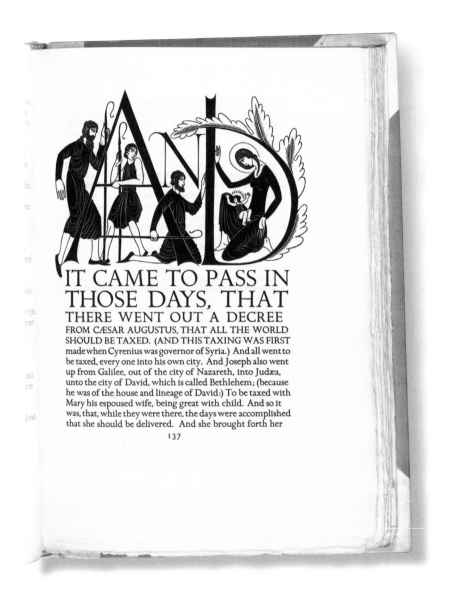

XLIX. *The Four Gospels of the Lord Jesus Christ [...] with decorations by Eric Gill*

Eric Gill, stone cutter and sculptor, book and type designer, was very much part of the arts and crafts movement in the early twentieth century. He led a community of the like-minded at Ditchling in Sussex from 1907 to 1924. The Four Gospels (1931) is one of his most ambitious and successful achievements, blending his own distinctive engravings with the Cockerel type he designed for the Golden Cockerel Press.

Acquired (probably by legal deposit) in 1932
N.T. Eng. 1931 c.1, p. 137

See p. 189

From 1789 all attempt at classification was abandoned and two new series begun, one BS. with no subject element in the shelfmark (*e.g.* **8° B 270 BS.** and **4° BS. 240**), and a supplementary one for the smaller quartos (*e.g.* **AS. 240**).

From 1824 as Selden End filled up, the 'year book' series was used for current accessions in octavo and housed in the Picture Gallery (now the Upper Reading Room). The books were numbered consecutively in each year, with shelfmarks from which the first two figures of the date had been dropped (*e.g.* **24.1**). Over 32,000 volumes in all subjects, acquired 1824–49, remain in this series.

In 1861, Bodley's Librarian H.O. Coxe re-introduced classification for new octavos and small quartos, based on the British Museum model, with eight three-figure numbers indicating broad subjects. The shelfmarks added a letter of the alphabet and a running number (*e.g.* **100 a. 154**). The classification was expanded in 1864, for example dividing Medicine (150) into three: medicine (151), surgery (160) and anatomy (165). New folios and large quartos were placed in similar classes, but named rather than numbered: **Arts, History, Physics, Poetry, Theology** and **Trades,** with similar shelfmarks (*e.g.* **Arts a.15**). Topography was omitted from these schemes and accessions were (from 1860) classified as additions to the Gough collection (with shelfmarks in the form **G.A. Oxon. 8° 132**). Drama was also omitted, accessions being added to the Malone collection; from 1883 to 1988 the fact that they were additions was recorded in the shelfmark **M. Adds.** Older books in octavo and small quarto, purchased between 1861 and 1883, were classified in a different one- and two-figure sequence, with shelfmarks in the form **35 c.24**.

E.W.B. Nicholson, appointed Bodley's Librarian in 1882, introduced in 1883 a much-extended classification which retained Coxe's sections, but subdivided them minutely. In all, Nicholson's system produced over 7000 sections. He retained the notation of three-figure numbers, but added one, two or occasionally more digits, which, although the point is omitted in the shelfmark, are regarded as decimals (*e.g.* **2589 e. 142**). He introduced seven size divisions, indicated in the shelfmark with letters of the alphabet: from 'a' for books over 20 inches to 'g' for those under 5 inches. Nicholson's scheme remained in use until the advent of on-line cataloguing in 1988, when the inclusion of subject headings in the searchable catalogue records rendered subject classification unnecessary.

From 1988 a simpler system was adopted for new accessions, which were divided into four 'classes': standard monographs (M), 'popular' monographs, including fiction and other lesser-used material to be outhoused (X), periodicals (P) and multi-volume works in progress (R). The number of size divisions was also reduced, to five. The shelfmark now consists of the classification, the last two digits of the year (for M and X classes only) a letter indicating the size and a running number. Current shelfmarks are thus in the form **M03 E.01298, P.D00147**.

From the mid-seventeenth century 'special collections' were not split up into the general classification, but retained as collections and assigned the name, usually abbreviated in the shelfmark, of the donor or previous owner. These 'named' collections are included in the list 'Principal Special Collections' on pp. 198–222. There remain a few shelfmarks which have been used at various periods for particular types of accessions. Those which survive are:

Antiq. (Antiquiora): antiquarian accessions, 1883–1936, with subdivisions by size, place of printing and date.

Arch. (Archivium): books which on account of their rarity, value, small size or the like would be unsuitably placed in the general classification.

Bib. , O.T., N.T., Apoc., Ps., C.P.: editions of the Bible, the Old Testament, the New Testament, the Apocrypha, the Psalms and the Book of Common Prayer, used 1883 onwards.

Caps.: antiquarian accessions in folio and large quarto, used 1860–83.

Delta: accessions of English and foreign quartos, 1824–61, then, 1861–83, older books in folio and large quarto.

Diss. (Dissertations): German, Dutch and and Scandinavian dissertations of the 17th, 18th and 19th centuries, many in Roman and German law, theology and history.

Don. (Donations): books presented by or through the Bodleian's Friends' organisations, 1925–82.

Mus. Bibl. (Museum Bibliothecae).

Mus. Bibl. II: editions of works by Thomas Hearne brought together from existing collections c.1860 and since added to.

Mus. Bibl. III: auction, booksellers' and library catalogues, 17th – 19th cent., brought together c.1860, some from existing collections, others current and purchased catalogues.

Pamph. (Bartholomew Pamphlets): a collection of about 50,000 English pamphlets of the period 1603–1740, collected by Humphrey Bartholomew of University College and presented by him to the Radcliffe Library in 1749

Rec. (Recentiores): books published after 1850 which would be unsuitably placed in the general classification.

Sermons: a collection of 570 English sermons, 17th– 19th cent., purchased in 1850.

Sigma: books of the 16th to 19th centuries, acquired 1826–50 and shelved in Selden End.

Slav. (Slavonic): used in the 19th cent. for Slavonic books and books on Eastern Europe.

Theta: used 1840–61 for multi-volume sets in quarto and octavo; 1845–61 for older books in folio; and 1923–36 for retrospective purchases of 18th- and 19th- cent. English books.

Trac. Luth. (Tractatus Lutherani): Latin and German tracts by or about Luther and the German reformers, 1518–50.

Vet. (Vetera): used since 1937 for antiquarian accessions, subdivided by country of printing and by period of printing.

Western manuscripts

Thomas Bodley decreed that manuscripts and printed books should be shelved together. Despite attempts by his first Librarian, Thomas James, to separate them, they remained together on the shelves, with the exception of a few particularly precious manuscripts which were kept in the cupboards (*Archivi*). James's successor, John Rous (Librarian from 1620 to 1652) began the process of arranging the manuscripts in separate series. Thomas Barlow (Librarian from 1652 to 1660) began in 1655 another series of manuscripts kept in the cupboard in his study (*in musaeo*). Miscellaneous donations and purchases were added to this series until 1884 and from 1728 were shelfmarked **MSS. e Mus.** In the mid-eighteenth century the various series of manuscripts begun by Rous were brought together into one sequence and shelfmarked **MSS. Bodley**.

The first large gifts of manuscripts – Roe (1628), Barocci (1629), Digby (1634) and Laud (1635–40) – were kept as separate collections and shelfmarked with their name. Throughout the seventeenth, eighteenth and nineteenth centuries and well into the twentieth this system continued, and collections of manuscripts were referenced with the name of their collector or donor (*e.g.* **MSS. Tanner, MSS. Douce, MSS. Bryce**).

With the fitting out of the new library room (the auctarium) in 1789, classical and biblical manuscripts were moved there from their existing locations. Those taken from the named collections were restored to them in the late nineteenth century; those removed from the MSS. Bodley series were kept together as **MSS. Auct.**

The general series of manuscript accessions (MSS. Bodley) was closed by H.O. Coxe around 1860, and a new series begun which in about 1877 was rearranged according to size and shelfmarked **MSS. Add. A – E**. This sequence was closed in 1887.

When E.W.B. Nicholson became Librarian in 1882, the new subject classification he planned for the Library encompassed manuscripts as well as printed books. Manuscripts on county history and topography were placed in a series **MSS. Top.** (Topography), subdivided into gen(eral), eccles(iastical), and into England, Scotland, Wales and Ireland, with divisions for the first three by counties. The volumes were arranged by size, indicated by the letters a to g. This produced shelfmarks in the form **MS. Top. gen. e. 23, MS. Top. Oxon. a. 41, MS. Top. Ireland b. 2**. The music manuscripts were arranged around 1885–7, following the transfer of the Music School library to the Bodleian in 1885, using the shelfmarks **MSS. Mus.** for general music manuscripts, **MSS. Mus. Sch.** for manuscripts transferred from the Music School, and **MSS. Mus. Sch. Ex.** for exercises submitted for Oxford degrees. They continue in use to the present.

In 1887 Nicholson introduced a classification, chiefly by language, for the miscellaneous manuscript accessions. The chief languages (English, Greek and Latin) were subdivided thus:

- **Eng(lish)** into bib(les), lit(urgies), th(eology), hist(ory), poet(ry) and misc(ellaneous), with lett(ers) added in 1928.
- **Gr(eek)** and **Lat(in)** into bib(les), liturg(ies), th(eology), class(ics) and misc(ellaneous).

Basque, Cornish, Dutch, French, German, Icelandic, Irish, Italian, Manx, Portuguese, Russian, Spanish, Swedish and Welsh were also assigned separate classifications. Each classification was divided by size (a–g). Additions were subsequently made: Autogr(aphs) in 1889, Breton in 1902, Lat(in) hist(ory) in 1923, Scand(inavian) in 1924 and Don(ations) in 1925. This produced shelfmarks in the form: **MS. Eng. lett. d. 148, MS. Lat. class. e. 4** and **MS. Cornish c. 3**.

In the second half of the twentieth century pressure on space, accelerated by the increasing size of the many accessions of collections of modern papers, led to a reduction in the number of collections named after their donor or previous owner. Many such collections, while catalogued as a collection, *e.g.* the Napier family papers, are shelfmarked and housed in the general series, *e.g.* MSS. Eng. lett., Eng. hist., Eng. misc. and French.

In 1989, in order to make best use of diminishing space in the bookstack, the subject divisions within the MSS. Eng. classification were abandoned and a new series **MSS. Eng.** begun. The number of divisions by size was reduced to five. Some classification by form, *e.g.* autographs, was also abandoned and post-1988 accessions of these materials are placed in the language classifications. The tradition of assigning the name of the donor or previous owner as the shelfmark for all major manuscript collections was also abandoned and in the last twenty years only the largest of such collections have been shelfmarked outside the general classifications. The series **MSS. Don.** has been retained for manuscripts given by or through the Library's Friends' organisations. For ease of consultation or storage, classification by form has been continued for charters, deposits, facsimiles, fiches, films, music, photographs, rolls, rubbings and theses.

Oriental collections

Most of the Oriental manuscripts in the Library are contained in the great named collections (Laud, Pococke, Oppenheimer, etc.), producing shelfmarks in the form **MS. Laud Or., MS. Pococke, MS. Opp.**, etc. The miscellaneous remainder were originally shelved with their Western counterparts until 1812, when they were separated and formed into the new series Bodley Or., producing the shelfmark **MS. Bodl. Or.**. The series lasted until 1883 and all new Oriental manuscript acquisitions were placed there, with the exception of the accessions of 1826-43, which seem to have been put into Caps. Or. (shelfmark **MS. Caps. Or.**), and Hebrew accessions in the period 1847-1883, which were classified as Oppenheimer Additions (shelfmark **MS. Opp. Add.**). The shelfmark **Opp. add.** without the prefix MS(S) indicates Hebrew printed books. As with Oriental manuscripts, no attempt was made to segregate Oriental from Western printed books until the middle of the nineteenth century, when the threefold classification **Ary.** (Aryan), **Sem.** (Semitic) and **Tur.** (Turanian) was introduced. (**Tur.** was used to cover everything that could not be classified as Aryan or Semitic.)

A new classification for Oriental materials was introduced in 1883, which is still in use, providing for various language sections: **Aeth.** (Ethiopian languages), **Arab.** (Arabic), **Aram.** (Aramaic), **Chin.** (Chinese), **Cor.** (Korean), **Heb.** (Hebrew), **Malay, Pers.** (Persian), etc., which are followed by a letter of the alphabet indicating the size of the item and a running number. These language categories are applied to manuscripts as well as printed books, the manuscript shelfmarks being always preceded by the prefix MS(S). The section **Or.**, which was introduced at the same time, provides a classification for printed works relating to Oriental languages in general, festschrifts, etc. Early and rare printed editions are currently classified into **Sinica** (Chinese, which also includes some manuscripts), **Nipponica** (Japanese) and **Vet. Or.** (all other Oriental languages).

Principal Special Collections

Collections described as ***Deposited*** are privately owned and, although generally available for study, may need prior permission for access from the owner or be subject to restrictions on copying and publication.

In the case of older collections, the entry heading in this list will normally be the same as the Bodleian shelfmark for that collection, but many later collections have been allocated to more than one shelfmark and should be accessed through the appropriate catalogues.

Abinger Papers of William Godwin (1756–1836), Mary Wollstonecraft Godwin (1759–97), Mary Wollstonecraft Shelley (1797–1851) and Percy Bysshe Shelley (1792–1822) and of their circle. *Deposited* by James, 8th Baron Abinger.

Acland Correspondence of the Acland family, chiefly of Sir Henry Wentworth Acland, 1st Bart. (1815–1900), Regius Professor of Medicine at Oxford, with some papers of his wife and children and of his brother-in-law William Charles Cotton (1813–79), first secretary of the Apiarian Society.

Addison Political papers of Christopher, 1st Viscount Addison (1869–1951). *Deposited.*

Aldiss Correspondence and papers of the author and critic Brian Aldiss (*b.*1925).

All Souls Title deeds of properties of All Souls College, Oxford, 12th – 19th cent. *Deposited.*

Allen Papers of P.S. Allen (1869–1933), President of Corpus Christi College, Oxford, with books from his library, including original editions of the works of Erasmus and some 2,000 items relating to him.

Anti-Apartheid Movement Papers of the British AAM, 20th cent. (In the Bodleian Library of Commonwealth and African Studies at Rhodes House.)

Anti-Slavery Society Correspondence and records from the early 19th cent. to the present day: still being added to. Includes the records of the Aborigines Protection Society. (In the Bodleian Library of Commonwealth and African studies at Rhodes House.)

Aris Correspondence and papers, 1960s–1999, of Michael Vaillancourt Aris (1946–99), mostly relating to his work in the field of Tibetan/Bhutanese and Himalayan studies.

Ashmole Manuscripts and books collected by Elias Ashmole (1617–92), antiquary and astrologer; the manuscripts mainly relating to heraldry, genealogy and astrology, including working papers of Ashmole himself, and of the astrologers Simon Forman (1552–1611), Richard Napier (1559–1634), John Dee (1527–1608), John Booker (1603–67) and William Lilly (1602–81); the books including works of astronomy, astrology and related subjects, contemporary pamphlets, tracts, poetry, sermons, newspapers and book catalogues, and books from the libraries of John Aubrey (1626–97), Edward Lhuyd (1660–1709) and Martin Lister (1638–1712).

Ashmolean Natural History Society Records of the Ashmolean Society, 1828–1901, the Oxfordshire Natural History Society and Field Club, 1880-1901, and of the Ashmolean Natural History Society which was formed by the amalgamation of the two societies, 1901–74. *Deposited.*

Asquith Personal and political papers of Herbert Asquith, 1st Earl of Oxford and Asquith (1852–1928), many from his period as Prime Minister, and of his wife Margot.

Association for the Education of Women in Oxford Papers of the Association, 1877–1922. (Further papers on the education of women in the University, including the meetings of women principals and papers of the Women Students' Property Committee, are *deposited*.)

Attlee Papers of Clement, 1st Earl Attlee (1883–1967), mainly notes for his Prime Ministerial speeches and broadcasts. *Deposited.*

Aubrey Manuscripts of the antiquary John Aubrey (1626–97).

Backhouse Chinese books donated by Sir Edmund Backhouse (1873–1944), Sinologist and authority on China. He made the first of a number of considerable donations in 1913.

Baker Papers of John Randal Baker (1900–84), cytologist.

Ballard Literary and historical manuscripts collected by the antiquary George Ballard (1705–55), including correspondence and papers of Arthur Charlett (1655–1722), Master of University College, Oxford.

Bankes Papers of Sir John Bankes (1589–1644) as Attorney-General, 1634–40.

Bannister Papers of H. M. Bannister (1854–1919) relating to plainsong and liturgy in the medieval church.

Barlow Manuscripts, chiefly medieval, collected by Thomas Barlow (1607–91), Bishop of Lincoln and from 1652 to 1660 Bodley's Librarian. For books from his library, see **Linc.** below.

Barocci Greek manuscripts of the 10th to the 17th centuries, collected by Giacomo Barocci of Venice, chiefly patristic and Byzantine theology and the works of grammarians and scholiasts.

Baskerville Notebooks of the historian Geoffrey Baskerville (1870–1944), chiefly relating to his *English Monks and the Suppression of the Monasteries* (London, 1937).

Beckford Correspondence, papers and music manuscripts of William Beckford (1760–1844); working papers of Boyd Alexander (1913–80) relating to Beckford.

Benson Literary papers of A.C. (1862–1915) and E.F. (1867–1940) Benson, and correspondence of Edward White Benson (1829–92), Archbishop of Canterbury.

E.C. Bentley Diaries, scrap-books and correspondence of the writer Edmund Clerihew Bentley (1876–1956).

Berlin Personal, academic and literary papers of Sir Isaiah Berlin (1909–97), philosopher and historian of ideas.

Bertie Papers relating to the estates of the Bertie family, Earls of Abingdon, in Berkshire and Oxfordshire, 14th – 20th cent.

Bickersteth Correspondence and papers of the Bickersteth family, 19th –20th cent., including the 'Bickersteth Diary' for 1914–18.

Birkbeck Historical and theological books, mainly 19th cent. and in Slavonic languages, collected by W.J. Birkbeck (1859–1916).

Blackman Papers of Geoffrey Emett Blackman (1903–80), agronomist.

Blakeway Manuscripts of John Brickdale Blakeway (1765–1826) relating to the history of Shropshire.

Bland Burges Correspondence and literary papers of Sir James Bland Burges (1752–1824), including some relating to his period as Under-Secretary of State at the Foreign Office, 1789–95. *Deposited.*

Blish Published works, literary manuscripts and correspondence of James Blish (1921–75).

Bliss 745 volumes, 16th – 19th cent., from the library of Philip Bliss (1787–1857), including books printed in Oxford, works relating to Oxford and Oxfordshire, editions of and commentaries on the Psalms, and works of 16th- and 17th-cent. poets; and notebooks of Bliss relating to the history of Oxford University.

Bonham Carter Correspondence and papers of Lady Violet Bonham Carter, Baroness Asquith of Yarnbury (1887–1969), Liberal political figure, with correspondence and papers of other members of her family.

Boreal. Collection of Scandinavian manuscripts, chiefly Icelandic, bought in 1828 from Finn Magnusen (1781–1848).

Bourne 18th-cent. printed music and manuscripts from the collection of Thomas William Bourne (*d.*1948).

Bow Group Records and published papers of the Bow Group, 1952–2000. *Deposited.*

Bowyer Books and manuscripts relating to the work of the jurist Sir George Bowyer (1811–83) on the statutes of Italian cities.

Boyd of Merton Papers of Alan Tindal Lennox-Boyd, 1st Viscount Boyd of Merton (1904–83), mainly relating to Rhodesia, and from the period after his resignation from the Cabinet in 1959.

Bradley Papers, with some correspondence, of James Bradley (1693–1762), Savilian Professor of Astronomy at Oxford and Astronomer Royal.

Brand Correspondence and papers of Robert Henry, Baron Brand (1878–1963), banker and public servant.

Brasenose College Manuscripts from the library of Brasenose College, Oxford. *Deposited.*

Brett Correspondence and papers of the non-juror Thomas Brett (1667–1724).

John Bridges Manuscript collections of the antiquary John Bridges (1666–1724) relating to Northamptonshire.

Robert Bridges Literary manuscripts, papers and correspondence of the Poet Laureate (1844–1930). *Deposited.*

British Association for the Advancement of Science Archives of the Association, 1851–1972, many relating to the organisation and proceedings of its annual meetings. *Deposited.*

J.C. Brooke Correspondence and field books of the herald and antiquary John Charles Brooke (1748–94).

Broxbourne Books and manuscripts collected by Albert Ehrman (1890–1969) as examples of fine bindings, 12th – 20th cent., with catalogues of printers, publishers, booksellers, auctioneers and libraries, and reference works on binding and printing history.

Bruce Arabic and Ethiopic manuscripts of James Bruce (1730–1794), explorer of the source of the Nile.

Bruce family Papers of the Bruce family, chiefly of Michael Bruce (1787–1861), M.P. and traveller.

Bryce Political, literary and personal papers of James, Viscount Bryce (1838–1922), British Ambassador to the United States, 1907–13.

Buchanan Books and manuscripts collected by Thomas Ryburn Buchanan (1846–1911), chiefly for their fine bindings, printing and illumination.

Burdett Papers of Sir Henry Burdett (1847–1920), chiefly relating to the Stock Exchange, hospitals and nursing.

Burdett-Coutts Papers of the politician Sir Francis Burdett (1770–1844) and of the banker Thomas Coutts (1735–1822).

Burgert Books produced by Hans Joachim Burgert (*b*.1928), German calligraphic printer, at the Burgert Handpresse from 1962.

John Burton Manuscript collections of the antiquary John Burton (1710–71) relating to Yorkshire.

Robert Burton 581 books (nearly 900 titles) from the library of the author of *The Anatomy of Melancholy*, for the most part English.

Butler Papers of Christine Violet Butler (1884–1982), mainly relating to her social work with young people in Oxford, with some family papers.

Butterworth Music manuscripts of the composer George Butterworth (1885–1916).

Buxton Books from the library of Edward John Mawby Buxton (1912–89), mainly works of English literature, notably those of Sir Philip Sidney, Samuel Daniel, Charles Cotton and P.B. Shelley, with some personal papers.

Bywater Books and manuscripts collected by Ingram Bywater (1840–1914), Regius Professor of Greek at Oxford, chiefly illustrative of the history of classical learning in Europe in the 16th and 17th cent.; his working papers and correspondence with classical scholars.

Cadoux Papers of Cecil John Cadoux (1883–1947), mainly relating to the Congregational Church, with letter-books of his father William H. Cadoux (*fl.* 1866–99), a general merchant in Turkey.

Callcott Papers of the painter Sir Augustus Wall Callcott (1779–1844) and of his wife Maria (1785–1842), author and traveller.

Canonici Greek, Latin, Biblical and liturgical manuscripts collected by Matteo Luigi Canonici (1727–*c*.1806). The Oriental manuscripts (mainly Hebrew) in this collection are separately classed as **Canonici Or.**

Carte Papers collected by the historian Thomas Carte (1686–1754), many relating to Ireland from the 16th to the 18th century, including papers of James Butler, 1st Duke of Ormonde (1610–88), Sir William Fitzwilliam (1526–99), Lord Deputy, and Sir John Davies (1569–1626), Attorney General.

Carte Calendar Unpublished calendar of the Carte papers, arranged chronologically, compiled by Edward Edwards (1812–86).

Carter Books collected by John Waynflete Carter (1905–75) as examples of 19th cent. publishers' bindings.

Cary Library and literary manuscripts and correspondence of Joyce Cary (1888–1957), including books by, about and presented to him, with some correspondence.

Casaubon Greek manuscripts collected by Isaac Casaubon (1559–1614), with some correspondence.

Castello Works of Arthur Rackham (1869–1939), one of the greatest of English book illustrators, including signed, limited editions, some with original art work; given by Simon J. Castello.

Catholic Apostolic Church Books and pamphlets, English, 19th and 20th cent., of the Catholic Apostolic Church.

Chandler Correspondence, business, personal and literary papers of Raymond Chandler (1888–1959). *Deposited.*

Chandra Shum Shere Collection of over 6,000 Sanskrit manuscripts presented in 1909 by the Maharajah Sir Chandra Shum Shere, Prime Minister of Nepal.

Chapman Papers of the scholar and editor R.W. Chapman (1881–1960).

Chaundy Papers of William Chaundy (1889–1966), mathematician.

Cherry Manuscripts collected by Francis Cherry (?1665–1713), nonjuror and antiquary.

Christ Church Manorial records and title deeds of properties of Christ Church, Oxford, 12th –19th cent. *Deposited.*

Church's Ministry among the Jews Archive of the Church's Ministry among the Jewish People, originally the London Society for Promoting Christianity among the Jews, 19th–20th cent. *Deposited.*

Clarendon Papers of members of the Hyde and Villiers families, 17th – 19th cent., chiefly of George William Frederick Villiers, 4th Earl of Clarendon (1800–70) as British Minister to Spain, Lord Lieutenant of Ireland and Foreign Secretary; also includes diplomatic correspondence and papers of Thomas Villiers, 1st Earl of Clarendon (1709–86). *Deposited.*

Clarendon Press Books published by the Clarendon Press, 1720–1892, arranged according to subject; 200 books of the 15th – 19th cent., chiefly texts of the classics and of the Fathers, some with manuscript editorial annotations; c.1,000 Clarendon Press file copies of books printed in the 18th and 19th centuries, mostly bound at the time in original boards or cloth bindings; manuscripts in the collection are chiefly working papers of scholars of the 18th and 19th centuries whose works were published by the Clarendon Press.

Clarendon State Papers Papers of Edward Hyde, 1st Earl of Clarendon (1609–74), chiefly relating to the Civil War, the Commonwealth and the Restoration.

Katherine Clarendon Diaries, correspondence and papers of Katherine, Lady Clarendon (1810–74), wife of the 4th Earl of Clarendon.

Andrew Clark Diaries and newspaper cuttings of Andrew Clark (1854–1922) relating to Essex, 1914–19, with antiquarian collections for Essex and Hertfordshire.

W.D. Clark Correspondence of Charles Townshend (1725–67), of George, 1st Earl Macartney (1737–1806), of Lady Louisa Stuart (1757–1851), of Lady Anna Maria Dawson (d.1866), of H.D. Erskine, Dean of Ripon (d.1858), and of members of the Strong family.

Wilfrid Clark Diaries and correspondence of Sir Wilfrid Edward Le Gros Clark (1895–1971), anatomist.

William Clark Diaries, correspondence, broadcasts and other papers of William Donaldson Clark (1916–85), many relating to his time at the *Observer.*

E. D. Clarke Greek, Latin and French manuscripts collected by Edward Daniel Clarke (1769–1822) during travels in Europe and Asia. The Oriental manuscripts (Arabic, Persian, etc.) in this collection are separately classed as **E.D. Clarke Or.**

S. Clarke Small collection of Arabic and Persian manuscripts chiefly in the hand of Samuel Clarke (1628–1669), Orientalist and first Printer to the University.

Clough Correspondence and literary manuscripts of A.H. Clough (1819–61).

Coghill Papers of Neville Coghill (1899–1980), Merton Professor of English Literature at Oxford.

Colefax Correspondence and books from the library of Sybil, Lady Colefax (1874–1940), society hostess and co-founder of the interior decoration firm Colefax & Fowler.

Collingwood Essays, lecture notes and other papers of Robin George Collingwood (1889–1943), philosopher and historian. *Deposited.*

Congreve Papers and correspondence of the positivist Richard Congreve (1818–99).

Conservative Party Archive Archive of the Conservative Party central administration, 19th – 20th cent. *Deposited.*

Coulson Personal and scientific lectures and papers of Charles Alfred Coulson (1910–74), mathematician and theoretical chemist.

Crampton Correspondence and papers of the diplomat Sir John Crampton (1805–86), mainly relating to Anglo-American affairs, Russia and the Crimean War and Spain.

Craven Estate and family papers of the Earls of Craven, 16th – 19th cent. *Deposited.*

Crawford Papers of the archaeologist O.G.S.Crawford (1886–1957).

Cripps Papers of Sir Stafford Cripps (1889–1952), statesman and lawyer.

Cromwell Greek manuscripts from the collection of Giacomo Barocci, owned and given by Oliver Cromwell.

Crook Correspondence and press cuttings of the Liberal politician William Montgomery Crook (1860–1945).

Crowe Correspondence of the diplomat Sir Eyre Crowe (1864–1925).

Crynes 16th –18th cent. books from the collection of Nathaniel Crynes (1688–1745), covering a wide range of historical subjects.

Curtis Personal and literary papers of Lionel Curtis (1872–1955), with papers of the Round Table organisation.

Curzon Books and manuscripts relating to Napoleon, collected and bequeathed by George, Marquess Curzon of Kedleston (1859–1925).

Darlington Personal and scientific correspondence and papers of Cyril Dean Darlington (1903–81), botanist and geneticist.

Dashwood Personal and official papers of members of the Dashwood family of West Wycombe, Bucks., 17th – 19th cent. *Deposited.*

Davidson Papers of John Colin Campbell, 1st Viscount Davidson (1889–1970), relating to the Indian States Enquiry Committee, 1931–9.

Davies Printed ephemera relating to American (primarily Presidential) elections 19th – 20th cent., collected by Philip and Rosamund Davies. (In the Vere Harmsworth Library.)

H.W.C. Davis Notes and lectures of the historian H.W.C. Davis (1874–1928), chiefly on English and European history.

Dawkins Syriac manuscripts named after the 18th-century traveller James Dawkins (1722–1757), who collected some, but by no means all, of them, presented by his brother in 1759.

Dawkins family Papers of the Dawkins family of Over Norton, Oxon., 18th – 19th cent., relating to their estates in Oxfordshire and Jamaica. *Deposited.*

Dawson Diaries, correspondence, and papers of George Geoffrey Dawson (1874–1944), editor of *The Times.*

Albinia de la Mare Palaeographical papers of Professor Albinia de la Mare (1932–2000).

Walter de la Mare Correspondence and literary papers of Walter de la Mare (1873 –1956).

de Bunsen Political and personal papers of Sir Maurice W. E. de Bunsen (1852–1932), diplomat, and of members of his family.

Dell Papers of the economist Sidney Dell (1918–90).

De Michele Diaries and correspondence of Charles Eastland De Michele (1810–98), with papers relating to the *Morning Post.*

Denyer Collection of English 16th-century Bibles and theological works bequeathed in 1825 by Eliza D. Denyer, widow of John Denyer (*d.*1806).

Dew Papers of the Dew family of Lower Heyford, Oxon., 19th – 20th cent., chiefly of George James Dew (1846–1928), local historian and overseer of the poor. *Deposited.*

Digby Manuscripts collected by Sir Kenelm Digby (1603–65), many relating to medieval theology and science, astronomy, astrology, and medicine. The Oriental manuscripts (Arabic and Hebrew) in this collection are separately classed as **Digby Or.**

Dobell Correspondence, diaries, literary papers and books of Bertram Dobell (1842–1914), bookseller and man of letters.

Dodds Working papers and correspondence of Eric Robertson Dodds (1893–1979), Regius Professor of Greek at Oxford.

Dodsworth Manuscript collections of Roger Dodsworth (1585–1654) relating to the antiquities, monastic houses, pedigrees and families of Yorkshire.

D'Orville Working manuscripts of Jacques Philippe D'Orville (1696–1751) on classical literature and languages.

Douce Manuscripts and books collected and bequeathed by Francis Douce (1757–1834): the manuscripts notable for many superb examples of medieval illumination, the books strong in history, biography, antiquities, manners, customs, the fine arts, travel, archaeology, witchcraft and the Dance of Death; children's books, chapbooks and similar ephemeral literature from Douce's collection, acquired after his death; correspondence and papers. The Oriental manuscripts (Persian, Egyptian, Malay, etc.) and paintings in this collection are separately classed as **Douce Or.**

Drower Mandaean manuscripts given to the Library in 1958 by Lady Ethel May Stefana Drower (1879–1972), writer on the Middle East, especially the language and religion of the Mandaeans.

Drummond-Hay Correspondence, diaries and other papers of members of the Drummond-Hay family, chiefly diplomats, 18th – 19th cent.

Dugdale Manuscript collections of Sir William Dugdale (1605–86), mainly transcripts from private archives and public records made by him for his *Baronage* and *Antiquities of Warwickshire.*

Dunston Books, and a few manuscripts, collected by F.W. Dunston (1850–1915), his sons and daughter of Donhead St. Mary, Wiltshire, including English literature, late 17th – early 20th cent., and children's books, mainly from the first half of the 19th cent., with some family papers.

Dyer Papers of Frederick William Dyer (*d.*1906), chiefly relating to 'Lingualumina', the universal language he invented.

Eckert Collection of Robert Paul Eckert (*d.*1966) relating to the poet Edward Thomas (1878–1917), including 190 books owned by or written by or about Thomas.

Edgeworth Correspondence and literary papers of the Edgeworth family, chiefly the novelist Maria Edgeworth (1768–1849), her father the writer Richard Lovell Edgeworth (1744–1817) and her step-brother the botanist Michael Pakenham Edgeworth (1812–81).

Eighty Club Minute books and membership and financial records of the London Eighty Club, 1881–1979.

Elliott Over 600 Persian manuscripts given in 1859 by John Bardoe Elliott of the Bengal Civil Service, including many items formerly belonging to Sir Gore Ouseley.

Ellis Papers and some correspondence of the classical scholar Robinson Ellis (1834–1913).

Elton Correspondence and papers of Charles Sutherland Elton (1900–91), animal ecologist.

Emmet Political papers of Evelyn, Baroness Emmet of Amberley (1899–1980).

Ensor Personal, political and academic papers of Sir Robert C.K.Ensor (1877–1958), journalist and historian. *Deposited.*

Evans-Wentz Papers of the anthropologist Walter Yeeling Evans-Wentz (1878–1965), many relating to folklore, Celtic and Tibetan studies and Buddhism.

Ewelme Muniments of the medieval almshouse at Ewelme, Oxon., with later administrative papers of the Ewelme Almshouse Charity, 14th – 19th cent. *Deposited.*

Fairbank Correspondence and papers of the calligrapher Alfred John Fairbank (1895–1982), including design and calligraphic work.

Fairfax Manuscripts of British medieval history and literature, collected and bequeathed by Thomas, 3rd Baron Fairfax (1612–71), with later correspondence and papers of the Fairfax family.

Farrar Music manuscripts of the composer Ernest Bristow Farrar (1885–1918).

Fell Medieval and antiquarian manuscripts collected and bequeathed by John Fell, Bishop of Oxford (1625–86).

Frederic Sutherland Ferguson Collection of 220 Scottish books of the 16th and 17th cents., bequeathed by Ferguson (1878–1967).

Howard Ferguson Autograph compositions and working notebooks of the composer Howard Ferguson (1908–99).

'Michael Field' Correspondence and literary papers of Katherine Harris Bradley (1846–1914) and Edith Emma Cooper (1862–1913).

Finch Letters, journals and commonplace books of the antiquary Robert Finch (1783–1830), with manuscripts collected by him.

Finzi Music manuscripts of the composer Gerald Finzi (1901–56).

Firth Manuscripts, books and broadside ballads, 17th – 19th cent., collected by Sir Charles Harding Firth (1857–1936), with some of his working papers and lectures.

Fisher Diaries, correspondence, speeches, lectures and notebooks of H.A.L. Fisher (1865–1940), Warden of New College, Oxford.

Fiske Music manuscripts of the composer and writer Roger Fiske (1910–87).

Ford Papers of Edward Brisco Ford (1901–88), geneticist.

Forster Printed works of the poet Edward Young (1683–1765), in the original and in translation, collected by Harold Bagley Forster (1913–85).

Fraser Persian and Sanskrit manuscripts collected by James Fraser (1713–1754) of the East India Company.

Gatliff Correspondence and papers of Herbert Evelyn Caulfeild Gatliff (1897–1977), many relating to his support of voluntary organisations such as the Youth Hostels Association, the Council for the Preservation of Rural England, the Ramblers' Association and the National Trust.

George-Brown Papers of George Alfred, Baron George-Brown (1914–85).

Gibson Material for the study of every stage of the process of making a printed book, collected by Strickland Gibson (1877–1958), Keeper of Printed Books in the Bodleian, for use in his course on bibliography.

Gilliat Works of Dame Edith Sitwell (1887–1964), poet and critic, and of Sir Osbert Sitwell (1892–1969), writer, mainly presentation copies, given by Mrs. E.G.V. Gilliat.

Gilpin Correspondence and literary manuscripts of William Gilpin (1724–1804), with some earlier and later family papers.

Gladstone 256 pamphlets on Homeric subjects from the library of W.E. Gladstone (1809–98), presented by Henry N. Gladstone in 1923.

Godwyn Books and pamphlets in English and general history, civil and ecclesiastical, published in the 18th cent., collected and bequeathed by Charles Godwyn (1700–70), Fellow of Balliol College, Oxford. (Further material has been added to this collection.)

Goodhart Correspondence, literary and academic papers of Arthur Lehman Goodhart (1891–1978), lawyer and Master of University College, Oxford.

Gore-Booth Correspondence and papers of Paul, Baron Gore-Booth (1909–84), diplomat, and of members of his family.

Gough Topographical collections – books, manuscripts, maps and prints – of Richard Gough (1735–1809), with manuscript and printed service books of the English Church before the Reformation, copper plates, used mainly for his *Sepulchral Monuments of Great Britain*, and (MSS. Gough Drawings-Gaignières), 16 volumes of drawings of monuments in French churches.

Grabe Manuscript *adversaria* of the theologian Johan Ernst Grabe (1666–1711).

Grahame Correspondence and literary papers of Kenneth Grahame (1859–1932) and of his wife, Elspeth.

Greaves Arabic and Persian manuscripts belonging to Thomas Greaves (1612–1676) and his brother John (1602–1652), purchased in 1678.

Greenwood Correspondence and papers of the politicians Arthur Greenwood (1880–1954) and Anthony, Baron Greenwood of Rossendale (1911–82).

Gregor Over 800 volumes of Esperanto material, published worldwide, collected by Douglas Gregor and donated by his widow.

Grey Correspondence and papers of Sir Charles Edward Grey (1785–1865), some relating to the West Indies and India, with papers of earlier and later members of the family.

Gwynne Diaries, correspondence and papers of Howell Arthur Gwynne (1865–1950), journalist. *Deposited.*

Hale Music manuscripts of the composer Alfred Hale (*d.c.*1960).

Hamilton 58 manuscripts from the library of the Carthusian monastery of Erfurt, collected by Sir William Hamilton (1788–1856).

Hammond Correspondence, diaries and other papers of the journalist and historian J. Lawrence Hammond (1872–1949) and of his wife and co-author Barbara (1873–1961).

Hanson Publications, papers, catalogues and bindings of the Edwards family of Halifax, Yorks., 18th – 20th cent, collected by Thomas William Hanson.

Hanworth Correspondence and papers of the judges Ernest Murray Pollock, 1st Viscount Hanworth (1861–1935) and Sir Jonathan Frederick Pollock (1783–1870).

Harcourt Political and family papers of Sir William Harcourt (1827–1904) and his son Lewis, 1st Viscount Harcourt (1863–1922), with estate papers of the Harcourt family of Nuneham Courtenay and Stanton Harcourt, Oxon. *Deposited.*

Harding Music (*c*.120,000 items), chapbooks, songbooks and poetry, drama, jestbooks, ballads and broadsides collected and bequeathed by Walter Newton Henry Harding (1883–1973) of Chicago.

Hardy Personal and scientific papers of Sir Alister Clavering Hardy (1896–1985), zoologist.

Harley Papers of John Laker Harley (1911–90), forest scientist.

Harris Papers of Geoffrey W. Harris (1913–71), Dr. Lee's Professor of Anatomy at Oxford.

Harwood Music manuscripts of the composer Basil Harwood (1859–1949).

Hatton Medieval manuscripts collected by Christopher, 1st Baron Hatton (1605–70). Near Eastern manuscripts in the collection are referenced **Hatton (Or.)**.

Hawker Sermons, literary manuscripts and correspondence of Robert Stephen Hawker (1803–75), Vicar of Morwenstow, Cornwall.

Hawkes Correspondence and papers of Professor Christopher Hawkes (1915–92), archaeologist.

Hearne's Diaries 150 volumes of diaries and notebooks of the antiquary Thomas Hearne (1678–1735).

Heber Correspondence and papers of Reginald Heber (1728–1804), Fellow of Brasenose College, Oxford and of his sons Richard (1773–1833), book-collector, and Reginald (1783–1826), Bishop of Calcutta.

Hemming Papers of Francis Hemming, mainly relating to the International Council for Non-Intervention in Spain, 1937–49. *Deposited*.

Herrick Exchequer papers, family and business correspondence of Sir William Herrick (1502–1563), including letters from his nephew Robert the poet (1591–1674), with papers of other members of the Herrick family of Leicestershire.

Hertford College Manuscripts from the library of Hertford College, Oxford. *Deposited*.

Hinton and Hunt Topographical collections of Henry Hinton (1749–1816), ironmonger, and James Hunt (1795–1857), both of Oxford.

Hodgkin Personal and scientific papers of Dame Dorothy Hodgkin (1910–94), biochemist.

Hodgson Sanskrit manuscripts collected by Brian Houghton Hodgson (1800–94), Resident in Nepal 1833–43, with some correspondence and papers.

Hogan Collected works, novels, short stories and articles, in all over 1,000 printed items, by or about Edgar Wallace (1875–1932), collected and given by John A. Hogan (*d*. 1993).

Holkham Over 800 printed works and important manuscripts from the library of the Earls of Leicester at Holkham Hall, Norfolk, including early works on law, and English literature and plays collected by 18th-cent. members of the family, and English and Italian literature collected by Thomas William Coke, 1st Earl of Leicester (1752–1842).

Holmes Collations of manuscripts of the Septuagint Version by the biblical scholar Robert Holmes (1748–1805).

Hope Newspapers and periodical essays collected by John Thomas Hope, mainly 18th cent.

Hopkins Literary manuscripts and a few personal papers of Gerard Manley Hopkins (1844–89).

Horsley Diaries, correspondence, music and other papers of four generations of the Horsley family, including the composer William Horsley (1774–1858) and the painters John Callcott Horsley (1817–1903) and Rosamund Horsley (1864–1949).

Howden Correspondence and papers of John Francis Caradoc, 1st Baron Howden (1759–1839), general, and his son John Hobart (1799–1873), diplomat and general.

Hughenden Personal, political, literary and family papers of Benjamin Disraeli, Earl of Beaconsfield (1804–81), with some papers of his father Isaac D'Israeli (1766–1848). *Deposited.*

Hume-Rothery Papers of William Hume-Rothery (1899–1968), metallurgist.

Huntington Arabic, Hebrew, Syriac and Coptic manuscripts collected by Robert Huntington (1636–1701), Fellow of Merton College. Huntington was resident chaplain to the Levant Company in Aleppo, 1670–80. He gave 35 manuscripts to the Library, whilst the bulk of his collection, over 600 volumes, was purchased in 1693.

Hyde Persian and Arabic manuscripts of Thomas Hyde (1636–1703), purchased in 1692. Hyde was Bodley's Librarian 1665–1701. He also held the posts of Laudian Professor of Arabic and Regius Professor of Hebrew.

Inverchapel Diplomatic papers of Archibald John Clark Kerr, Baron Inverchapel (1882–1951). *Deposited.*

Jacobs 300 printed foreign dissertations on classical subjects from the library of Professor Friedrich C.W. Jacobs (1764–1847).

James 43 volumes of notes and extracts, mainly relating to the pre-Reformation church in England, by Richard James (1592–1638), Fellow of Corpus Christi College, Oxford.

Jerome K. Jerome Literary manuscripts of Jerome K. Jerome (1859–1927) and presentation copies of his books.

Jessel About 3,400 volumes relating to playing cards, card games, games of chance, fortune-telling by cards and card-tricks, 16th – 20th cent., collected and bequeathed by Frederic Jessel (*d.*1934).

Jesus College Manuscripts from the library of Jesus College, Oxford. *Deposited.*

Joachim Lectures and notebooks of H.H. Joachim (1868–1938), Wykeham Professor of Logic at Oxford.

Johnson Printed ephemera collection formed by John de Monins Johnson (1882–1956), with a large collection of books, pamphlets and manuscripts, mainly English.

Johnston and Frank Manuscript collection of Nathaniel Johnston (1627–1705) and Richard Frank (1698–1762), chiefly relating to the history and antiquities of Yorkshire.

Jones Manuscripts collected by Henry Jones, Vicar of Sunningwell, Berks. (*d.* 1707), chiefly historical and of the 16th and 17th centuries.

Juel-Jensen Printed translations of works by the writer Bruce Chatwin (1940–89).

Juel-Jensen Drayton Some 340 editions of works by and about Michael Drayton (1563–1631) collected and given by Dr. Bent Juel-Jensen.

Junius Anglo-Saxon manuscripts and philological collections of Francis Junius (1589–1677).

Kafka Literary manuscripts, *Tagebücher* and letters of Franz Kafka (1883–1924), in part **deposited**.

Kelmscott Press 60 items, mainly works printed at the Kelmscott Press by William Morris (1834–96).

Kendrew Correspondence and papers of Sir John Cowdery Kendrew (1917–97), molecular biologist.

Kennicott Hebrew biblical manuscripts of Benjamin Kennicott (1718–1783), originally held by the Radcliffe Library, of which he was Librarian.

Kettlewell Correspondence of Henry B.D. Kettlewell (1907–79), lepidopterist and geneticist. *Deposited.*

Kierkegaard Some 80 printed works, 19th and 20th cent., by and about the Danish philosopher and theologian Søren Aabye Kierkegaard (1813–55).

Kimberley Political and personal correspondence and papers of John Wodehouse, 1st Earl of Kimberley (1826–1902).

Lambe Notes on the Arabic language by James Lambe (1599–1664), given to the Bodleian in 1669.

Lambert Correspondence and working papers of Jack Walter Lambert (1917–86), literary editor.

Langbaine *Adversaria* of Gerard Langbaine (1609–58), Provost of Queen's College, Oxford, with descriptions of Bodleian and Oxford College manuscripts and notes concerning the arrangement of the books in the Bodleian.

Latey Correspondence and papers (including BBC radio scripts) of Maurice Brinsmead Latey (1915–91).

Laud Wide-ranging manuscript collections of William Laud (1573–1645), Archbishop of Canterbury, including many from churches and religious houses in Germany, notably Würzburg, Mainz, Eberbach and Lorsch. Oriental manuscripts are separately classed as **Laud Or.**

Lawn Personal papers of Dr. Brian Lawn (*d.*2001), proofs of his learned publications and his catalogued library of manuscripts (Oriental and Western) and books.

Lawrence Papers of T.E. Lawrence (1888–1935), 'Lawrence of Arabia', with papers of his brother Professor A.W. Lawrence (1900–91) relating to him.

Lee 160 printed works mainly relating to Dutch law and history, 17th – 20th cent., collected and given by Professor Robert Warden Lee (1868–1958).

Legge Academic and family papers of James Legge (1815–97), first Professor of Chinese at Oxford.

C.S. Lewis Literary manuscripts, correspondence, photographs, essays and notebooks of C.S.Lewis (1898–1963), mainly *deposited*.

Lewis family Correspondence of Elizabeth, Lady Lewis (1844–1931), wife of Sir George Henry Lewis, 1st Bart. (1833–1911), with papers of other members of the family.

Library Records Archives of the Bodleian Library, Oxford, 17th – 20th cent.

Libri Hungarici 416 volumes, mainly 1700–1830, on the civil and ecclesiastical history, and topography of Hungary and South-Eastern Europe.

Libri Polonici Some 1,600 volumes about Poland, with particular reference to its cultural history and the Reformation, and to the development of education, for the most part from the collection of the historian Józef Andrzej Łukaszewicz (1797–1873).

Linc. Tracts and pamphlets of the reign of Charles I and of the Civil War and Interregnum, with many theological works, from the library of Thomas Barlow (1607–91), Bishop of Lincoln.

Lincoln College Manuscripts from the library of Lincoln College, Oxford. *Deposited.*

Lister Books and manuscripts, mainly 17th cent., on medicine, anatomy, natural philosophy, botany and travels, from the library of Martin Lister (1638–1712). A small number of Arabic manuscripts is separately classed as **Lister Or.**

Locke Journals, correspondence, notebooks and other papers of the philosopher John Locke (1632–1704), and the 'King moiety' of his library.

Lovelace Byron Correspondence and papers of Anne Isabella, Lady Byron (1792–1860), her parents, her daughter Ada, Countess of Lovelace (1815–52) and her grandson Ralph Milbanke, 2nd Earl of Lovelace (1839–1906). *Deposited.*

Lugard Papers of John Daltry, Baron Lugard (1858–1945), Governor of Hong Kong and Governor-General of Nigeria. (In the Bodleian Library of Commonwealth and African Studies at Rhodes House.)

Lyell 100 medieval manuscripts and some later manuscripts from the collection of James Patrick Ronaldson Lyell (1871–1948), solicitor, with some of his working papers.

Macartney Correspondence of George, 1st Earl Macartney (1737–1806) as Governor and President of Fort St. George, Madras.

C.A. Macartney Papers of the historian Carlile Aylmer Macartney (1895–1978), chiefly relating to Hungary in the inter-war period and during the Second World War.

Macdonnell Papers of Anthony Patrick, 1st Baron Macdonnell of Swinford (1844–1925), many relating to India and Ireland.

McGhee 32 printed works of Roman Catholic theology, 1770–1850, collected and presented by the Rev. Robert James McGhee (1789–1822).

Maclean Correspondence and papers of Sir Donald Maclean (1864–1932), politician. *Deposited.*

Macmillan Political papers of Harold Macmillan, 1st Earl of Stockton (1894–1986). *Deposited.*

MacNeice Correspondence and literary papers of Louis MacNeice (1907–63), with some papers of his father John Frederick MacNeice (*d.*1942), Bishop of Down, Connor and Dromore – partly *deposited.*

Madden Journal, 1819–72, of Sir Frederic Madden (1801–73), Keeper of Manuscripts in the British Museum.

Malone Collection of Elizabethan, Jacobean and Caroline literature, especially drama, mainly printed and a few manuscripts, formed by Edmund Malone (1741–1812), with some of his letters and papers. Accessions of printed English drama were from *c.*1860 added to the Malone collection and (from 1883 to 1988) given the shelfmark M. adds.

Manning Some 500 books on the antiquities and history of the city, county and university of Oxford, with 87 portfolios of local engravings and drawings, collected and bequeathed by Percy Manning (*d.* 1917), with his manuscript collections chiefly on sports, pastimes and folklore of Oxford.

Mansfield Over 500 volumes mainly relating to the Congregational Church, from the Library of Mansfield College, Oxford, including Dutch and German pamphlets, sermons and tracts.

Mansfield College Manuscripts from the library of Mansfield College, Oxford. *Deposited.*

Marlborough Vicar's Library The Vicar's Library, St. Mary's, Marlborough, Wiltshire, chiefly put together by William White (1604–78), mainly theology, works of scholarship and schoolbooks. *Deposited.*

Marsh Arabic manuscripts (chiefly) bequeathed to the Bodleian in 1713 by Narcissus Marsh (1638–1713), Archbishop of Armagh. The collection contains some 270 manuscripts formerly belonging to the Dutch Orientalist Jacob Golius.

Marshall Books and manuscripts collected and bequeathed by Thomas Marshall (1621–85), Rector of Lincoln College, Oxford, including contemporary Protestant theology and works on Anglo–Saxon and Middle Eastern languages. The Oriental manuscripts in this collection (Arabic, Coptic, Hebrew, etc.) are separately classed at **Marshall Or.**

Marvin Correspondence and papers of Francis Sydney Marvin (1863–1943), positivist.

Masefield Papers of John Masefield (1878–1967), Poet Laureate, mainly *deposited.*

Mason Some 8,000 volumes, including plate books and editions de luxe, 16th – 19th cent., purchased with money bequeathed by Robert Mason (1783–1841) of Queen's College, Oxford.

Mather Over 170 printed works by or about the New England divines, Cotton (1663–1728) and Increase (1639–1723) Mather, collected by Henry Octavius Coxe (1811–81), Bodley's Librarian.

Mavrogordato Diaries, literary papers and correspondence of John Mavrogordato (1882–1970), Bywater and Sotheby Professor of Byzantine and Modern Greek at Oxford. *Deposited.*

Max Müller Correspondence and academic and personal papers of Friedrich Max Müller (1823–1900), first Professor of Classical Philology at Oxford.

Max Müller Memorial Sanskrit manuscripts purchased in India in 1907–08 for the administrators of the Max Müller Memorial Fund.

Meerman Some 1,500 volumes from the library of Gerard Meerman (*d.* 1771) and his son John, including works on foreign history and law, and classics, 16th – 19th cent.

Kurt Mendelssohn Papers of the physicist Kurt Alfred Georg Mendelssohn (1906–80).

M. Deneke Mendelssohn Personal papers, drawing books, correspondence, music manuscripts and printed music of Felix Mendelssohn Bartholdy (1809–47).

Mendham Italian and Spanish manuscripts, chiefly relating to the Council of Trent, collected and bequeathed by the Rev. Joseph Mendham (1769–1856).

Michael Large collection of Hebrew manuscripts of Heimann Joseph Michael (1792–1846), Hebrew scholar from Hamburg, purchased in 1848.

Midland and Oxford Circuit Records of the Midland and Oxford [Assize] Circuit, 19th – 20th cent., including papers of its Bar Mess Association. *Deposited.*

Milford Music manuscripts of the composer Robin Humphrey Milford (1903–59).

Mill Sanskrit manuscripts collected by William Hodge Mill (1792–1853), Principal of Bishop's College, Calcutta and, from 1848, Regius Professor of Hebrew at Cambridge.

Mill House Press Some 50 books printed at the Mill House Press, Stanford Dingley, Reading, Berks., 1926–71.

Milne Papers of Edward Arthur Milne (1896–1950), mathematician and natural philosopher.

Milner Personal and official papers of Alfred, Viscount Milner (1854–1925), mainly relating to South Africa and the First World War. *Deposited.*

Milner adds. Papers relating to the compilation of Cecil Headlam, *The Milner Papers* (London, 1931–3) with some papers of Lord Milner as Secretary of State for the Colonies.

Violet Milner Papers of Violet, Viscountess Milner (1872–1958), with correspondence, family and estate papers of the Maxse family.

Minn Topographical collections of Henry Minn (1870–1961) relating to Oxford, including many photographs – some by Henry William Taunt (1842–1922) and Sarah Angelina Acland (1849–1930) – with transcripts and extracts from records.

Monckton and **Monckton Trustees** Personal and official papers of Walter, 1st Viscount Monckton of Brenchley (1891–1965), including papers relating to the Abdication Crisis of 1936, India and the Ministry of Information. *Deposited.*

Monk Bretton Papers of three generations of the Dodson family: letterbooks and case notebooks of the judge, Sir John Dodson (1780–1858); diaries and political papers of John George Dodson, 1st Baron Monk-Bretton (1825–97), and diaries and diplomatic papers of John William Dodson, 2nd Baron Monk-Bretton (1869–1933). *Deposited.*

Monro Over 1,000 printed works of Homeric studies, mainly 19th cent., from the library of David Binning Monro (1836–1905), Provost of Oriel College, and presented in his memory.

Monson Correspondence of Sir Edward John Monson (1834–1909) relating to his diplomatic postings throughout Europe.

Montagu Literary manuscripts, autograph letters and 700 printed works collected and bequeathed by Captain Montagu Montagu, R.N. (*d.* 1863), including 90 editions of the Psalter, classical and French literature and grangerised volumes of topography and biography.

Montgomery Correspondence, papers and music manuscripts of Robert Bruce Montgomery (1921–78) who wrote as Edmund Crispin.

Moorcock Printed editions and translations of the works of Michael Moorcock (*b.*1939), novelist, writer of science fiction and heroic fantasy, with some *deposited* working papers.

Morley Diaries, correspondence and papers of John, 1st Viscount Morley (1838–1923), with papers of his biographer, the economist F. W. Hirst (1873–1953).

Mortara 1,400 volumes, 16th – 19th cent., from the library of Conte Alessandro Mortara, rich in rare 16th-cent. editions of Italian authors.

Moss Col. William E. Moss (1875–1953) made many donations of books and manuscripts; on his death his widow presented his collection of books and papers on book-binding and on William Blake.

Gilbert Murray Correspondence and papers of Gilbert Murray (1866–1957), Regius Professor of Greek at Oxford and internationalist.

H.J.R. Murray Books, correspondence and papers relating to chess and other board games collected and given by Harold James Ruthven Murray (1868–1955). His collection of Arabic, Hebrew, Turkish and other Oriental manuscripts is separately classed at **H.J. Murray Or.**

Sir James Murray Correspondence and some papers of Sir James Augustus Henry Murray (1837–1915), lexicographer.

Music School Manuscript and printed music of the 16th – 18th cent., formerly in the Oxford Music School, including the foundation gift of William Heather in 1627.

Music School Exercises Oxford B.Mus. and D.Mus. compositional 'exercises' from the mid-18th century to the present day.

Myres Correspondence, lectures and other papers of Sir John Linton Myres (1869–1954), Wykeham Professor of Ancient History at Oxford.

Nalson State Papers, mainly 1640–60, used by John Nalson (?1637–1686) in *An Impartial Collection of the Great Affairs of State* (London, 1682–3).

Napier Papers of the Napier family, chiefly of Sir William Francis Patrick Napier (1785–1860), general and historian, his brother Sir Charles James Napier (1782–1853), general and colonial governor, and their father Col. George Napier (1751–1804).

E.J. Nathan Correspondence, diaries and other papers of Edward Jonah Nathan (*fl.* 1898–1962), relating to the Chinese Engineering and Mining Company and the Kailan Mining Administration.

Matthew Nathan Papers of Sir Matthew Nathan (1862–1939), Governor successively of the Gold Coast, Hong Kong, Natal and Queensland. (Part of the collection is in the Bodleian Library of Commonwealth and African Studies at Rhodes House.)

Nevinson Journals of Henry Woodd Nevinson (1860–1949), essayist, philanthropist and journalist – see also **Sharp**.

New College Manuscripts from the library of New College, Oxford. *Deposited.*

Nichols Newspapers Collection of London newspapers, 1672–1737, formed by John Nichols (1745–1820).

Noble Correspondence, sermons and antiquarian papers of Mark Noble (1754–1827).

North Papers of the North family, Barons North and Earls of Guilford, 13th – 20th cent., kept at Wroxton Abbey, Oxon., the principal seat of the Earls of Guilford until 1932. The largest section comprises the estate and personal papers of Francis North, 1st Earl of Guilford (1704–90).

Officina Bodoni About 100 books printed by Giovanni Mardersteig at the Officina Bodoni in Montagnola and Verona, 1923–77.

Ogston Papers of Alexander George Ogston (1911–96), biochemist.

Opie Collection of some 20,000 works for children formed by Iona and Peter Opie, 16th – 20th cent., with some personal and working papers.

Oppenheimer Extensive collection of Hebrew and Yiddish manuscripts and printed books formed by David ben Abraham Oppenheimer (1664–1735), Chief Rabbi of Prague, bought in 1829.

Oriel College Manuscripts from the library of Oriel College, Oxford. *Deposited.*

Ouseley Persian manuscripts collected by Sir William Ouseley (1767–1842) and his brother Sir Gore Ouseley (1770–1844). Sir Gore's manuscripts are referenced **Ouseley Adds.**

Oxford Barbers Records of the guild of Oxford Barber Surgeons, 17th – 19th cent.

Oxford Enzyme Group Papers of the Group, 1968–88.

Oxford University Press, Printer's Library Some 2,000 books printed in Oxford from 1585 to the 20th century.

Oxford University Press, Type Specimens Over 300 type specimens, the majority either English or Scottish.

Oxfordshire Architectural and Historical Society Records of the Society, 1835–1969, with some earlier manuscripts relating to the history and heraldry of the area.

Palmer Business correspondence, mainly letter-books, and papers of John Palmer (1766–1836), East Indies merchant.

Parker Music manuscripts of the composer Clifton Parker (1905–89).

Parry Drafts and fair copies of the works of Sir Hubert Parry (1848–1918), composer and musical historian.

Pattison Diaries, commonplace books, sermons and correspondence of Mark Pattison (1813–84), Rector of Lincoln College, Oxford.

Peake Literary manuscripts and notebooks of Mervyn Peake (1911–68). *Deposited.*

Peierls Correspondence of Sir Rudolf Ernst Peierls (1907–97), theoretical physicist.

Percy Literary and antiquarian papers and correspondence of Thomas Percy (1729–1811), Bishop of Dromore, and some 120 books from his library, including annotated copies of Goldsmith, Johnson and other 18th–cent. authors.

Perham Papers of Dame Margery Perham (1895–1982), writer and lecturer on African affairs. (In the Bodleian Library of Commonwealth and African Studies at Rhodes House.)

Perrott 9 historical and heraldic manuscripts collected by Thomas Perrott (*fl.* 1710–27), including a letter-book, 1584–6, of Sir John Perrot (1527–1592) as Lord Deputy of Ireland.

Peters Papers of Sir Rudolph Albert Peters (1889–1982), biochemist.

Pettingell Collection of 19th-cent. 'penny dreadful' publications formed by Frank Pettingell (1891–1966).

Phillipps-Munby Working papers of A.N.L. Munby (1913–74) concerning his *Phillipps Studies* (5 vols., Cambridge, 1951–60) and the history and location of manuscripts collected by Sir Thomas Phillipps.

Phillipps-Robinson Topographical collections and personal correspondence and papers of Sir Thomas Phillipps (1792–1872), presented by Lionel and Philip Robinson.

Phillips Papers of Sir David Clifton Phillips (*b.*1924), biophysicist.

Pigott Diaries, correspondence and albums of Harriet Pigott (1775–1846), authoress.

Pococke Arabic, Hebrew and other Oriental manuscripts of Edward Pococke (1604–1691), first Laudian Professor of Arabic at Oxford and later Regius Professor of Hebrew. He was chaplain to the Levant Company in Aleppo and resident in Constantinople.

Pollard Working papers and correspondence of Graham Pollard (1903–76), bibliographer, with records of the antiquarian booksellers Birrell & Garnett, 1927–39.

Ponsonby Political correspondence of Arthur A.W.H. Ponsonby, 1st Baron Ponsonby of Shulbrede (1871–1946).

Porter Research notebooks of Rodney Robert Porter (1917–85), biochemist.

Powell 170 works on science, theology and education from the library of Baden Powell (1796–1860), Savilian Professor of Geometry at Oxford.

Primrose League Records of the Primrose League, mainly minute books, 19th – 20th cent.

Pringle Research notebooks and lectures of John William Sutton Pringle (1912–82), zoologist.

Prior Papers of Arthur Norman Prior (1914–69), philosopher.

Pym Literary papers, diaries and correspondence of Barbara Pym (1913–80).

Queen's College Title deeds of properties of The Queen's College, Oxford, 12th – 18th cent. *Deposited*.

Radcliffe Printed works on architecture, the classics, history, literature and theology from the Radcliffe Library, Oxford.

Radcliffe Papers of the Radcliffe Trust, many relating to the Radcliffe Observatory, Infirmary and Library in Oxford, 18th – 20th cent., with earlier title deeds. *Deposited*.

Radcliffe Records Records of the Radcliffe Library, 18th – 20th cent.

Radcliffe Trust Miscellaneous manuscripts, 13th – 20th cent., from the Radcliffe Library, Oxford, including 12 volumes of letters to the botanist and antiquary Richard Richardson (1663–1741), and 60 dissertations submitted for the degree of Doctor of Medicine at Oxford, 1859–95.

Rawlinson Over 5,000 manuscripts, 8th – 18th cent., and some 1,800 books, 16th –18th cent., collected and given or bequeathed by the antiquary and non-juror Richard Rawlinson (1690–1755), mainly relating to theology, English literature and history, antiquities, topography, heraldry and law, with almanacs, 1607–1747; the manuscripts including papers of John Thurloe (1616–68), as Secretary of State to Oliver and Richard Cromwell, papers of Samuel Pepys (1633–1703) as Secretary to the Admiralty, sermons and other papers of many non-jurors (high churchmen who refused the oath of allegiance to William and Mary after their accession in 1688), 17th- and 18th-century correspondence of, among others, Thomas Hearne (1678–1755), Isaac Vossius (1618–89) and Rawlinson himself, 17th-century poetical collections, and biblical, liturgical and classical manuscripts. The Oriental manuscripts in this collection (Arabic, Hebrew, Turkish, etc.) are separately classed as **Rawlinson Or.**

Reggio Hebrew manuscripts of Isaac Samuel Reggio (1784–1855), Italian rabbi of Gorizia.

Rennell of Rodd Official and personal papers of James, 1st Baron Rennell of Rodd (1858–1941), with family papers of the 18th and 19th cents.

Rhodes Business records and some personal papers of Cecil Rhodes (1853–1902), including all versions of his will. (*Deposited* by the Rhodes Trustees at the Bodleian Library of Commonwealth and African Studies at Rhodes House.)

Richards Papers of Sir Rex Edward Richards (*b.* 1922), chemist and biophysicist.

Richardson Papers of Hugh Richardson (1905–2000), Indian administrator and Tibetologist, dating from his period as head of the British and Indian Missions in Lhasa, 1936–40 and 1946–50, together with academic papers and correspondence, 1950–2000.

Rigaud Correspondence and notebooks of Stephen Peter Rigaud (1774–1839), Savilian Professor first of Geometry, then of Astronomy, at Oxford, with books from his library.

Risley Papers of the Risley, Barber and Cotton families, including title deeds and estate papers, 15th – 19th cent., and diaries of the Rev. W.C. Risley, 1834–69. *Deposited.*

Roe Greek manuscripts, 10th – 17th cent., collected and given by Sir Thomas Roe (1581–1644).

Rogers Correspondence and papers of James E. Thorold Rogers (1823–90), political economist, and of members of his family.

Ross Some 1,000 works of and about Oscar Wilde (1856–1900) or relating to literary movements in England in the 1890s, collected by Walter Edwin Ledger (*d.* 1931) and named after Wilde's friend Robert Baldwin Ross (1869–1918). *Deposited.*

Roxburghe Club Collection of Roxburghe Club publications from 1814.

Rumbold Journals, correspondence and diplomatic papers of Sir Horace Rumbold (1829–1913) and Sir Horace George Rumbold (1869–1941). *Deposited.*

Russell Papers of the Russell family of Swallowfield, Berks., mainly 19th cent., many relating to India.

Ryder Papers, correspondence and printed books of John Ryder (1923–2001), book designer; the collection is strong in private press material, letter-design, calligraphy and book illustration.

Rylands Manuscripts collected and compiled by William Harry Rylands (1847–1922), chiefly relating to heraldry, freemasonry and genealogy.

Sadler Correspondence and papers of Sir Michael Ernest Sadler (1861–1943), some relating to the Department of Education, 1896–1903, the Oxford Preservation Trust, 1925–41, and the Bodleian Library (of which Sadler was a Curator), 1924–40.

St. Amand 600 books, mainly contemporary editions of the classics and of the writings of modern Latin scholars, from the library of James St. Amand (1687–1754), with his notes on classical authors and letters to him from foreign scholars.

St. Edmund Hall Manuscripts from the library of St. Edmund Hall, Oxford. *Deposited.*

Sale Arabic and Persian manuscripts of George Sale (1697?–1736), translator of the first English version of the Qur'an.

Sancroft 140 commonplace books of William Sancroft (1617–93), Archbishop of Canterbury. Much of his correspondence survives in the **Tanner** collection.

Sandars Papers of John Satterfield Sandars (1853–1934), private secretary to A.J. Balfour, many of whose papers are included in this collection.

Sankey Correspondence and papers of John, Viscount Sankey (1866–1948), many relating to his period as Lord Chancellor and to the Indian Round Table Conference.

Savile Manuscripts and books collected by Sir Henry Savile (1549–1622), which formed the library serving the Professors of Astronomy and of Geometry, enhanced by successive holders of the Chairs; with estate papers relating to the properties with which the Savilian foundation was endowed.

Schuster Papers of Sir George Schuster (1881–1982), financial adviser to governments and educationist.

Scicluna Books on the history of Malta and the Order of St. John of Jerusalem collected and given by Sir Hannibal Publius Scicluna (1880–1981). (In the Bodleian Library of Commonwealth and African Studies at Rhodes House.)

Selborne Correspondence and papers of William Waldegrave Palmer, 2nd Earl of Selborne (1859–1942) and Roundell Cecil Palmer, 3rd Earl (1887–1971).

Selby Diplomatic, literary, business and family correspondence of Sir Walford Selby (1881–1965).

Selden Books and manuscripts from the collection of John Selden (1584–1654): the books including many 16th- and 17th-cent. works in classical and foreign languages, on medicine, science, theology, history, law and Hebrew literature; the manuscripts mainly mathematical, astronomical, astrological and Greek.

Shackleton Some 1,000 volumes by and about Charles de Secondat, Baron de Montesquieu (1689–1755) collected and bequeathed by Robert Shackleton (1919-86), Bodley's Librarian, with 8 related English and French manuscripts and some working papers.

Sharp Correspondence and papers of Evelyn Sharp (1869–1955), author and journalist, with some of her husband Henry Woodd Nevinson (1856–1941).

Shelley Drafts and fair copies of Shelley's poems and prose works with some correspondence; correspondence and literary papers of his wife Mary Wollstonecraft Shelley (1797–1851) and papers of and relating to his family and friends.

Sherwood Music manuscripts of the composer Percy Sherwood (1866–1939).

Shrivenham Over 400 textbooks of the 1930s and 1940s collected for the American servicemen's university at Shrivenham, Berks., including works on science, engineering, geography, American history and literature.

Shuttleworth 378 volumes of editions of Sheridan's plays, music for them and songs in them, with works on Sheridan, presented by Bertram Shuttleworth in 1934.

Sidgwick and Jackson Letter-books and files of correspondence of the publishers Sidgwick and Jackson, 20th cent.

Simon Personal and political correspondence and papers of John Allsebrook, 1st Viscount Simon (1873–1954).

Smith Notes, extracts and correspondence of the non-juror Thomas Smith (1638–1710).

Smith newsbooks Early newsbooks, corantos and newspapers collected and presented by George Smith of Great Bedwyn, Wilts. (1871–1963).

Society for the Propagation of the Gospel Archive of the SPG, the oldest Anglican missionary society, and of the Universities' Mission to Central Africa, 18th – 20th cent. (*Deposited* in the Bodleian Library of Commonwealth and African Studies at Rhodes House.)

Society for the Protection of Science and Learning Archive of the Society, 20th cent.

Soddy Biographical and scientific papers of Frederick Soddy (1877–1956), chemist.

Somerville Correspondence, scientific and family papers of Mary Somerville (1780–1872), writer on science. *Deposited.*

Spalding Journals, literary papers and correspondence of Philip Anthony Spalding (1911–89), writer.

Stanbrook Abbey Papers, including proofs, relating to the Stanbrook Abbey Press, 20th cent.

Stein Correspondence, notebooks, field diaries, personal diaries and other papers of Sir Aurel Stein (1862–1943), explorer and archaeologist. The Oriental manuscripts in this collection (mainly Sanskrit) are separately classed as **Stein Or.**

Stephens Correspondence of the art critic Frederic George Stephens (1828–1907), much of it with fellow members of the Pre-Raphaelite Brotherhood.

Stokes Diaries, correspondence and political papers of Richard Rapier Stokes (1897–1957), Labour MP for Ipswich.

Strachey Papers of Christopher Strachey (1916–75), computer scientist.

Stuart Papers of Sir Louis Stuart (1870–1949), mainly papers of the Indian Empire Society and the India Services Pensioners' Association.

Stukeley Correspondence, diaries, topographical and antiquarian papers of William Stukeley (1687–1765).

Sturt Journals, letters, maps and watercolours of Charles Sturt's three expeditions into the interior of Australia, 1828–9, 1829–30 and 1844–6. (In the Bodleian Library of Commonwealth and African Studies at Rhodes House.)

Sutherland 35 illustrated biographical and historical works, enriched with additional engravings by Alexander Hendras Sutherland (*d.* 1820) and his widow.

Sutton Papers of Leslie Ernest Sutton (1906–92), chemist.

Talbot Estate and personal papers of the Talbot de Malahide family of Co. Dublin, 13th – 20th cent.

Tanner Manuscripts collected by Thomas Tanner (1674–1735), Bishop of St. Asaph, including correspondence and papers of Archbishop Sancroft and of John Nalson; some 960 volumes from his library, mainly 16th and 17th cent., including important examples of early English printing, theological works by the Reformers and their opponents, and pamphlets of the Civil War and interregnum. Near Eastern manuscripts in the collection are referenced **Tanner (Or.).**

Tauchnitz Some 1,300 volumes of British and American authors, mainly fiction, published in the series begun by Bernhard Tauchnitz junior in Leipzig in 1841.

Taylor Correspondence, diaries and literary papers of Sir Henry Taylor (1800–86), author of *Philip Van Artevelde*, and his family.

Tenbury Manuscript and printed music from the library of St. Michael's College, Tenbury Wells, including early musical treatises, opera scores, first editions of major 19th-cent. composers and much sacred music.

Tercentenary Manuscripts, correspondence and papers relating to the celebration of the tercentenary of the Bodleian in 1902, including illuminated addresses.

E.J. Thompson Correspondence, literary and family papers of Edward John Thompson (1886–1946).

T.W. Thompson Papers of Thomas William Thompson (*d.*1968), folklorist, mainly relating to Gypsies, their language and folk tales.

Thomson Literary papers, diaries and correspondence of James Thomson (1834–82), poet and pessimist.

Thorn-Drury Some 70 volumes of late 17th-cent. English poetical texts, from the library of George Thorn-Drury, heavily annotated by him.

Thurston Arabic and Persian (mostly) manuscripts of which only a handful were donated by William Thurston, a London merchant, in 1661. The provenance of many of the others remains unknown.

Tinbergen Papers of Nikolaas Tinbergen (1907–88), ethnologist.

Todhunter-Allen Collection including county atlases of England and Wales, 17th – 19th cent., and large scale county maps of the 18th and early 19th cent., formed by Hugh Todhunter and G.E.H. Allen of Liverpool.

Tolkien Literary and academic papers of the author and scholar J.R.R. Tolkien (1892–1973) – partly *deposited*.

Arnold Toynbee Correspondence and literary papers of Arnold Joseph Toynbee (1889–1975), author, scholar and historian.

Paget Toynbee Books and manuscripts collected and given or bequeathed by the Dante scholar Paget Jackson Toynbee (1855–1932), including 16th-cent. editions of Boccaccio and Petrarch, manuscripts, editions and translations of Dante, other works of Italian literature and works from the library of Horace Walpole, 4th Earl of Orford, with related papers and correspondence.

Trinity College Manuscripts from the library of Trinity College, Oxford. *Deposited.*

Tucker Correspondence and papers of the Tucker family of Weymouth, Dorset, much relating to the quarrying of stone on Portland, mainly 18th cent.

Twyne and **Twyne-Langbaine** Transcripts, extracts and notes relating to the university and city of Oxford, made by and for Brian Twyne (1579?–1644); arranged, listed and bound by Gerard Langbaine (1609–58).

Tyson Printed music and books from the library of Alan Tyson (1926–2000), including many first editions of Haydn, Mozart, Beethoven and Schubert.

United Nations Career Records Project Replies to questionnaires, and memoirs of men and women who served in the United Nations Organisation and its agencies, 20th cent.

University College Manuscripts from the library of University College, Oxford. *Deposited.*

University College Over 100 scarce works of 15th – 17th cent., presented by the Master and Fellows of University College, Oxford, 1923–35.

University College II Around 200 volumes on various subjects discarded by the College and over 1,000 volumes of mainly theological works published in the 17th century. *Deposited.*

Vaughan Correspondence, lectures and other papers of Henry Halford Vaughan (1811–85), Regius Professor of Modern History at Oxford.

Villari Correspondence and diaries of Linda Villari (*d.* 1915), author, and her son Luigi.

Viner Working library, mainly legal works, of Charles Viner (1678–1756), with transcripts and notes for his *A General Abridgement of Law and Equity* (23 vols., Aldershot, 1741–57). (Held at the Bodleian Law Library.)

Wain The author's own file copies of the publications of John Barrington Wain (1925–94), both in English and in translation.

Waismann Papers of the philosopher Friedrich Waismann (1896–1959).

A. Walker Arabic, Persian and Sanskrit manuscripts of Alexander Walker (1764–1831), soldier and administrator in India.

Ernest Walker Music manuscripts of the composer and writer Ernest Walker (1870–1949).

J. Walker Collections of John Walker (1674–1747) for his *Account of the Numbers and Suffering of the Clergy of the Church of England … in the Late Times of the Grand Rebellion* (London, 1714), including many original returns.

Walpole Collection of published works (mainly first editions), manuscripts and letters of English writers of fiction, poetry and *belles lettres* of the 1890s, formed by Sir Hugh Seymour Walpole (1884–1941).

Ward Papers of Irene, Baroness Ward of North Tyneside (1895–1980).

Wardrop Georgian manuscripts, printed books and papers of Sir Oliver Wardrop (1864–1948), Chief British Commissioner of Transcaucasia 1919–21, and his sister Marjorie (1869–1909). Sir Oliver established the Wardrop Collection in 1910 to commemorate his sister's name and he continued to add to it until his death.

Warton Antiquarian, classical and literary papers and sermons of Thomas Warton (1728–90), Thomas Warton (1688–1745), Professor of Poetry, and James Ingram (1774–1850). *Deposited.*

Wedgwood Correspondence, personal and literary papers of Dame Veronica Wedgwood (1910–97), historian.

Weld Papers of the Weld family, including title deeds for their estates in Staffordshire, Oxfordshire and Derbyshire, 13th – 18th cent. *Deposited.*

Welensky Papers of Sir Roy Welensky (1907–91), Prime Minister of the Federation of Rhodesia and Nyasaland. (In the Bodleian Library of Commonwealth and African Studies at Rhodes House.)

Whinfield Manuscripts of the Persian scholar and translator of Omar Khayyam Sir Edward Whinfield (1836–1922).

221

Wight Printed and manuscript English music, 17th- and 18th- cent., from the collection of Osborne Wight (*d.*1800).

Wilberforce Correspondence and papers of the philanthropist William Wilberforce (1759–1833) and his sons Samuel (1805–73), Bishop of Oxford and Winchester, and Robert Isaac (1802–57), Archdeacon of East Riding.

Wilkinson Sketchbooks, correspondence, archaeological and personal papers of Sir John Gardner Wilkinson (1797–1875), many relating to his Egyptological work. *Deposited.*

Willis Manuscript collections of the antiquary Browne Willis (1682–1760), mainly relating to the cathedrals of England and Wales, and to Buckinghamshire.

Harold Wilson Political papers of Harold, Baron Wilson of Rievaulx (1916–95).

H. H. Wilson Sanskrit manuscripts collected by Horace Hayman Wilson (1786–1860), first Boden Professor of Sanskrit at Oxford.

Windham Club Minute books, agenda for meetings and book of rules of the Windham Club, 1849–1954.

Winterton Diaries, correspondence and political papers of Edward Turnour, 6th Earl Winterton (1883–1962).

Wood Collections of Anthony Wood (1632–95): 25 medieval manuscripts, his working papers for the history of the city, university and county of Oxford, his diary for 1657–95, and some 960 volumes, mainly 17th cent., including books printed at Oxford or written by Oxford men, a series of almanacs, 1629–95, newspapers, pamphlets, chapbooks, ballads, broadsheets, book catalogues and prospectuses.

Woods Papers of Donald Devereux Woods (1912–64), microbiologist.

Woodforde Papers of members of the Woodforde family, 17th – 19th cent., including the diaries of James 'Parson' Woodforde (1740–1803).

Woolton Political papers of Frederick Marquis, 1st Earl of Woolton (1883–1964), including papers as Minister of Food, Minister of Reconstruction and Chairman of the Conservative Party.

Worthington-Evans Political papers of Sir Worthington Laming Worthington-Evans (1868–1931), 1st Bart.

Wright Papers of Joseph Wright (1855–1930) and his wife, including his annotations and corrections to his *English Dialect Dictionary* (London & New York, 1896–1901).

Wykeham Musgrave Estate papers of the Wykeham Musgrave family of Chinnor, Oxon., mainly 17th – 19th cent. *Deposited.*

Zimmern Correspondence and papers of Sir Alfred Zimmern (1879–1957), mainly relating to his work for international peace.

Index

The Index contains entries for the following where they are mentioned in the text of the Guide, the bibliographies, the illustration captions or the list of principal special collections:

- Authors and sponsors (including organisations and institutions) of works and bodies of material.
- Former owners of collections.
- Donors of collections.
- Names of collections where different from those of owner or donor.
- Other individuals or organisations important to the growth of the Library, e.g. Bodley's Librarians, academics, sources of funding.
- Titles of important works or bodies of material with no named author.
- Special categories and formats of material, e.g. newspapers, illuminated manuscripts, photographs, pamphlets, dissertations.
- Subjects covered by holdings mentioned, including academic disciplines; countries and other localities; individuals; organisations; events; and specialised topics.

Roman numerals refer to illustrations

Abingdon, Earls of 39, 199
Abinger, James, 8th Baron 198
Aborigines 73, 157-8, 198
Academic Assistance Council 66
Aceh, Sultan of 178
Ackermann, Rudolf 112
Acland, Sir Henry 90-1, 198
Acland, Sarah Angelina 173, 213
Acta eruditorum 98
Adams, William 146
Adams Papers 152
Adcock, Fleur 157
Addison, Christopher, 1st Viscount 198
Admiralty charts 75
Adversaria 28
Aesop 43
Africa 159-62, 176, 215, 219
African-American writers 154
Agincourt Song 81
Agriculture 92, 94, 200

Ainslie, Thomas 155
Akbar, Emperor 136, 176
al-Hariri 176, XXIX
al-Idrisi 128, 176
al-Jazari 176
al-Sufi 129, 176, 185
Albania 76, 120
Alcaeus 25
Alchemy 33, 89
Aldeburgh Festival 85
Aldersey, Thomas 54
Aldine Press 29, 59, 107, 171
Aldiss, Brian 45, 198
Aldus Manutius, *see* Aldine Press
Aleni, Giulio 141
Alentiak language 111
Alexander Library, Department of Zoology 95
Alexander, Boyd 199
Alexander Romance 102
Alfonso X, King of Castile 112

Alfred, King 52
All Souls College, Oxford 69, 198
Allen, G.E.H. 220
Allen, Mr and Mrs H.M. 77
Allen, P.S. 99, 198
Allen, Thomas 27, 88
Almanacs 66, 216, 222
American Communist Party 123
American Fiction 1774-1850 154
American literature 45, 152-4, 218-9
American Revolution 152
American War of Independence 151
Amis, Kingsley 45
Anatomy 90, 94-5, 203, 208, 211
Anglican Church, *see* Church of England
Anglo-Boer War 161
Anglo-Norman literature 102, XXII
Anglo-Saxon Chronicle 31
Anglo-Saxon language 45, 209, 212
Anglo-Saxon literature 43
Animal ecology 205
Annals of Inisfallen 32, V
Annals of Ulster 32
Annuals 49
Ansell, David 36
Anthropology 91, 93-5, 205
Anti-Apartheid Movement 161-2, 177, 198,
    XXXVIII
Antico, Andrea 84
Anti-Slavery Society 153, 160, 198
Anti-War Committee, Oxford University 36
Antonelli, Cardinal Giacomo 108
Antonelli, Count Pietro 108
Apiarian Society 198
Apollonius of Perga 129
Arabian Nights 130
Arabic 88, 112, 127-31, 176, 185, 201, 203, 207,
    209-12, 214, 216-18, 220-1
Aramaic 121, 123-4
Archaeology 39, 116, 168, 175, 203, 208, 219, 222
Architecture 154, 167-9, 171-3, 216, XLI
Arethas of Patrae 27
Ariosto, Ludovico 106
Aris, Michael 139, 198
Aristotle 58-60
Armenia 125-6, 175, XXVIII
Armenian literature 125-6
Armenian Patriarchate, Jerusalem 131
Art 106, 115, 135-7, 146, 154, 167, 172, 174-9,
    201, 219
Ashbery, John 154
Ashmole, Elias 33, 39, 40, 54, 88-9, 96, 169-70,
    198
Ashmolean Library 25 *see also* Sackler Library
Ashmolean Museum 25, 33, 91, 174
Ashmolean Natural History Society 199
Askew, David 170
Asquith, Herbert, 1st Earl of Oxford and
    Asquith 34-5, 199
Asquith, Margot, Countess of Oxford and
    Asquith 37, 199
Association for the Education of Women in
    Oxford 66, 199

Astrology 33, 89, 198, 218
Astronomy 88-9, 128-30, 198, 200, 218
Astrophysics 95
Atlases 76-7, 104, 220
Attlee, Clement, 1st Earl 34
Attwood, Margaret 155
Aubrey, John 33, 39, 198-9
Audebert, Jean Baptiste 90
Auden, W.H. 45
Audubon, John James 171
Augustine, St 51, 53
Aung San Suu Kyi 139
Austen, Jane 44
Austin, J.L. 59-60
Australia 71, 73, 157-8, 219
Australian literature 157
Austria 71, 100
Avebury, Wilts. 39, 168
Aydelotte-Kieffer-Smith Collection 152
Azeri 132

Bach, Johann Sebastian 85
Backhouse, Sir Edmund 143, 148, 178, 185, 199
Bacon, Sir Francis 59
Bacon, Roger 58
Bahtiyar-name 130
Baker, John Randal 199
Balfe, Michael William 82
Balfour, Arthur J., 1st Earl 218, XIV
Balfour, Lady Frances 66
Balfour, Honor 35
Ballads 37, 44, 165-6, 171, 180, 206, 222
Ballard, George 199
Baltic States 117
Bandinel, Bulkeley, Bodley's Librarian 17, 53,
    106, 111
Bankes, Sir John 33, 153, 199
Banking 200-1
Bannister, H.M. 199
Barber family 217
Barbour, Ruth 29
Barker, Christopher 183
Barlow, Thomas, Bodley's Librarian and Bishop
    of Lincoln 31, 53, 195, 199, 211
Barocci Collection 27, 52, 199, 203
Barozzi, Francesco and Iacopo 27
Bartholdy, Felix Mendelssohn, *see* Mendelssohn,
    Felix
Bartholomew, Humphrey 33, 174, 194
Bashkir 132
Basire, James 169
Baskerville, Geoffrey 37, 199
Baskin, Leonard 171
Bastiat, Frédéric 63
Batrachomyomachia 27
Batten Organ Book 82
BBC, *see* British Broadcasting Corporation
Beckford, William 199
Beckington, Thomas, Bishop of Bath and Wells
    33
Beckley manor. Oxon. 39
Bede, Venerable 32, 52
Beekeeping 198

Beethoven, Ludwig van 83, 85, 220
Belarus 117
Benedictines 56
Beneš, Edvard 118
Benfactors' Register II
Bennett, William Sterndale 82
Benson, Arthur Christopher 199
Benson, Edward Frederic 199
Benson, Edward White, Archbishop of
    Canterbury 199
Bentley, Edmund Clerihew 199
Bentley, Richard 29
Berkshire 38-9, 168-70
Berlin, Sir Isaiah 60-1, 199
Berlioz, Hector 84
Bernard of Clairvaux 51
Bernard, Edward 89
Bernardelli, Harro 66
Bertie family 39, 199
Besler, Basilius 171
Beveridge, William H., Baron 66
Bewick, Thomas 171
Bhupal Singh XLIV
Bhutan 198
Bible 43, 51-5, 103, 111, 116, 124-6, 149, 151,
    175, 183, 194-5, 204, 208-10, 216
Bibliographical Society of London 188
Bibliography 115-16, 118, 187-91, 206, 216
Bibliography Room 189-90
Bickersteth family 199
Bidpai 128
Bihzad 130, 176
Bill, John 16, 102, 106, 110, XXIV
Bindings 104, 182-6, 201-2, 208, 213, XLVI,
    XLVII, XLVIII
Biochemistry 92, 94, 208, 214-16
Biology 94
Biophysics 216-17
Birkbeck, W.J. 116, 200
Birrell and Garnett 216
Bishop, Sir Henry 82
Black Literature 1827-1949 154
Blackman, Geoffrey Emmett 200
Blackstone, Sir William 69, 71-2, 74
Blake, William 171, 213
Blakeway, John 39, 200
Blish, James 200
Bliss, Philip 38, 54, 200
Blockbooks 171
Blow, John 82
Blundell, Michael 161
Bly, Robert 154
Board games 214
Boccaccio, Giovanni 106-8, 220, XXIII
Boden, Col. Joseph 136
Bodleian Japanese Library 46, 62, 64, 70, 75,
    145-7
Bodleian Law Library 62, 67, 70-4, 115-16, 135,
    154-5, 158-9
Bodleian Library of Commonwealth and African
    Studies 62, 67, 75, 135, 154-5, 157-62, 176
Bodleian Library Record 188
Bodleian Quarterly Record 188

Bodley, Sir Thomas 12, 15-16, 19, 20, 24, 42,
    51, 68, 88, 98, 102, 106, 110, 121, 127, 141,
    173-4, 195, I, II, III
Bodoni 107, 189, 214
Boethius 27, 57
Bohemia 118
Boileau, Nicolas 103
Bonham Carter, Lady Violet, Baroness Asquith
    of Yarnbury 200
Boniface VIII, Pope 69
Bonn, Moritz 6
Bonnet, Paul XLVII
Book of Curiosities 77, 130
Booker, John 198
Bookplates 166
Books of Hours 53-4
Booksellers 50, 166, 201, 204, 216
Bosworth, Joseph 46
Botanic Garden, Oxord 95
Botany 90, 93-4, 204-5, 211, 217
Boudan, Louis XLII
Bourne, Thomas W. 200
Bow Group 200
Bower, Lieut. H. 136
Bowyer, Sir George 106, 200
Boyce, William 80, 82, 86
Bracton, Henry de 68
Bradley, Francis Herbert 59
Bradley, James 200
Bradley, Katherine Harris 206
Bradshaw, Henry 188
Brahe, Tycho 88
Brand, Robert Henry, Baron 200
Braque, Georges 171
Brasenose College, Oxford 200
Brason, Paul 174
Brass rubbings 38, 169
Braun, Georg 76
Brazil 108
Brehon laws 68
Brennan, Christopher 157
Breton, John le 68
Brett, Thomas 55, 200
Breydenbach, Bernhard von 76, 170
Bridgeman, Charles 168
Bridges, John 39, 200
Bridges, Robert 44, 200
Bridgnorth Collection 165
Brister Collection 166
British Anti-Apartheid Movement 161-2, 177,
    198
British Association for the Advancement of
    Science 95, 200
British Broadcasting Corporation 85, 116, 210
British Commonwealth 70-2, 75, 154-62
British history 31-41, VI, VII
British Library 22-3, 85, 123, 139, 149, 188
British Museum 211
British Museum Library 22
British politics 31-41, 64-5
British Standards 94
Britton 68
Broadcasting 35-6, 85, 116, 210

Brooke, John Charles 170, 200
Brown, George Alfred, Baron George-Brown 207
Browning, Robert 45
Broxbourne Library 76, 183, 186, 189, 201, XLVII
Bruce, James 124, 127, 130, 201
Bruce, Michael 201
Bruni, Leonardo 58
Bryant, Andrew 77
Bryce, Mrs Annan 37
Bryce, James, Viscount 35, 153
Buache, Philippe 77-8
Buchan, Alastair 65
Buchanan, Thomas R. 104, 183, 201
Buckinghamshire 39, 168, 222
Buckler, John Chessell 168, 180
Buddhism 148, 177-8, 185, 205, XXXI, XXXII, XLVIII
Bulgaria 64, 76, 119
Bulgarian Academy of Sciences 119
Burdett, Sir Francis 201
Burdett, Sir Henry 64, 201
Burgert, Hans Joachim 201
Burges, Sir James Bland 200
Burley, Walter 58
Burma 135, 139, 178
Burn, J.H. 104
Burton, John 39, 201
Burton, Robert 20, 31, 42-3, 190, 201
Burton, William 31
Buryat 149
Business and FinancialPapers 1780- 1939 64
Butler, Arthur Gray 173
Butler, Christine Violet 201
Butler, Samuel (1835-1902) 45
Butterworth, George 82, 201
Buxton, Edward J.M. 44, 201
Buxton, Sir Thomas Fowell 160
Byron, Anne Isabella, Lady 211
Byron, George Gordon Noel, Lord 174, 180
Bywater, Ingram 28, 29, 201
Byzantine chant 81
Byzantine literature 27-8
Byzantine liturgy 52
Byzantine manuscripts 25, 30, 57, 167, 199

Cabinet papers 36
Cadoux, Cecil J. 201
Cadoux, William H. 201
'Caedmon Manuscript' 43
Cairo Genizah 123
Calcidius 57
Caldecott, Randolph 171
Callaghan, James, Baron Callaghan of Cardiff 34
Callcott, Sir Augustus 201
Callcott, Maria 201
Calligraphy 176, 201, 206, 217
Callimachus 26
Cambodia 139
Cambridge University Library 85, 145
Cameron, Julia Margaret 173
Campaign for Nuclear Disarmament 65

Canada 71, 73, 154-5
Canadian literature 155
Canonici, Matteo Luigi 17, 27, 52-3, 58, 89, 107, 119, 122, 167, 175, 201, XXIII, XXVI
Canterbury, Province of 54, 68
Card games 165, 209
Carroll, Lewis 48-9, 59
Carshuni 127
Carte, Thomas 32, 201
Carter, John W. 169, 183, 186, 189, 202
Cartography 75-9, 130
Cartoons 37, 65, 104, 172
Cartwright, Thomas III
Cary, Joyce 45, 202
Casaubon, Isaac 28, 202
Castello, Simon J. 49, 202
Castiglione, Giuseppe 142
Castle, Barbara, Baroness 37
Catalogues of the general Bodleian collections 13-15, 42, 51, 69, 188-91
Cathedrals 222
Catullus 26-7
Caucasus 117, 126, 132, 221
Caxton, William 43
Celtic studies 205
Census Bureau (US) 152
Census reports 67, 152, 157, 159
Central Asia 132, 149
Cervantes, Miguel de 110, XXIV
Chagatay 132
Chalmers, George 151
Chandler, Raymond 202
Chandra Shum Shere, Maharajah 137, 202
Channel Islands 71
Chanson de Roland 102, 105, XXII
Chapbooks 103, 222
Chapman, R.W. 202
Charles I, King 32-3, 173, 211
Charles II, King 32-3
Charles the Bold, Duke of Burgundy 103
Charlett, Arthur 199
Charters 38, 40
Chatham House 65
Chatwin, Bruce 209
Chaucer, Geoffrey 42
Chaundy, William 202
Chemical Library 89
Chemistry 89-90, 92, 94-5, 217, 219-20
Cherry, Francis 202
Cheshire 39
Chess 214
Chester, Rev. Greville John 124
Child, Reginald 95
Children's books 48-50, 163, 205, 214, X
Chile 113
China 64, 76, 84, 132, 141-5, 149, 178, 185, 199, 210, 214, XXXIII
Chō, Queen Dowager 148, 179, XXXV
Choniates, Niketas 52
Chopin, Frédéric 83-4
Christ Church, Oxford 38, 202
Christian Orient 125-7, 175
Church monuments 103, 168-70, 207

Church of England 32, 54-5, 221
Church's Ministry among the Jewish People 202
Chuvash 132
Cicero 26, 57
Cimarosa, Domenico 82
Cinema 154
Civil War 31-2, 41, 43, 53-4, 77, 211, 219
Clarendon, Edward Hyde, 1st Earl of 32, 40, 202
Clarendon, George Villiers, 4th Earl of 34, 112, 153, 202
Clarendon, Katherine Villiers, Lady 37, 202
Clarendon, Thomas Villiers, 1st Earl of 202
Clarendon Press 28, 124, 202
Clarendon State Papers 32, 40, 202
Clark, Andrew 39, 202
Clark, Sir Wilfred Le Gros 95, 203
Clark, Wyndham Damer 203
Clark, William Donaldson 35-6, 65, 153, 203
Clarke, Edward D. 27, 108, 203
Clarke, Samuel 203
Clarke, W.N. 39
Clarkson, Thomas 160
Classical studies 25-30, 57-9, 104, 201, 204, 209, 212, 214, 216-18, 222, IV
Clemenceau, Georges 36
Clement V, Pope 69
Clinical medicine 94
Clough, Arthur Hugh 44, 203
COBOP 67
Coconuts 95
Codex Bodley 110
Codex Brucianus 124
Codex Ebnerianus 52
Codex Laud 110, XXV
Codex Mendoza 110
Codex Selden 111
Coghill, Neville 203
Coke, Sir Edward 69
Coke, Sir John 32
Coldstream, Sir William 174
Colefax, Sybil, Lady 203
Collingwood, R.G. 59, 203
Colonial Service 160
Comenius Library, University of Lancaster 118
Comics 49, XI
Commission on Civil Rights (US) 152
Committee on Slavery 160
Communist Party of the Soviet Union 117
Computer manuals 94
Computing science 94-5, 219
Concert programmes 85
Congregational Church 54, 201, 212
Congress, US 152
Congreve, Richard 59, 203
Conington, John 29
Conservative Party 222
Conservative Party Archive 36, 64, 203
Constitutiones provinciales 68
Contemporary Scientific Archives Centre 95
Continental Congress 151
Cooper, Emma Edith 206
Co-ordinating Committee for Refugees 66
Copperplates 172

Coptic 124-5, 175, 209, 212
Copyright Acts 21-3
Cornwall 39
Corpus Christi College, Oxford 59, 198
Cotton, Charles 44, 201
Cotton, William Charles 198
Cotton family 217
Coulson, Charles A. 95, 203
Council for the Preservation of Rural England 206
Council of Confederate Catholics 32
Council of Europe 67
County maps 76-7
Court rolls 39
Coutts, Thomas 201
Cowen, Sir Frederick 82
Coxe, Henry O., Bodley's Librarian 17, 113, 193, 195, 212
Crampton, Sir John 35, 112, 153, 203
Crane, Stephen 154
Crane, Walter 171
Craster, Ann 174
Craster, Sir Edmund, Bodley's Librarian 43, 174
Craven, Earls of 203
Crawford, O.G.S. 203
Crevenna, Pietro Antonio 17, 29, 103
Crewe, Nathaniel, Lord, Bishop of Durham 17
Crimea 169, 173, 203
Criminology 70-1
Cripps, Sir Stafford 203
Crispin, Edmund 213
Croatia 119
Croft, William 82
Cromie, St George 100
Cromwell, Oliver 27, 203, 216
Cromwell, Richard 216
Crook, William Montgomery 203
Crowe, Sir Eyre 35, 203
Crynes, Nathaniel 33, 203
Culham Laboratory 94
Cumnor manor, Berks. 39
Curtis, Lionel 63, 162, 203
Curzon, George, Marquis Curzon of Kedleston 104, 172, 204
Custodian of Alien Property 93
Cytology 199
Czech Republic 64, 118
Czechoslovakia 76, 118

Dance of Death 99, 171, 205
Daniel, Rev. C.H.O. 189
Daniel, Samuel 44, 201
Danilewicz-Zieli ska, Maria 118
Dante Alighieri 106-8, 220
Danube Basin 119
Daoism 144
Daresbury Laboratory 94
Darlington, Cyril Dean 204
Dashwood family 204
Daventry Priory, Northants. 38
Davidson, John Colin Campbell, 1st Viscount 204
Davies, Sir John 32, 201

Davies, Philip and Rosamund 153
Davis, H.W.C. 37, 204
Dawkins, James 204
Dawson, Lady Anna Maria 203
Dawson, Geoffrey 35, 204
de Beer, E.S. 54
de Bunsen, Sir Maurice 204
De Chirico, Giorgio 171
de la Mare, Albinia 109, 204
de la Mare, Walter 204
De Michele, Charles 204
Dee, John 89, 198
Deedes, Sir Wyndham 66
Deir el-Bala'izah 124-5
Dejevsky, Nikolai 116
Dell, Edmund 35
Dell, Sidney 35, 64, 204
Dentistry 94
Denyer, Eliza D. 204
Design 172, 206
Devon 39
Dew, George James 166, 173, 204
Dickinson, Emily 154
Digby, Sir Kenelm 31, 88, 102, 108, 128, 204, XXII
Dillenius, Johann Jacob 171
Dingley, Thomas 169
Dioscorides 130, 176
Disraeli, Benjamin, Earl of Beaconsfield 34, 41, 209
D'Israeli, Isaac 209
Dissertations 17, 54, 73, 85, 92, 99, 104, 194, 209, 216
Dobell, Bertram 204
Dobson, Rosemary 157
Dodds, Eric R. 204
Dodson, Sir John 69, 213
Dodsworth, Roger 39, 205
Dominicans 52
Donato, Pietro, Bishop of Padua 107
Donne, John 44, 54
Dormer, Sir Michael 106
Dorpat, University of 117
D'Orville, Jacques Philippe 27-8, 108, 205
Douce, Francis 29, 34, 40, 43-4, 49, 53-4, 76-7, 99-100, 103, 105, 108, 124-5, 136, 139, 142, 166, 167, 183, 187, 205, XL, XLIV, XLVI
Douglas, Frederick 34
Doves Press 171
Doyle, General Sir Charles 34, 112
Drawings 39, 103-4, 161, 168-9, 176, 211, XLI, XLII
Drayton, Michael 44, 209
Drower, Lady Ethel May Stefana 127, 205
Druids 39
Drummond-Hay family 205
Dubs, Homer 144
Dugdale, Sir William 39, 170, 205
Dulac, Edmund 49
Duns Scotus 58
Dunstan, St 27
Dunston, F.W., and family 44-5, 166, 189, 205
Durand, William, the Elder 69
Dürer, Albrecht 171

Dutch East India Company 141, 147
Dutch East Indies 139
Dutton, Geoffrey 157
Dyer, Frederick William 205

Eagle 49, XI
Early American Imprints 152
Early American Newspapers 152
Earth sciences 94
Earth Sciences, Department of, Library 95
East Asia 141-50
East India Company 136, 147
East Indies 215
Eastern Art Library 135, 146, 167, 174-5
Eastern Europe 71-2, 76, 84, 115-20
Eccles, John 82
Eckert, Robert P. 205
Eckhart, Meister 100
Economics 63-4, 66, 104, 115, 213
Edgeworth, Maria 205
Edgeworth, Richard Lovell 205
Edizioni dell'Elefante 107
Edkins, Joseph 142
Education 49, 199, 216, 217
Education, Department of 217
Edward VIII, King 37, 213
Edwards family, Halifax 207
Egypt 25-6, 36, 124-5, 130-1, 222
Egypt Exploration Fund 124, IV
Ehrman, Albert 183, 189, 201, XLVII
Eighteenth Century Russian Books 116
Eighty Club 205
Elections 65, 153, 161, 165, 204
Elias, Norbert 66
Eliot, John 151
Eliot, T.S. 45
Elizabeth I, Queen 183
Ellacombe, Canon H.N. 174
Elliott, John B. 129, 205
Ellis, Robinson 205
Elton, Charles S.
Emblem books 171
Emden, A.B. 77
Emerton, Wolseley Partridge 64
Emmet, Evelyn, Baroness 205
Engineering 92, 94
Engineering Science, Department of, Library 95
English dialects 46, 222
English Historical Review 37
English language and linguistics 45-6, 222
English literature 42-7, 201, 205, 208, 211, 216-17, 219, 221, VIII, IX
Engravings 104, 168-9, 172, 174, 211
Ensor, Sir Robert C.K. 205
Environmental studies 75
Ephemera 50, 65, 100, 153, 163-6, 172, 204, 209
Epictetus 28, 57
Erasmus, Desiderius 99, 198
Erfurt 52, 207
Eritrea 108
Erskine, H.D., Dean of Ripon 203
Esperanto 207
Essex 39, 202

Essex, Robert Devereux, 2nd Earl of 110
Estonia 117
Ethiopia 108, 127, 175, 181, 185, 201
Ethnology 91, 220
Euclid 26-7
Euripides 25, 30
European Community, *see* European Union
European Documentation Centre 67
European Space Agency 67, 95
European Union 67, 70-1
Eusebius 26
Evans, Edwin 142
Evans, Major H.F. Owen 169-70
Evans-Wentz, Walter Y. 205, XLVIII
Ewelme, Oxon. 205
Exeter Cathedral 27, 51, 182, XII

Fabian Colonial Bureau 160
Fabian Society 65
Fairbank, Alfred J. 29, 109, 206
Fairfax, Thomas, 3rd Baron 31, 206
Farrar, Ernest 82, 206
Farrar, Sir George 161
Fascism 107
Federal Writers' Program 152
Fell, John, Bishop of Oxford 45, 206
Fenton, Roger 173
Ferguson, Frederic Sutherland 206
Ferguson, Howard 82, 206
Fernández de Lizardi, José Joaquín 112
Ficino, Marsilio 58
Field, Michael, *pseud.* 44, 206
Finch, Rev. Col. Robert 107, 206
Finzi, Gerald 82, 206
Firdawsi 129, 176
Firth, Sir Charles Harding 37, 166, 172, 206
Fischer, Hugo 66
Fisher, H.A.L. 37, 206
Fiske, Roger 82, 206
Fitzgerald, Edward 129
Fitzwilliam, John 54
Fitzwilliam, Sir William 32, 201
Fitzwilliam Museum, Cambridge 85
Flanders 53, 102, 167
Flora Graeca 171, 180
Folk music 84
Folklore 206, 211, 220
Food and Agriculture Organisation 35, 67, 95
Ford, Edward B. 206
Ford, James 39
Foreign Broadcast Information Service 116
Forestry 92, 94, 208
Forman, Simon 33, 89, 198
Forrest, David 157
Forrest-Heather partbooks 81
Forster, Harold B. 206
Fortescue, Sir John 52
Fowler, Thomas 59
France 50, 53, 64, 71, 84, 92, 102-5, 167, 183, 207, 218
Franciscans 37, 52
Frank, Richard 39, 209
Frankfurt Book Fair 98
Franklin, Jane, Lady 35

Fraser, James 130, 206
Freeman, E.A. 37
Freemasonry 217
French literature 103, 213, XXII
Frewin, Richard 90
Friends of the Bodleian 30, 76, 83, 104, 130, 144, 147, 174, 194
Frost, Robert 154
Frobisher, Sir Martin XLIII
Furney, Richard 39, XV

Gafurius 84
Gaignat, L.J. 103
Gaignières, François-Roger de 103, 169, XLII
Gaisford, Thomas 29
Gallery Five 165
Galuppi, Baldassare 82
Gandy, Henry 54
Garden cities 172
Gardiner, Mary 165
Garrett-Jones, C. 95
Garter, Order of the 33
Gatliff, Herbert 206
Gehenna Press 171
Gelehrte Estnische Gesellschaft 117
Gender studies 65-6
Genealogy 33, 198, 205, 217
Genetics 204, 206, 210
Genizah 123
Geographical Information Systems 78
Geography 75-9, 94, 115-16, 176
Geography and Map Reading Room 75, 78
Geology 90
Geomorphology 94
George IV, King 26
George-Brown, George Alfred, Baron 206
Georgia (Transcaucasia) 117, 126, 175, 222
Gerald Coke Collection 85
Gerard, John 170
German Democratic Republic 99
German literature 99-100, XXI
Germany 50, 53-4, 64, 71, 76, 82, 84, 92-3, 98-101, 167, 182, 212
Gibbes, Charles Sydney 117
Gibbon, Edward 29
Gibbs, James 90
Gibraltar 34
Gibson, Edmund, Bishop of London 55
Gibson, Strickland 164, 190, 206
Gill, Eric 172, XLIX
Gilliat, Mrs E.G.V. 45, 206
Gilpin, William 169, 206
Ginsberg, Allen 154
Gladstone, Henry N. 29, 207
Gladstone, William Ewart 29, 207
Glanville, John 106
Gloucestershire 39
Glover, Sir Robert 33
Glyndebourne Festival 85
Godwin, Mary Wollstonecraft 198
Godwin, William 198
Godwyn, Rev. Charles 22, 33, 207
Goethe, J.W. von 100-1
Gold Coast 214

Golden Cockerel Press 171, XLIX
Golden Jubilee (2002) 165
Goldsmith, Oliver 215
Golius, Jacob 212
Gonzaga, Eleonora 108
Goodhart, Arthur L. 69, 153, 207
Gore-Booth, Paul, Baron 35, 207
Gough Map, 77-8, XVII
Gough, Richard 39, 53, 76-7, 99, 103, 166, 168-9,
    172, 180, 207, XVII, XLII
Gould, John 171
Government documents, see Official publications
Grabe, Johan E. 28, 207
Grahame, Kenneth 45, 49-50, 207, X
Graphic design 172
Gratian 69, XVI
Greaves, John 128, 207
Greaves, Thomas 128, 207
Greece, Ancient, see Classical studies
Greek Patriarchate (Jerusalem) 131
Green, T.H. 59
Greenaway, Kate 171
Greene, Sir Hugh 35
Greene, Maurice 80, 82
Greenhill, Joseph 22
Greenwood, Anthony, Baron 207
Greenwood, Arthur 207
Greenwood, Christopher and John 77
Gregor, Douglas 207
Gregory the Great, St 51
Grey, Sir Charles E. 207
Griffith Institute, Oxford 125
The Guardian 37
Guilford, Earls of 34, 39, 215
Gutenberg Bible 17
Gutteridge, Richard 99
Gutteridge-Micklem Collection 99-101
Gwynne, Howell A. 207
Gypsies 46, 220

Habsburg Empire 119
Hailey, W. Malcolm, Baron 153
Hale, Alfred 82, 207
Hallam, Thomas 46
Halley, Edmund 129
Hamilton, Sir William 52, 207
Hammarskjöld, Dag 35-6
Hammond, J. Lawrence 207
Hammond, Thomas 86
Handel, George Frederick 80, 82
Handley-Derry, Leo 44
Hanson, Thomas W. 189, 207
Hanworth, Ernest Murray Pollock, 1st Viscount
    69, 207
Harcourt family 39
Harcourt, Lewis, 1st Viscount 34, 207
Harcourt, Sir William 34, 207
Harding Collection 81, 83-4, 86, 103, 208, XIX
Harding First-Line Song Index 86
Harding, Walter N.H. 81, 208, XIX
Hardy, Sir Alister 208
Hardy, G.H. 95
Hardy, Thomas 45

Harley, John L. 208
Harris, Geoffrey W. 208
Harris, Sir John 153
Harvard University Library 111
Harwell Laboratory 94
Harwood, Basil 82, 208
Hatton, Christopher, 1st Baron 52, 208
Hawke, Bob 158
Hawker, Robert Stephen 55, 208
Hawkes, Christopher 208
Hawley, Capt. R.B. 169
Hawthorne, Nathaniel 154
Haydn, Joseph 82, 84, 220
Hayek, Friedrich von 66
Hayes, William and Philip 82
Headington manor, Oxon. 39
Headlam, Cecil 213
Health trusts 94
Health, Department of 94
Hearne, Thomas 19, 31-2, 38, 40, 51, 54, 194,
    208, 216
Heather, William 214
Heber, Reginald, Bishop of Calcutta (1783-1826)
    208
Heber, Reginald (1728-1804) 208
Heber, Richard 208
Hebrew 121-3, 175, 181, 184, 209-10, 212-18,
    XXVII
Heidenheim Troper 81
Heinsius, Nicholas 28
Hemming, Francis 208
Henri III, King of France 104
Henry VIII, King 33
Heraldry 33, 169-70, 180, 198, 201, 215-17
Herculanaeum 26
Heritage Lottery Fund 83, 130
Herodotus 28
Herrick, Robert 208
Herrick, Sir William 33, 208
Hertford College, Oxford 208
Hertfordshire 202
Hevelius, Johannes 76, 170
Hickes, George 54
Higden, Ranulf 31
Hilliard, Nicholas 174
Himalayas 135, 138-9, 198
Hinazuru 179
Hindi 137-8
Hinton, Henry 38, 169, 180, 208
Hirst, F.W. 213
Hispanic studies 110-14
Hispano-Arabic science 112
Historical bibliography 187-91
Historiographical Institute, Tokyo 147
History, see British history, under countries, and
    Principal Special Collections passim
History of the book 104, 187-91
Hobson, John Atkinson 64
Hodgkin, Dame Dorothy 95, 208
Hodgson, Brian H. 208
Hodgson, Shadwell Holloway 59
Hodson, Henry Vincent 63
Hoernle, A.F.R. 136-7

Hogan, John A. 45, 208
Hogenberg, Francis 76
Hogg, Thomas Jefferson 47
Holdsworth, Richard 54
Holkham Hall 28, 69, 107-8, 208
Holman, William 39
Holmes, Robert 208
Holy Land 76-7
Holywell Music Room, Oxford 85
Homer 26, 28-9, 99, 207, 213
Hone, Nathaniel 174
Hong Kong 211, 214
Hooke Library 46
Hope Collection (Ashmolean Museum) 174
Hope, F.W. 33
Hope, John T. 208
Hopkins, Gerard Manley 44, 47, 208
Horace 26
Hornbooks 49
Horsley family 83, 209
Horsley, William 82, 209
Hospitals 201
Houdon, Michael 155
Howden, John Francis Caradoc, 1st Baron 34, 209
Howden, John Hobart Caradoc, 2nd Baron 112, 209
Howe, Sir Geoffrey 35
Howell, Lawrence 54
Huddleston, Trevor, Archbishop 162, 177
Hugh of Saint-Victor 51
Hughenden Collection 209
Hughes, Ted 171
Hume-Rothery, William 209
Humfrey, Duke of Gloucester 58, 60-1, 108-9
Hungarian literature 115
Hungary 64, 76, 118-19, 210
Hunt, James 38, 180, 208
Huntington, Robert 121, 124, 127-9, 209
Huxley, Elspeth 161
Hyde, Thomas 17, 21, 128, 209
Hyde family 202
Hyderabad 34, 37
Hydrographic Office 76, 78
Hypnerotomachie Poliphili 171
Hywel Dda, Laws of 68

Ibrahim Sultan 176
Iceland 200
Illuminated manuscripts 52-3, 100, 102-3, 107, 111, 119, 129, 135-7, 167-8, 175-9, 201, 205, XVI, XXIII, XXV-XXXII, XXXIV-V
Illustrated books 43, 49-50, 83, 155, 170-1, 178, 180, 202, 217, 220
Imperial Academy of Sciences (Russia) 115, 132
Inayat Khan 176
Incunabula 29, 53, 58, 69, 76, 99, 102, 122, 182, 184, 189
Index librorum prohibitorum 110
India 36, 62, 64, 131, 135-8, 176, 181, 204, 207, 211, 213, 218
India Services Pensioners' Association 219
Indian Empire Society 219

Indian Institute Library 18, 46, 62, 64, 67, 70, 75, 126, 135-6, 148
Indian Round Table Conference 218
Indian States Enquiry Committee 204
Indonesia 181
Industrial technology 94
Ingram, James 221
Inklings 45
Inner Asia 138
Innys, John and William 21
Inquisition 110
Institute for Chinese Studies, Library 62, 144
Institute for Microfilmed Hebrew Manuscripts, Jerusalem 122
Interior decoration 203
International Atomic Energy Agency 67, 95
International Council for Non-Intervention in Spain 208
International Exhibition, London (1884) 143
International Exhibition, Philadelphia (1876) 143
International Labour Organisation 67
International Monetary Fund 67
International relations 64-5, 101, 108, 112, 116, 153, 222
Inuit 73
Inventaires sommaires 104
Inverchapel, Archibald Clark Kerr, 1st Baron 209
Ipsden manor, Oxon. 39
Iran 125-6, 131 *see also* Persia
Iranian Oral History Collection 131
Ireland 32, 34, 36, 57, 67, 71, 201, 211, 215, 220, V
Isaac ben Solomon ibn Sahula XXVII
Islamic collections 127-32, 176, 181, 185, XXIX, XXX, XLV
Islamic law 70
Isle of Man 71
Ismail, Khedive of Egypt 131
Istanbul 181, XLV
Isum, John 82
Italian literature 106-7, 208, 213, 220, XXIII
Italy 53, 58, 64, 69, 71, 82, 84, 106-9, 167, 175, 182, 200, 212-14

Jablonski, Paul Ernst 124
Jackson, Gilbert 174
Jackson, W. Hatchett 92
Jacobs, Friedrich 29, 209
Jacobus de Voragine 53
Jaina manuscripts 137
Jamaica 204
James I, King of England, VI of Scotland 32, 178
James I, King of Scotland 43
James II, King 32
James, Richard 209
James, Thomas, Bodley's Librarian 16, 20, 51, 68, 88, 102, 110, 174, 195
Jameson Raid 159
Jami 128, 176
Japan 46, 62, 64, 145-7, 150, 178-9, 185, XXXIV
Japan Foundation 147
Japanese Friends of the Bodleian 147
Java 139, 178

Jehan de Grise 102
Jenkins, Roy, Lord Jenkins of Hillhead 65
Jenson, Nicholaus 29
Jerome, Jerome K. 209
Jerome, St 26
Jerusalem 131
Jessel, Frederic 209
Jesuits 147
Jesus College, Oxford 68, 209
Jews 121-3, 202
Jiménez de Cisneros, Francisco, Cardinal 111
Joachim, H.H. 59, 209
Johannes Scotus Erigena 57
John Johnson Collection 50, 65, 85, 103, 163-6,
    172-3, 183, 189, 209, XIV, XXXIX
John, Augustus 174
Johnson, Jane 50
Johnson, John de Monins 163, 190, 209
Johnson, Samuel 215
Johnston, Henry 168-9
Johnston, Nathaniel 39, 209
Jones, Arthur Creech 160
Jones, Henry 209
Jones, John Pike 39
Jones, Thomas 63
Jonson, Ben 42
Joseph, Sir Keith 65
Jowett, Benjamin 29
Jowett Society 60
Juel-Jensen, Bent 44, 95, 209
Junius, Francis 45, 100-1, 209
Justinian 69
Juvenal 26

Kafka, Franz 100-1, 210, XXI
Kahn-Freund, Sir Otto 73
Kalighat paintings 174
Kalilah wa-Dimnah 176, 185
Kalmuck 149
Kalthoeber, Samuel 184
Karamanlidika 131
Kaser, Michael 64
Kazakh 132
Kazan 132
Keen, Barbara 37
Kelmscott Press 171, 210
Kendrew, Sir John C. 210
Kennicott Bible 175, 181, 185
Kennicott, Benjamin 210
Kenya, XXXVII
Kerr, Archibald Clark, 1st Baron Inverchapel 209
Ketel, Cornelis XLIII
Kettlewell, Henry B.D. 210
Keynes, John Maynard 63, 66
Kidd, John 90
Kierkegaard, Søren 54, 210
Kimberley 161
Kimberley, John Wodehouse, 1st Earl of 34, 210
Kingsborough, Edward King, Viscount 112
Kirchenkampf 100
Kirgiz 132
Kishore, Naval 138
Kohn-Bramstedt, Ernst 66

Koran 127, 130, 176, 217
Korea 147-8, 179, XXXV
Kripke, Saul 60
Kroetsch, Robert 155
Kroner, Fritz

La Fontaine, Jean de 103
Labor Department (US) 152
Labour Party 36
Ladakh, 138
Ladysmith 161
Lamb, Lady Caroline 180
Lambe, James 210
Lambert, Jack W. 210
Lancashire 39
Lancaster, University of 118
Langbaine, Gerard 28, 210, 220
Lantern slides 161
Laos 139
Larkin, Philip 45, 47
Latey, Maurice 35, 210
Latin America 62, 64, 110-14
Latin American Centre 113
Latin language and literature, *see* Classical
    studies
Latvia 117
Laud, William, Archbishop of Canterbury 21,
    26-7, 31, 52, 55, 88, 100-1, 122, 125, 127-8,
    135, 139, 141, 167, 173, 210, XXV
Law 62, 68-73, 99, 115-16, 118-19, 135, 154-5,
    158-9, 208, 212, 217-18, 221, XV, XVI
Law Library, *see* Bodleian Law Library
Law, Major J.S. 137
Lawes, William 82
Lawn, Brian 210
Lawrence, A.W. 210
Lawrence, T. E. 45, 47, 210
Lawson, Henry 157
The Lay of Havelock the Dane 43
Le Sueur, Hubert 173
League of Nations 65, 67
Lebanon 125
Ledger, Walter E. 217
Lee, Robert, Clarenceux King-of-Arms 170
Lee, Robert Warden 69, 210
Legal deposit 16, 20-4, 67, 71, 80, 83, 92, 94,
    151, 170, III
Legge, James 142, 210
Leicester, Earls of 28, 76, 107-8, 208
Leland, John 31
Lennox-Boyd, Alan Tindal, 1st Viscount Boyd of
    Merton 200
Lenthall, William 32
Leofric Missal 53, 81, XII
Lepidoptera 210
Les enfaunces de Jesu Christ 102
Lettische Literaerische Gesellschaft 117
Leverhulme Trust 145
Lewis, C.S. 45, 210
Lewis family 210
Lexicography 46, 214, 222
Lhuyd, Edward 198
Library Records 210

Libri Hungarici 118, 210
Libri Polonici 117-18, 211
Lichfield, Staffs. 39
Liddell, Henry, Dean of Christ Church 29
Lilly, William 89, 198
Lin Qing 178
Linacre College, Oxford 60
Lincoln College, Oxford 211-12, 215
Lindsay, Norman 157
Lingualumina 205
Linguistics 45-6, 93, 205, 207, 212, 220
Linnell, John 171
Lister, Martin 76, 89, 172, 198, 211
Literae Humaniores, School of 59
Lithuania 117
Little, A.G. 37
Little magazines 154, 157
Liturgical works 53-4, 80-1, 86, 125, 199, 216, XII
Livingstone, David 159-61
Livres d'artiste 170-1, 180
Livy 26
Lloyd, William Forster 63
Lobel, Edgar 29
Local history, British 38-9
Locke, John 48, 58, 60-1, 76, 153, 211
Lodovico III Gonzaga, Marquess of Mantua 108
Logic 59
Lombard, Peter 53
London Eighty Club 205
Lovelace, Ada, Countess of 211
Lovelace, Ralph Milbanke, 2nd Earl of 211
Lowe, E.A. 29
Ludlow, Edmund 33
Lugard, John Daltry, Baron 161-2, 211
Łukaszewicz, Józef 117, 211
Luther, Martin 54, 98, 195
Lydgate, John 42
Lyell, James P.R. 100, 112, 211

Macartney, C.A. 119, 211
Macartney, George, 1st Earl 34, 203, 211
McCullagh, James 155
Macdonnell, Anthony Patrick, 1st Baron 211
McGhee, Rev. Robert J. 211
Mack Smith, Denis 107
Mackenzie, Frederick 168
Mackenzie, W.J.M. 65
Maclean, Sir Donald 211
Macmillan, Harold , 1st Earl of Stockton 34, 211, VII
MacNeice, John, Bishop of Down, Connor and Dromore 211
MacNeice, Louis 45, 211
Macray, W.D. 12, 43
Madan, Falconer, Bodley's Librarian 188
Madden, Sir Frederic 211
Madras 34, 213
Magna Carta, XV
Magnus, Edward 174
Magnusen, Finn 200
Maimonides 121
Maine, Charles d'Anjou, Count of 103

Malan, Rev. Solomon Caesar 126, 137, 147-8
Malaria 95
Malaya 139, 178
Malchair, J.B. 168
Malmesbury, William of 58
Malone, Edmund 21, 34, 42, 44, 166, 211, VIII
Malta 218
Manchu 148
Mandaeans 127, 205
Mandela, Nelson 177
Mann, Arthur 35
Mannheim, Karl 66
Manning, Henry, Cardinal 55
Manning, Percy 38, 173, 211
Mansfield, Katherine 157
Mansfield College, Oxford 54, 212
Maoris 157
Maps 75-9, 128, 130, 176, 220, XVII, XXXIII
Marathi 137
Marbeck, John 81
Mardersteig, Giovanni 107, 189, 214
Margaret of York 103
Maria Theresa of Austria, Queen of France 104
Marillier, Christabel 82
Marlborough Vicar's Library 54, 212
Marlowe, Christopher 42
Marsh, Narcissus, Archbishop of Armagh 125, 129, 139, 141, 212, XXIX
Marshall, Thomas 45, 53, 124-5, 212
Martianus Capella 57
Marvin, Edith 37
Marvin, Francis S. 212
Mary I, Queen 51
Mary II, Queen 217
Masaryk, Tomáš 118
Mascarenhas Collection 110
Masculinity: Men Defining Men and Gentlemen 66
Masefield, John 45, 212
Mason, Robert 212
Materials 94
Mathematics 88-9, 94-5, 130, 137, 202-3, 213, 218
Mather, Cotton 54, 212
Mather, Increase 54, 212
Matisse, Henri 172
Mavrogordato, John 212
Maxse family 213
Mayekiso, Moses XXXVIII
Mechitarists, 126
Medici Press 131
Medicine 33, 88-97, 130, 198, 201, 211, 218, XX
Meerman, Gerard 69, 99, 212
Meerman, Johan 27, 99, 212
Mellon, Paul 58
Mellor, Charles 161
Melville, Herman 154
Mendelssohn, Felix 81, 83-4, 86-7, 100, 169, 174, 212, XVIII
Mendelssohn, Kurt A.G. 212
Mendelssohn, M. Deneke, Collection 81, 83, 100, 169, 212, XVIII
Mendham, Rev. Joseph 212
Metallurgy 94, 209
Meteorology 75, 88

Mexico 110-12, 114, 168, XXV
Michael, Heimann Joseph 122, 175, 212
Micklem, Nathaniel 99
Microbiology 222
Middle East 76, 121-34, 205, 212
Middle English literature 43
Midland and Oxford Circuit 212
Miélot, Jean 103
Milan 69
Milford, Robin H. 82, 212
Military Censor 99
Milkayak language 111
Mill House Press 213
Mill, John Stuart 63
Mill, William H. 136, 213
Milles, Jeremiah 39
Milne, A.A. 49
Milne, Christopher Robin 48
Milne, Edward A. 213
Milne, William 143
Milner, Alfred, Viscount 162, 213
Milner, Violet, Viscountess 35, 162, 213
Milton, John 30, 59
Mineralogy 90
Mining 214
Ministry of Food 222
Ministry of Information 213
Ministry of Reconstruction 222
Minn, Henry 38, 169, 173, 213
Mirouer historial abregie de la France 103
Missionaries 142-3, 146, 149, 153, 155, 158,
   161, 219
Mitchinson, John 169
Moldavia 119, XXVI
Moldova 117
Molecular biology 210
Monasteries 199, 205
Monckton, Walter, 1st Viscount 36, 69, 213
Mongolia 148-9
Monier-Williams, Sir Monier 136-7
Le Moniteur 104
Monitoring reports 116
Monk-Bretton, John G. Dodson, 1st Baron 213
Monk-Bretton, John W. Dodson, 2nd Baron 213
Monmouth, Duke of VI
Monro, David Binning 29, 99, 213
Monson, Sir Edward J. 213
Montagu, Capt. Montagu 103, 106, 172, 174, 213
Montague, Edward Wortley 130
Montesquieu, Charles de Secondat, Baron de
   103, 218
Montgomery, Robert Bruce 82, 213
Moorcock, Michael 213
Morley, John, 1st Viscount 213
Morning Freiheit 123
The Morning Post 204
Morocco 131
Morris, William 210
Morrison, Robert 143
Mortara, Count Alessandro 106, 213
Moseley, H.N. 150, 179
Moser, Sir Claus 66
Moss, Col. William 183, 186, 213

Movement writers 45
Mozarabic Breviary 111
Mozart, Wolfgang Amadeus 82, 84-5, 87, 220
Mughal art 135-6, 176-7
Müller, Friedrich Max 136, 147, 212
Mumford, Lewis 66
Munby, A.N.L. 215
Murbach Hymnal 100
Murray, Dr Elizabeth 46
Murray, Gilbert 28, 64-5, 214
Murray, Harold J.R. 214
Murray, Sir James 46, 214
Murrow, Ed 36
Musaeus 27
Music 80-7, 115, 118, 135, 199-201, 206-8, 212-
   15, 218-22, XVIII, XIX
Music Faculty Library 80-1
Music hall 83
Music School, Oxford 80, 82, 84, 214
Music societies 85
Müteferrika, brahim 131
Myres, Sir John Linton 214

Nalanda, University of 137, XXXI
Nalson, John 32, 214, 219
Namibia Support Committee 162
Napier, General Sir Charles J. 214
Napier, Col. George 214
Napier, Richard 33, 198
Napier, General Sir William F.P. 37, 112, 214
Napoleon I, Emperor 41, 104, 172, 177, 204
Nara-ehon 147, 178, XXXIV
Natal 214
Nathan, Edward J. 214
Nathan, Sir Matthew 214
National Art Collections Fund 130
National Diet Library (Tokyo) 147
National Institute of Informatics (Japan) 147
National Library of Scotland 85
National Palace Museum (Taipei) 144
National Review 36
National Trust 206
Native rights 73
Nattes, J.C. 168
Natural history 90, 95, 171, 199
Navigation 76-7, 141
Nazi Party 99
Near East 121-34, 220
Nennius 31
Nepal 208
Netherlands 50, 54, 92, 182, 210, 212
Neubauer, Adolf 122
Neurolinguistics 46
Nevai 130, 176, XXX
Nevinson, Henry Woodd 214, 218
New College, Oxford 52, 58, 206, 214
New Deal 152
New Opportunities Fund 137
New Zealand 71, 157-8
Newspapers 33, 38-9, 64, 116-19, 145, 152, 155,
   157, 159, 198, 208, 214, 219, 222
Newton, Sir Isaac XX
Nian Xiyao 142

Nicholas, Herbert 153
Nichols, John 33, 214
Nicholson, E.W.B., Bodley's Librarian 23, 91-2,
    125, 136, 193, 195
Nielsen, Kay 49
Nigeria 159, 161, 211
Nile, River 201
Nissan Institute of Japanese Studies 145, 147
Noble, Mark 214
Non-jurors 54-5, 200, 202, 216, 218
North America 151-6, 172
North, Barons 34, 39, 153, 214
North, Francis, 1st Earl of Guilford 34, 214
North, Frederick, 2nd Earl of Guilford 34, 153
Northamptonshire 39, 200
Notitia Dignitatum 107
Nove, Alexander 64
Nowell, Lawrence 45
Nuremberg Chronicle 171
Nuremberg tribunals 99
Nursery rhymes 48-9
Nursing 201
Nyasaland 221

The Observer 203
Ocharte, Pedro 111
Ockham, William of 58
OECD 67
Office of National Statistics 94
Official publications 62, 67, 94-5, 116, 118, 138,
    145, 152, 154-5, 157, 159
Officina Bodoni 107, 189, 214
Ogilby, John 161
Ogston, Alexander G. 214
Oldham, J.B. 183
Omar Khayyam 129, 221
Opera 81-2, 84-6, 103
Ophthalmology 92
Opie Collection of Children's Literature 48-50,
    215
Opie, Iona and Peter 48-9, 214
Oppenheimer, Rabbi David ben Abraham 17,
    121, 175, 184, 215, XXVII
Ordnance Survey 75-6, 78
Organic chemistry 92
Organisation for Economic Co-operation and
    Development 67
Oriel College, Oxford 215
Oriental Collections, Department of 75, 167
Oriental Institute Library 62
Oriental studies 62, 115, 121-50, 174-9, 184-5,
    197
Origen Society 60
Ormesby Psalter 53
Ormonde, James Butler, 1st Duke of 32, 201
'Ormulum' 43
Ornithology 90, 93, 95, 171
Oseney Abbey, Oxford 38
Osler, Sir William 130
Osler Society 95
Ossetian 132
Ostrog Bible 116
Otto, Cardinal 68

Ottobuono, Cardinal 68
Ottoman Empire 130-1, 176, 185, XXX, XLV *see
    also* Turkey
Ouseley, Sir Frederick 81, 86
Ouseley, Sir Gore 129, 136, 185, 205, 215
Ouseley, Sir William 129, 215
Ovid 27
Oxford, city of 38, 40, 65, 77, 88, 166, 168, 173,
    188, 200-1, 211, 213, 221, 222
Oxford, University of 38, 40, 168-9, 173, 200,
    211, 221, 222
Oxford Barber Surgeons 215
Oxford Bibliographical Society 188
Oxford Colonial Archives Project 160, XXXVII
Oxford Colonial Records Project 160
Oxford Constituency Labour Party 65
Oxford Development Records Project 160
Oxford Digital Library 165
Oxford Enzyme Group 215
Oxford Lectures for Ladies 66
Oxford Mathematical and Physical Society 95
Oxford Medical Club 95
Oxford Philosophy 59
Oxford Preservation Trust 217
Oxford University Junior Scientific Club 95
Oxford University Philosophical Society 60
Oxford University Press 188, 215
Oxford University Scientific Society 95
Oxford University societies 165
Oxfordshire 38-40, 65-6, 168-70, 173, 200, 204,
    212, 222
Oxfordshire Architectural and Historical Society
    215
Oxfordshire Natural History Society and Field
    Club 199

Pachelbel, Johann 82
Pacifism 36
Paint technology 94
Painting aids 171
Paintings 158, 161, 172-4, 176-7, XXXVII,
    XLIV, XLV
Pakenham, Michael 205
Pakistan 135
Palaeography 204
Pali 137-8, XXXII
Palmer, John 215
Pamphlets 17, 31-4, 38, 53, 73, 91, 93, 99-100,
    112, 151, 194, 198, 212, 219, 222
Panizzi, Sir Anthony 22
Paper technology 94
Papyri 25-6, 52, 124, 130, 133
'Parallel press' 117
Paris Peace Conference 35
Park, Mungo 159
Parker, Clifton 82, 215
Parliamentary papers 67, 71, 99, 116, 118-19, 155,
    157, 159
Parma 108
Parry, Sir Hubert 82, 215
Parthenia 80
Past and Present 37
Pathology 92, 94

Patristic texts 51-3, 55, 199
Pattison, Mark 28, 55, 215
Peace, Charles XIV
Peake, Mervyn 215
Peierls, Sir Rudolf 95, 215
Pembroke, William Herbert, 3rd Earl of 27
Peninsular War 37
'Penny dreadfuls' 44, 215
Pepys, Samuel 32, 216
Percy, Thomas, Bishop of Dromore 215
Perham, Dame Margery 162, 215
Perrot, Sir John 215
Perrott, Thomas 215
Persia 128-31, 176, 185, 203, 205-7, 209, 215,
    217, 220-1 *see also* Iran
Peter Lombard 53
Peterborough Chronicle 31
Peters, Sir Rudolph 215
Petrarch 106-7, 220
Petrie, Sir Flinders 124-5
Petrucci, Ottaviano 84
Petrus de Unzola 69
Pettingell, Frank 44, 215
Pharmacology 92, 94
Philip the Good, Duke of Burgundy 103
Philip, Ian 12, 43
Philips, Sir David C. 216
Phillipps, Sir Thomas 38, 40, 169, 215-6
Philosophy 57-60, 104, 115, 203, 209-12, 216,
    221, XIII
Philosophy Library 46, 59-60
Philosophy of language 46
Philosophy of religion 55
Philosophy of science 60
Philosophy, Politics and Economics, School of
    58-9
Philostratus 28
Photius 27
Photographs 29, 38, 126, 155, 160-1, 168-9, 172-
    3, 176, 181, 183, 210
Photography 154, 173
Physical geography 75, 94
Physics 88, 94, 212, 216
Physics, Department of, Library 95
Physiology 90, 94-5
Physiology, Department of, Library 95
Picasso, Pablo 171-2, XLVII
Pictorial resources 83, 161, 167-81
Pigott, Harriet 216
Pindar, Paul 128
Pinelli, Maffeo 17, 29, 184
Piri Reis 176
Pisan, Christine de 43
Pizarro, Francisco 112
Plant sciences 90, 94
Plant Sciences Library 95
Plato 26-7, 57-8
Plaut, Theodor 66
A play-book for children... 48
Playing cards 165, 209
Pliny 29
Plot, Robert 89
Pococke, Edward 121, 125-6, 128, 139, 216

Poland 17, 64, 76, 117-18, 211
Polish Academy 118
Political and Satirical Prints 165
Politics 34-7, 64-5 *see also under countries, and*
    Principal Special Collections *passim*
Pollard, Graham 182, 216
Pollock, Sir Jonathan 69, 207
Ponsonby, Arthur A.W.H., 1st Baron 216
Poole, Henry Ward 112
Pope, Alexander 45
Porson, Richard 29
Porter, Rodney R. 216
Portland 34, 220
Portland, Ivy Cavendish Bentinck, Duchess of 32
Portolans 77
Portraits 37, 167, 172-4, 181, I, XLIII
Portugal 110-14, 141
Portuguese literature 111
Posters XXXVIII-XXXIX
Potter, Beatrix 49
Pound, Ezra 154
Powell, Baden 216
Prakrit 137-8
Pre-Raphaelite Brotherhood 219
Presidency, US 152, 204
Press cuttings 85, 119
Press Licensing Act 21
Press summaries 116
Price, H.H. 60
Prichard, H.A. 59
Primatology 95
Primrose League 216
Pringle, John W.S. 216
Printed ephemera 50, 65, 100, 153, 163-6, 172,
    180, 204
Printer's Library, Oxford University Press 188,
    215
Printing 94, 154, 165, 172, 188-90, 201, 206,
    215, 217, 219
Prints 39, 165, 171-2, 180
Prior, Arthur N. 60, 216
Priscian 26
Private presses 165, 170-2, 210, 213, 217, 219
Proctor, Robert 188
Programmes 85
Psycholinguistics 46
Psychology 62, 94
Ptolemy (Claudius Ptolemaeus) 76
Ptolemy II Philadelphus 25
Public health 91
Publishing 115, 154, 201-2, 218
Purcell, Henry 80, 82
Puttenham, George 42
Pym, Barbara 45, 216

Quakers 54
The Queen's College, Oxford 210, 216
Queensland 214
Quine, W.V. 60
Qur'an 127, 130, 176, 217

Rackham, Arthur 49, 171, 202
Radcliffe, Dr John 88, 90, XX

Radcliffe Camera 90-1
Radcliffe Infirmary 216
Radcliffe Library 33, 72, 90-1, 93, 216, XX
Radcliffe Observatory 216
Radcliffe Science Library 18, 46, 60, 62, 67, 75, 91-6
Radcliffe Trust 216
Radio Free Europe 116
Radio Liberty 116
Radnor, William Bouverie, Earl of 103
Ramblers' Association 206
Rawlinson, Richard 32, 42-3, 53-4, 69, 89, 103, 108, 166, 172, 174, 187, 216, V, VI
Red Decree 142
Redman, Richard, Bishop of Ely 33
Reformation 53-4, 211, 219
Reggio, Isaac Samuel 217
Reichenau Sacramentary 100
Reilly, Sir Patrick 35
Rennell of Rodd, James, 1st Baron 217
Repton, Humphry 168, XLI
Rhodes House Library 18, 151, 153, 159 *see also* Bodleian Library of Commonwealth and African Studies *and* Vere Harmsworth Library
Rhodes, Cecil 159, 217
Rhodesia 200, 221
Ricardo, David 63
Richards, Sir Rex 217
Richardson, Henry Handel 157
Richardson, Hugh 139, 217
Richardson, Richard 93, 216
Ricketts, Charles 172
Rickman, Thomas 168
Rigaud, Stephen 89, 217
Risley family 217
Risorgimento 107
Robinson, Lionel and Philip 216
Rock music 83
Roe, Sir Thomas 27, 217
Rogers, J.E. Thorold 63, 173, 217
Roman de la Rose 103
Roman law 71
Romania 64, 76, 119
Rome, Ancient, *see* Classical studies
Rosenthal, Harold 85
Ross, Robert 45, 217
Rothermere American Institute 151
Rotton, Capt. Guy 177
Round Table 162, 203
Rous, John, Bodley's Librarian 195
Routh, Martin 29
Rowe Music Library 85
Roxburghe Club 217
Royal College of Music 85
Royal Institute of International Affairs 65
Royal Printing Archive 165
Royal Society Catalogue of Scientific Papers 92
Rule of St Benedict 52
Rumbold, Sir Horace (1829-1913) 35, 217
Rumbold, Sir Horace George (1869-1941) 217
Rushworth, John 41
Russell, Charles 34

Russell family 218
Russia 50, 64, 71, 115-20, 132, 203 *see also* USSR
Russian and Eurasian Studies Centre, St Antony's College 115
Russian Revolution 117, 132
Rustaveli, Shota 175
Ryder, John 107, 166, 189, 217
Rylands, William H. 170, 217
Ryle, Gilbert 60

Sackler Library 25, 135, 167, 175
Sacre rappresentazioni 53
Sa'di 176
Sadler, Sir Michael E. 217
Sadler partbooks 81
Saga-bon 146
Saibante, Giovanni 28
St Amand, James 28, 217
St Antony's College, Oxford 113, 115
St Catherine's Monastery, Mount Sinai 131
St Edmund Hall, Oxford 217
St Frideswide's Priory, Oxford 38
St Helena 104, 159, 177
St John of Jerusalem, Order of 218
St Michael's College, Tenbury Wells 81, 220
Saladin 129
Sale, George 130, 217
Sallust 26
Samizdat 117-18
Sancroft, William, Archbishop of Canterbury 32, 54, 218-219
Sandars, John S. 218
Sankey, John, Viscount 218
Sanskrit 135-7, 148, 202, 206, 208, 212, 219, 221-2, XXXI
Santiago de Compostela 112
Sappho 25
Saris, John 146
Satow, Sir Ernest 147
Savile, Sir Henry 76, 147, 218
Savile Library 89
Saxton, Christopher 77
Say, Jean-Baptiste 63
Sayce, Archibald Henry 124
Sayings of Jesus 26, IV
Scandinavia 54, 92, 200
Schiller, Friedrich von 101
Schlagintweit, Emil 138
Schnebbelie, Jacob 169
Schoeffer, Peter XVI
School of Geography and the Environment 75
School of Oriental and African Studies 145
Schubert, Franz 83-4, 220
Schuster, Sir George 218
Scicluna, Sir Hannibal 218
Science 88-97, 130, 216, 218-19
Science fiction 213
Science Museum Library 93
Scotland 71, 183, 206
Scott, George C. 106
Scott, Michael 162
Scott, Sir Walter 45
Seckersen, Austin 95

Seillière Collection 183
Selborne, Maud, Countess of 37
Selborne, Roundell C. Palmer, 3rd Earl of 65, 218
Selborne, William Palmer, 2nd Earl of 162, 218
Selby, Sir Walford 218
Selden, John 27, 31, 45, 69, 76, 88, 110-11, 122, 125, 128, 141, 146, 168, 187, 218
Sendak, Maurice 171
Seneca 26
Senior, Nassau William 63
Serbia 119
Sermons 52, 54-5, 195, 198, 208, 212, 214, 216, 221
Sèvres Agreement 36
Settle, Elkanah 186
Sex and Sexuality, 1640-1940 66
Shackleton, Robert, Bodley's Librarian 103, 174, 218
Shakespeare, William 20, 42, 44, 47, VIII
Sharafnamah 176
Sharp, Evelyn 37, 218
Shaw, Sir Run Run 145
Shel-dkar Monastery 138
Shelfmarks 192-7
Shelley, Jane, Lady 44
Shelley, Mary Wollstonecraft 198, 218
Shelley, Percy Bysshe 44, 47, 174, 198, 201, 218, IX
Shelley-Rolls, Sir John 44
Sheridan, Richard Brinsley 218
Sherwood, Percy 82, 218
Shrivenham American University 218
Shropshire 39, 200
Shuttleworth, Bertram 218
Sidgwick and Jackson 218
Sidney, Sir Philip 44, 47, 201
Sidonius Apollinaris 26
ik pattr 137
Simon, John A., 1st Viscount 218
Sinica Collection 185
Sitwell, Dame Edith 45, 206
Sitwell, Sir Osbert 45, 206
Sitwell, Sir Sacheverell 45
Sixteenth and Seventeenth Century Russian Books 116
Skrine, Rev. Vivian Eccles 124
Slavery 34, 152, 160, 198, 222
Slavonic countries 62, 115-20, 200, XXVI
Slovakia 64, 118
Smith, Adam 63
Smith, George (1871-1963) 219
Smith, George Ivan 35
Smith, Thomas (non-juror) 218
Social Democratic Party 65
Social policy 65-6
Social sciences 62-7
Social work 65-6, 201
Society for the Propagation of the Gospel, *see* United Society for the Propagation of the Gospel
Society for the Protection of Science and Learning 66-7, 219

Sociology 65-6, 104, 115
Soddy, Frederick 95, 219
Solinus 26
Somers, Phoebe 161, XXXVII
Somerville, Mary 95, 219
Somerville College, Oxford 95
Songs 44, 81, 83-4, 86, 103
Sonmans, Willem 174
Sound recordings 80
South Africa 36, 71, 159, 161-2, 213, XXXVIII
South Asia 135-8, 177, 181, XXXI
South East Asia 139, 178, 181, XXXII
South English Legendary 43
Southey, Robert 111
Spaher, Michael 171
Spain 34, 71, 110-14, 182, 203, 208, 212
Spalding, Philip A. 219
Spanish literature 110-11, XXIV
Spencer, Herbert 65
Spinckes, Nathaniel 54
Spokes, Peter S. 38, 169
Sport 211
Sri Lanka 135
Stainer, John 82
Stanbrook Abbey Press 165, 219
Stanley, Sylvia 35
Star Chamber 21
State Department (US) 152
Stationers' Company 16, 20-3, 42-3, 49, 187, III
Stationery Office 67
Statistics 94, 115-16, 118-19
Stein, Sir Marc Aurel 137, 219
Steinschneider, Moritz 122
Stephens, Frederic G. 219
Stevenson, Robert Louis 45
Stock Exchange 64, 201
Stokes, Richard R. 219
Stonehenge 39, 168
Strachey, Christopher 95, 219
Strong family 203
Stuart, Sir Louis 219
Stuart, Lady Louisa 203
Stubbs, George 171
Stukeley, William 39, 168, 180, 219
Sturt, Charles 158, 219
Suez crisis 36
Suffolk 39
Suffragettes 37, 66, XIV
Sullivan, Sir Arthur 82
Supreme Court (US) 154
Surrey 39
Sutherland, Alexander H. 174, 219
Sūtras 148, 177, 185
Sutton, Leslie E. 219
Swaminarayan, Lord 137
Swann, Emma 169
Switzerland 92, 98
Syriac 127, 175, 204, 209

Tajik 132
Talbot, William Henry Fox 173
Talbot de Malahide family 219
Tamil 137

Tanis 124

Tanner, Thomas, Bishop of St Asaph 32, 53-4, 219, XXXVI

Tappan, Lewis 153

Tashkent 132

Tasso, Torquato 106

Tatar 132

Tauchnitz editions 45, 219

Taunt, Henry W. 213

Taverner, John 81

Tavistock, Wriothesley Russell, Marquis of, afterwards Duke of Bedford 82

Taylor Institution Library 99, 102, 106, 111, 113, 115-16, 155

Taylor, Sir Henry 220

Technology 88-97

Telegu 135

Temple, Charles 161

Tenbury Collection 81, 86-7, 220

Tennyson, Alfred, Lord 45

Tercentenary Collection 220

Terence 26

Tern Press 165

Textile manufacture 94

Thailand 139, 178, XXXII

Theology 51-6, 99, 104, 110-11, 210-12, 216- 21

Theon: letter 25

Theoretical chemistry 95, 203

Theoretical physics 215

Theses, see Dissertations

Third Reich 99

Thomas à Kempis 53

Thomas Aquinas 53

Thomas, Edward 205

Thompson, E.P. 36

Thompson, Edward J. 220

Thompson, Thomas W. 46

Thomson, James 44, 220

Thorn-Drury, George 44, 220

Thou, Jacques Auguste de 183

Thurloe, John 32, 216

Thurston, William 141, 220

Tibet 138-9, 148, 177-8, 185, 198, 205, 217, XLVIII

Ticknor, George 111

The Times 204

Tinbergen, Nikolaas 220

Todhunter, Hugh 221

Todhunter-Allen Collection 77-8, 220

Tokugawa Ieyasu, Sh gun 146

Tolkien, J.R.R. 45, 47, 49, 169, 220

Topography 38-9, 77, 99, 106-7, 118, 168, 173, 207-8, 213-14, 216-17, 219

Tottell, Richard 72

Town planning 172

Townshend, Charles 203

Toynbee, Arnold 220

Toynbee, Paget 107, 220

Toyota City 147

Toys and games 50, 165

Tracts 31-2, 37, 53-5, 98, 143, 151, 195, 198, 212

Trade Cards 165

Trades and Professions Prints 165

Tradescant, John, Senior and Junior 89

Transcaucasia, see Caucasus

Travel 75-9, 90, 101, 108, 112, 147, 152, 169, 211

Trent, Council of 212

Trinity College, Oxford 220

Tristan 102

Trollope, Mark, Bishop in Korea 148, XXXV

Tucker, Edward 34, 220

Turkey 201 see also Ottoman Empire

Turkic languages 131-2

Turkish 127-8, 130-2, 214, 217

Turkmen 132

Turner, Capt. Samuel 138

Twyne, Brian 38, 220

Twyne, Thomas 88

Tylor, Sir Edward Burnett 93

Type specimens 190, 215

Tyson, Alan 81, 84, 220

Uighur 130, 132

UKOP 67

Ukraine 117

Ulugh Beg 128

UNESCO 35, 67

UNICEF 35

United Nations 35, 65-7

United Nations Career Records Project 35, 65, 220

United Society for the Propagation of the Gospel 153, 155, 158, 219

United States of America 36, 70-3, 81, 83, 84, 151-4, 201, 203, 218, XXXVI

Universities' Mission to Central Africa 161, 219

University College, Oxford 52, 199, 207, 221

University College London 154

University Museum of Natural History 95

Unzola, Petrus de 69

Upper Canada Clergy Society 155

Urashima 147, 178, XXXIV

USSR 64, 72, 76, 94, 115, 117, 126, 132 see also Russia

Uzbek 132

Vaisey, David, Bodley's Librarian 174

Valdivia, Luis de 111

Vallière, Duc de la 103

Van Heyningen, W.E. 95

Vanandetsi, Thomas, Archbishop 126

Vaughan, Henry H. 37, 221

Venice 69

Vere Harmsworth Library 62, 67, 70, 75, 151-4

Vernon, Col. Edward 43

'Vernon Manuscript' 43

Vesalius, Andreas 171

Veterinary medicine 94

Victoria, Queen 48

Videos 147

Vietnam 139

Villari, Linda 108, 221

Villiers family 202

Vilnius 117

Viner, Charles 72, 74, 221

Viney, Robert 146

Virgil 26
Vitruvius 171
Voltaire (François-Marie Arouet) 105
Vossius, Isaac 28, 216

Waghenaer, L.J. 76
Wagner, Richard 101
Wain, John 221
Waismann, Friedrich 221
Wales 71
Walker, General Alexander 130, 136, 221
Walker, Ernest 82, 221
Walker, John 221
Walker, Sir William 136
Wallace, Edgar 45, 208
Waller, Horace 160
Wallingford Priory, Berks. 38
Walpole, Horace, 1st Earl of Orford 220
Walpole, Sir Hugh 45, 221
Walther, Heinrich 184
Wanley partbooks 81
Ward, Irene, Baroness 37, 221
Ward, Mary Augusta 66
Ward, Thomas 108
Wardrop, James 29, 109
Wardrop, Marjory 126, 134, 221
Wardrop, Sir Oliver 126, 134, 221
Waring, Lady Clementine 174
Warner, John, Bishop of Rochester 54
Warton, Thomas (1688-1745) 221
Warton, Thomas (1728-90) 221
Warwickshire 39, 205
Watson, John 39
Weaver, Mike 173
Webb, F. Gilbert 85
Wedgwood, Dame Veronica 221
Weld family 221
Welensky, Sir Roy 161, 221
Wesley, Samuel 82
West Indies 204, 207
Western European Union 67
Westwood, J.O. 169
Wey, William 112
Whinfield, Sir Edward 221
White, George XXXIII
White, Patrick 157
White, William 54, 212
Whitman, Walt 154
Wight, John 72
Wight, Osborne 80, 222
Wilberforce, Samuel, Bishop of Oxford 55, 222
Wilberforce, Robert I. 55, 222
Wilberforce, William 34, 160, 222
Wilde, Oscar 45, 217
Wilkinson, Sir John Gardner 180, 222
Willement, Thomas 170
William III, King 217
William of Malmesbury 57
William of Ockham 58
Williams, Carlos 154
Williams, Charles 45
Williams, George 90
Williams, Philip Maynard 65

Williams, Shirley, Baroness 65
Willis, Browne 39, 222
Wilson, Charles Joseph 93
Wilson, Harold, Baron Wilson of Rievaulx 34, 37, 222
Wilson, Horace H. 136, 222
Wilson, John 82
Wiltshire 39s
Winchester Troper 53, 81
Windham Club 222
Winterton, Edward Turnour, 6th Earl 222
Witchcraft 205
Wittgenstein, Ludwig 59, 100, XIII
Woide, Charles Geoffrey 124
Wolfe, General James 155
Women Advising Women 66
Women Students' Property Committee 199
Women's rights 37, 66, XIV
Wood, Anthony 33, 38, 40, 166, 190, 222
Woodcock, George 155
Woodforde, Rev. James 55, 222
Woods, Donald D. 222
Woolton, Frederick Marquis, 1st Earl of 34, 40, 222
Worcester, John Tiptoft, Earl of 108
World Health Organisation 67, 95
World Trade Organisation 67
World War I 35, 39, 213
Worthington-Evans, Sir Worthington L. 222
Wotton, Thomas 88
Wren, Sir Christopher 89
Wright, Joseph 46, 222
Wright, Judith 157
Writing masters' copy books 103
Wyclif, John 52, 56
Wykeham Musgrave family 222
Wylie, Alexander 142, 147

'Yankee Doodle' XIX
Yeats, William Butler 45
Yiddish 101, 121-3, 215
Yorkshire 39, 169, 201, 205, 209
Young, Edward 206
Younghusband Expedition 138
Youth Hostels Association 206
Yu Xiangdou 141
Yugoslavia 64, 119

Zheng He 141
Zimmern, Sir Alfred 65-6, 222
Zoology 90, 95, 208, 216
Zoology, Department of, Library 95